A Philosophy of Belonging

D1452478

THE BEGINNING AND THE BEYOND OF POLITICS

Series editors: James R. Stoner and David Walsh

The series is in continuity with the grand tradition of political philosophy that was revitalized by the scholars who, after the Second World War, taught us to return to the past as a means of understanding the present. We are convinced that legal and constitutional issues cannot be addressed without acknowledging the metaphysical dimensions that underpin them. Questions of order arise within a cosmos that invites us to wonder about its beginning and its end, while drawing out the consequences for the way we order our lives together. God and man, world and society are the abiding partners within the community of being in which we find ourselves. Without limiting authors to any particular framework we welcome all who wish to investigate politics in the widest possible horizon.

JAMES GREENAWAY

A Philosophy of Belonging

PERSONS, POLITICS, COSMOS

University of Notre Dame Press
Notre Dame, Indiana

University of Notre Dame Press
Notre Dame, Indiana 46556
undpress.nd.edu

All Rights Reserved

Copyright © 2023 by the University of Notre Dame

Published in the United States of America

Library of Congress Control Number: 2023937446

ISBN: 978-0-268-20601-7 (Hardback)
ISBN: 978-0-268-20602-4 (Paperback)
ISBN: 978-0-268-20603-1 (WebPDF)
ISBN: 978-0-268-20600-0 (Epub)

To my parents, Ann and Jim

Who, in life and death, bear witness to the
meaning of presence in absence

CONTENTS

PREFACE

I wonder whether the reader has ever experienced homesickness. If so, then she or he may understand why a book about belonging might have begun in a period of homesickness. I had emigrated from rural Ulster to south central Texas with my wife and children at the age of thirty-nine. At thirty-nine, mind you, one has already lived half a lifetime. One has grown roots. The elements of a place, natural and human, have become one's own. We were fleeing neither a tyrannical regime nor economic hardship, and unlike most of my compatriots over the centuries, we were not compelled by circumstance to leave, but driven by a desire to explore a once-in-a-lifetime opportunity that had opened up.

We arrived and got busy learning how things Texan work, learning our new roles, and learning how to survive. It took about two years to begin to feel like we were doing more than merely surviving. We were beginning to find our feet again, and it was about then that I became aware that homesickness was setting in. The climate of Texas had demonstrated its mild winters and beautiful springs, but also its hot, grinding summers that drag on mercilessly until October. I found the vastness of the wide-open spaces between Texan towns to be impressive and unnerving at the same time. Where Ireland's distances are small in comparison to Texas, the history is long and stretches seamlessly back beyond the great megalithic structures in our landscape. By contrast, the historical memory in Texas is short. The inversion of scale according to place and time was not easy to get used to, and after two years, I realized that I had merely adjusted to living on the surface of things; not belonging, just getting along.

Homesickness is a most uncanny feeling, because it renders the inconspicuousness of belonging conspicuous by its absence.

I am, by nature, circumstance, or grace, a philosopher. Inevitably, I began to ask, what do the philosophers have to say about belonging? Alas, it proved to be very difficult to find much philosophical work in the area of belonging. Apart from some contemporary thought on the theme of "home," philosophers have seemingly not paid much attention to belonging. This stands in stark contrast to the social scientists, whose work on belonging is voluminous. At the time, I found this to be strange, but it was because of this that the notion of writing a book on belonging first raised itself in my mind. It occurred to me that by the research and writing involved in a book-length study, I might overcome my homesickness. This proved to be partially true. Homesickness means that we are yearning for home and that home still lives meaningfully within us. Positively, our belonging remains intact, but negatively, and precisely because we still belong, separation and distance hurt. The harshness of homesickness—like all coming to terms—did eventually abate, not because belonging diminished, but because in time, and in an affection that I barely noticed growing, roots did begin to go down in new soil. Seemingly, the contours of home do expand, horizons do open, and the wheel just keeps on rolling. Old friends abide as new friends come in. In a more extensive belonging, the times and places between us are enriched by the spirit of encounter and memory. Regardless of distance or proximity, we're all growing older together, but it is in togetherness that we begin to belong more deeply to the mystery of existence that holds us.

If the writing of this book proved to be a partial means for my overcoming of homesickness, then there was also the welcome of the people and places of Texas, for which I am deeply grateful. Indeed, the day I harvested my first Texan cabbage, I knew I finally belonged.

ACKNOWLEDGMENTS

I wrote this book with two men in mind: Paul Flynn and Michael Foley. Both are friends of mine from Ireland; both highly intelligent, gifted, and generous; and oddly, both interested in the philosophical career that took me away from them and their families. I wanted to write a book that we might all talk about together. We'll see.

Glenn "Chip" Hughes, professor emeritus in St. Mary's University, has been an inspiration and buddy, a mentor, support, and delight for years. His humor and his penetrating insights, always evident in our conversations, have directly helped me formulate much of what lay unarticulated in my thought about belonging, simply because his philosophical interests and existential concerns have also been mine to a large degree. To him in particular I owe a debt of gratitude. Lunches with Conrad Kaczkowski over the years proved to be decisive occasions in which the narrowness of my horizons has been constantly enlarged. His suggestions and generosity, his love of teaching and learning, his relentless pursuit of self-appropriation, his concern for others, and his existential openness to the mystery that is God—combined with a robust impatience with mediocrity and nonsense—have kept me on the ropes. I cannot imagine writing this book without his friendship. Steve Calogero and Andy Brei of St. Mary's have always kept their doors open to me, often joining me in thinking about belonging. Thanks to them, I have had a model of philosophical friendship to draw upon. Dean Chris Frost and Provost Aaron Tyler of St. Mary's approved my sabbatical of Spring 2020 when I finally sat down to write the first draft of the manuscript. I thank them for their faith in me.

To the various members of the Eric Voegelin Society, I should first apologize. They have been an audience of friendly critics over the years, having to listen and respond to my papers and presentations about themes related to the present work. It was among them that I first tried to crystallize my thoughts on the significance of belonging that eventually made their way into these chapters. I am grateful that they have put up with me. In particular, I'd like to thank David Walsh, Steve McGuire, John McNerney, Lee Trepanier, Gustavo Santos, and Paul Caringella. A special word of thanks goes to two more people. First, Brendan Purcell, professor emeritus of University College Dublin, whose lectures, writings, humor, self-giving, and friendship continue to have a formative influence on me. Second, I am grateful to Tilo Schabert, professor emeritus of the University of Erlangen-Nuremburg, whom I got to know after a wonderful day together in Boston some years ago. He has continually expressed interest and encouragement for this project, centered as he has been on cosmological significance in politics and architecture.

David Walsh of Catholic University of America and Jim Stoner of Louisiana State University are editors of this series, The Beginning and Beyond of Politics, and both welcomed my book proposal right at the start. Steve Wrinn and Rachel Kindler of University of Notre Dame Press have been exceptionally generous with their patience, support, and availability over these years, always making time for me when I had questions or needed help. The copyediting of the manuscript for this book was expertly completed by Bob Banning. His swift, erudite, and lavish responses to the text and to my questions are the mark of a true professional.

It remains the case that the welcome of old friends like Kevin Dillon and Nick Kelly has never diminished over the years. Our spontaneous picking-up-where-we-left-off is such a strong marker of our belonging that their lives remain for me a constant source of wonderment and joy. A book on belonging, at a minimum, needed to take account of that.

Lastly, heartfelt thanks to my wife, Wendy, who has borne the brunt of my philosophical enthusiasms over the years, and to my children, Andrew, Isabella, Isaac, and Sarah. As with all families, we continue to learn how to live out the meaning of belonging, day by day, year by year.

Introduction

Everyone belongs somewhere or with someone. We know, for example, that we belong to places and to times, and we know that we belong to other people and to our communities. Indeed, they belong to us too. We buy or inherit or are gifted things and artifacts. We may even have a sense that we have found our niche in the great scheme of things, especially when things are going well for us. But even if that sounds like empty-headed mysticism, and even if we feel as though we *do not* belong anywhere and to anyone, then at the very least there are ways in which we can think about how we belong to ourselves. In this book, we set out to explore the meaning of belonging, allowing for the probability that much about belonging remains elusive. Involved in every inquiry is the personal concern that our own belonging has for us. It is no mere academic issue to love one's children, to support one's nation in an international sports tournament, to be moved to the bottom of one's soul at the plight of innocent people suffering in a distant place or time, or to seek the forgiveness of neighbor or God or one's own self after a gross act of inauthenticity, recklessness, or destruction. A cursory glance at this book's table of contents reveals just how expansive the meaning of belonging is, and how bound up it is with one's very existence.

However, we need to be careful since the concern with belonging has been co-opted by various partisans across the political spectrum at different times. After the ideological horrors of the twentieth century, our eyes are wide open. Nor are we naïve about the dangers that factions pose much closer to our own day and to our own polities. As a result, suspicion hangs over the very topic of belonging. After all, belonging to a particular group often involves a deliberate choice not to belong to some other group. For many, it is not clear how belonging could mean anything other than narrow-minded prejudice, or how belonging could avoid becoming a means of inequitably excluding others for the sake of the favored in-group. Yet there is much more at stake than the political or cultural movements of the day. What is at stake in belonging is the subject of our study.

Let us briefly refer to the etymological derivation of the verb "to belong." We note that while one can overestimate the value of etymology, one can underestimate it too. Etymology often uncovers subtle lines of meaning that have been operative in our thinking and discourse for a long time. It excavates the original core of meaning in the particular term, and its continuing adequacy as a term today indicates not only the endurance of that core but its course of development that proves instructive. The verb "to belong" is linked to the Old English word *gelang*.[1] This word, *gelang*, suggests what we already recognize in our most fulfilling relationships. Firstly, *lang*, although of uncertain meaning, gives rise to the later term *longen*, whose meaning can be expressed as "to go along with." Thus, the -*long* in our modern word "belong" bears an original meaning of relatedness, a sense of fitting, a proximity to what is right or good or proper. Secondly, the *be*- in "belong" does not derive from the verb "to be," but is, rather, a modern linguistic rendition of the *ge*- in *gelang*. *Ge*- is an Old English intensifying prefix attached to the root word. Thus, *be*- intensifies the sense of relatedness in -*long* into being *really* related or being *very* fitted to what is proper and good. Indeed, the *be*- in "belonging" is evocative of what is at stake in belonging, in finding "a fit." Etymologically speaking, when we genuinely belong, when we find that we are *really* related to what is right, we experience something like "the perfect fit," a relation worthy of our time and effort, or even of our entire life. The term "belonging" then suggests a grasp of this sense of perfection as a fit suited to us.

So much for etymology! Back here in the messiness of our concretely lived relationships, surely we are entitled to ask, Where is that perfection? What would a perfect fit even feel like? In this study, I will treat belonging not primarily as a startling experience of fitting perfectly, like one's waist in a pair of jeans, but as a familiarity that—because it is so familiar—is rarely an object of scrutiny until something is amiss or the fit becomes less fitting. Belonging is more like a foundation that sets us up to go about our daily business. The people, places, times, and things of our belonging constitute something like a frame within which we live our lives. Whatever degree of perfection inheres in our belonging, we barely perceive it until the fit becomes noticeably imperfect. In addition, we know that we don't belong everywhere or in every situation, and when we find that we don't belong, not only is the lack of a fit obvious, but we may have lost or failed at the perfection that belonging seemed to promise. The death of a loved one, rejection or betrayal by a lover, social censure, faltering relationships with friends and family, our own choice to move on or to move away, the demolition of a home or a place that was held as sacred: belonging that fails or comes to an end can be so painful that it amounts to being personally undone. Our frame collapses. When we do not belong, we are adrift. Nothing holds us, nothing reaches us. It is not hard to discern the connection between despair and the experience of not-belonging.

What is interesting is that, in spite of what appears to be its centrality, belonging has not often appeared on the radar of philosophers. What has been discussed by a small handful of modern and contemporary thinkers is a notion of home appearing variously as *Heimat*, homeland, homestead, *oikos*, and hospitality. The social scientists, on the other hand, have been very busy. They have studied, analyzed, and discoursed at length about belonging under many names and rubrics for a long time. Therefore, it is not surprising to find that, within the field of philosophy, it is the political philosophers who have produced the most sustained consideration of themes related to belonging, for the most part in the course of tackling the problems that nationhood generates.

Yet the relative silence of philosophers in general has been offset by two centuries of concentration on the antonym of "belonging," "alienation." It is alienation that has commanded the imagination of philosophers, rather than belonging. This raises some interesting questions about the nature of modern and postmodern philosophy and about the predilections of those who become philosophers in our day. It is not my task to suggest answers to these questions about philosophy and philosophers, but to put the focus upon the meaning of belonging itself, in its own right. However, in doing so, I make one suggestion that relates to philosophy's muteness on belonging that the reader can think about as they proceed through the book: Belonging has not been a conspicuous theme in philosophy because philosophy moves intellectually *within* the horizons that the experience of belonging has opened.

Such an experience we can be confident in describing as primordial. "Primordiality" springs from two Latin terms, *primus* (first) and *ordiri* (to begin), and so, I venture to suggest that philosophers have not noticed the primordiality of belonging because they have overlooked the primordiality that gives rise to philosophy.[2] The primordiality of belonging, I suggest, is the very condition of philosophy. It may be a controversial suggestion, one that I flesh out in the course of the book, but perhaps not more so than the claim of both Plato and Aristotle that philosophy begins in wonderment. Without wonderment at the cosmos, the conditions that give rise to philosophy in its reaching out to the cosmos simply do not exist for the philosopher. The awe and admiration that wonderment signifies are moments of experience when the soul was figuratively caught or suspended. Wonderment is the arresting of the soul, the Parmenidean glimpse of being, that goes on to seek its expression in the philosopher as a question in search of an answer. Philosophy, as the love of wisdom, is a tension that lives more in the question than in the answer, and my suggestion is that belonging, much like wonderment, is the condition for questioning.

The philosopher, then, responsive to the experience of wonderment, has already assumed belonging and begins from there. Only when we find ourselves in situations where the belonging we took for granted is in jeopardy does Hegel's Owl of Minerva take flight. When what we have belonged to begins to fade away, when what we hold as our own is being steadily diminished by foolishness or thoughtlessness, or when the heights of what we took to be a form of perfection are being reduced to rubble, the dusk of alienation sets in. We begin to notice what we never really noticed because in slipping away, our foundations become unsteady. At times such as these, philosophy begins to grapple more consciously with the conditions of its own possibility. What we exist within is rarely a thing to be scrutinized because what we exist within is the very condition of scrutinizing. Often, it is only when our belonging has been debased or denied that it becomes visible. Thus, the modern philosophical concern with alienation is more deeply a grappling with the tensions of existence by which we belong in being. Not to belong is to lose the cosmos, and there can be no greater alienation. Alienation is a horror because the bond and order of belonging that extend our lives into ever more meaningful relationships have been violated or lost. The philosophical concern with alienation has been well judged. Alienation points to a prior belonging that has been lost, and the loss can amount to losing the meaning of one's personal existence. In many cases, philosophical works on alienation reveal themselves to be more deeply works that are haunted by belonging.

The effort to establish how we belong, and what we belong to, is surely a philosophy of belonging, and it is worth suggesting here that there have been philosophies more clearly discernible as "philosophies of belonging" in the Western oeuvre. Largely consonant with the efflorescence of Neoplatonism from the early medieval period onward, "philosophies of belonging" typically did not lose sight of the mystery that holds all things.[3] Many of the most well-known thinkers and mystics of this era—Plotinus, the Pseudo-Dionysius, Eriugena, Bernard of Clairvaux, Hildegard of Bingen, Elizabeth of Schönau, Mechthild of Magdeburg, Meister Eckhart, Marguerite Porete, Bridget of Sweden, Julian of Norwich, Catherine of Sienna, and so on—evince a deep yearning for an ineffable, primordial, transcendent-divine unity, of which we are already part. The sense of intimacy in and beyond the cosmos is almost palpable in their works. They are mystics because they are drawn to the mystery of existence in which they, and all persons and things, belong. Certainly not every medieval mystic can be considered a Neoplatonist; still less can every Neoplatonist be considered Christian; but early medieval philosophy developed dominantly among the Neoplatonists, even as the christological and Trinitarian debates in Christianity were being settled. Painting Neoplatonism with a broad brush, we might say that what generally characterizes it as a pattern of thought is an intimacy of presence of things to one another in the cosmos that, together, have emerged into existence as partners in cosmological communion, together in the great *exitus* of divine substance from the simplicity and unsullied divinity of "The One," and in its *reditus* back toward Oneness at the end of all things. The relentless driving flow of being from the Alpha to the Omega is a great flow of belonging. It is the life of the cosmos that implicates everyone and everything in its bond and order.

On the smaller scale of individual persons, Neoplatonist thought concerns itself with the attunement of the soul toward the divine flow in which we already exist. Neoplatonism may have had its moment in early and middle centuries of the medieval era—the whiff of pantheism lingering in the air—and this moment may well have been superseded by other moments and schools and dominant concerns within the career of both philosophy and theology, but the mysteriousness of existence and the yearning for perfection, presence, and communion remain as threads of meaning that do not pass away. Belonging is as important to us today as it ever was.

In continuity with our ancient predecessors, we can symbolize the experience of belonging within the cosmos in terms of a fourfold relationality, or a primordial orientation toward four fields of reality that constitute the Whole: there are persons and communities, there is the natural world, there is one's own self, and there is the mystery of being we routinely name as God. We are (1) in relation to other human beings, of course, and it is this relation that usually jumps to mind when we think about belonging. However, as mentioned above, there are also times and places and things that we belong to, or that belong to us. This means that (2) we are also in relation to the astrophysical reality of the world around us. One of the most overlooked relations is (3) the relation we have with ourselves. Self-belonging, like belonging in general, seems rarely to become conspicuous until we find that we are out of sync with ourselves, in need of therapy, in need of taking ourselves in hand, in need of self-recovery. Self-forgiveness, deep-seated traumas, willed forgetfulness of dimensions of the self are all facets of brokenness in the self-relation. Clearly, when our self-relation is unstable, this can impact the integrity of other relations. There is (4) another relation that is abidingly present but that is too often ignored or rationalized as something that can be set aside when inconvenient. This is the relation with mystery—or, better said, with the mystery that we encounter in the fact of our existence: we exist, but are not the foundation or explanation of our own existence; and nothing exists from itself. Existence is intrinsically mysterious, and the intrinsicality of mystery pervades every aspect of life, simmering below the surface of things only to erupt at times in its consoling divine height or in its troubling abyssal depths. The givenness of one's own existence, and the inevitability and unforeseeableness of one's own death, remind us that existence is not a commodity and never free of mystery. The source of this mystery, which has been grasped as both impersonal and personal, has many names, the most familiar of which is "God." Each person is a hub of these four elemental axes of relationality. As personal existence extends in these four directions, so does belonging emerge from these four relations: others, world, self, and mystery. The enhancement of our personhood involves the enrichment of belonging; and the enrichment of belonging implicates each of the four, while the disintegration of personhood always involves the dissipation of oneself as the hub that makes sense of their interconnectedness.

It is hard to imagine that happiness and a meaningful life could be possible in the absence of belonging and relationality. Aristotle, we remember, famously argues that the highest good is *eudaimonia*, translated typically into English as "happiness." However, *eudaimonia* also connotes flourishing, well-being, and meaningfulness in life. The term itself captures a spread of meaning that can be clunkily symbolized as "happiness-meaningfulness." Coming to know oneself as a person, or to know one's society, to grasp how things work, or to grasp one's place or purpose within the mystery of the cosmos is also to know what constitutes *eudaimonia* for us. For Aristotle, this knowledge renders us metaphorical archers who now have a target to aim at.[4] Happiness-meaningfulness is the good everyone wants for its own sake, and all other goods for the sake of it. We want wealth when we are poor because we want to be happy, he writes. We want health when we are sick because we want to be happy. The reason anyone wants a friend is because everyone wants to have a happy, meaningful life. I suggest that another hermeneutical accent that is already implicit in the search for meaning and happiness is belonging. For the purposes of this study, let us acknowledge *eudaimonia* as a complex that encompasses belonging: happiness-meaningfulness-belonging. Evidence for this claim by Aristotle can be found in book 19 of St. Augustine's *City of God*. Augustine begins, "Anyone who joins me in an examination, however slight, of human affairs, and the human nature we all share, recognizes that just as there is no man who does not wish for joy, so there is no man who does not wish for peace."[5] Joy and peace, for Augustine, seem to be the primary desires operative in the soul of every person. Joy and peace are what everyone desires for their own sake, and everything else for the sake of these. Augustine is employing a more differentiated symbolization of the range of meaning in Aristotle's more compact *eudaimonia*. He presents many diverse examples of human activity, at different levels of moral worthiness, and proceeds to demonstrate that all of these activities are manifestations of the eudaimonic desire for joy and peace. The unjust man, like the just man, is ultimately seeking peace, albeit through ignoble or nefarious means. Augustine then takes the analysis a step further when he writes that there is an encompassing bond and order, synonymous with an order of peace, that all things exist within: "It comes to this, then: a man who has learnt to prefer right to wrong and the rightly ordered to the perverted, sees that the peace of the unjust, compared to the peace of the just, is not worthy even of the name of peace. Yet even what is perverted must of necessity be in, or derived from, or associated with—that is, in a sense, at peace with—some part of the order of things among which it has its being or of which it consists. Otherwise it would not exist at all."[6]

In seeking peace, everyone seeks the good of existence: their own and others. Everyone and everything is seeking peace because existence is wrought within the encompassing order of peace. Everything—parts of bodies and parts of souls, the whole of a creature, all creatures, the entirety of the cosmos—is engaged for its very existence in the pursuit of the underlying order of peace that holds it and sustains it. At this point in Augustine's narrative, it is evident that "peace" is no longer the most adequate symbol, and he makes a final clarification in chapter 13. Peace is more deeply articulated as one's own place in the cosmos, and Augustine formulates this as *tranquillitas ordinis*. "The peace of the whole universe is the tranquillity of order—and order is the arrangement of things equal and unequal in a pattern which assigns to each its proper position."[7] *Tranquillitas ordinis* is a symbol equivalent to belonging. It raises an existential ambiguity that can only be resolved in the personal living of life: we owe our existence to the emergence of the astrophysical *universe* because we are embodied and therefore subject to suffering and to the mortal predicament of death; yet we also seem to exist in something more, which we name the *cosmos*, understood as the primordial, abiding communion of all things whose undergirding "peace" endures, and in which we participate for the fullest realization of *eudaimonia*. The meanings of "universe" and "cosmos" overlap in every person, but these are not the same. This book explores the existential ambiguity of the "in-between." To exist in between a universe and a cosmos is a way to think about belonging.

I propose to discuss belonging under two titles: "Presence" and "Communion." Presence, of course, means more than mere physical (or "positional") proximity. It is the word we give to the possibility of belonging. The section "Presence" is composed of three chapters, each of which discusses a type of presence fundamental to belonging. What presence brings out is that human existence is an "in-between" reality. I have just mentioned the universe and the cosmos, but we can also think about human existence in between the immanent dimension of things and the transcendent dimension of things. By "transcendence" is intended an intelligible meaningfulness of what remains beyond any capacity we have for final knowing or mastering. The origin of the universe, the fact of the intelligibility of the universe, the divine ground of being, life after death, and so forth are all sources of meaning and wonderment that draw us in wonderment and questioning but elude final answers that would bring to an end our desire to know. Correlatively then, immanence is what is amenable to our understanding, knowing, valuing, and making. Both immanence and transcendence constitute the proper domain of the human person, who exists as an in-between reality, gathering both dimensions of reality into their own personhood. That is, the person is both transcendence and immanence, not as a duality but as an immanence-in-transcendence and transcendence-in-immanence. Such is the in-between reality of the person that I discuss below. Thus, "Presence" is the section that is concerned with the existence of individual persons and what renders us inherently in search of belonging. "Communion" is the second major section of the book. Also composed of three chapters, "Communion" examines belonging as it manifests itself among persons in community. It is the section that considers the manner of existing in communion in both more and less intimate sets of relations.

Throughout both sections, I highlight the lodestone of belonging: sacredness. I am concerned to discuss how it is that our belonging brings us into encounter with sacredness and how it is that by belonging we participate in what is sacred. By sacredness, I do not necessarily intend divinity; still less am I divinizing what is not divine. But that which is sacred to the human heart is what is given as, received as, and held to be of absolute value. Our spouses, children, parents, friends; our neighborhoods, cities, nations; houses, schools, churches; memories, histories, and shrines; humanity and existence itself: in our belonging, we already know quite a lot about absolute value and about what it asks of us if we would properly belong. This is the sacredness that I will pay attention to. I am concerned to differentiate between the things that are experienced as sacred and things as profane, and between what can be known in itself and what can be known only heuristically as mystery at the border of transcendence. Our claims of sacredness and perfection are not ontological claims, but dimensions of meaning that manifest themselves in our relationships. In the apparent ordinariness of raising a family, for example, what is the value of this child to the parent? In the apparent ordinariness of married life, what is the value of our marital covenant? In the apparent ordinariness of friendship, what is the value of my friend, he who, with me, talks and laughs, but must age and suffer and pass away, irreplaceable in his uniqueness, yet subject to the common fate of all things? Intrinsic to presence and communion is an absolute value, a flash of perfection in our midst that our belonging always strains for, yet remains centered in. In this study we will see that "sacredness" is a term that pivots easily between human and divine, immanent and transcendent, time and eternity. The ease of pivoting is explicable in that our belonging extends to the cosmos itself, where not only do we find our place and role *within* the cosmos, but we find that the cosmos, in a significant sense, inheres *in* us.

The reader should be aware that I have "picked" my way through a vast field of symbolism and thought in order to render the experience of belonging intelligible in a single volume in a way that made sense. No doubt, any reader of this book could think of other important philosophers and works and relevant areas of development that do not appear here. What I have offered is intended merely as a contribution, drawn from my professional and existential background, and delimited by my own limitations. Clearly, there is scope for further selections and further thought, refinement, and adaptation. Moreover, there is always the risk in discussing so broad a topic as a whole that the various "parts" may appear somewhat insubstantial in comparison with a scholarly monograph on a single thinker, work, school, or era.

Mine, however, is intended as a study of a central human experience—perhaps the central experience—whose breadth and multifariousness are participated in by every human being. I have taken what I consider to be pertinent soundings from some of the most significant thinkers, primarily from modern and contemporary philosophy. I am exploring as many aspects of belonging as seem crucial to me, and I inevitably have had to spread my net widely. However, I hope that the reader will not be disappointed at the extent to which each of various philosophers' thoughts are discussed in relation to belonging. I have aimed to do justice to the topic in a single volume. I have found it to be a worthy topic, and as the book moves forward, the reader will notice that my viewpoint moves with it. Therefore, I will return occasionally to various aspects of belonging from the perspective of later discussions in order to shed further, hopefully richer, meaning on those aspects that was not available in the earlier discussions.

The first chapter is a survey of contemporary philosophical work directly relevant to belonging: Martin Heidegger, Emmanuel Levinas, René Girard, and Linn Miller's adaptation of Søren Kierkegaard. Here, much of what is important in the meaning of belonging is presented through considering the works of these thinkers. In the shadow of the Third Reich, the controversial effort of Heidegger to think through the existential significance of *Heimat* is one that is discussed in light of Levinas's response to Heidegger. The tension between Heidegger's "enclosure" and the openness of Levinas's "threshold" is one that is rich for the meaning and potential of belonging and one that just about everybody will already have experienced. Girard's work on belonging moves mostly on a sociological level as he explores power dynamics within and between groups, and this is heightened by Miller's work as she considers the meaning of both belonging and "misrelation" in the context of the nonindigenous population of postcolonial Australia. Inevitably, given the nature of the study, only a clipped account of each of these thinkers' work is presented inasmuch as it bears on the theme of belonging. But in some ways, I have aimed to extend their insights through the rest of the book.

The second chapter brings together the foundational insights from the first chapter with a proposed phenomenological hermeneutic in order to propel the discussion forward in the more explicit direction of belonging itself. The aim is to understand what the experience of belonging means, to be able to point out what the conditions of belonging are, and how we know when those conditions have been met. Here a preliminary interpretive framework is offered: we belong when we both *exist-from* someone or something and *exist-toward* that someone or something. To exist-from is to find that someone or something is already a constitutive part of one's own self, that, living or dead, present or absent, that person, community, time, place, or object has already become part of who we take ourselves to be, is the one by whom or that by which we have come to know ourselves—as a spouse, as a parent, as a friend; as a colleague, a neighbor, a citizen; as a fellow human being who shares in the universal predicament of human flourishing and suffering; as participants in the process of the cosmos. Yet existing-from someone or something else is not sufficient for belonging. There is always the possibility of indifference, of falling out of love, of prideful ambition, and all that would bar the way to finding oneself at home and that would impact belonging. To belong is also dependent upon existing-toward that someone or something. This is fundamentally an attitude of care, of loving attentiveness, of desire to share in the life or being of another and to have them share in one's own. Existence-toward is not sufficient by itself for belonging. When we yearn for what will not receive us or we face rejection or betrayal, we undergo the bitter experience of heartbreak. Existence-from and existence-toward comprise the first two structures of belonging, but I also discuss an inherent tension, which Eric Voegelin has elucidated in his theory of consciousness: *metaxy*. *Metaxy* is the Greek term for the "in-between" mentioned above, existence as participation in both the immanent dimensions of the cosmos and the transcendent dimension of the cosmos. In the presence of the cosmos, which holds both transcendence and immanence as dimensions of itself, it is the human being as *metaxy* who can mediate an abiding sacredness in the midst of depravity, disintegration, and death.

Chapter 3 begins the sequence of three chapters on presence. It is concerned with the cosmos as primordial presence. The cosmos was experienced by the ancients as an enchanted place, compactly containing within itself immortal gods, mortal humans, and the world. The distinction of all things from all other things within that experience of the cosmos was less clear than their sameness. This

sameness is called "compact" because the rivers, trees, fields, mountains, oceans, and skies, as well as animals, individuals, societies, and
the gods all share in a sameness of substance together. Indeed, the
cosmos of the ancients was a world "full of gods." The cosmos is
discussed as a form of presence because each of us exists in the presence of the conditions that govern all things. In the epochal process
of differentiation of that compactness from sameness to distinction
or autonomy, cosmological presence does not disappear, even when
the myths of "intracosmic" existence and belonging give way to
both spiritual revelation and the intellectual *theoria* of philosophy
and science, whose horizons have been opened by the opening of
immanence and transcendence as dimensions of meaning. Since this
differentiation occurs nowhere but in human consciousness, I focus
on the presence of the cosmos in personhood. Certainly, we exist *in*
the cosmos, but there is an important sense in which we exist *as* the
cosmos; or indeed, as embassies of the cosmos.

Chapter 4 takes on the discussion of personhood more directly.
The traditional language includes the terms "subject" and "self."
While both of these terms are taken seriously, I argue that the term
"person" gathers the respective shades of meaning of "subject" and
"self" within its own meaning. We are subjects because the cosmos
is what remains abidingly present to persons in respect of their consciousness and bodiliness. Cosmological presence is what we remain
subject to, and it fortifies the notion of person as a subject in a primordial way: our lives are lived in the in-between of mortal time and
the immortal timelessness of the truth of truths, the good of goods,
and the beauty of beautiful things. Cosmological presence is the infinite surplus beyond what can be experienced, the source of possibilities impossible to count. The person is also a self—self-determining
and autonomous—who must choose their way and the pattern of
their own life. The subject-self is present in the cosmos and to others
by way of consciousness and the flesh. The chapter then first considers presence and belonging by way of consciousness. I consider self-
presence, intentional presence, and luminous presence by engaging
the work of Bernard Lonergan and Eric Voegelin. The chapter then
turns to embodiment, and to the originality of Maurice Merleau-
Ponty's thought on "the flesh of the world." There are themes of intersecting immanence and transcendence within the works discussed

in this chapter, all of which indicate the crucial importance of conscious and incarnate presence for the belonging of persons.

Chapter 5 is anchored in the role that love plays in presence. A helpful image here is to consider love as the engine of belonging, the *energeia* that joins existence-from and existence-toward and that drives the opening within our own limitedness heuristically toward unlimitedness. As with the emotion that carries concern for belonging and with the intelligibility that knows belonging, love has an affective-intelligent character. Presence in love brings feeling and knowing together in a unity of belonging in between lover and beloved. To love is to acknowledge what exists already as a good, and yet to strain toward that good in desire. The chapter begins with Plato's *Symposium* and in particular with Socrates's speech in honor of Eros, the in-between reality that bridges the gulf between god and mortal man. In love gods and mortals are present to one another, and in love do mortals attain to the immortality that is no stranger to them, but lives within them as love. Love is *metaxy*, a meaning that resonates in Aristotle's work. I look at two areas in Aristotle's thought that tell us about love as presence: friendship and the reaching out for knowledge. I bring the focus back to contemporary thought with Levinas's thought on love, desire, sex, and the good, as well as with David Walsh's renovation of personalism that embraces persons human and persons divine.

The part entitled "Communion" begins with chapter 6 and runs through chapters 7 and 8. Presence is not yet belonging, but by presence, we anticipate the communion that is the accomplishment of belonging. Belonging is always oriented toward the communion from which it emerges and by which it is sustained. Chapter 6 sets out to establish what constitutes genuine community, which I signify by the term *communitas*. *Communitas* points toward the communion at its heart. The types of community are as diverse as the people whose communion constitutes them. They range from the intimacy of the family to the less than intimate *communitas* that is a society. This chapter is thus organized around the meaning of *communitas* and the meaning of communion. I enlist the philosophical services of Lonergan once again. That a *communitas* exists at all is testament to the communion that it lives by. Lonergan—sober, competent, and

wide-eyed—draws us into a consideration of the difficulties and genuine accomplishment that he calls common meaning, but he also gives
an account of the permanent fracture lines that every *communitas*
must attend to, caught as it is in the dialectic between intelligence on
the one hand and the spontaneous intersubjectivity of social groups
on the other. The great twentieth-century thinkers on communion
are Martin Buber and Gabriel Marcel, but I have been able to draw on
only a fragment of their work that rolls the task of the study forward.
Primarily recognized by his work on I-Thou relations, Buber's I-It is
what I have chosen to adapt for the purposes of the chapter, developing a meaning that is latent within the symbol and its social—rather
than interpersonal—context. Combining this with a discussion of his
work on the nature of citizenship and social relations, the chapter
suggests that Buber provides us the tools we need to talk meaningfully about the social *communitas* as a communion that respects distance rather than proximity. Marcel's work connects well with earlier
chapters on the cosmos and embodiment, but with an added emphasis on communion, while Jacques Maritain's thought on persons and
the common good remains a touchstone for any study of communion
and human dignity in the concrete context of persons in *communitas*.

Chapter 7 turns toward specifically political *communitas* in order
to think about the meaning of political communion. This inevitably
engages us in thinking about more than intersubjective groups and
enterprise associations (as Michael Oakeshott names them, in contrast
to civil associations), and brings us into the field of thought on what
constitutes the political *communitas*. There are three main parts to this
chapter. The first part deals with politics in the mode of the ancient,
cosmological myth where politics is the name given to the imitation
of the gods' provision for mortals. Thus, cosmological politics sees
the political role as divinely representative and salvific, the lines between political and divine obligations not yet drawn. I draw upon
two cosmological myths to elaborate the compact primordiality that
the political role must respond to. The overall point in this part
of the chapter that charts accomplishments in the development from
compactness to differentiation is the establishing of order as the first,
most fundamental political good. The second part of the chapter
takes this further. The differentiation of order as the foundational

political good is the discovery of the further political goods, and it is precisely these that bring an aggregate of individuals together as a people. The study follows St. Augustine's political insight that agreement on political goods, as objects loved in common, is the communion that forms a *communitas*. I finish the chapter by thinking about the approaches in political theory to an understanding of the nation as the modern political *communitas*. The two main camps— perennialists and modernists—focus on different, but occasionally complementary aspects of nations, their development, and the unique dynamism of national belonging. The discussion points toward the continuing importance of nationhood at a time when supranational bodies appear to carry greater moral, if not political, authority. While the nation continues to be the best guarantor of the specifically political existence of the *communitas*, forgetfulness of the political goods that bring about communion is the danger that does not pass away.

Chapter 8 formally concludes the study on belonging by attempting to illuminate a horizon of meaning that is seldom mentioned, but has already made itself felt as a sacredness, by way of presence and communion. Belonging reaches out for its consummation, its completion, its perfection. Belonging strains toward the perfection that lives within it. We want to realize the good of our marriages and our family units, of our friendships, communities, and of humanity. Few of us are tempted to think we can capture perfection, which would be to perform an apocalypse. Yet we do value the perfection we glimpse and love as present in those we belong to and who belong to us. I have named the movement of our belonging from and toward the good of that belonging as sacramental. Everyone who knows the immeasurable value of those whom we belong to, and of the places and things and times that chronicle the sacredness of love and life together, also knows the limitless value that belonging occasions in our lives and relationships. Indeed, sacramentality is the name we have given to the bond and order that sustains us in communion and that commissions us to think, speak, and act in communion with those we belong to: children, lovers, neighbors, compatriots; homesteads, localities, nations; eras, times, and timelessness. We experience and know ourselves partly from these, and toward these are our affection and prudential liberty directed. The chapter begins with an account of sacramentality from Thomas Aquinas, and his thought on the meaning of the Eucharist as the exemplar of a communion consummated and consummating sharpens the point. The meaning of wisdom, according to Aristotle, and the meaning of the philosopher's death, according to Plato, metaphysically extend our insights on sacramentality. Matrimony gives us in another exemplar, a familiar instance of a communion with its own unique consummation that is simultaneously bounded in immanence by the flesh and consciousness of two spouses yet, precisely because of flesh and consciousness, also participates in the timeless, transcendent mystery of being and the begetting of beings. I follow along with Kierkegaard from his philosophical commentary on marriage in *Either/Or*. Again, what is ordinary is revealed to be a sacramental extraordinariness in our midst. The intimacy of matrimonial belonging is a clear example of a consummation, but less intimate types of communion drive toward their own kind of consummation too. I choose to complete this meditation on belonging as sacramental by briefly considering the meaning of human existence as historical and pointing toward what is genuinely universal and sacramental about a humanity of persons and communities in history.

Finally, our study concludes with a short epilogue about alienation. It is my contention that experiencing, understanding, and judging that we do not belong, while wanting to belong, is not the same as a repudiation of the very possibility of belonging; and the outcomes are very different. The former I simply call not-belonging, and the latter, unbelonging. Both are forms of alienation, of course, but there is a need for some delineation. If not-belonging can lead to despair, its remedy is to find another avenue toward belonging. Not-belonging is, by its desire, an affirmation of belonging. On the contrary, it is unbelonging that tends to become ideological, make grand sociological claims against genuine belonging, history, and the cosmos, and can deteriorate into nihilistic destruction whose primary victims are unsurprisingly individual persons and their communities—the bearers of belonging, history, and the cosmos. The term "alienation" then is not particularly helpful since it compactly encompasses a spectrum of meaning that brings not-belonging and unbelonging together under one title. It is this that often gives ideology an apparently moral cover, up to and including the justification of violence. The epilogue briefly discusses the problems associated with alienation in the context of the insights on belonging that have arisen in the course of the book, relying upon Voegelin again, but also Albert Camus and Friedrich Nietzsche.

Levinas once wrote that philosophy, as "love of wisdom," is better comprehended as the "wisdom of love."[8] Let the reader judge whether the wisdom that is love, the wisdom that is driven by love in its movement in the direction of perfection, is not the tranquillity of order that brings us into a belonging that is worth our very lives.

CHAPTER ONE

Belonging as a Philosophical Theme

This opening chapter aims to provide a survey of some of the philosophical literature related to belonging. It is a matter of fact that we are confronted by a relative paucity of writings on the theme of belonging among philosophers. The paucity is startling, relative to the abundant output from social scientists on belonging, but also from philosophers on alienation, which one may regard as the contrary of belonging. The primary task here is to discuss some of these philosophical writings on belonging that have proved to be influential.

BELONGING AS A PHILOSOPHICAL THEME

It is surely a marker of the richness of belonging that various branches of the human and social sciences have been busy analyzing, quantifying, and interpreting its dimensions. For example, in the field of education, Karen F. Osterman writes that belonging is "a psychological concept, defined as a feeling of connectedness or a feeling that one is cared for by others. . . . It involves the need to feel securely connected with others in the environment and to experience oneself as worthy of love and respect." She adds, "In an organizational setting, the feeling of belonging or relatedness can be defined as a sense of community."[1] Sociologist Gabriele Pollini treats belonging as a type of involvement, similar to Osterman's "connectedness": "It is necessary to distinguish four different dimensions or states in the involvement of individuals in the context of human relations: territorial location, ecological participation, social belonging, and cultural conformity."[2] Anthropologist Nadia Lovell presents her account of belonging by suggesting that it is powerfully linked to territory and functions as a way of remembering, and therefore "instrumental in the construction of collective memory surrounding place."[3] For Lovell, memory persists even when a group is displaced, invoking the persistence of belonging in the absence of territory. The literature in psychology is also vast.[4] The task at hand is not to continue to survey the literature of the sciences on the topic but merely to note that these fields have been explicitly engaged with the human phenomenon of belonging, and any brief glance at the literature will be enough to see how full and fruitful their work continues to be.[5]

Then there are the philosophers. For their own reasons, philosophers seem less inclined to concern themselves directly with belonging, which has rarely become thematic in their work. Of course, there are some notable exceptions. To these exceptions, one does well to acknowledge the entire question of the nation and national belonging which has exercised the intellectual energies of many political philosophers, particularly in the modern era. To the question of national belonging I will return in chapter 7. Furthermore, the problem of alienation is more deeply understood as an indirect concern with belonging, or more precisely, with the problem of not-belonging. For now though, we must make our start. Let us consider four contemporary, representative philosophers who have grappled with belonging in ways that are both political and, as it turns out, more foundational than politics: Martin Heidegger, Emmanuel Levinas, René Girard, and Linn Miller.

Heidegger

Is philosophy possessed by a spirit of homelessness? Martin Heidegger's suspicion is that it is, and in this he follows G. W. F. Hegel. For Hegel, Socrates first and fundamentally set "the principle of subjectivity . . . the absolute inherent independence of Thought" as the characteristic of what would later become Western thinking.[6] While Socrates dwelled in Athens, was obedient to its laws, and found his city worthy of his incessant stinging, Hegel nonetheless suggests that "though Socrates himself continued to perform his duties as a citizen, it was not the actual State and its religion, but the world of Thought that was his true home."[7] In this interpretation, the "world of Thought" has become the principle of subjectivity in classical and subsequent Western philosophy, which then for Heidegger has also become a principle of philosophic homelessness in the world. For Heidegger, subjectivity takes on a further nihilistic character in the trajectory of modern philosophic thought through Descartes, Kant, and Nietzsche.[8] Heidegger is concerned to address this homelessness and to show what homeland or *Heimat* beckons to the human being who is *Dasein*, who exists *Da* or "there," in nearness to Being. *Dasein* is thus being-in-the-world, but it is precisely this being-in-the-world that opens up a turbulence that can become profoundly disturbing. On the face of it, being-in-the-world suggests anchorage, embeddedness, and belonging; but by being *in* the world, by being submerged *by* the world, one senses being locked into a field of meaning that is not authentically one's own, but belongs to "the-They." "The-They" is Heidegger's symbol for the noise of inauthentic existence, a technologizing force that tranquilizes and lulls us into empty gestures and uniformity, an "enframing" that is always at work to tell us in advance what must be done, and where and when and how. The problem of authenticity then is to achieve authentic existence in a world that is not of one's own making. *Dasein* is concerned to the bottom of its being with authenticity. It wants to belong, but not at the price that "the-They" command. It urgently seeks more than a refuge—indeed, a homeland or *Heimat*. Homelessness is clearly a turbulence, an anxiety, that wracks *Dasein* and causes misery; but it is also an anxiety that is crucial to overcoming the lack of authentic personhood that characterizes the state of being-in-the-world. To the extent that anxiety or angst is experienced, homelessness is recognized, and authenticity becomes a possibility. Why is this? For Heidegger, "uncanniness" (*Unheimlichkeit*) is the anxious experience that attends to a mode of existence that Heidegger names as Being-toward-death. Death, for Heidegger, is not the event of ceasing to exist—the common lot of all things—but is the condition of *Dasein*'s authentic life. One's death is the irrefragable bar of authenticity: nobody else owns one's death, nobody can take away one's death in an act of theft or charity, and nobody else's death gives an adequate understanding of one's own death.⁹ Being-toward-death is an anxiety or dread that underscores *Dasein*'s authenticity and irreplaceability. In this sense, only a human being can know their mortality; only a human being can die. It also means that, for Heidegger, *Dasein* exists in an ongoing state of homelessness that disturbs being-in-the-world, but that also drives one continually to live an unfinished seeking: we are always in search of a home in which we yearn to belong.

Heidegger's dalliance with the National Socialists was, of course, his most infamous lapse, and it occurred at a time in his career when he was grappling with the basic homelessness of *Dasein*. In this period, the *Volk* seemed like a possible—and no doubt, ideologically expedient—setting for a homecoming: the achievement of an approximate rootedness could perhaps be accomplished by belonging in a *Volk*, with each *Volk* involved in the agonistic struggle to realize its own essence. "Only in communicating and in struggling does the power of destiny become free."¹⁰ The battle to realize its own destiny is a battle that literally takes "place." History is the story of a *Volk* in a particular place, and history can only happen in this place. "The *polis* is the site of history, the Here, *in* which, *out of* which and *for which* history happens. To this site of history belong the gods, the temples, the priests, the celebrations, the games, the poets, the thinkers, the ruler, the council of elders, the assembly of the people, the armed forces, and the ships."¹¹

Place as a bounded space was the location of the homeland, the locale of the *Volk* where *Dasein* can find an abode at last. As opposed to a universal cosmopolitanism, as envisaged by Immanuel Kant among others, only the place of the more local or national *Volk* can properly be a home.¹² Since cosmopolitanism is a way to talk about all the peoples at one time, it must overlook the "essence" of any of them. If cosmopolitanism avoids group essentialism, its inclusiveness masks its participation in subjectivity's philosophic loneliness. In the scope of Heidegger's career, the detour into *Volk*-essentialism proved to be a relatively short-lived project in his search for a resolution to the problem of inauthenticity. He had hoped to establish that *Volk* was the remedy to subjectivity's homelessness and that authenticity could be achieved at least at the level of one's own people, at the level of rootedness in a place and time, but what he came to realize was that the reality of a *Volk* stood in need of some clarification, which it would not yield in practice. He had to differentiate between a rootless people who do not modulate themselves in an agonistic manner and a rooted *Volk* who do, battling constantly to refine and glorify their spirit. But where in the world was a rooted *Volk* to be found? Even the Germans, he concluded, did not fit the bill since too few experienced the struggle of Being by which authenticity is achieved. *Volk*, as an anticipated homeland of *Dasein*, fell short. Overall, the political direction of his pursuit of a proper dwelling fell short too. He later wrote that "every nationalism is metaphysically an anthropologism, and as such subjectivism."[13]

Heidegger's later career detached itself from the political and centered more squarely on the meaning of dwelling. It is by dwelling that Being is disclosed, and disclosed not in a moment but in a process that extends in time and place. Dwelling is thus an event (*Ereignis*) in which *Dasein* is "enowned" by Being: *Dasein* does not disclose Being, but is gradually disclosed by Being. This is the "turn" (*Kehre*) in his work, a turning that Heidegger himself claims, though it occurred in his thinking, occurred in Being first, manifesting itself in his thinking and writing and in the writing and thinking of others.[14] In *Building Dwelling Thinking*, he writes, "Human being consists in dwelling and, indeed, dwelling in the sense of the stay of mortals on the earth. But 'on the earth' already means 'under the sky.' Both of these also mean 'remaining before the divinities' and include a 'belonging to men's being with one another.' By a primal oneness the four—earth, sky, divinities and mortals—belong together in one."[15]

The fourfold is, arguably, Heidegger's way of setting forth our dwelling in Being, or what I will refer to in this book as "the cosmos." What Heidegger means by each of earth, sky, divinities, and mortals is not to be taken at face value. Earth and sky seem to suggest the natural rhythms that implicate the conditions of dwelling on the earth; divinities and mortals suggest the cultural appropriation of such conditions: the divinities are witnesses to all that is and is yet to come, while mortals give witness to death. These are poles of the fourfold of dwelling, and they point toward what is disclosed in between nature and culture, between givenness and an invitation to enter into a panoply of meaning for the sake of receiving, between mortality and the language of mortality that seems to elude death. Thus, the lasting and passing of the cosmos. Heidegger's concerns are clearly continuous with his earlier work, even if the enowning of *Dasein* by Being amounts to a radical disruption of perspective. However conceived, Heidegger achieves the insight—or the insight of Being manifests itself in his writings—that the fourfold is our foundational belonging in place and time *that is always more than* a restriction to a place or time; instead the disruption of perspective affords a heuristic glimpse of the placeless and timeless cosmos that nonetheless reaches into place and time. Effectively, by dwelling here and now we learn how to dwell in such a way that dwelling becomes both our mode of being and Being's mode of "holding sway."[16] To dwell is to be; to lose one's dwelling is to plunge into a vacuum that quickly fills itself with machination and technology and the oblivion that is the-They. Dwelling is no minor matter, a detail of life, but what existence depends upon in every conceivable sense. Our existence is underpinned, disturbed, and illuminated by dwelling, because dwelling amounts to an eruption of Being within the privacy of the enclosure.

According to commentators like John D. Caputo and Theodore Kisiel, there is a tension that runs through the corpus of Heidegger's work. It is a tension between self-containment and scattering, where that which is close is what is familiar or intimate, and does not find its opposite in that which is remote, but in what is alien and always threatens dispersion and "de-severance." Another commentator, Paul Harrison, sets out three figures of self-containment, of "mineness" (*Jemeinigkeit*), and ultimately of dwelling that appear in different phases of Heidegger's career. Each of these three figures demonstrates an attempt to establish belonging appropriate for *Dasein*.[17] The first is the craftsman, discussed in *Being and Time*, and the craftsman's tools in his workshop. The "readiness-to-hand" of the craftsman's tools is their "fit." They belong not in the first instance to the world as *things*, but to their place in *my* field of belonging. That is, the readiness-to-hand of tools is their already-constituted meanings as equipment for the making of jewelry, toys, and so on in my meaning-saturated dwelling. As Heidegger puts it, in using equipment, artifacts, or things, in employing their "manipulability" as a thing already meant for some functional purpose, we are at work. "The work which we chiefly encounter in our concernful dealings—the work that is to be found when one is 'at work' on something . . . has a usability which belongs to it essentially; in this usability it lets us encounter already the 'towards-which' for which *it* is usable."[18]

We may say that the "towards-which" aims at *home*, becomes a *homewardness*, because it is already concerned with, even constituted by, the meaning of home. The stuff of our lives, the things we pick up and use for commonsensical purposes, are already impregnated with meaning. Their services constitute for us, in the first place, a serviceability of home. For example, a car is a repository of meaning that one may assert in legal terms or emotionally or by aesthetic sensibilities, and so on. A directedness, intentionality, and care for one's car may be evident in that one wants to drive it to work, to church, to the store, and home again. Its functionality is at the service of one's meaningful activities. However, one's car also communicates the meaning of my belonging in this time and place. One may own different cars at different times, but each is a chronicle of the years in which the owner negotiates the primordial conditions of living, growing older, loving, and suffering as existence in the cosmos. It is a *Jemeinigkeit* and expresses something of the meaning of dwelling. My car is rooted in the meaningful matrix of my life, and not only derives its meaning for me from that matrix but reflects that very meaning in its usability for me. It is a small example, but as "ready-to-hand," the car belongs among the paraphernalia and purposes of a life. It is only on those occasions when the car breaks down, when the screwdriver cannot be found, when the pen is stuck behind the sofa, that their handiness becomes explicit. Heidegger remarks, "When an assignment to some particular 'towards-this' has been thus circumspectively aroused, we catch sight of the 'towards-this' itself, and along with it everything connected with the work—the whole workshop—as that wherein concern always dwells."[19]

The second figure that Harrison discusses is the cabinetmaker's apprentice from the lecture "What Calls for Thinking?"[20] Here, the question relates to what must be learned by the apprentice. The apprentice is not merely learning how to use tools, practicing cutting and engraving, or gathering knowledge about the furniture he is to build. "If he is to become a true cabinet maker, he makes himself answer and respond above all to the different kinds of wood and to the shapes slumbering within the wood—to wood as it enters into man's dwelling with all the hidden riches of its essence."[21] Handicraft that is learned by the apprentice is neither outward nor inward form, but the relatedness of wood to dwelling. By handicraft, a homeland proper to *human* being is maintained; by means of handicraft, Being discloses itself to *Dasein*. In this case, handicraft is a means of attunement by which *Dasein* brings forth Being in the wood, in the cabinet, as an act responsive to Being's disclosure of itself as dwelling.

The third figure comes from "Building Dwelling Thinking," in which Heidegger describes how a hut in the Black Forest is constructed because there is already dwelling in the sense of the anticipation that it is *here* that dwelling can be accomplished. What is needed is the self-possession of the hut builder, the look in his eye, the movement of his hand. Without this, there is no measure for building, no landscape to be grasped. The peasant may have built the dwelling, but it is more accurate to admit that "the dwelling of peasants" built the structure, which was placed "on the wind-sheltered mountain slope, looking south, among the meadows close to the spring. . . . It did not forget the altar corner behind the community table; it made room in its chamber for the hollowed places of childbed and the 'tree of the dead'. . . and in this way it designed for the different generations under one roof the character of their journey through time."[22]

The specter of National Socialism hovers close to Heidegger's work, including his thought on dwelling, which extends throughout his career. For some, it infests his work. While it is true that his work is able to accommodate much of the occult and malevolent spirit that animated Hitler, and dovetails neatly with the Nazi objective of broadening *Lebensraum* for the Germanic peoples, it would be self-defeating to arrogate genuine insights into the meaning of belonging to a branch of Nazism, with all of its horrors and inhumanity. While much of Heidegger's thought on the meaning of dwelling risks fetishing place and time, and his fourfold hesitates—in spite of what is suggested by its symbolism—to open into a transcendent dimension of meaning, there remains much of value in his examination of rootedness and the yearning to come home. Not everyone who experiences homesickness, who is sentimental about a time and place, or who is aware of their family's rootedness in a region finds themselves goosestepping to the tune of *Horst-Wessel-Lied*. Belonging remains a legitimate concern in philosophy. Jettisoning the entirety of Heidegger's work on dwelling at one fell swoop and burning it as so much radical-right-wing rubbish is not going to be helpful. In spite of the man, the work on belonging remains as one of the most significant contributions in the philosophical pursuit of the meaning of belonging. Heidegger reminds us that intelligibility relies upon the prior inaccessibility of mystery against which it is unveiled: "Freedom is that which conceals in a way that opens to light, in whose clearing shimmers the veil that hides the essential occurrence of all truth and lets the veil appear as what veils."[23] So too does belonging depend upon a tension between the here-and-now and what appears as no more than a point of light, inaccessible but orientational in its lambency. In his lecture on Hölderlin's *Der Ister*, the river (Danube) is a figure of both a place of home and a place of journey. He writes, "*coming to be* at home in one's own itself entails that human beings are initially and for a long time, and sometimes forever, not at home."[24] For the later Heidegger, the meaning of belonging is not the achievement of some final state, the achievement of a *Volk*-ish enclosure against the world. Experientially, the disclosure of Being in *Dasein* ebbs and flows. Rather, the meaning of belonging extends to the tensions and turbulences of the struggle to allow Being to achieve home through its enowning of the dweller. Dwelling is a struggle that may be embodied in the particularity of this place and this time, but the dwelling that we think would enclose a home against the world when we shut the door seems also to be the site into which the protean presence of Being becomes richly manifest. The yearning to find the belonging of home, as a remedy for existential loneliness and angst, binds this or that particular home into the larger, unfinished process of belonging in Being.

Levinas

Emmanuel Levinas offers an account of dwelling in his *Totality and Infinity* that in some ways is continuous and complementary to Heidegger, and in other ways is a stark contrast and refutation. Levinas writes that "the privileged role of the home does not consist in being the end of human activity but in being its condition, and in this sense its commencement. . . . Man abides in the world as having come to it from a private domain, from being at home with himself, to which at each moment he can retire."[25] Furthermore, the privilege of home is that it is here where the inwardness of privacy and intimacy opens. Although the home is characterized primarily by such inwardness, Levinas stresses that it is also related necessarily to what is outside of itself in the world of objects. "Concretely speaking the dwelling is not situated in the objective world, but the objective world is situated by relation to my dwelling."[26] Here is a similarity to Heidegger's account of dwelling that fortifies the *Da* of *Dasein.* It relates all distance and modulations of space to an "originary distance" that is achieved in dwelling. Because I belong here, all that is beyond here subsists in a distance inflected by its relation to my dwelling. "Circulating between visibility and invisibility, one is always bound for the interior of which one's home, one's corner, one's tent, or one's cave is the vestibule."[27]

He describes the home as a "utopia in which the 'I' recollects itself in dwelling at home with itself," a home that is founded upon hospitality for its inhabitant. The home is essentially hospitable.[28] However, unlike in Heidegger, this hospitality of home acts more like a threshold than as an enclosure. For Levinas, the Other inevitably comes into my proximity and regards me by his or her look. The Other is the one whose look asks for a hospitality that seems to draw me from my "vestibule" and, in this, dares me to open the enclosure with a newer, richer sense of home, itself teetering on the edge of the "an-archic" or unrooted. Contrary to Heidegger's emphasis on place, Levinas writes, "The 'vision' of the face as face is a certain mode of sojourning in a home, or . . . a certain form of economic life. No human or interhuman relationship can be enacted outside of economy; no face can be approached with empty hands and closed home. Recollection in a home open to the Other—hospitality—is the concrete and initial fact of human recollection and separation; it coincides with the Desire for the Other absolutely transcendent. The chosen home is the very opposite of a root."[29]

In light of Levinas's figure of home as a threshold between exteriority and interiority, privileged and hospitable to inhabitants and to the alterity or sheer otherness of the stranger, Heidegger's notion of dwelling becomes conspicuous for its missing something. Where Heidegger sought a rootedness for *Dasein*, Levinas finds dwelling in both rootedness and unrootedness, where unrootedness is the welcome to the Other who can be known neither in advance of their advent nor in encounter. The Other escapes being finally known, yet is the occasion for hospitality. In fact, within the full scope of Levinas's work, it is the hospitality of unrootedness (or exteriority) that is emphasized as the proper home of persons. I discuss this below, but the encounter with the Other is an encounter with absolute "alterity," one of Levinas's symbols for the transcendent otherness that the face of that Other communicates.

The response to the face that regards me is always an ethical response, a response that opens my inward subjectivity and puts me beyond it. Levinas identifies subjectivism as the problem to be overcome. Contra Heidegger, Levinas's notion of dwelling is ultimately arrived at through encountering, opening to, and welcoming the ungraspable and unfathomable alterity of the Other. The primacy is always an ethical primacy: the "I" must respond to the Other, regardless of any metaphysics of a homeless, lonely subjectivism; and dwelling must be the accommodation of this response. Where Heidegger emphasizes particular places and times—even the particular *Volk*—Levinas's essential openness pushes the notion of dwelling toward a universal embrace that suspends or transcends time and place, and even the subjectivity of the self. Levinas's work emerged, of course, from the shadow of Heidegger, a shadow whose reach had accustomed us to thinking of dwelling as what can be assimilated to the self to the exclusion of others, whether by *Dasein* or by Being through *Dasein*. (Levinas calls such assimilation "totalization.") Indeed, for Heidegger, assimilation and enclosure seem to be the very conditions of *Dasein*'s ability to recollect itself (or to be recollected in Being). There is little that would allow Levinas's "Other" to call into question the *Da* of *Dasein*, and to shift dwelling from an entrenched sovereignty of the particular to an opening through which alterity could draw one to a wider, more universal belonging. However, it is also fair to note that Heidegger's work on dwelling is animated by a pervasive sense of the inexhaustible, and there may be more of a complementarity between Heidegger's work and Levinas's than is generally acknowledged. From *Unheimlichkeit* (uncanniness), the "not-yet," and *Angst*, to the "sometimes forever never at home," Heidegger leaves open the possibility of the unassimilable as a dimension of dwelling that is highlighted in the work of Levinas.

If there remains something incomplete in Heidegger's particularistic emphasis, it might be said that Levinas is at risk of demoting the interior sacredness and domesticity of the home to an exclusive possessiveness by his emphasis on a contrasting universal hospitality. Furthermore, if Levinas considers the home as something of a threshold, and unrootedness as the larger field of dwelling, the idea of homecoming seems to become problematic. Homecoming was a central concern, or perhaps a yearning desire, for Heidegger, one that recalls the troubled journey of Ulysses, who overcame so many fantastic obstacles over a protracted time because he was determined to come home. Yet Levinas is more partial to Abraham, who journeys in his own soul from interiority to exteriority. "To the myth of Ulysses returning to Ithaca, we wish to oppose the story of Abraham who leaves his fatherland forever for a yet unknown land."[30] It is Abraham who, Levinas tells us, responds to the call of God by journeying into alterity, paradoxically making his home beyond his home, learning to belong in the taking leave of a particular place. Heidegger's Ulysses returns to the interiority of the particular; Levinas's Abraham departs for the exteriority of the universal.

One is inclined to think that it was because Abraham had already learned something about dwelling, home, and belonging that he knew what leaving the particular would mean. He could journey out into an apparent unrootedness because he was already rooted, not so much in the universal, but in a transcendent intimacy with God. Spiritual belonging was the motive force that drew Abraham from the particular homeland of Ur toward the homeland that could become, in some transcendent sense, the home of all. Perhaps Abraham, having learned to belong in the particular, was existentially prepared to heed the call of God to expand his belonging for the sake of the universal: a universal people would be a people not by ethnicity, a common (profane) memory, borders, or ideas, but by a belonging in immediacy to God; they would be a people whose belonging could become constitutive of history itself.[31] In his "vestibule," Abraham had learned what dwelling is, so that the command of God to uproot and be unrooted in the world was not a loss of dwelling, but a swelling and surplus of dwelling that could embrace what Levinas calls exteriority. Abraham could make his self-sacrificial journey and glorify God with his faith and fidelity because he had already learned to belong in the domestic sacredness of home, which effulgent sacredness could no longer be restricted to domesticity. Abraham knew how to belong because his departure for the universal was predicated upon the prior particular affection for a home that had grounded him and where he was able to receive the call of the universal.

The "privilege" of a home is surely not a Heideggerian enclosure, but it is in the place and time of the enclosure where the seed of hospitality can safely germinate in order that the dwelling itself become a threshold and the inhabitants can venture out to welcome the Other who comes. Still, if Abraham and Ulysses represent the elemental going out and coming home of the dwelling, it means that each is made possible by the threshold.[32] There are neither welcomes nor homecomings without thresholds, and, pushing the metaphor further, one dares to say that only the enclosure can unenclose itself by means of its own threshold. The hospitality of home depends upon interior enclosures and thresholds both.

René Girard

René Girard approaches belonging from another direction entirely. He veers away from dwelling, the locus of Heidegger and Levinas, and points to a different problem that is associated with belonging: violence. Belonging begets violence within groups and among groups. Within the totality of one's life, there are many groups to which we will belong (and not belong). This is due, Girard writes, to many simultaneous relationships, each of which contributes in its own way to one's identity. Such relationships may range from weak to strong, from involuntary to voluntary, from the hierarchically arranged to the variable and unstable, and from the administrative to the private and concealed. Thus, "our social identity is an intertwining and intermingling of relationships of belonging so numerous and diverse that together they constitute something unique: an individual being that we are the only one to possess."[33]

The very act of belonging, he contends, involves either an external violence of exclusion of others not in the group or the internal violence of rivalry among those who desire the same thing within the group, or both. "The more desirable the relationship of belonging is or appears to be, the more bitterly the violence of exclusion is experienced by the excluded. . . . While the violence of exclusion is nowadays very visible and hotly debated, . . . it is not the only violence associated with relationships of belonging. Neither is it the most widespread or the worst. There is another form of violence of which we are largely unaware and that can be said to exist inside relationships of belonging."[34] The mechanism that binds, and then prevents the disintegration of belonging within the group, is the ritual of scapegoating and sacrificial violence.[35] There is, he argues, utility in both the strength and the weakening of bonds of belonging. The strength is the sacred and ancient rootedness of man; the weakening of bonds leads to less exclusion with regard to those previously outside the group, and less ostracism of those inside, which is an essentially positive phenomenon. For example, Girard looks to Proust as one of the great "specialists in human relations" and draws some observations from Proust's account of Combray (the idyllic village setting beside the sea in *Swann's Way* where the narrator spent time on holiday as a child) and the "salon Verdurin" (the home of M. and Mme. Verdurin, who hosted parties for a conspicuously select group of individuals; these were often caustic affairs, especially if one demurred from the dominant opinion).[36] Both of these are paradigms of "small, enclosed worlds" or "scale models," which, while providing a rootedness, also employ rituals to banish what they would not or could not contain. However, the tone of belonging in each differs, according to Girard: patriotism marks the former, while chauvinism the latter. Belonging, for Girard, is intrinsically exclusionary and hierarchical, and always either actively or passively violent. When these relationships are strong, they do not "fuel violence," even if they are experienced by the excluded as implicitly violent. However, belonging is more complicated than simply gauging the relative strengths and weaknesses of the relationships. Relationships of belonging, since they are not static, are always vulnerable to atrophy. Therefore, even an apparently strong relationship can employ violence to mask its weakness.[37]

Girard makes the related point that a sense of belonging weakens as it widens, as it does under the conditions of contemporary globalization. That is, many of our relationships have a global reach, and distance—nonproximity—works to dilute the experience of belonging and its attendant problems. This is a positive-sum consequence of globalization. Since belonging for Girard is inherently a source of violence, the process of globalizing relationships works as a remedy in overcoming belonging. Nonetheless, the remedy is not without its own problems. The weakening of belonging in an increasingly globalized world entails consequences that are themselves the source of further violence. On the global stage, "while the weakening of relationships of belonging paves the way for increasing global unification, such unification entails an increase in rivalry."[38] Girard suggests that mechanisms used to prevent violence within the in-groups—of which some will persist, even if in weaker or smaller forms—will become less available, leading to irregular, if bitter, spasms of violence. Globalization is not a new form or a diluted form of belonging. It is a not-belonging aimed at universality, whose by-product is a world with evermore dislocated or unrooted people who occasionally turn to violence because the mechanisms of the group that would hold them in check have disappeared. Globalization would seem to replace the violence born of exclusionary belonging with the violence born of not belonging. The presence or absence of belonging seems to testify to a violence inherent in interpersonal and social relationships, according to Girard.

Girard has begun to think through the dynamics of belonging (already quite an original undertaking outside the social sciences)—especially in a world of immense and increasingly globalized communication—and to highlight the problems of violence, exclusion, and disintegration, as well as raising the possibility of an internationalist identity as a partial solution to these problems.[39] However, to my mind, Girard seems also to have missed something rather important. His emphasis on the exclusion of those not in the in-group and on the inner rivalry among the in-group members suggests that his focus is less on belonging and more on alienation and on the architecture of power. He is beginning from a dynamic rooted in individual and group estrangement whereby all relationships are no more than utilities for managing the acquisition of advantages and the avoidance of disadvantages, and this estrangement is itself a consequence of "mimetic rivalry." Mimetic rivalry is Girard's theory that human beings desire an object only because other human beings also desire that object. The object in question is desirable primarily because other human beings desire it. Thus it is that our desires are dependent upon some model who can mediate the desirability of an object to us and make clear why we would also desire it. It's not hard to see that, if this is a basic anthropological starting point, we are immersed in a hopeless sea of rivalry with others, where even the mediating model becomes a rival. There is something approximately Hobbesian in Girard's anthropology of "mimetic rivalry." Hobbes claimed that "if two men desire the same thing, which nevertheless they cannot both enjoy, they become enemies" in the state of nature, which only an enforceable social compact can remedy under pain of death.[40] In a similar vein, Girard writes, "If we desire the same things, we feel close to one another, and this closeness, which constitutes agreement on the spiritual level, can become disagreement on the concrete level. Indeed, there are two possibilities: either the object that two or more of us desire can be shared and we agree to share it, in which case there is no conflict; or the object is one that we cannot or will not share, in which case conflict is inevitable."[41] "Archaic" societies, Girard argues, are constituted by rituals (or implicit social contracts, to employ the language of classical liberalism) such as scapegoating and blood sacrifice. These are mechanisms employed to manage and mediate the savage tendency toward mimetic rivalry among individuals in the group, and thus they function to keep the group intact. "All social relationships of belonging," writes Girard, "originate in ritual and sacrifice."[42] The mechanisms that limit the worst effects of mimetic rivalry are like a useful violence to curb the untrammeled violence born of mimetic desire.

While not wanting to dismiss the natural proclivity of individuals and groups to savagery, from archaic times to the present, it is worth keeping in mind that there may be other proclivities. One of these is the human proclivity for meaning, and furthermore, such a proclivity seeks its expression in belonging—or, more precisely, in different types of belonging. The possibility of a relationship of belonging between and among persons and peoples that might satisfy not only the yearning for meaning—that is, belonging as something like contentment rather than power—but might do so in a nonviolent way seems almost laughable in the light of Girard's analysis, which he admits remains schematic and simplified.[43]

Girard correctly diagnoses the ugliness and violence of power relations as forces that often characterize the social phenomenon of group belonging and exclusion, but what is left unattended to in his analysis is the personal experience of belonging itself that extends to social, political, and cultural belonging. Unfortunately, what Girard's analysis comes to sounds less like a matrix of belonging among persons and peoples and more like a set of ritualistic mechanisms to salve the passionate power urges among group members. There is, I argue, much more to the experience and existential significance of belonging than appears in Girard's critical postmodernist account, which, unsurprisingly, takes the social phenomenon of the group as the adequate level of analysis rather than, as I will argue, the dynamics of personhood. For example, he comments, "Christians used to believe—and still do—in the existence of the individual person, inseparable from her relationships of belonging but neither lost in the mass of those relationships nor, even more so, melded with any single one of them such as, for example, her race."[44] This is a useful insight into Girard's thinking since it raises three points of criticism in regard to his work overall: (1) that personhood is no more than a belief, mythical rather than concretely real; (2) that such a belief is easily collapsible; and (3) that identity politics is the most salient aspect of belonging. It is the contention of this book that Girard is wrong on all three counts.

Linn Miller

I include Linn Miller here because she considers belonging not only in relation to geographic or sociohistorical conditions but also as a self-relation: belonging to one's own self. Looking to the thinking of Søren Kierkegaard, she writes, "Kierkegaard offers a philosophical anthropology of being-in-the-world from which I draw the notion of 'belonging *qua* correct relation.'"[45] Miller's analysis is therefore both situational and more than situational.

She begins by identifying the concrete crisis of belonging in contemporary Australia among nonindigenous Australians of Anglo-Celtic backgrounds as an existential crisis. She sets herself the task of articulating a conceptual apparatus "by which 'belonging' itself and thus 'true belonging' might be grasped."[46] The situation in Australia is equivalent to many postcolonial societies elsewhere. On the one hand, many nonindigenous Australians are skeptical of the claim that their right to belong rivals that of the indigenous, while on the other, there is frustration that the place they experience today and for generations as home should be in question as a necessary result of colonization that occurred centuries ago. Feelings in postcolonial societies run high, but Miller is adamant that belonging and identity are not dependent upon feelings alone: "I now take it to be the case that belonging proper is something much deeper than that which pure emotion can guarantee; it has to be something rather more ontological—something more fundamental to who and what we are. Rather, it might be stated that belonging is in some way part of what constitutes our identity, whether we are explicitly aware of it or not."[47] Pushing past Girard's presentation of belonging as a structure of power within or between groups, Miller identifies the key issue of belonging as how we exist in the world; and furthermore, how we exist in the world is our very identity. "It is the 'we' and the 'us' that are fundamentally at stake here."[48] We belong by way of social connections, and/or historical connections, and/or geographical connections to our communities, histories, and localities respectively. Belonging is a "state of being" in which we are related to the world in one or some of these three ways. The experience of belonging is the experience of a fit: belonging is a right or correct relation to the world. It is about experiencing oneself as fitting in the relation. That is, one experiences belonging as a dimension of one's own self; this is *how* I am in the world, this is *how* I fit.

Miller deals with belonging at the level of the person, extending the analysis to the sociopolitical and historical level. In this regard, she reminds us of Kierkegaard's term "transparency," in which—in order to know something—one must first "have a clarity that creates the possibility of seeing into something."[49] Transparency is a condition of the self as conscious of its own true being. Contrary to the absolute independence of subjectivity that vexed Hegel and Heidegger, Kierkegaard considered subjectivity to be crucial to belonging because it is only in subjectivity that the truth of one's being-in-relation can be known and lived and that transparency becomes possible.[50] The connection (the belonging) between knowing oneself and being oneself is one that is not only rooted in the subject, but concretely lived.[51] Miller employs the term "authenticity" in this regard. To be authentic is to disclose the connection between knowing and being in one's life by the manner in which one lives one's life. One lives the truth of one's being when one is conscious of the conditions of one's life: one's limitations and one's potentialities in the light of how we relate to our world and how we find ourselves in the world. Miller might have underlined at this point that this self-understanding is a self-belonging that bears upon how we belong to the world around us. Nevertheless, belonging, as a concrete expression of the subject's being in the world, is how one can live authentically and transparently. Belonging—geographically, socially, historically—is a truth of the conditions of any person's life. To be an authentic self is to be correctly related to the world in which one finds oneself and to know oneself as being already in relation to that world. It appears that, in discussing belonging, one is also engaging in a philosophical anthropology. What, after all, is a human person and a human community that the tension between belonging and not-belonging is so important? Miller's answer is that the importance is grasped in how it "constitutes our identity, whether we are explicitly aware of it or not."

She writes that "Kierkegaard expresses this through a philosophical anthropology in which the self is a synthesis constituted by the finite and the infinite," where the finite includes such realities as those qualities that we have inherited from our parents and those relations to the world that she has already outlined. Then there is "the infinite." One way to describe the infinite with regard to the human subject is that we are also called to a paradoxical participation in what is infinite and what overcomes our inherited finite limitations. Kierkegaard's word is the "eternal," whereby one lives in such a manner that each decision and each self-manifestation has eternal consequences. To live infinitely is to be able to take a risk with all of one's life—with all the passion of the infinite, as Kierkegaard would say—that who one is, and how one belongs, matters more than can be known by any objective measure.[52] Miller concludes that "belonging is to be in accordance with who we are in ourselves as well as who we are in-the-world."[53] The transparent or authentic self integrates both the finite and the infinite. The transparent or authentic self has integrity as a finite being with obvious finite limitations but lives in the mode of the infinite, which is Kierkegaard's way of writing about what Miller calls (rather more pragmatically) "correct relation."

The Australian crisis of identity among some of the nonindigenous is an experience of a nonfit or something less than a good fit. The problem of belonging for them lies in not being able to achieve a rightful connection to the world in which they find themselves. Presumably, this has a twofold meaning: on the one hand, the problem lies in how the nonindigenous relate to the indigenous peoples, and/or to the historical events of their own Anglo-Celtic past, particularly as involved in the European discovery and colonization of Australia, and/or to the geographical reality of the place; but on the other, crucially, it also lies in how they relate to themselves as nonindigenous. Miller discusses Kierkegaard's notion of despair and finds that the Australian crisis of "misrelation" among many of the nonindigenous is experienced as a "pathology of the spirit," a pathology that points to the existential condition of not-belonging as an inauthentic mode of existence. The distinction between belonging and not-belonging is always more than situational, because it penetrates to how one finds one's own self, one's own place, and one's own worth in the world.

There is much of merit in Miller's account of belonging, derived from the concreteness of the Australian predicament. Discussing the panoply of sociopolitical meanings as a manifestation of a deeper existential crisis, rooted in the person first, is essentially correct; and moving within the orbit of Kierkegaard's work is enormously helpful. Miller pits belonging (as a correct relation) and despair (in finding that one does not belong) against each other as opposites, but what keeps belonging and despair in tension with each other is that each is always a possibility of the other; or, better, because belonging and despair are possibilities of any human person, belonging and not-belonging are poles of an existential tension, intrinsic to the personhood of anyone. Miller's work is a fruitful stopping point in my brief survey of thought on belonging because it is operative at the stratum of philosophical anthropology. She demonstrates that what is implicated in any sociopolitical crisis is the deeper existential truth that every person faces: Who am I? In relation to myself and to world, who do I take myself to be?[54] These questions of personal and social existence are, fundamentally, questions of belonging. Social science and power-focused critical theorists only get us so far, lacking, as they do, adequate tools to handle the problems of personhood. Thus, it falls to philosophy to handle the dynamics of personhood in the human search for meaning, fundamental to which is the endlessly textured reality of belonging.

FROM HEIDEGGER, let us merely say that "dwelling" is the key term that encapsulates a rich set of possibilities that can be brought to fruition as something like a place to call one's own, and yet a base from which to journey out into what is not one's own with the hope or expectation of returning, unwinding, resting, and drawing apart. For Levinas, the meaning of dwelling is perfected in its having a threshold. A threshold, we learn, is a liminal region that, in housing an inner sanctum, all the more affords the privilege of extending hospitality. As Aristotle argued about generosity, only those who have property have something they can be generous with.[55] So too, only those who have achieved a dwelling have what is required to offer hospitality. Furthermore, both Heidegger and Levinas invoke that which is more than property and that which is more than a political regime of property in their notions of dwelling. In their own ways, both are grappling with what transcends, and yet seems to hold, amplify, and animate dwelling, that which becomes manifest in unfathomable ways in the articulation of dwelling. For Heidegger, this is Being; for Levinas, this is exteriority (or what is beyond Being, which I will discuss in chapter 5).

Girard makes clear the problems that pertain to social groups and local factions. His consideration lays bare the tendency to violence that comes from attempting to formulate the meaning of belonging within a solely sociopolitical frame where the most salient characteristic is mimetic desire. The work of Miller provides a timely remediation, reminding us of relationality and concentrating the locus of a "right relation" in the authenticity of one's own personhood. With Miller, we come to the thorny but necessary zone of personhood. While personhood may be less readily amenable to objective measures and markers, it is also the only appropriate level at which to consider the meaning of belonging. Indeed, it is only at the level of the person—and not the biases of social groups—that the meaning of belonging is realized.

CHAPTER TWO

A Hermeneutic of Belonging

The task of this chapter is to understand better the experience of belonging. What do we mean when we say, *I belong*? This means that we must begin with the *experience* of belonging, rather than with either a definition or some matter-of-fact membership in a group. We must begin experientially because, although we often take our belonging for granted, belonging is apprehended affectively before its meaning is either understood and articulated in words or judged to be a matter of fact. We know this from bitter experience: when we are unexpectedly deprived of someone who belongs to us, or even some thing that was ours. Too often we experience the value of belonging in a heightened way when we are losing it, or sadly, once we have finally lost it. Wittgenstein reminds us of an oversight that we may be inclined to make in any inquiry: "One keeps forgetting to go right down to the foundations. One doesn't put the question marks deep enough down."[1] Keeping this in mind, one would be remiss in failing to attend to experience first since it is in the experience that the foundational material or data for understanding the meaning and determining the reality of belonging is first encountered. If we can recognize what is foundational in the experience of belonging, what is crucial to the sense or feeling of belonging, then we can also recognize it as structuring the experience of belonging. If we can grasp the structures, then we can proceed to a fuller understanding of what our belonging means to us.

Why would we undertake the effort to establish what is required for an understanding of belonging? The answer lies in the empirical observation that belonging is as complex and multivalent as any person or community and, as such, presents enormously difficult impediments to a firm understanding. For example, we can often feel welcome or unwelcome in a situation long before we have achieved any understanding of why that is; or indeed, we may begin to experience "mixed feelings" about a relationship or some set of circumstances without precisely knowing the reasons. Belonging can often be complicated and frustrating, while under different circumstances belonging is simple, comfortable, and obvious. It is an experience that can range from a deep sense of being at home—in the right place, with the right person or persons, safe, refreshed, surrounded by what is familiar—to having a resentful, troubled spirit at odds with one's surroundings or predicament, even to the extent that one seriously doubts that one belongs at all. Belonging, it appears, is a name that we can give to an experience in which people, places, or things matter to the extent that we regard ourselves in the light of these people, places, and things. We can delight in, rest with, or rail against our belonging, because whom or what we belong to already matters to us. The term "belonging" provides an arc of meaning over many simple and complicated experiences that we attempt to understand in order to grasp who we are and what we live in relation to. Belonging, it seems, is an intrinsically heuristic notion: that is, it invites much contemplation but thwarts any uniform, final, and exhaustive grasp. We ought to underestimate neither the thicket of issues that belonging raises nor the benefit of achieving some insight that can steer us as we enter into such a thicket. It is for such an insight that this chapter aims. If a hermeneutic can be found, an interpretive framework by which we can render our experiences of belonging intelligible, then it will be possible to make some meaningful claims about belonging in the chapters ahead.

STRUCTURES OF BELONGING

As Linn Miller emphasized, belonging can be experienced as a powerful feeling of a fit: that one fits here and now, with these people or this person, or that some object or role fits with oneself. Belonging is clearly a feeling of identity and purpose, Yet the experience of belonging can also be unassuming, inconspicuous, and, as mentioned above, often taken for granted. While there are times when we feel that we obviously belong somewhere or with someone—when our belonging has become patent and explicit (manifest as pride in our children's achievements or as love for an ailing parent, for example)—more often our fit with things, with others, with a place, and so on has become so familiar and so second-nature that our belonging does not feel like anything in particular. It does not stand out—it is not, or is no longer, ecstatic—because it is the very frame that structures how we are already relating to the people, places, times, and things of our lives. It provides the template of meaning, or the unspoken background against which we enact our daily business. Belonging can simply form the pattern in which we live out most of our days. It is what we would otherwise refer to as "normality." Belonging is what "being at home" feels like: comfortable, predictable, secure, intimate, understated, foundational, ordinary, yet open to occasional eruptions of extraordinariness. Keeping in mind both Heidegger's and Levinas's thoughts on "dwelling," when we are "at home" we are primarily attending to the daily and the domestic, to the jejune and the commonsensical. Nor is belonging restricted to our domicile, but extends to the domiciles of neighbors and friends, to the workplace and the school, or to any of the typical settings in which our lives unfold. When we are "not at home," the familiar and the commonsensical are anything but; and strange times, places, and tasks—the panoply of the uncanny—require much emotional, intellectual, and moral effort to make sense of. Belonging is a state we find ourselves in that does not often draw attention to itself except when our "being at home" is being highlighted or jeopardized, or when circumstances change and our own lives are consequently pulled in another direction away from home.

In seeking to ascertain in the experience of belonging what the requirements are that have been met so that we can confidently acknowledge that we belong, we must not be distracted by the potentially unlimited number of people, places, times, things, and circumstantial variables that invoke a sense of belonging and that color belonging in endless ways. Rather, we must pay attention to what it is that is being colored. That is, we must pay attention to how each of these variables is being experienced qua belonging and what it is about belonging (even in its understatedness, its implicitness) that means so much to who we are already. In doing so, we can begin to notice—as Miller tells us in her adaptation of Kierkegaard's thought—*how we are* in the sense of how we relate, *who we take ourselves to be* in our relating, and the *quality* or *authenticity* or *truthfulness of the relation* as we live it. One must begin to notice one's own self. Within this or that relation, who am I that these obligations hold me, that these affections draw me (or indeed that these people annoy me), that I would manifest myself in this relation and to the world as I do? How we belong in a particular relation is partly who we are. Belonging generally is nothing less than a mode of our existence, and therefore, the question of belonging inevitably becomes a question of existence. We suspect that our being sons and daughters, friends, spouses, colleagues, neighbors, participants in faith and civic communities, citizens, and so on constitutes in large part the meaning of our lives.

In order to grasp what is intelligible in the experience of belonging, and in order to discuss why belonging is fundamentally important, one has no choice but to attempt a phenomenology of belonging. If a rudimentary, but basically adequate, phenomenological framework can be established, one will be able to discern the minimum requirements of belonging and proceed to understand and affirm what it means to belong. In developing a phenomenology of belonging, attentiveness to the range of experiences that arise between the poles of what we can call "home" and "homelessness" becomes crucial. Belonging seems to be an experience of a fit to a greater or lesser degree, but of course, when something is a good fit, it does not normally draw attention to itself. The quiet contentment of a fit—you belong to me, I belong to you, these objects here at hand belong to us—seldom falls within the orbit of *problems*. The experience of belonging by itself is not problematic: when we belong we are, in some significant sense, at home, which is where we want to be or how we want to be. Our existential need for meaning is being met when we have the abiding deep contentment of home; and conversely, belonging becomes problematic when we lose the contentment of home or when we begin not to belong to a particular home. Homelessness, exile, exclusion all involve the loss or lack of a home, and the quiet contentment of a fit—especially when it was presumed or anticipated—is conspicuously, and perhaps painfully, absent. That is certainly experienced as problematic. Indeed, as we have seen, it is this loss or lack of a home, this nonfitting, that becomes a new source of violence in Girard's concern with mimetic rivalry in an increasingly globalized world.

Let us then proceed with this conspicuousness—the experience of not-belonging—which provides us with not only the impetus to consider the importance of belonging but also a path toward grasping the requirements for belonging that are not being met. Belonging, since it is a fit, since it is the air we breathe and the ground we stand upon, is harder to probe. Not-belonging, always conspicuous and sometimes harsh, brings the experience of belonging to our attention by way of contrast. Most often, it is only when we lose or miss the contentment of belonging that we notice that we are without it. This was Heidegger's point when he wrote about an assignment or a task becoming explicit at the moment when the equipment needed to bring about a successful completion has become unusable for some reason.[2] Similarly with the experience of not-belonging; it is the "fit" that now becomes explicit as that which is diminished or missing. An inverse phenomenology of belonging can be uncovered by following the stark contours of what not-belonging can mean to us. Not-belonging always involves a phenomenological conspicuousness. There is a gap between me and the person or people where I had anticipated the relation to be a fit. It is not easy to overlook that one does not belong in a given situation, and the disturbing discovery of a gap is one that radiates the experience of not-belonging. Let us consider a preliminary description of some of those stark contours now that inversely chart the contours of belonging itself.

On the one hand, there are situations in which we do not want to belong to someone or something: this is not our place, this feels wrong, I don't belong to you, I belong elsewhere, with others, I am just passing through. In such situations, there is an unmistakable discomfort and a desire to propel oneself away from a situation of not-belonging, from what is alien, or has become alien in the course of developments. Perhaps we grew tired of a social situation, a job, a dreary place; perhaps we gained an insight that changes the meaning of a relationship, perhaps insults were leveled or damages inflicted that uprooted the foundations unalterably. Perhaps I will not, or cannot, forgive. Perhaps the lure of a new home evokes a greater desire to leave than to stay. Perhaps we never particularly liked some aspect of what we belonged to from the start, and now we find the courage to admit that. Not wanting to belong can stem from a myriad of reasons, and we choose to renounce our belonging, whole or in part.

On the other hand, not-belonging can variously be experienced as a sharply painful rejection from the other or as a missing out on what is proper or good that I had anticipated or to which I felt entitled. That is, sometimes I want to belong here, with you, in this place, at this time, among these objects and accoutrements; but the problem is that I am not wanted or needed. When the desire to belong to someone, to some group, to some organization or thing is met with a refusal of that belonging—that one simply does not belong, not now, not ever, not here, not to you, not with them—the realization of not-belonging comes as a blow. We want to come in here, to put down our roots, but are shut out. Being cast adrift while others are rooted in the firm soil we crave is unpleasant, or possibly catastrophic. It constitutes an exclusion whose affective impact one does not recover from too readily, if at all. Concretely, most of us can recall relationships that we wanted to keep or renew but that ended, where one once belonged to another but no longer belongs. There have been job interviews that did not work out, advice rejected, snubs from neighbors, damaging falsities whispered by colleagues around the institution, and so forth. The resulting effect was rough and the experience not to be forgotten. Historically, we can think about those who were actually uprooted, invaded, evicted, exiled, whose place is lost and who simply have nowhere left to belong. We can think about a people, a nation, a religion, a race, or about those with limitations or disabilities, or about those whose faces have not yet been seen and who are simply not wanted, or who will no longer be tolerated, or who are cast out or annihilated, their belonging renounced.

In order to belong, it is not enough that I want to belong. It is clear that the *claim* or the *desire* to belong—which may burn like a fire within me—is not by itself sufficient to actually establish my belonging. Something more is needed. In addition to my desire to belong, you must also accept, reciprocate, or acknowledge my desire in some appropriately meaningful way. My desire to belong must read its welcome in the eyes of the one(s) to whom I look, a door left open for me, a place to rest that awaits me. If I have the desire to belong, and that desire has grounds for anticipating hospitality that are concretely realized, then I may indeed experience a belonging. Whoever you, they, or it may be, I must know that my affection is already meeting with who or what can welcome, gather, and accommodate me. Then, phenomenologically speaking, I am at home; or at least, with a home to call my own somewhere, I find that I am homeward-bound.

This of course is a generalized characterization of the dramatic tension that subsists between belonging and not-belonging—the particulars of which are as multifarious as are the persons or peoples or places or times or objects involved—but from this tension I now suggest the following as an operative hermeneutic. In order to belong, two requirements must be met. Let us call these phenomenological structures of belonging, and let us name them "existence-toward" and "existence-from."

Existence-Toward and Existence-From

To belong is partly, but necessarily, to relate to someone or something intentionally. It is to exist in tension *toward* someone or something by reason and emotion. I am conscious of, and I aim toward, someone or something with whom I am experiencing some kind of an affinity. I want to belong, and this wanting or tension-toward is what we can identify as a conditional structure of belonging. Let us name it *existence-toward*. In its absence, my connection with here, with you, with something is no more than a meaningless duty or coercive undertaking or a dissimulation on my part, due perhaps to a failure of nerve or lack of personal authenticity. Substantively, I strain away from here, from you, from this, because I do not want to belong. While my busyness and demeanor may suggest to some that I belong here, in fact I yearn to be elsewhere. What you see is merely an outward appearance. If I do not exist-toward someone or something, if I do not desire this or you or them or here in the affectivity of my heart, or if I can find no legitimate reason for remaining where I do not want to be, then I do not belong. I am dissembling and I am lying, and what you are encountering is the persona I have adopted for the purposes. Rather than belonging, I may be living out my lack of virtue and sincerity, my lack of imagination, my abundance of fear; and if I remain rather than clear the air, take myself in hand, and leave, I am transacting my self-destruction and perhaps yours too. Belonging then has this particular structural orientation: I must *exist-toward* what I am in relation with. Here is where I want or aim to be. This is what I know I need to do. Here is the promise or contract or vow that I have pledged myself to. I exist-toward someone or something; and without this structure, I simply do not belong.

The other structure of belonging is that we find that we have something of the other already within us, as a constitutive part of who we are, of who we take ourselves to be. We find that we belong because we already derive meaning from someone or something. Under this structural orientation, I *exist-from* what was already—or has become—some part of myself, in the sense of constituting part of my self-understanding. Something or someone is, to some degree, formative of my ground, my foundation, my self-understanding. I exist-from them, and I cannot be who I am without them. Either the spouse, parents, siblings, friends, children, communities, places, times, and so on to which I belong preexist me and formed the world of meaning into which I came, from which I emerged, in which I grew up, and by which I was molded, or they exist alongside me now because this is how my life has gone, and they are all the good fruits and bad outcomes of my choices. They welcomed me, they bore me, they chose me, they pledged themselves to me, they are flesh of my flesh; or they challenged and provoked me, they denigrated me, they took advantage of me; and I exist-from them because my relation to them is so significant that I cannot be who I am without them. Present or absent, alive or dead, they exist within me because I carry them as part of me, and to lose them would be to lose part of myself. Who I am reflects them. Those I exist-from bear a meaning for me that was, from the beginning, or has now become, a structure of my own self-experience, self-understanding, and self-appropriation. For example, to know oneself as daughter or son, wife or husband, sister or brother, master or servant, critic, enemy, friend, or lover is to exist from the ground of meaning that the other person has generated for me, in relation to me. Who they are for me is, again phenomenologically speaking, a measure of how I experience myself and come to know my own self. We can say the same of places and times and things. When people die, times change, friends move on, lovers betray, new opportunities collapse, things break down, I am the one who is partly dismantled. And when they smile to welcome me home, when forgiveness has purified a resentful, broken soul, I am restored.

Existence-from and *existence-toward* are, then, the two conditional structures that constitute the tension of belonging that we must explore in this study. They are simultaneous orientations in the one experience of belonging. Therefore it makes no sense to prioritize one over the other or to make either of them a condition of the other. Together they seem to compose the phenomenological structures of belonging, and as rudimentary and heuristic, they invite further insights and refinements. When we belong, we exist in a mode of tension *toward* something or someone that *already* holds us and uniquely constitutes what we are in significant ways. These structures are not the same, though they converge. We know this because we know we do not belong when one of the structures is removed. When we do belong, whom or what we exist-toward is whom or what we find we are already existing-from; whom or what we exist-from (our children, our parents, our friends, our colleagues, our generation, our province, etc.) is what is already constitutive of us, and we find we exist-toward this too in love, responsibility, duty, covenant. Belonging results from, and derives its flexibility and dynamism from, these two very fundamental orientations: to exist in tension-toward and to exist in tension-from. As we proceed in this study, it will be clear that belonging is inevitably a conservative concern, but that its dynamism is always also pushing toward what is new, exciting, deep, refreshing, holy, beautiful. Belonging is the human mode of existence. It is existence as threshold: settled and fitting, we flourish; but our lives and relationships are always probing and promising to spill out of their well-worn grooves to bring us like Abraham from the familiarity of Ur to the possibilities of Canaan.

Belonging as Problematic

Homelessness as Not-Belonging

As presented here, these structures of existence-toward and existence-from are simple and ideal. Together, they provide us with an operative hermeneutic by which we can begin to recognize belonging and assess the quality of that belonging.

We may exist in a state of tension-toward someone or something—for example, longing, yearning to belong, reaching out—but without achieving an *existence-from*, we remain in suspense. For example, we desire the acceptance of a lover, we want to become friends with someone, or we long for the recognition of a group or the forgiveness of one against whom we have trespassed. However, if we are refused, then in that refusal of whom or what we exist-toward, we do not belong. We find no welcome. If our longing remains, we exist in something not unlike limbo. If we do not attend to our unrequited longing, limbo can turn to shame or to despair.[3] We have not achieved an *oikos* or "home" *to exist-from*. The ground to which we want to relate "homewardly" does not await us, or awaits us no longer. We are kept at a distance. It is fundamentally a homelessness in which our longing remains unfulfilled or unreciprocated, and we find ourselves dangling fruitlessly.

On the other hand, what we exist-from may be secure, but the problem arises with desire or *existence-toward*. A diminishing tension-toward leads to displacement. Any person can "outgrow" a relationship, a place, a time, a community. We know from life-experience what it means to move on; and it is to displace oneself. Obviously, outgrowing someone or something is not necessarily negative, but it is not without pathos either. Children leave their parents, new interests open possibilities of opportunities and new friends that come at the cost of current friends. Of course, fantasy can jeopardize reality, and faraway fields are always greener. Pride or ambition can trample over the bonds that have held us. Desiring what is merely alluring but without substance can destroy the substantially real and familiar. The longing or the tension in *existence-toward* someone or something that already holds us can become colder, more stale, less passionate, less meaningful for many reasons. Obviously, something may come to light that changes our desire: betrayal, a series or pattern of ignoble choices in the home, a loss of faith, the arrival of a burdensome set of new requirements in an institution. In this case, our *existence-toward* can simply collapse. Belonging here may no longer be worth our effort or worthy of our affection. It would, however, be a mistake to think that old homes mean nothing to us anymore. On the contrary, they still reverberate within us. Their meaning for us has constituted part of who we are and how we understand ourselves. We still *exist-from* them. In the absence of some noxious upheaval or devastating violation, the diminishing of *existence-toward* does not necessarily become a rejection in loathing or in the blandness of uncaring. In simply outgrowing a home, we leave without rejection even if we

leave with some relief. Not-belonging becomes the problem of finding a new belonging, a new home; and in the meantime, we are homeless, even if ours is a chosen homelessness.

When the ties of *existence-toward* loosen, that relaxation yields
the same result as not being received in *existence-from*. It is homelessness, but not like limbo. Instead, it is a homelessness suggestive of an
exodus or emigration from a home that once held us to the possibility
of a new home. In both of these archetypal cases—limbo and exodus—
belonging remains our central concern, highlighting our state of not-
belonging as precisely the problem to be addressed.[4]

Corruptibility
If there is some further utility to such a hermeneutic, then it surely
must include grounds by which we can name corruptions, and perhaps
learn to navigate myriad complexities. This hermeneutic is preliminary
and simple, but the reality of belonging is often complicated, vigor-
ous, and turbulent. St. Augustine reminds us that every good—including the good of belonging—can be corrupted.[5] We must be careful. On
the personal level, there are the problems that follow from neuroses,
traumas, and prejudices that arise from situational backgrounds, life
events, and encounters. There are complexities in the psychological
makeup of the person, such as those laid out in the Myers-Briggs tests
or OCEAN personality traits. Belonging itself can be abused and corrupted. In the case of Stockholm Syndrome, for instance, we know
that long-term or distressing experiences of abuse and enslavement
can generate an irrational tension *toward* that which holds the victims
(what these victims, in their bondage, exist-from), where it is not un-
common for them to evince a loyalty to their captors or, once released
from their grip, to return to them. Kidnapped and battered persons,
victims of cult-mentality, whole peoples submerged in the tide of sociopolitical or commercial propaganda, and so on sometimes evince a
distorted affection, trust, or even devotion toward their tormentors
and manipulators that is far from healthy in either a psychogenic or
existential sense. Abuse from those we exist-from scars us deeply, and
perversions can twist us into dependency where we can exist-toward
the perverters or the manner of the perversions. In every conceivable
type of relationship, there exists the potential for endless corruptions

of belonging, and the resultant sadness, woundedness, and victim-hood can bring us to the end of the road.

The corruptions of belonging, if we are prepared to look for them, will be found in the sources of meaning that we exist-from and/or the sources of meaning we exist-toward. However, while we can become stuck in a cancerous web that our belonging has degenerated into, it is wrong to conclude that belonging is therefore intrinsically pestilential or pathological in personal or social ways. It is the company we keep — or that keeps us — that can be perilous. Belonging is the good that can be corrupted when not properly tended, and as a mode of existence, its corruption can lead to the corruption of one's life. Belonging can be dangerous because much is always at stake. Each person flourishes and disintegrates through the complexity of our relatedness to other people, places, times, and things. Belonging, if not cultivated, nurtured, and consequently allowed to "grow the soul," risks degradation in a manifold of ways.[6] Belonging — as an open reception of the other at the same time as an open giving to the other — is always vulnerable to being sullied. Yet when tended properly and with care, such belong-ing is a healer and, for some, maybe even a redeemer. Recovery from destructive patterns of belonging comes not from solipsistic atomism and withdrawal — which surely fuels the negativity of alienation — but from patterns of belonging that nourish the meaning of our personal humanity and affirm our lives on a scale that ranges from material to spiritual well-being. It is possible to diagnose malignant situations that pervert the affective experience of belonging by understanding what is intelligible, and by affirming what is reasonable and good, in the circumstances of our belonging.

Restriction to the Sociopolitical

On a sociopolitical level, Bernice Johnson Reagon points out a prob-lem of belonging that not only indicates the limitations I suggested in Heidegger's yearning for an enclosed dwelling but complements Girard's thesis of intergroup and intragroup rivalry and exclusion. As she puts it, "home" for some can be experienced as a "barred room."[7] The internal problem with "barred rooms" is that they provide a "nurturing space" for a while, but "they ultimately provide an illu-sion of community based on isolation and the freezing of difference."[8]

Belonging is further complicated by what Mariana Ortega refers to as "multiplicitous selfhood." Various demographic identity markers, such as skin color, religion, sexual identity, ethnicity, and so on create conflicts in belonging. Some aspects of one's own self face a "barred room" that otherwise would not be barred. The multiplicitous self becomes a "world-traveler" in the sense of traveling between worlds. Ortega writes: "Given the complexity of the selves as well as the complexity of spaces of belonging (in terms of their members as well as criteria for membership), there is no sense in which one can be said to fully belong. There are only different senses of belonging depending on which markers of identity are chosen. Full membership and belonging—the safe, comfortable home—is indeed an imaginary space in need of demystification."[9]

Ortega is partly right in that there are "different senses of belonging" that are appropriate to various places (and the local "politics of location"), but it is not clear what it would mean "to fully belong." Perhaps in this context full belonging might mean some kind of demographic homogeny that one shares, but beyond being an individual member of some larger social grouping, it is not clear what the source of Ortega's criticism is. Is a demystified social membership sufficient to satisfy the personal yearning to belong? To say that one cannot fully belong might, in the end, make some kind of sense if one keeps the analysis on a sociopolitical level, whose subject matter is restricted to the uneasy juxtapositions of those demographic social markers. Since social reality is an inherently pluralistic and intersectional field, one might agree with Ortega and yet be tempted to ask whether there is not something more to belonging than one's inclusion within an identity group and the status of that identity-group within the power struggles of the still larger, if fragmented, society. Beyond the sociopolitical level of analysis, full belonging—whatever that may be—remains an open question. Within the person, belonging seems to be experienced as a tension between the heuristic orientations, existence-from and existence-toward, and because of these, there are important reasons why we should widen our concerns with belonging beyond the sociopolitical level. The chapters below explore such reasons. While sociopolitical reality is a primary source of meaning, it does not exhaust all of a person's life.

On reading Ortega's account of belonging—or better, its nonrealization—I find a tone that suggests sorrow, a touch of resentment, and perhaps some yearning. Only she could speak to that, but it may be that her and others' dissatisfaction at the failure to achieve full belonging in any given society is more accurately an inevitable outcome of the restriction of analysis—that is driven, after all, by the deepest intimations of the human heart—to the field sociopolitical reality. Where the most salient characteristic in many fields of analysis is power, it is that very power that sets the ceiling on insight. The sense of a poor return on intellectual investment perhaps arises from a lingering, ever-present, and never-quite-eradicable sense of the meaning of "home" as transcending the meaning that is engendered by framing belonging in a limited way as merely a function of identity politics and factionalism. Ortega writes: "Despite the problems associated with the notions of home, belonging, and location, there is no denying the power that the notion of home has in producing sentiments of safety, comfort, and belonging."[10] Perhaps Heidegger's notion of the "uncanny" as the "not-at-home" is bound up with Ortega's frustration at the failure "to fully belong" because belonging not only embraces but also transcends the social and political aspects of our lives. In spite of the tendency of contemporary critical theory to think about belonging in sociopolitical categories, the "power" of belonging is not reducible to power politics and cannot be captured or exhausted by those categories.[11]

METAXY

To belong is one of deepest desires of the human heart, and in order to belong a person exists-toward other persons, places, and things, while she or he also exists-from these. Such is the heuristic approach to belonging that this chapter has undertaken. Yet, one might still ask, Why is it so? What is this quality of personhood that configures us in such a manner that our belonging matters? In using the language of tension to express what is intelligible in the experience of belonging, I am deliberately adapting the language that Eric Voegelin has emphasized in his exegesis of philosophical thought on consciousness.

Voegelin suggests that in consciousness there is a foundational tension whereby it is not so much that consciousness is *in* tension, but that consciousness *is* tension. Indeed, what I have named as the tension of belonging—journeying between the shifting sources of home and homelessness in the restlessness of existing-from and existing-toward—is derived from the relation in which human existence stands to the encompassing cosmos. We relate to the cosmos as participants; the primordiality of human existence is participation. Between the divine ordering "height" and the abyssal cosmic "depth," all things come into existence. From the direction of the divine pole of sacred mystery, human consciousness experiences a draw (*helkein*), while it also experiences itself as engaged in a search (*zetesis*), like a question reaching out for its answer, toward the source of the draw or tug.[12] *Helkein* and *zetesis* symbolize one and the same tension, but name the difference in human experience of that tension. Voegelin employs the symbol *metaxy* (in-between), from Plato's *Symposium* and *Philebus*, to symbolize this state of being in tension.

> It remains a mystery how man, in the temporal dimension of being (Plato's *thnetos*), can experience eternal being. There is, then, a need for a mediator who interprets and reports to the gods what is happening among men, and to men, what is happening among gods. The role of mediator is attributed by Plato to "a very powerful spirit," for the entire realm of the spiritual (*pan to daimonion*) lies between (*metaxy*) God and man. . . . The experience of being does not occur in world time from whose perspective the experience of eternity is hard to comprehend; instead it is allowed to take place where it is experienced, in the "in-between," the *metaxy* of Plato, which is neither time nor eternity.[13]

In the metaxy, human beings experience themselves in between poles that are variously described: life and death, perfection and imperfection, knowledge and ignorance, divine and human, immortality and mortality.[14] "The in-between—the metaxy—is not an empty space between the poles of the tension but the 'realm of the spiritual'; it is the reality of 'man's converse with the gods' . . . , the mutual participation (*methexis, metalepsis*) of human in divine, and divine in human, reality."[15]

While the accent of experience sometimes falls on *being drawn toward*, and sometimes on *being in search of*, both directional indices reveal the in-between, metaxic tension that is already constitutive of consciousness. Belonging, then, is another way to think about existence and consciousness as metaxy. We find our belonging when we exist-from what already constitutes us while existing-toward this in bonds of affection. The Platonic *helkein* exercised upon us is equivalent to existence-from, since we find ourselves in love, possessed by the spirit of the beloved, and sustained by the reality of what holds us; and the *zetesis* is equivalent to the intentionality of existing-toward the source of the draw in wondering, questioning, conceiving, affirming, choosing, acting, and loving. Belonging is a recognizable and abiding tension in the midst of ordinary life that grounds and motivates us and that announces itself to us both in joy and in times of crisis; while it is also by the tension of belonging that we become aware of our perennially reaching out for meaning in the metaxy. So, while the metaxy is the central insight that accounts for the tension that is belonging, it is belonging that gives us experiential access to the primordial meaning of existence in metaxic tension.

It is worth saying that the metaxy is neither merely an idiosyncrasy restricted to some of Plato's writings nor an arcane direction in the oeuvre of Voegelin's thought. What is needed to make sense of the predicament of existence and belonging as tension in the metaxy is a shift of perspective that comprehends persons (and derivatively, societies and history) as participants in an encompassing cosmos, rather than atomized modern egos floating in an arbitrary universe. *Metaxy* is the name we can give to consciousness, to the soul, to the reality of the person, as the metaphorical zone where the sacred and the profane intersect. The fifteenth-century Christian bishop, philosopher, astronomer, and polymath Nicholas of Cusa provides an example of the ubiquity of the metaxy in his work on *concordantia*: "Man is therefore God, but not absolutely, since he is a man. Hence he is a human god. Man is also the world, but he is not everything by contraction, since he is a man. Man is therefore a microcosm or, in truth, a human world. Thus, the region of humanity itself encloses God and the universal region in its human power."[16] Cusa should be read in a manner appropriate to a descriptive account of participatory existence. Each person paradoxically straddles both the incorporeal, unseen, abiding, and transcendent dimension of reality that generates, sustains, and pervades the cosmos and, simultaneously, the corporeal, visible, concrete, flourishing, and perishing dimension in which we live out our mortality. For Cusa, the in-between existence of each person harmonizes both transcendent and immanent dimensions of reality and brings them into "concordance" by participation in both because the person already belongs in both. Because we exist in between the poles of divine height and the cosmic depth, our existence is essentially a share in both, and our intellect a *capax omnium*.

The metaxy, the in-between tension of existence, is therefore the underlying dynamism of consciousness that moves each person for belonging. Our two phenomenological structures of existence-from and existence-toward are expressive of the primordiality of this dynamism by which we exist. Writing about human participatory existence in the metaxy at all times, Glenn Hughes argues that this is "a constant in historical meaning, and the human participant in history can become aware of this fact because in consciousness there is always an awareness of 'eternity,' of timeless divine presence, though the type or quality of that awareness varies with the historical stages or conditions of the search for the ground."[17] I will discuss this further in the next chapter, but for the purposes of this chapter, familiarity with the symbol of the metaxy is crucial. It denotes the experiential tension, relatedness, direction, and belonging of existence. It expresses our need and our desire to belong, and what that need and desire are grounded in; and conversely, the experience of belonging is the key that unlocks the fundamental metaxic character of our own personal existence, opening what seemed closed in us and unveiling horizons of meaning we hardly suspected.

BELONGING, THEN, IS A TENSION. The tension of belonging is how we exist because our existence is a fourfold set of relationalities. We exist firstly in relation to others, secondly in relation to the astrophysical and biological world around us, thirdly in relation to the divine and cosmic *mystery* that is existence, and fourthly (and perhaps most crucially) in relation to our own selves. We exist in between the variously experienced fields of reality, as a hub, as a participant, as a partner. Just as the existence of every person is neither static nor one-dimensional, but dynamic, dramatic, affective, intellectual, moral, spiritual, and profoundly complex, so too is the multivalent experience of belonging. I proposed an elementary hermeneutic that identifies two structures or orientations that seem formally to structure the apparently limitless descriptions of the tension of belonging: *existence-from* and *existence-toward*. Where a "home" remains desirable, we exist-toward it in affection; but we also exist-from it since it welcomes us, it has received us, and we fundamentally know ourselves by that home. One's belonging in any relationship or any set of relationalities is always in question, always in motion, always in tension. Yet here is our center, the home where our roots go down to anchor us. Belonging may be in motion, but to the extent that our relationships are genuinely relationships of belonging, we too are borne along in motion.

THE TIME HAS COME to put this preliminary hermeneutic to the test. In the chapters to follow, I will be concerned with the meaning of presence. If the orienting structures of existence-from and existence-toward can afford us some insight in interpreting the experience of belonging, it is because these structures are also the conditions of belonging. Now we must think about the significance of presence, which is the encounter with reality that opens the possibility of belonging by rendering those conditions operative. It is by presence that one is potentially unlocked from solitude and liberated for belonging. I will unfold the metaxic character of belonging by thinking about presence and personhood before proceeding to extend the analysis to sociality in community, politics, and history. That is, before we would consider sociopolitical belonging, we must first explore belonging at the personal level because it is only here that the meaning of presence and belonging can be experienced, grasped, and affirmed as real. If we can make clear to ourselves in the following section what is significant about personal existence as, first, participation in the abiding presence of the cosmos, second, presence by way of consciousness and the flesh, and third, presence in love, then we will more richly be able to consider community in the next section as a belonging nested within, and emergent from, the fullness of meaningful presence.

PART 1

Presence

CHAPTER THREE

Of the Cosmos

This chapter considers the cosmos as the abiding presence of a primordial totality that always holds us and of which we are always part. By "the cosmos" is meant the ordered totality of all things in which we exist, the Whole of which we are a part. I will approach the meaning of the cosmos as a kind of presence. "Cosmological presence" begins with experiencing and acknowledging the primordiality of our own personal mortality. We know that we will not always be here; we experience ourselves getting older. We are also aware of the wheel of life and death, the coming into this world and the going out of it. By cosmological presence, I intend the significance of being contingently alive, and in that significance, something precious, a value beyond any cost-benefit measures. My claim is that by cosmological presence, we discern our mortality as what unfolds against a backdrop that is not itself mortal. Our lives must pass, but we love as though we endure. The value of our lives and the value of the lives of those we love are unrestricted by the fact of death and the fact that nothing persists. They are transcendent values, sacred values. So, by "cosmos," I intend a bond and an order, the totality that encompasses us, present in modes of both sacred and secular values, as an intersection of time and timelessness, as a metaxy of mortality and immortality. Cosmos is primarily a presence because, under the conditions of existence in the cosmos, we live, suffer and flourish, and pass away; yet through it all, we are participating in what does not pass away. By our very existence we participate in the primordiality of cosmological presence.

I begin this first section on Presence with the cosmos because it is primordial presence. Not only is the person "in the cosmos" along with everything else, but for the pursuit of the meaning of belonging it is crucial to underscore that it is only "in the person" that there can be a cosmos. Ours is a moving viewpoint, and in later chapters, we will be in a position to elucidate this claim further. In this chapter, I shift emphasis from the language of "experience" to the language of presence that speaks itself through persons. Indeed, I will conclude that each person is, metaphorically speaking, an *embassy* of the cosmos, that personhood alone is what gives expression to cosmological presence, and that it is the person who exists precisely as a mediation of the cosmos. In order to arrive there, I divide this chapter into three parts: the first considers mythopoeic existence in the cosmos, where all gods, mortals, societies, and things are fused together; the second considers the process of differentiation that loosens this compactness; and the third considers personal existence as the paradoxical reality in which the part brings forth the Whole.

PRIMORDIAL COMPACTNESS: EXISTENCE IN THE COSMOS

The first task then bears upon the meaning of belonging in the cosmos and the significance of our place, purpose, and role within the Whole. While such propositions sound mystical or vaguely religious to contemporary ears, they capture something so crucially important that an understanding of humanity is woefully inadequate without it. To speak of the cosmos as presence is already to point toward our existence within the primordial totality of all things, and always as a unique part of that totality. To recall presence in an encompassing cosmos is to engage in *anamnesis* or recollection, an effort to recover one's own personhood as more than an autonomous unit within the Whole, to perceive oneself as a participant in the unity and emergence of all that is.[1] Let me begin with clarifying the meaning of "cosmos" and "cosmological," before discussing the dramatic importance of anamnetic recollection, which will occupy us for the rest of the chapter.

The Cosmos as Sacred Drama

In the most general sense, the cosmos is a totality of reality, but emphatically, this does not mean an accumulation of objects. Nor does "cosmos" bear the same meaning as "universe." Gregor Sebba writes, "Our dictionaries define 'cosmos' as 'the universe as an ordered whole or system.' This fits the original Greek meaning of 'cosmos' as 'order' and especially 'world order,' but the modern conception lacks what the ancient one had: the view that this order is divine and divinely created." Sebba continues, "For us [moderns], the presence of the universe is a fact, no more."[2] Louis Dupré asks, "What did the Greeks of the classical era understand by *kosmos*? Clearly, its meaning of ordered totality exceeded that of the physical universe we now call cosmos."[3] Furthermore, Glenn Hughes writes that the cosmos "does not represent simply another entity.... The Greek *kosmos* means 'the ordered Whole of reality,' ... the common matrix assumed 'behind' the variegated things of experience."[4] The cosmos as "common matrix" is not merely what we exist within but also what we abidingly exist as part of.

For mythological, pretheoretical societies (i.e., prephilosophical and prerevelatory societies of, typically, ancient and prehistorical times), the cosmos as common matrix—the background that gives rise to, holds, sustains, and gathers in all that exists—was not an object of metaphysical abstraction and knowledge, but was the experiential context or setting for the mythopoeic drama of life in which everyone and everything was already implicated and had their role to play. The cosmos was the Whole whose common matrix was the foundation or *Urgrund* from which everything already existed, and to the extent that human societies attuned themselves to the order of the cosmos by ritual and liturgical symbolism, they were assured of their place, their life, their belonging. In such societies, existence, mystery, and reality were symbolized in the form of dramatic myth, in which immortal gods, demons, demigods, mortals, animals, plants, and inanimate things existed together, one with another within the same cosmological order. Rather than an aggregate of facts to be known, the cosmos was saturated with enacted meaning and sacredness. It was experienced as an unfolding drama by its players, who were already enacting their role. Cosmological existence was the participation, by the very living of one's life, in an encompassing, sacred order. It was participation as dramatic attunement—rather than theoretical knowledge or revelatory scripture—that unveiled life itself as oriented toward substantive belonging within an overarching and interpenetrating order of sacredness. Cosmological belonging, as attunement, was therefore grasped as the only viable direction of culture, since the alternative represented the collapse into, or the eruption of, primordial chaos. Importantly, the drama of existence was heightened by the ever-present threat of chaos that could be realized if one failed to participate in the sacredness of the common matrix. With the presence of cosmological sacredness, there necessarily arose the copresent risk of diabolical chaos in the inevitable violations and lapses to which human existence is always prone.

This remains a relevant insight because the primordial experience of belonging in a sacred cosmological order endures as a genuine experience at all times. The primary difficulty with such a contention is that cosmological belonging is a subtle experience and easily overlooked, or indeed, easily dismissed by cynicism. However, if the "common matrix" of reality "was not itself an object of cosmological mythic thought," as Hughes points out, there is little reason to think that contemporary thinkers and the cynics among us would be inclined to speculate on it either.[5] The cosmos as presence, as an order of primordial belonging in a common matrix, often goes unnoticed. *Anamnesis* or recollection of the cosmos reminds us that we are already rooted in the Whole, which is abidingly present, and that we are invited by the norms of our own lives to find and deepen our belonging as participants in the Whole that holds and sustains us.

The cosmos is a presence of sacredness, and it is to this sacredness that our belonging tends. To belong within the totality of the abiding cosmos is to acknowledge that our belonging is already subject to two kinds of condition. Following Eric Voegelin, we can call these the conditions of passing and lasting.[6] Always inhering in the cosmos, they are bound up with an order of sacredness that governs existence. The condition of cosmological passing includes all the characteristics of emergence and mortality: conception, birth, maturity, decline, death, with all of the attendant flourishing and suffering that pertain to sentient beings. The condition of cosmological lasting includes all that intelligence, reason, and love aim at: it includes truth, goodness, and the beauty that inspires every wonderment and praise and that suspends mere ordinariness in its uncovering of dimensions of extraordinariness.

Of course, truth, goodness, and beauty are traditionally referred to as the transcendentals, and they are transcendentals of intelligibility just as much as they are "indices" of what grounds the intelligible. Thus it is that, while truth, goodness, and beauty communicate an intelligible order that saturates the metaxy of existence, consciousness, and belonging, they also point toward what mystics such as the Pseudo-Dionysius characterized as a "darkness which is above the intellect."[7] Cosmological presence is presence in the metaxy between conditions of lasting and passing that we can symbolize variously as mystery and knowledge, wisdom and ignorance, time and timelessness. Life passes, and death enacts the limit of every life, but always in the presence of what does not pass and what cannot be exhausted. Such is the cosmos, opening us to the pathos of life and death while also invoking the urgency of attunement to what does not pass.[8] Voegelin writes, "One man lasts while others pass away, and he passes away while others last on. All human beings are outlasted by the society of which they are members, and societies pass while the world lasts. And the world not only is outlasted by the gods but is perhaps even created by them. . . . A first ray of meaning falls on the role of man in the drama of being insofar as the success of the actor depends upon his attunement to the more lasting and comprehensive orders of society, the world, and God."[9] The world with its seasons and celestial revolutions itself partakes of the highest, sacred order. The role a person or society plays is aimed at attunement to the lasting order of the cosmos, an order symbolized adequately by the gods. The condition of passing inherent in the cosmos is not itself an evil and is not itself a chaos, but is a condition of cosmological presence. In ritual and liturgical attunement to the sacredness of what does not pass, even those who must pass stand in the light of what is everlasting, which overarches each of their temporal moments. We already exist-from the cosmos since it gave rise to us in time, but by necessity we must exist-toward it in attunement or we lose even our hold on time and perish untimely. The sacredness of the cosmological order is its necessity. There is no higher value since sacredness is the absolute, and there is no other source of life and order.

At first glance, the condition of passing communicates mere temporariness, a meaning that contrasts with the meaning of the condition of lasting. However, it is because of this temporariness, because we must die, that our mortal passing raises the stakes and enriches our participation in what lasts; and what lasts radiates a wisdom and consolation to mortality. Even the most distracted and cynical among us must, in the end, contend with the concrete mortality of ourselves and others. We live our lives aware that suffering and flourishing are real and that life is short, and yet somehow we know we must get up, greet the day, and go into the world to edify and beautify, as we speak the truth to one another, and to enact the good that seeks thriving and the alleviation of unnecessary misery. Under the conditions of lasting and passing, home unveils its necessity: home is a mirror of what lasts, and so it can shelter us from caprice, from the vagaries of the ephemeral. Home functions as a microcosmos, bolstering us with solidity and purpose when we are supine and listless and refreshing us with the permanence of its fertile soil so that we may be propelled outward again to navigate the anguish and joy of the passing world. Home is consecrated ground because it reconciles us to the reality of cosmological presence: it is home that gathers together the conditions of lasting and passing in intimate and familiar ways. Home is where life begins; it is where the generations come and go, where mistakes are made and rectified, where success finds its measure; it is the chronicle of ordinariness in whose own story the mundane gives way to the sacred. To recall home with all of our heart is to recover the cosmos. As microcosmos, home is a mirror of the timeless "common matrix" out of which our lives emerge in time, a heightening of existence and belonging. As time passes, home is where we find a way, worthy of ourselves, to bear witness to what does not pass.

Consubstantiality: Intimacy in the Cosmological Community

Prior to philosophy and revelation, ancient societies symbolized their presence and participation in the cosmos in ways that suggested an interwovenness of all things, a unity of substance. All things were "located" within the cosmos. There was no symbolization of a field of reality beyond the cosmos. The cosmos, rather, was where all immortals, mortals, and animate and inanimate fields of reality were to be found. In this sense, the cosmos was the Whole in the most comprehensive sense. For the ancients, the dramatic emphasis lay upon the Whole as a harmonious bond of communion among all things and as an order of sacredness, all of which could be violated. Thus it was that fantastic images and stories arose: shape-shifting, divine interventions, demonic eruptions of chaos and heroic conflict for the sake of order, and so on. Such unity of cosmological substance was so emphatic that it took precedence over the autonomy and formal distinction of types of things from each other, a development that had to await the theoretical thinking that had not yet arrived.

In a cosmos full of gods and their erratic, powerful ways, what importance could there be in a recognition of the partial autonomy and relative distinction among things? When a tree with a twisted trunk is held to be a soul who transgressed a divine ordinance, to what extent is it even a tree? Or a mortal individual? When the wind blows, or the river rises, or the fires rage, are we confronting elemental physical realities in their massiveness, or has there been an outburst of divine fury? When gods can take the shape of animals or mortals or celestial bodies, how secure is knowledge? When Athena commands Odysseus to use his eloquence to turn his army around and return to battle, or when Aphrodite whisks Paris away from certain death at the hands of Menelaus to his "fragrant, perfumed bed," allowing the war to continue, to what extent are political events even human?[10] The existence of the world hinges upon the metaxic context of ritual and liturgy. That is, order comes not from knowledge, which is never guaranteed, but from the attunement of ritual drama and liturgy to that which lasts. Order comes from the alignment of mortals and gods. Voegelin writes, "God and man, world and society form a primordial community of being."[11] The "primordial community of being" is not a body of knowledge, but a belonging, precariously made, unmade, and recovered again through ritual action. A "primordial community" refers to the intimate experience of an interfusing and interpenetration of each of these four primordial partners with each other. Sharing the same common matrix, the immortal gods, mortal men, and the world are more same than different. The character of cosmological existence is more than an interrelationality between discrete things; rather, it is an intimacy of belonging together in the sacred Whole of the cosmological substance. Voegelin calls this "consubstantiality."

The primordial community is a compact symbol that expresses the intimate communion of all fields of reality with every other. While it holds latent within it the later differentiation of each constituent or partner from the other (just as the later differentiation holds inherent within things their consubstantiality with other things), ancient mythological consciousness seems to have found meaning dominantly in the underpinning oneness, the common matrix, that holds all things as entwined together for their existence, rather than in their separateness from each other. Cosmological consubstantiality was the overriding presence that framed the drama of existence and the meaning of society and culture. As such, it did not become particularly conspicuous. Myth symbolizes the meaning of existence as a drama *within* the cosmological whole, where the dramatic exploits of a character more deeply symbolize the struggle to attune the world to the sacred order of the cosmos as a whole. In this sense, myth is a remembering and re-presenting of the sacredness of that which lasts (and derivatively, the sacredness of what passes in its attunement to what lasts). It is everybody's business, so to speak. In the absence of the later differentiations of genera in reality—physical, chemical, biological, psychological, noetic, and revelatory— and under the dominance of consubstantial oneness, there were no obvious barriers to conceiving the transubstantiation of one body or level of reality into another. Theoretically, there were not yet "things" as such, but all bodies were bound up with the primordial struggle between *kosmos* and *chaos*, the choices of each player letting one or other of these flow. Before *theoria*, the pursuit of knowledge was ancillary to the life-giving alignment among the primordial partners whose communion constituted the cosmos. What we might refer to today as magic or enchantment was characteristic of the experience of consubstantiality in cosmological consciousness—that is, awareness of the cosmos as a drama within which one must play one's role for the sake of existence itself. Voegelin describes the context: "[All things exist] in a charmed community where everything that meets us has force and will and feelings, where animals and plants can be men and gods, where men can be divine and gods are kings, where the feathery morning sky is the falcon Horus and the Sun And Moon are his eyes, where the underground sameness of being is a conductor for magic currents of good and evil forces."[12] It is not hard to see that the experience of living within such

a mysterious, intimate, and flowing cosmos is a sacred drama of belonging with and among the primordial partners in the community
of being, to the extent that it is a cosmos (and not a chaos). In the
cosmological experience of reality, "God and man, world and society"
are the four fields of reality that are always consubstantially present,
and their consubstantiality is not an experience of an amalgam, like
various self-contained items gathered together like fruit in a bowl. All
partners in the primordial community are intimately entangled with
each other because they all subsist within the same common matrix.
None can be unraveled from the other without losing their own hold
on existence, since their primordial belonging is the sacred foundation
of all lasting and passing.

Mircea Eliade discusses why the defining characteristic of the cosmos was the abiding presence of the sacred and, conversely, why the
defining characteristic of chaos was the absence of the sacred: "If every
inhabited territory is a cosmos, this is precisely because it was first
consecrated, because, in one way or another, it is the work of the gods
or is in communication with the world of the gods."[13] To belong in a
territory is to make the cosmos present or to come into the presence
of an order of sacredness. Only by sacredness do we have a cosmos.
Consequently, to belong—to a place, to a society, to a world—is always
to belong in the cosmos and its intrinsic sacredness. It is a cosmos of
primordial partners whose presence in and with one another is itself
a sacred order revealing "absolute reality and at the same [making]
orientation possible."[14] In belonging, time and place have been consecrated, and are continually consecrated, to timeless order that binds
the cosmos. Timelessness, the divine mode of lasting, is what orders
and binds the passing.

On the other hand, where we do not yet have a cosmos, we do
not yet have either sacredness or belonging. Eliade writes, "An unknown, foreign, and unoccupied territory . . . still shares in the fluid
and larval modality of chaos. By occupying it and, above all, by set-
tling in it, man symbolically transforms it into a cosmos through a
ritual repetition of the cosmogony."[15] Through dramatic ritual, time
and place are consecrated to a timeless order that underpins life. Life
can be lost, but it is restored by way of ritual participation in, and
an anamnetic recollection of, the founding of the cosmos. According to Eliade, we can belong to the cosmos because there is sacred

center, an *omphalos* (navel, central point), a hallowed place in our presence.[16] "Every religious festival, any liturgical time, represents the reactualization of a sacred event that took place in a mythical past, 'in the beginning.'"[17] Indeed, "reality is saturated with divine presence, because the origins of things are manifest in the cosmos."[18] For the cosmological mind, exile was a punishment worse than death, because death occurs within the conditions of the cosmos. Death has its place within the sacred order of lasting and passing. To be exiled, however, was to be cast into the jaws of the unsacred chaos that lay just outside the walls. To belong to a cosmologically attuned society was to belong to the sacredness of the cosmos that already held us, and to this sacredness all were oriented for the sake of life.

TRANSCENDENCE AND IMMANENCE: DIFFERENTIATING THE COSMOS AS BOND AND ORDER

The mythic expression of cosmological belonging is eventually superseded by philosophic and scientific theory, as well as revelatory religion. Reasons for this will be discussed below. I want to emphasize here that mythic symbolization of the truth of existence and belonging is not so much denied by later symbolizations as it is refined and clarified. For example, I have been discussing truth in mythic form in the above section, but I have been discussing it theoretically rather than mythically in order to conceptualize and affirm it in a way suited to our theoretically inclined minds. There are two points to be made. First, this does not erase our need for myth, for finding a way to communicate the meaning of what cannot be fully grasped by intelligence and reasonably affirmed by judgment. The human "place" is the metaxy, and we are always confronted by mystery, which, when it becomes conspicuous, can only be expressed in a mythos. Second, the superseding of myth by theory and revelation is not so much a swapping of one symbolization for another as it is a development of human consciousness. What I have called "cosmological presence" is a conceptual referent of a series of experiences that had been symbolized mythopoeically in its array of magical, dynamic, and evocative images and that we are able to render theoretically intelligible with philosophical precision. I called attention to the sacredness of order in which life and death occur, in which existence is always subject to the conditions of lasting and passing. Ours is no longer the pretheoretical and mythopoeic consciousness of our ancestors, but what is crucial for an understanding of belonging is that there is no reason to assume that our existence is somehow exempt from cosmological presence. Under more developed circumstances—where we can better differentiate between the knowable and the inherently mysterious—the primordial experience of the cosmos is nonetheless still *our* primordial experience: we still live and die, we still suffer and flourish, even as we continue to enact the drama of our own lives from and toward what does not change: absolute values we discover in places, persons, principles, virtues, convictions, hopes, all of which function as mirrors of what does not pass. In this section, I want to demonstrate the enduring importance of cosmological presence in a way that is equal to the level of our time.

For context, specifically human beings have been around for well over one hundred thousand years, according to the archaeological anthropologists. The dates keep being adjusted with new research and discoveries, but presumably mythic symbolization has been around for as long as we have.[19] Yet our mode of thinking and symbolizing the truth of existence and belonging is no longer restricted to the mythic. We today are, of course, beneficiaries of the developments in theory and revelation and are successors to those in whom the irruptions or "leaps in being" occurred. The time frame of all this development has come to be known as an "axis time" or as the "Axial Age," coined first by Karl Jaspers.[20] We can squabble about when this window of time opened and when it closed, about how it occurred relatively simultaneously across vast spaces, or about what is included and what is not, but for the purposes of this study, the term "Axial Age" is a useful heuristic term that points generally to a unit of emergent meaning within the metaxy of consciousness, existence, and belonging. Speaking generally, we live within the horizons set by this axial window in the wisdoms of Taoism, Buddhism, the Vedic writings of the Upanishads, the Hebrew prophets, the Greek philosophers, and nothing precludes us from including Christianity and Islam. Quoting from Jaspers, Voegelin writes, "This axis would have to be the time when 'the formation of humanity [*Menschein*]' happened with 'such overwhelming fertility' that the result would be empirically convincing both for the West and Asia and for all men at large, regardless of this or that faith, and thus could become 'for all peoples the common basis of historical self-understanding.'" [21] From China through India, and through to Israel and Greece, mythopoeic consciousness began to quicken with the unfurling of fecund possibilities within its "intracosmic" narrative. If the myth began to fall short as a suitable symbolization of truth, it was due to developments in human consciousness that sought a truth in a form not available in myth.

Dissolution of Cosmological Compactness

Voegelin writes that the mythic style of truth is fundamentally unstable because the communion between the primordial partners—God and man, world and society—is not adequately symbolized in the myth. It was a style of truth that was susceptible to disintegration by its very nature. In the cosmological myth, we have seen how the existence of each partner as a field of reality is experienced and symbolized as "intracosmic" because the gods, mortals, societies, and the world itself are bound together within the one cosmic order. This means that the sacred order of the cosmos itself is a function of the Whole. Within the compact mythopoeic consciousness of ancient peoples, the intracosmic bond of sacredness was sufficiently compelling. That is, the cosmos itself was its own sacred ground. The first, and most crucial, development of consciousness is the gradual recognition that the ground, the *arche*, the origin of the cosmos can neither be the cosmos itself nor be contained within the cosmos.

Whatever the sacred ground of the cosmos may be, it cannot be another existent with the cosmos because the Whole cannot exist from a constituent part that remains less than the whole. Existents are located within, and find their place as part of, the Whole. Nor is the cosmos itself another existent within some other putative Whole. This creeping conceptual instability began to disturb the compactness of intracosmic existence when the sacredness of the lasting divine ground of the whole was increasingly recognized as "nonexistent," or beyond the various existents to hand.[22] The ground cannot be another one of those existents but, by contrast, has a mode of "nonexistence" or is more-than-existence. Since perceivably existent "things" like plants, animals, and mortals can die, the apparently more enduring partners in the compact cosmological myth, such as "the universe and the gods, assume the function of the non-existent ground," writes Voegelin.[23] Since the universe and the gods are not subject to perishing in the way existent things are, but seem to endure, they more closely approximate to the enduring sacred ground of the cosmos than do other, more "existent" things. They are, to be crude, fitting representatives of the nonperishing ground of the cosmos.

However, since "the astrophysical universe must be recognized as too much existent to function as the non-existent ground of reality, and the gods are discovered as too little existent to form a realm of intracosmic things," mythic symbolization begins to shed its authority as the symbolic vehicle that effectively communicates the truth of the cosmos.[24] For example, the "unseemliness" of the deportment of the mythic gods of the Greeks was enough for someone like Xenophanes to reject them as the divine ground. As an early philosopher (ca. 530 BCE), he could write, "But mortals believe the gods to be created by birth, and to have their own (mortals') raiment, voice and body. But if oxen (and horses) and lions had hands or could draw with hands and create works of art like those made by men, horses would draw pictures of gods like horses, and oxen of gods like oxen." Furthermore, "Both Homer and Hesiod have attributed to the gods all things that are shameful and a reproach among mankind: theft, adultery, and mutual deception."[25] The gods have insufficient authority to represent the sacredness of the cosmological order. Instead, "There is one god, among gods and men the greatest, not at all like mortals in body or in mind. He sees as a whole, thinks as a whole, and hears as a whole. But without toil he sets everything in motion, by the thought of his mind. And he always remains in the same place, not moving at all, nor is it fitting for him to change his position at different times."[26]

As far as the astrophysical universe is concerned, it also ceased to function as a likely candidate for the nonexistent ground of all that is, especially when it later came to greater theoretical clarity, replete with its own autonomous structures. The universe, after all, comes to share too much in the nature of an existent "thing" to be the source of itself. The "nonexistent" ground of reality begins to suggest itself as supracosmic and transcendent of the Whole, rather than simply intracosmic. Rather than banishing the cosmos as the bond that holds all things and the order that structures all things, one might well advance the argument that the development of consciousness has enhanced the mystery of existence exponentially by diminishing the experience of an intracosmic world full of gods as the "ground of being."

The Differentiation of Consciousness and *Theoria*

We have seen how the compact consubstantiality of all things within the cosmos dominated mythic consciousness, but in the Axial Age this compactness began to shift and loosen, and its emphasis began to pivot toward the autonomous existence and distinction of each thing. Voegelin calls the development of consciousness a process of differentiation. The differentiation of consciousness has obviously resulted in a growth of scientific and philosophical knowledge about the world and ourselves, but "differentiating knowledge does not dissolve the bond of being between God and world, which we call the cosmos."[27] In the process of differentiation in consciousness, the cosmos as a common matrix remained, but individual things and their relations became the prominent focus of attention as objects of knowledge, opening the speculative realms of nature and form.[28] One's belonging was no longer tied to a membership within a cosmologically attuned culture, sanctified by liturgical symbolization. Rather than securing the existence and belonging of all by ritual reenactment and the consecration of a place, Axial Age irruptions across the world seemed to suggest an inversion: now it was that each person could respond to the order of the cosmos, an order of sacredness and presence, by an authority present within themselves. From the security of a world full of gods and political regimes of cosmic-divine rulers with sacramental powers, the spiritual upheaval in consciousness began to move in the more fraught direction of personal accountability. That is, the emergence of the individual person is emphatically part of the process of differentiation, but one that highlights relationality as constitutive of personal existence: relations with other persons, with other things, with oneself, and with the cosmos out of which one has come and toward which one veers in the interiority of one's life.

Cosmological presence does not disappear with the cosmological myth, but manifests itself in the interior reality of personhood. Instead of regarding individuals merely as members of a society ritually attuned to cosmological order—where the quality of that social attunement was paramount in imbuing all members with a derivative sacred value—one was now encountering in the other, him- or herself, a depth resonating with the depth of the cosmos. In the shift of horizon opened by Axial Age developments in consciousness, the individual soul was now potentially the locus into which the cosmos itself had already "flowed" and from which it was always mediated. To violate the person, in acts of "theft, adultery, and mutual deception," amounted to breaking the bond and order of the cosmos. Of course, insights once achieved take time to be communicated, to be accepted, and to gain personal, social, and historical traction. The discovery of what we might later call personal dignity does not eradicate the possibility of chaos, but only raises the stakes. Recognition and reverence of the immeasurable cosmological depth of personhood are subject to a time lag, and it is in time that such an insight must grind its arduous way through the vicissitudes of history into law and politics, into ethics and religion, and into interpersonal relations. Yet it remains that an insight gained is an insight that cannot be ungained or reversed, even if ignored.

Let us briefly consider the significance of the differentiation of consciousness as it occurred in history in order to show that the primary experience of belonging in the presence of the cosmos persists even under differentiation conditions. Differentiation "dissociates" gods and man, world and society from their consubstantial intimacy with one another as the primordial bond and order toward an understanding of their meaning as different fields of reality. Hughes stresses that "the elemental differentiation that breaks the authority of the cosmological myth is the imaginative and conceptual separation of world and divinity."[29] He goes on to quote words by Voegelin that are worth reproducing here. Differentiation is the process that "dissolves the image of reality produced by the primary cosmic experience. A de-divinized world takes the place of a cosmos full of gods, and correlatively, the divine is concentrated into a world-transcendent ground of being. . . . 'Immanent' and 'transcendent' are the spatio-metaphorical indices attributed to realms of reality that have become, respectively, the world of things in space and time, and the divine being of the ground beyond space and time."[30] The opening of transcendence and immanence from mythic compactness is the "spatio-metaphorical" relocation of mystery from an intracosmic realm of a world full of gods to a divine ground or foundation (*arche*) "beyond" both the world and gods.

As alluded to above, what this meant in practice was another opening: the opening of *theoria*, of philosophy and science, of the possibility of grasping the intelligibility of things in their own right as autonomous realities. A dedivinized world is a world that can operate according to its own laws and norms, appropriate to the various natures or forms of existent things, because, unlike the mythopoeic examples we find in Homer's *Iliad* and *Odyssey*, for instance, the world is no longer conceived to be the playground of the gods. Nor is the political order of society fused with the divine order of the gods, in the sense of the *Enuma Elish* or the Egyptian theologies. In the epochal differentiation of Christianity, as an eminent counterexample, the things of Caesar are explicitly differentiated from the things of God, differentiating a realm of political things with its own autonomous structure from a realm of spiritual things.[31] The divine kingship of the pharaoh or the cosmic-divine empire of Babylon is superseded by the mundane nature of the political on the one hand and the charismatic and sacramental community of the church on the other. *Theoria* rationally discovers and clarifies the autonomous realities of things and thereby opens the cosmos from its mythic compactness to its transcendent and immanent dimensions.

Autonomy, however, is only one consequence of the development of consciousness and its knowledge. The cosmos has not vanished, but it too has been differentiated. Voegelin clarifies the meaning of cosmological order under differentiated conditions as a threefold order: "The experience of being differentiates the order of things (a) in their autonomy, (b) in their relation to one another, and (c) in their relation to their origin."[32] Autonomy then is one part of the cosmological order. There is also the bond among autonomous things and between all things and the mysterious ground of their existence. The "origin" or ground from which all things exist transcends those things by necessity. The origin is not rightly considered another object or a place within the catalog of objects and places, but as the necessary source they exist-from and as the telos they exist-toward. The primary experience of the cosmos is a primacy of belonging in the most profound sense. Only through meditation on one's own troubled, restless conscience, the pure desire to know, and the yearning to belong does one begin to make sense of the cosmos as the presence of a bond and order in which one is already implicated.[33] John J. Ranieri, commenting on the intimate presence of the ground in consciousness, notes that there is no "detached, Archimedean point from which humans might coolly ask questions about the ground of existence as if they somehow stood apart from it all."[34] Glenn Hughes writes that, "since Voegelin knows that most people never explicitly concern themselves with the 'ground of being' at all, one might ask what he means by this assertion. He means that the desire to know is, generally and comprehensively, a human being's search for the meaning of his or her own existence."[35] For the human being, desire, restlessness, and the yearning for home function as something like an opening toward the transcendent ground. To the extent that people begin to question and seek the meaning of their lives, they find themselves on a quest for the ground. "But since no-one's existence is the cause of itself, the meaning of anyone's existence is ultimately to be found only in the cause of all existence. Therefore, any search for meaning is ipso facto a search for that ultimate cause, whether this fact is recognized or not."[36]

Cosmos and Being

Although the two terms "cosmos" and "being" are loosely interchangeable, I am obviously using "cosmos." I choose to retain the use of "cosmos" in this study in preference to "being." I recognize that "cosmos" is an outdated term, freighted with distracting mythopoeic images and lacking the precision that "being" (the more differentiated term) can offer. However, "cosmos" communicates a meaning of bond and order more evocatively than "being," which is, by contrast, quite sterile. Belonging is, after all, an experience and understanding of bond and order, of being held on the one hand and, on the other, having direction and purpose. I have spoken here of "cosmological presence," as manifest in the conditions of passing and lasting, because belonging mediates not merely the meaning of one's personal life and death but life and death as events within an overarching order of lasting and passing. As the meaning of belonging potentially contains such emphatically meaningful experiences, "cosmos" is the more suitable term. Voegelin underscores this: "For the cosmos may very well be dissociated by the experience of Being into a divine and worldly being, but that differentiating knowledge does not dissolve the bond of being between God and world, which we call cosmos."[37] It is this "bond of being" that I want to focus on. By itself, the term "being" involves the ongoing, theoretical delineation of the primordial bond and order of the cosmos. That is, it continues to elucidate (1) the immanent autonomous natures of all things that exist, (2) the immanent relations between and among them; and (3) the intimate and abiding presence of the transcendent-divine origin as a dimension of existence. Yet it is my focus on the drama of existence and belonging that suggests the use of the older term. Belonging is the human mode of existence; it is a tension between lasting and passing. "Cosmos" and "cosmological" semantically convey such tension more effectively than the more abstract terms "being" or "ontological."

Historically, the symbol "cosmos" typically dropped out of favor in *theoria* (for example, in metaphysics and theology), the symbol "being" replacing it as the more adequate term for a differentiated intellectual and spiritual environment. The earliest philosophical meditations on the meaning of "being," early in the historical process of differentiation, still move within the experiential orbit of cosmological bond and its order of lasting and passing. For example, the Ionian Anaximenes wrote, "As our soul, being air, holds us together as a ruling principle, so do breath and air embrace the whole universe." Breath and air give life to individual beings and seem to guarantee the life or being of the whole universe. Voegelin comments, "Thus he [Anaximenes] seems also to posit an element as the nature that governs being and possibly even produces the gods . . . ; on the other hand, with characteristic vacillation, the tradition has him say that the air is god."[38] Voegelin continues,

> In retrospect, the [material] speculation of Anaximenes still runs very close to the cosmological speculation of the Egyptian [mythic] type; however, when we look ahead, there seems to loom the possibility of an unmythical god (for air is not one of the gods, but God) as the origin of being, which would relieve the elements of the responsibility of playing the role of *arche* [ground of being]. . . . Experience of being and experience of transcendence thus are closely linked with each other. . . . Only in the light of the experience of transcendence, do God, as well as

the things of the world, gain that relative autonomy that makes it possible to bring them to the common denominator of being.[39]

I wish to comment on three aspects of the differentiation involved in moving symbolically from "cosmos" to "being," all of which implicate belonging and presence.

The Tension of Transcendence and Immanence

Voegelin points out, "There are no things that are merely immanent." Immanence is intelligible only in tension with transcendence, and transcendence can only be ignored or imaginatively forgotten, but never abolished.[40] However, Hughes points out that there is a danger inherent in the language symbols used to refer to transcendent meaning. It is a danger that has led to a ubiquitous blunder. "'Beyondness' of the divine will be taken to refer to some kind of spatial separation or absence: world 'here,' God 'out there.'"[41] Immanence and transcendence are dimensions of the meaning of being that differentiated the intracosmic compactness of the cosmos. They are neither places nor times but characterize the bond and order of all things as a tension that pertains in between them. For shorthand, immanence relates to the autonomous existence of things in space and time and to the relations of autonomous things with one another in space and time. Transcendence, then, relates to the unknowable, "nonexistent" origin or necessary ground of the things that exist, the mystery of their very existence that they carry with them in the mode of spatiotemporality. To mistake transcendence as a place—even as a very, very, very remote place "up there"—is to blunder. Remoteness is not the meaning of transcendence since transcendence is not what is removed, but what remains intimately and abidingly present. Moreover, to talk of "merely immanent" things is also to commit a philosophical gaffe. The conscious differentiation from cosmological compactness results in an opening of reality toward both transcendence and immanence as meaningful dimensions of being, and to eclipse the one is to collapse the tension between them. Not only is one pole of the tension lost, but in the loss of the tension entirely, both poles are lost. Furthermore, if immanence and transcendence are differentiated dimensions of what was compactly experienced in the cosmos, then it follows that the meaning of the cosmos (or its differentiated successor, being) is lost. "Mere immanence" is mere nihilism. It is a nonsense because mere immanence is not a mode of existence. "To immanentize" is to engage in the imaginative forgetfulness of transcendence, and in such an engagement, one embarks upon a self-alienation from the presence of the encompassing and engendering cosmos. In imagining that there is nothing we exist-from and nothing we exist-toward, we begin to obliviate ourselves.

The most devastating consequence of the blunder then is to sever our relation with the mysteriousness of being, our metaxic belonging in the cosmos, which is always the tension of our transcendent *and* immanent existence. It is to alienate oneself from the primordiality of one's own existence (1) as always emergent *from* the bond or communion of the cosmos and its transcendent-divine ground, and (2) as ordered *toward* the sacred order of lasting and passing. The compact truth expressed in myth is that primordial partners in the communion of the cosmos are bound up with each other in an ordered flow of lasting and passing. To speak of the "cosmos" is to remember anamnetically the bond by which we are continuous with the entire, unexplained world of contingent, passing and existent things and persons around us; and it is to humble ourselves before the supervening, governing, and sacred order of cosmological lasting and passing to which all are subject. To speak of the bond and order of the cosmos is not to ignore differentiated insights. Instead, it is to recover the "common matrix" as that within which we—and all that exists according to its autonomous nature—always live and move and have our being. To speak of belonging in the cosmos is to recover that matrix in which the autonomous nature of anything is not the final measure of its existence.

To belong in the cosmos is to participate in the grand, continual emergence of reality in all of its variety. Differentiation cancels neither the cosmos nor cosmological belonging, but secures our knowledge of things in their autonomous existence and in their relation to one another, in a range that extends across the emergent genera of physical, chemical, biological, psychological, and intellectual realities. And crucially, while the differentiation of consciousness opens and gives us access to the immanent structures of things through theoretical knowledge, it also holds them against the larger ocean of unsurpassable mystery. Mystery indeed symbolizes both the abyssal depths *from which* all things in the range of reality continually emerge and the divine height *toward which* they exist.[42] Differentiation results in the recalibration of how we take things to belong in the cosmos, but the broadening of knowledge does not collapse existential tension with mystery. Mystery remains as the indefatigable horizon of existence in the cosmos. The metaphorical depth and height is itself a needed mythos that provides the background limit against which the human act of intelligence can successfully grasp the intelligibility of things. Ever-increasing knowledge of the autonomous natures of things and of the relations of those things to each other merely pushes out the boundaries of the intelligible, but does not quash the mystery of the ground. Mystery—as the cosmological depth and transcendent-divine height—encompasses the intelligibility of all things insofar as they exist and remains as the inscrutable boundary of intelligibility.[43]

The World-Transcendent God and the Intimacy of Being
In the revelatory tradition of Israel, God announces the name by which He is to be called:

> Moses [said] to God, "If I go to the Israelites and say to them, 'The God of your ancestors has sent me to you,' and they ask me, 'What is his name?' what do I tell them?" God replied to Moses: I am who I am. Then he added: This is what you will tell the Israelites: I AM has sent me to you. God spoke further to Moses: This is what you will say to the Israelites: The LORD, the God of your ancestors, the God of Abraham, the God of Isaac, and the God of Jacob, has sent me to you. This is my name forever; this is my title for all generations.[44]

God reveals that his proper name is Being. The two salient characteristics of the tetragrammaton, YHWH, are that God is a personal reality and that this personal reality preeminently, foundationally, and always is. The name of God indicates that the essence of God must be, in some primary way, being.

In the noetic tradition of ancient Hellas, Parmenides experiences a similar but impersonal encounter:

Come, I will tell you—and you must accept my word when you
have heard it—the ways of inquiry which alone are to be thought:
the one that IT IS, and it is not possible for IT NOT TO BE,
is the way of credibility, for it follows Truth; the other, that IT
IS NOT, and that IT is bound NOT TO BE; this I tell you is a
path that cannot be explored; for you could neither recognise that
which is NOT, nor express it. For it is the same to think and to
be.... There is only one other description of the way remaining,
(*namely*), that (*What Is*) Is. To this way there are very many sign-
posts: that Being has no coming-into-being and no destruction,
for it is whole of limb, without motion, and without end. And it
never Was, nor Will Be, because it Is now, a Whole all together,
One, continuous.[45]

The fragments of Parmenides representatively symbolize the character of the Hellenic encounter with being. Transported in a mystical
experience by the goddess, through the "gates of the ways of Night
and Day," Parmenides catches a glimpse of the vision of divine, eternal being (by his *nous* as a faculty of his soul). In unpacking the vision of being for its significance, he reasons (by his *logos* as a second
faculty of the soul) that IT IS is the ultimate ground of all that exists;
and since truth is its companion, thinking and being are the same.

The obvious difference between the two experiences is that in
revelation to Moses, being is a personal divine reality, whereas in the
Hellenic experience, being signifies an impersonal divine reality. The
obvious similarity is emphatically that being signifies the divine origin and ground of beings. In the medieval Christian development of
thought in light of revelation and noetic philosophy, something of
a consensus among disparate philosophers arose that demonstrated
that "God" is a term approximately convertible with the idea of being.
Being is one of the "divine names," with Goodness or Perfection or
Wisdom. For example, Augustine offers an early "ontological" argument for God's existence, and in this he refers to God as that to
which nothing is superior. "God" is the name for whatever ranks
highest above mind and reason. He identifies truth and number
and wisdom as something like the very architecture of being, rank-
ing higher than mind and reason. So, God is either these or is what
makes them possible.[46] In his *City of God*, he writes, "For God is

existence in a supreme degree—he supremely *is*—and he is therefore immutable. Hence he gave existence to the creatures he made out of nothing."[47] Anselm famously names God as "that than which nothing greater can be conceived," on the basis of God as convertible with being. God-as-being is qualitatively different from God-as-a-being since the perfection or supremacy of God-as-being is not one of degree (like Gaunilo's image of an island), but one of ontological necessity.[48] From the early patristic and philosophical writings, the nomination of God as being was fundamental in developing an analogical understanding of God as subsisting of himself. In later scholasticism, the perfection of God was expressed by the term *aseitas*: that his essence and his existence are the same. God's essence is his existence, not received or contingent upon anyone or anything else. Thomas Aquinas explains that "every essence or quiddity can be understood without this feature: that something be understood pertaining to its existence. For I can understand what human being or phoenix is, and yet be ignorant whether they have existence in the world. Therefore, it is clear that existence differs from the essence or quiddity. This conclusion holds unless, perhaps, there is some thing whose quiddity is its own existence itself. This thing whose quiddity is its own existence itself can only be one and primary . . . and this is the First Cause, which is God."[49] God is being in a preeminent sense because the condition of passing that governs the mortality of our existence rests upon what necessarily is, what does not come into being or pass away. Mortal, contingent existence—as with all existent things in the cosmos, in "being"—does not contain within itself its own ground. "God" is the name we give to the divine ground, or "first cause," of all contingency. The meaning of divine perfection includes God-as-being in this foundational, necessary sense: God's essence and his existence necessarily lack nothing. It does not make sense then to search for the ground of God beyond himself.[50] Thomas Aquinas argues that, of all the names applicable to God, "He Who Is" is the most appropriate. He quotes John Damascene: "'HE WHO IS, is the principal of all names applied to God; for comprehending all in itself, it contains existence itself as an infinite and indeterminate sea of substance.' . . . [Furthermore] it signifies present existence; and this above all properly applies to God, whose existence knows not past or future, as Augustine says" (*De Trinitate* 5).[51] Damascene's "sea of substance" is the infinite fecundity of divine existence and essence and the source of all the attributes that, *quoad nos* (or, proportionate to our knowing), we predicate of the aseity of God: simplicity, perfection, goodness, infinity, ubiquity, immutability, eternity, and unity.[52] All the names of God, as the Pseudo-Dionysus told us, are merely human terms—proportionate as always to the level of human knowing—aimed at rendering God intelligible. While such attributes of God really do indicate something of God, nonetheless, the perfection of God surpasses all names.[53] It's worth saying that there are two modes of predicating names of God: cataphasis and apophasis. In the cataphatic mode, it is reasonable to predicate positively that the name "God" is approximately convertible with being, since both God and being, as heuristic terms, transcend the existence of beings. In the apophatic mode, it is reasonable to deny that the name "God" is convertible with being, since the transcendence of God as the divine origin of all being suggests that God is beyond being. We are in the semantic territory of transcendental border problems. Whether positively or negatively, both modes heuristically grasp and underscore that God is the divine ground of all being. Etienne Gilson writes,

> Beyond all sensible images, all conceptual determinations, God affirms Himself as the absolute act of being in its pure actuality. Our concept of God, a mere feeble analogue of a reality which overflows it in every direction, can be made explicit only in the judgment: Being is Being, an absolute positing of that which, lying beyond every object, contains in itself the sufficient reason of objects. And that is why we can rightly say that the very excess of positivity which hides the divine being from our eyes, is nevertheless the light which lights up all the rest.[54]

The symbol "being," differentiated from the compactness of "cosmos," clearly retained the cosmological intimacy of the sacred order of lasting and passing. This order is intimate because, from the perspective of the person, there is hardly a more apt term for the impact of cosmological presence on our lives: existence and belonging in between the lasting and passing conditions to which all beings are subject. The sacredness of being is still the sacredness of the cosmos, even if the meaning of being signifies a more differentiated range of existence and belonging than the more compact meaning of the cosmos in mythopoesis. From a strictly philosophical perspective, and abstracting from all revelatory traditions, God, Being, Cosmos are functionally coterminous. As heuristic terms, they each invite contemplation and consecration, because they signify the presence of mystery as the limit and foundation of our lives. Nor is that limit and foundation "out there," at a distance. God, Being, Cosmos, in their semantically different ways, name the intelligibility of reality in which our existence and belonging are already our personal share.[55] Reality, we can descriptively imagine, extends from the mystery of astrophysical emergence to the transcendent-divine ground. Existence is our share in the real. It turns out that, in superseding the myth in the unfolding symbolism of philosophy and revelation, we did not exit the cosmos. Rather, we find that we are "immersed" even more thickly in the reality of God and the perfection of Being. If the experiential discovery of transcendence and immanence opened the cosmos, then where is this experience to be found? Nowhere but in the soul, and so it is that in the intimacy of every soul the cosmos is present. The primary experience of the cosmos is a universal structure of every soul, because to exist is to belong in between the conditions of lasting and passing.

DIVINE PRESENCE AND THE COSMOS IN PERSONHOOD

Cosmological presence is not presence in the sense of proximity, nor does it connote an idling or a "standing by" in some passive and juxtapositional sense. Rather, the cosmos—which is neither a thing nor a compendium of things—can be said to be what we exist within as participants, or can be said to be what has presence in the interiority of human personhood. In either case, its presence is hardly conspicuous, since it is like the very air we breathe. On those rare occasions when the cosmos does become conspicuous, it acquires the character of uncanniness, as Heidegger highlighted—a movement or "flow of presence" that breaks in upon us.[56] Put another way, cosmological presence may be like an *overflowing* from its transcendent, eternally generative, limitless ground through the various immanent fields of reality. What seemed at first like a tidy relocation of divine reality to a transcendent realm of reality, and like the dedivinization of the world as a result of differentiation, has not resulted in a collapse of the cosmos.

The key term here is "divine reality." Philosophically, "the divine" is another heuristic term that points to the transcendent pole of mystery and lasting, the origin and end of all immanent reality. The creative movements of "outpouring," "*exitus et reditus*," and "flux" have characterized reflections on transcendent-divine reality since the beginnings of theology. Voegelin remarks in his reading of Plato's *Timaeus* that the divine "cannot be discerned by itself alone; there is no participation in 'the divine' but through the exploration of the 'things' in which it is discerned as formatively present."[57] "The divine" does not present itself as some object to be experienced, understood, and affirmed as real. Within the immanent realm of objects, the divine flow presents itself as already having flowed, as always leaving something proportionate to our knowing in its wake as an indication. The term "divine" is an index of both the ineffable presence and (thus we could just as well say) absence of "God." The uncanniness is that the ordinariness of mundane objects becomes problematic in the flow of divine presence. They exist, but why should they? The various "cosmological" proofs or ways to God, most famously from Aquinas, are examples of reasoning from the problem of ordinary existence in the direction of divine reality. What all ordinariness, or all immanent things, have in common is the problem of their existence as a matter of fact. The fact that they exist calls for an explanation; since nothing in existence has drawn itself into existence, nothing is the cause of itself. I referred to this above, but all things exist contingently, as an unexplained matter of fact; and this very matter of fact points toward some cause or generative ground that necessarily is its own ground primarily, and the ground of all being secondarily.

This inability to grasp an understanding of a divine "object" is neither a failure of differentiating consciousness nor a return to cosmological mythopoesis, but a recognition of the uncontainable character of the transcendent-divine God, the cosmological partner in the primordial community of being whose "overflow" is what brings forth, holds, and sustains the other partners in existence and gathers them in again. Glenn Hughes writes, "Explicit appreciation of transcendence dissolves belief in the traditional cosmological gods as adequate symbols of divine ultimacy, but it leaves intact the fundamental experience of divine formative presence in the things of the world, and it does not eliminate the human need to symbolize that presence through imaginative figuration."[58] Cosmological presence is a divine flow that illuminates as sacred the bond and order that has implicated the very fact of the existence of the things, the times, the places, and the persons we encounter. "Human being," Hughes emphasizes, "is where that intersection [of timelessness with time] comes to self-recognition and self-realization, where the flow of eternal divine presence orients temporal existence, through human consciousness, toward timeless meaning and truth."[59] Cosmological presence is a dimension of existence itself, a sacredness that our belonging not only takes account of but gives us meaningful access to.

We are not floating in a vacuum. On the one hand, cosmological presence as a dimension of existence can mean that we are living, suffering, flourishing, and passing within the richness of an ever lush and divinely saturated cosmos. On the other hand, cosmological presence increasingly means that divine presence "flows" within or through our own existence as a partner in the cosmos. As a dimension of the existence of things, cosmological presence illuminates the existence of the person. It is less a passive background against which we exist, and more an active luminosity within one's very personhood.[60] To seek and be drawn toward the luminous presence of the cosmos and its divine overflow is what commissions the person to think, speak, and act on behalf of the cosmos. I will speak about what thinking, speaking, and acting on behalf of the cosmos means in the next chapter. For now, it suffices to consider the person as potentially something of an embassy of the cosmos itself. The presence of the cosmos is the constant that we necessarily exist-from, and it is the beacon that we can choose to exist-toward in love of truth, goodness, and beauty. In paradoxical language, we can say that we carry the cosmos within us because the existence of each person is already a participation in the cosmos whose scope of transcendent-divine being, creativity, and outpouring on the one hand and immanent becoming on the other are also the scope of personhood. Persons do not merely exist, but can belong in the cosmos when they choose to turn their souls—Plato's *periagoge*—to the flowing presence of cosmological divine sacredness in their most intimate being.

Modes of Divine Presence

Voegelin writes that the divine sacredness of the cosmos is experienced as though from two directions: "the Beginning" and "the Beyond." Both of these, the Beginning and the Beyond, become increasingly conspicuous in the historical process of differentiation. "The Beyond," he writes, "is present in the immediate experience of movements in the psyche; while the presence of the divine Beginning is mediated through the experience of the existence and intelligible structure of things in the cosmos."[61] Furthermore, both directions of divine presence in its "overflow" through the cosmos have for their articulation their own set of language symbols. In the mode of the Beginning, the experience of divine being is present as wonder and awe. In the mode of the Beyond, we have "the language of seeking, searching, and questioning, of ignorance and knowledge concerning the divine ground, of futility, absurdity, anxiety, and alienation of existence, of being moved to seek and question, of being drawn toward the ground, of turning around, of return, illumination, and rebirth."[62]

Divine presence experienced as the Beyond is normally "experienced only in its *formative* presence, in its Parousia."[63] "The movement toward the Beyond of the cosmos can become fully articulate only when the Beyond itself has revealed itself. Only when man has become conscious of divine reality as moving his humanity, not through its presence in the cosmos, but through a presence reaching into his soul from the Beyond, can his response become luminous as the immortalizing countermovement toward the Beyond."[64] Divine presence encountered in the direction of the Beyond becomes present in the mode of utter transcendence, yet paradoxically is experienced in the most intimate stirrings of the soul.

I will explore cosmological presence from the direction of the transcendent Beyond in the following chapters where it becomes apparent in consciousness and love in particular. However, where transcendence is unveiled as present as an intersecting dimension of some apparently immanent reality, we have the direction of the Beginning. In the mode of the Beginning, divine presence is glimpsed by virtue of the existence of the things of the world; in the realm of nature, as the magnificent interrelated and symbiotic whole of those things bound together for the sake of their existence; and in the emphatic vastness of the order of sacredness that governs all passing things, set against the abiding mystery of the inscrutable, transcendent ground that holds them all. In storytelling, in liturgy and ritual, in the philosophical pursuit of wisdom, in experiences of beauty and the sublime, we recollect cosmological presence again and again. Recall, above, the renewal that mythopoeic, cosmological societies effected through the regular ritual reenactment of the time of the Beginning. Divine presence pervading the cosmos is the sacredness of the Beginning, not as an event in time, but as the establishing of time and the necessity in which time itself bides. Ritual, liturgy, and festivity "remember" the Beginning that we exist-from, and must exist-toward for the sake of life. The Beginning is always present as the very bond and order of the cosmos, and forgetfulness of this amounts to tearing the fragile fabric of the cosmos, a rupture through which the bond of the cosmos is undone and the chaos of disorder floods in.

A mythos is always required for the experience of divine being in the mode of the Beginning, because here the mystery of existence— existence in between the abyssal depths and the formative divine height—cries out for an explanation: Why is there something? Why are things constituted as they are? And what is the purpose of it all? Creation myths address questions such as these, just as the cosmological proofs of *theoria* do, but unlike those proofs, creation myths are rich with images that are richly invested with feeling and give us immediate access to the meaning of creation. The creative actions of the creator-god(s) or demiurge, rendered dramatically intelligible through the myth, communicate meaning for existence, essence, and purpose.[65] The creation myth seeks to address the specific human need for meaning amid the prevailing, foundational mystery of the cosmos. Encountered in the direction of the Beginning, divine presence in the cosmos is mediated by the existence of things that belong in the cosmos. Let us briefly consider the cosmological presence of divine reality from the direction of the Beginning, not mythopoeically, but in the differentiated environment of *theoria*.

The Person in the Universe

The question of divine presence from the metaphorical direction of the Beginning is not the question about the physical beginnings of things in the astrophysical universe. The "first cause" of metaphysical arguments is qualitatively different from the sequence of secondary causes that we know as naturally and humanly occurring.[66] In one way, the first cause is first in the sense that it alone must be uncaused. Yet this alone is not why it is first. The first cause, as intrinsically generative, might also be thought to be first in the sense of starting a falling domino sequence since it brings forth the entire set of autonomous and interrelated astrophysical processes. Still, this is insufficient. The priority of the first cause is also its sustaining in existence the entire set of emergent, interlocking realities that give rise to the things of the astrophysical universe. That is, the first cause is also presence. This is cosmological presence, rather than astrophysical presence. Divine being is not present in the universe as a puppet player, as an agent operating mechanisms. Still, there can be no secondary causes, no beginnings, without the ultimate Beginning.[67] That Beginning before time is a presence that abides in the passing of time.

The astrophysical process, as a matter of fact, is proportionate to human knowing. The burgeoning development of the sciences is witness to this. Since the process of astrophysical reality is proportionate to human knowing, the task of *theoria* is twofold: to discover the truths of the autonomous structures of beings—the correlations among properties of things and the probabilities of their schemes of recurrence and development—and to point to the mystery of the very existence of those proportionate truths. The former is the task of science, the latter is that of philosophy. The generation of knowledge of "proportionate being" (or being that can be known) demarcates the boundary with the transcendent mystery that is not proportionate to our knowing and therefore cannot be known. In this way, *theoria* indirectly raises the question of the Beginning. The quantitative vastness of time and space cannot answer the qualitatively human question about why there is temporal universe at all, but knowledge of vastness does serve to stoke the wonder that asks question in the face of mystery. The primary experience of lasting and passing in the cosmos, the mysterious bond of God and world, and the sacred order by which all things emerge and exist as what they are remain as the source of wonder, awe, and the deepest questioning. Belonging thrives by the richness of its symbols. Creation myths or the philosophers' myths of Plato are equipped to handle mystery and imaginatively symbolize a truth of cosmological presence that one can live by.[68] Even in the drive of *theoria* toward knowledge, there remains the need for an overarching mythos that makes sense of the drive. In order to belong in the cosmos, we remain in need of both theory and mythos because, behind achievements in knowledge, so redolent of scientific and technological progress, there abides the unsettling mystery of the universe's existence—indeed, one's own existence—which cannot be escaped.

Let us pass from myth for now to consider what *theoria* can tell us of the human belonging in between the universe and the cosmos. On the side of the organic emergence of the human being, there is continuity with the larger astrophysical emergence, while the symbolic life of the human person in philosophy and revelation involves the being drawn (*helkein*) and the seeking (*zetesis*) of the meaning of the cosmos, conspicuous in his or her yearning to belong. The process of the universe is the process that carries us into physical existence; to know its story is to know our story too. A scientific example will frame this nicely: the element carbon, essential for life as we know it, could emerge only after having been cooked up in the heat of the death throes of the first generation of stars in a process known as nucleosynthesis.[69] Science can tell us that the emergence of human life depended upon a preceding series of astrophysical, chemical, biological, botanical, zoological, and psychological developments. In terms of metaphysics, *theoria* considers the various levels of reality—from material to spiritual levels—heuristically as an emergent sequence of increasingly higher integrations of incidental outcomes left unsystematized by the lower levels over vast amounts of time.

This process of emergence is what Bernard Lonergan calls "emergent probability."[70] In terms of science, the task of *theoria* is to grasp and affirm the truth of the content of any reality at its own particular level in the sequence. Effectively, the functioning of earlier schemes of recurrence in the series—for example, the physical and the chemical—fulfills the conditions for the possibility of the functioning of later schemes. The universe as process can be grasped as proportionate to human knowing in that science affirms systematic correlations as its classical laws and records the statistical probability of nonsystematic divergences of events from ideal frequencies. The probability of anomalies occurring in any particular level of reality, in spite of laws that systematize properties of things, is relatively high over immense periods of time and over vast spaces and matter through the universe; but the probability of those emergent anomalies surviving as a new scheme of recurrence is relatively low. Emergent probability is not a process of straight lines and astrophysical inevitabilities; evolutionary emergences can occur at any or all levels of the process, but there are also evolutionary dead ends. As long as those new, higher schemes do survive or recur—let's say, the survival of biological reality as a systematization of incidental outcomes from the lower manifolds of chemical and physical reality—they in their turn provide the conditions for the statistical possibility of a still further scheme emerging and surviving. The higher schemes of recurrence, emerging from the lower schemes, also occur as a functioning of the laws that govern that lower scheme. The higher, though they are a distinct scheme by virtue of operating according to their own laws, must "sublate" or incorporate the lower laws into the functioning of their own laws. Lonergan states that this sublation involves a phenomenon where a scheme of recurrence obeys the laws of lower levels of schemes of recurrence while also conforming to a new set of laws.[71] So, chemical reality is stable according to the laws that chemistry has identified, but depends for its existence on fulfilling the necessary operation of physical laws.

Brendan Purcell, commenting on Lonergan's theory of emergent probability, writes, "This unfolding sequence of events exhibits a series where the earlier levels can function without the later ones, but the later ones depend on the earlier."[72] What this means is that there cannot be any series of botanical reality, such as sequoias or nettles, unless there is already a prior biochemical series that we find, for example, in cells and subcellular realties like genes. The lower biochemical does not depend upon the higher botanical, but the botanical depends upon the biochemical as its foundation, just as there is no biochemical series without the prior chemical and physical. However, and crucially, the higher series are not simply epiphenomena of the lower, and cannot be adequately explained by the sciences that take a lower series as their object. For example, a chemist does nothing more than advance fallacious concepts when reducing generically psychological reality, for example, to chemicals. Even if chemical laws are operative in the *psyche*, chemistry does not explain psychological reality, which is its own level, requiring its own sciences of terms and relations. While there is no psychological behavior without a foundation in the prior existence of chemical and other lower series, psychological phenomena cannot be rendered intelligible at their own level in the emergent series of reality by the norms adequate to rendering a lower series intelligible. Intelligible form in chemical reality is not intelligible form in psychological reality. That is, the terms and relations of the higher series must be explained at their own level, according the methods appropriate to those higher levels. Purcell, quoting Lonergan, describes these developments as "'a linked sequence of dynamic and increasingly higher integrations.' And since such sets of dynamic interactions between levels are recurrent, from plants through lower to higher animals . . . up to man, it's possible to form a viewpoint of the entire sequence, with lower levels providing the materials for the next highest level. That overall insight is into 'the immanent design or order' of the universe."[73]

The Cosmos in the Person

The emergence of the human person belongs within this process of emergent probability. That is, on an immanent level, every human being "houses," for her and his very existence, the full functioning of laws from physical and chemical to biological and psychological levels of reality. However, every human being is also constituted by the operations of wondering, inquiring, questioning, conceiving, judging, affirming, deliberating, choosing, acting, and loving. Myth and *theoria* and, in a different way, revelation are all outcomes of generically human reality. The belonging of each of us is implicated on the one hand by our continuity with the recurrence of all schemes of recurrence in the astrophysical universe, gathered intrinsically into the ordinariness of our own personal lives; but on the other hand, the highest laws or schemes that pertain generically only to human existence implicate the transcendent mystery in which emergent process is nested. Human reality is a metaxic reality that is fully participatory in a cosmos whose abiding presence includes both astrophysical immanence and the flow of transcendent-divine mystery. The passing and lasting of the cosmos, the dimensions of immanence and transcendence, are realized in every human person. In this way, each of us is a hub of the cosmos. The person bears the weight and dignity and stature of the cosmos, and in this way becomes an embassy.

Of course, from the viewpoint of emergent probability, the chance of human emergence within the larger astrophysical schemes of recurrence is statistically, almost infinitely, small. The existence of any one of us is already subject to the outcome of billions of years of these recurrent and successful series. Each of us is, in some sense, a vastly ancient creature, existing as a consequence of the process of the universe from its beginnings, carrying that process forward in every affirmation of life. Yet this is not all. Each of us is an ancient creature in a further sense too. That is, it belongs only to the human reality of personhood to come to know and tell the story—the mythos—of the universe in its Beginning. Alone among all that exists in the cosmos, only the human person can wonder about the Beginning of beginnings. Lonergan's emergent probability is an explanatory theory that can take account of the intelligible sets of terms and relations among the emergent series of astrophysical reality. It cannot account, however, for intelligibility itself, nor for the very existence of a process of emergence in the first place.

What we are left with is an account of how we belong to the astrophysical material process of reality and how we exist within the abiding mystery of its emergence. It belongs to the human scheme—that is, preeminently, to the individual person—to navigate existence at the metaxic intersection of the knowable and the unknowable, to be a scientist, a metaphysician, and a mythmaking storyteller, to live according to the natural laws of the universe while living out the mysterious bond and order of the cosmos. It is the person who, immanently structured with the process of the universe, nevertheless transcends the immanence of the universe in wonderment and the asking of questions. Indeed, it is the person, whose life is bound and ordered by the two cosmological conditions of lasting and passing, who thereby mediates the cosmos. Since the role is to mediate the Whole, a mediator must be the point at which the Whole is opened and becomes present. This is quite a claim, and one that is taken up in the next and subsequent chapters in various ways relevant to belonging. In encountering another person, we are encountering the foundational flow of cosmological presence from the Beginning; bodies and souls, we are touching the cosmos that floods the interpersonal spaces between us. In this way, each person potentially becomes an embassy of the cosmos.

I HAVE TRACED THE COSMOS from the totality within which all things exist to the totality that is present in the life of the person. The cosmos is not a magnitude of matter; for that, we have the universe. The cosmos is a Whole that is foundationally present in the matter-of-fact existence of things and is formatively present as constitutive of personhood. Declarations like this are easy, so it will be my task in the next chapters to verify and anchor the claim in exploring how human belonging, in all of its multifariousness, is always also a belonging of the cosmos. I say "of the cosmos" because, not only do we make our homes with one another in places and times, all set within an over-arching cosmological bond and order, but we more deeply become the cosmos for one another. Home is the microcosmos, and we bear our home in all journeying outward and homeward. In telling truth, enacting goodness, and loving beauty, our world of belonging tran-scends the passing of time and place, and death itself; and we find that our lives reach out for, and are received in some meaningful sense by, the transcendent-divine ground that we have sprung from. This "find-ing" is what one may call an "anamnetic recovery" of the cosmos, whose possibility is vouchsafed by cosmological presence. This pres-ence is a dimension of all presence since it foundationally and forma-tively underpins all existence. By its abiding presence, we *re*cover the cosmos and *dis*cover that is only by a belonging "of the cosmos" that we authentically live out the high dignity of personhood.

CHAPTER FOUR

By Way of Consciousness
and the Flesh

The cosmos is what we always exist-from. It is a bond of mutual interdependence of all things and an order of lasting and passing from
which life and death issue. It is what we exist-toward too if we would
reconcile ourselves to a belonging, primordial and profound. Present
not as an object, a thing to be known, the cosmos is the very possibility of the existence of things and of belonging. The turning toward
the cosmos is not necessarily a turning toward what lies outward,
but more primordially a turning toward one's own existence, or an
opening into one's own interiority, where the luminosity of mystery
abides. Cosmological presence is a luminosity that commissions the
person to be an embassy of the sacred. In this chapter, I will ask the
reader to think with me about the connection between sacredness and
belonging in the concreteness of our lives. Since this study is a moving, but enlarging viewpoint, I will now need to bring the insights of
the previous chapter to personhood. I will need to drill down more
deeply to make those necessary connections between presence as
cosmological and presence as personal. Therefore, I must consider
personhood, and I will do so by concentrating on consciousness and
embodiment. The literature is vast, so I will circumscribe the range
and draw upon representative thinkers who point us in a fruitful
direction, but who also leave the door open to still other insights.
Bernard Lonergan's critical realism provides a method for examining

consciousness as a mode of participation in being, while Maurice Merleau-Ponty's work on embodiment gives us a solid foundation for thinking about participation in what he calls "the flesh of the world."[1] By way of consciousness and the flesh, each human person is present to him- or herself and to others, as well as present in the divine height and abyssal depth of the cosmos.

I will begin the discussion with consciousness. Whether referred to as "the soul" or as some other signifier of interiority, consciousness is an obvious and enduring concern in philosophy. Since the end of the nineteenth century, however, an emphasis on intentionality has revolutionized thinking on consciousness. I choose to rely on Bernard Lonergan's guide, not to the exclusion of others, but for three reasons. First, Lonergan's thought follows in the classical-Christian tradition, a venerable heritage of 2500 years of substantive thought that takes both immanence and transcendence seriously. Moreover, Lonergan adapts this tradition in general, and the thought of Thomas Aquinas in particular, to the horizon of the contemporary mind and its achievements in the natural, social, and human sciences. Second, his "Generalized Empirical Method" provides an excellent philosophic channel through which to think about our own personal interiority and, crucially, without abstracting the exteriority of the body or the world. Indeed, for Lonergan, "genuine objectivity is the fruit of authentic subjectivity."[2] Third, Lonergan's method is a phenomenological analysis that holds on to what is largely omitted among phenomenologists: a phenomenology of inquiry itself. According to Jeremy D. Wilkins, Edmund Husserl's work on intentionality gives us a phenomenology of perception, while the hermeneutical method in Heidegger's writings and through the later writings of Hans-Georg Gadamer and Paul Ricoeur functions as a phenomenology of language.

The reason a phenomenology of inquiry is essential is that it deals with the problem of judgment: without judgment, we cannot affirm the real; we do not move from conceptual ideas to being.[3] Without a concern for judgment, we cannot affirm the concrete world, and the danger of becoming indifferent to the predicament of the world—in its flourishing and suffering—arises, leaving us pristine in our subjectivity, but otherwise alone and adrift. To belong, then, is about more than perception and language; in order for there to be a home, there is an affirmation that is required of us. I will also discuss Eric Voegelin's work on luminosity as a structure of consciousness that complements Lonergan's work on intentionality and gives us a way to think again about cosmological presence as a dimension of our own existence and belonging.

After consciousness, I turn to consider embodiment, and it is the highly original work of Maurice Merleau-Ponty that will guide us here. His work on embodiment converges in significant ways with Lonergan's and Voegelin's work on consciousness. His is an anthropology of integration, whereby interiority and exteriority are already encompassed by the deeper reality of incarnate personhood, and incarnate personhood itself is encompassed by the "flesh of the world." Merleau-Ponty demonstrates that the body is already speaking a primordial language, pregnant with the meaning of cosmological presence and belonging, even as it comes into the presence of other incarnate realities.

I will begin, however, with a preliminary consideration of the subject who is also a self, hopefully enhancing conventional language by taking into account the meaning of cosmological presence. This will prime the subsequent discussion of personal presence in consciousness and flesh.

THE PERSON AS SUBJECT-SELF

"Subjects" and "selves" are standard symbols for symbolizing individual persons. In recognizing that the person is both a subject and a self, we can usefully communicate that the person exists-from (as a subject, subjected to) a manifold of reality in the cosmos, while she and he also exist-toward that manifold of reality (as an intentional, autonomous self who desires to know and who wills to love). As subject-selves, in consciousness and in embodiment, persons live out the tension of their existence and belonging.

It is worth briefly remarking at this point that much modern and contemporary thought on personhood centers on the notion of autonomy. Autonomy names an aspect of the self-relation, which is one of the relations differentiated in the Axial Age that compose the order of the cosmos. With autonomy, the self is understood to be, literally, a law unto itself. Such was the view originally advanced by Kant and later by John Stuart Mill among others.[4] Autonomy means to be under one's own law or norm or rule. For sure, it is a reasonable place to begin a consideration of the person: we all make choices, and thereby set rules for ourselves, act according to our own norms, and measure the quality of our actions by the same. A recognition of human dignity always involves a recognition of the autonomy of any person as self-determining. Self-determining autonomy drives the moral claim of any person to achieve a dignified life for him- or herself, and indeed it is self-determination that is raised to harrowing conspicuousness when others deliberately foreclose one's autonomy. However, if autonomy is a choice of the self, it is also already a primordial relation etched into the fabric of the cosmos that binds and orders all things; and autonomy is the relation that is manifest in self-determination, the deliberate obstruction of which can be deeply problematic in ways that are personal and sociopolitical, and always cosmological.

On the other hand, since autonomy and "selfhood" do not indicate all the relationality that personhood is capable of, the one who would compress a version of their own personhood into autonomous selfhood alone, imaginatively and assertively sundering themselves from cosmological presence for the sake of unfettered mastery, subject to no one and to no thing, has also alienated him- or herself. No longer is a cosmological bond and order acknowledged by the person who knows him- or herself to exist entirely in the mode of autonomous selfhood.[5] Cosmological order includes autonomy but also relationality with other persons and things, as well as with the transcendent origin of all persons and things. The precise problem with the idea of unalloyed, pure selfhood is that one loses the cosmos. There is little incentive to look beyond autonomy to what would limit autonomy. Since the person really is an autonomous self, though, personhood is always exposed to the danger of forgetting the abiding presence of the cosmos and of overlooking our intrinsic subjection to the cosmological conditions of lasting and passing. Reminders of contingent existence can be unwelcome intrusions into the splendor of the self because not only is mortality a biological limitation of life, but the necessity of transcendent-divine mystery reminds us that our knowing is restricted to proportionate being. Cosmological order, composed of relatedness to self, to all others, and to the necessary origin of all things, is enhanced or diminished according to how cultivated any of those relations are. If the cosmos is presence, and if such presence widens the horizon of existential meaning for the person, then it becomes even more tangibly present in our relations with others. And if it is the person who can mediate the presence of the cosmos, then it is other persons who can mediate its presence to us, reminding us of the primordiality of relationality. We are subject to other persons, times and places, things and events in our proximity, locally, socioculturally, politically, and historically. Our subjection is precisely where the thought of Emmanuel Levinas, for example, begins and ends: "The self is a *sub-jectum*: it is under the weight of the universe."[6]

We are under the weight of the universe, yet it falls to each of us to navigate our way under such a weight. Each person is a subject-self, a hub in which subjection and self-determination meet. In belonging to a family, for example, I freely choose some good on behalf of my family, whose value was already set as a condition of, and a boundary to, my freedom. The presence of my family, or of my friend, or indeed of a stranger, is already the condition that I exist-from. How I choose to respond to that condition, to exist-toward that condition, is both the unfolding and enriching of my autonomy. All of the conditions, all that we are subjected to, demarcate where our autonomous selves begin from, on the one hand, and on the other, set boundaries to autonomous self-determination. The person is always an emergent reality, because one strives to enact one's personhood in each situation to which one is subjected. There are no selves who are not also subjects. Levinas writes in *Existence and Existents*, "The freedom of the present finds a limit in the responsibility for which it is the condition. This is the most profound paradox in the concept of freedom: its synthetic bond with its own negation. A free being alone is responsible, that is, already not free."[7] Levinas reminds us that our freedom is already bounded by our responsibilities, that it is not freedom without those responsibilities. Freedom becomes an empty gesture of licentiousness, or perhaps a cultic fetish, in the absence of responsibility. Nor does responsibility make sense, but becomes a degrading tyranny, if not already grounded in essential freedom. Freedom and responsibility are not set side by side in a happy contiguity but, as Levinas shows, are dialectically bound up with one another to the point of paradox.[8]

There are still other ways of talking about our being subjects that make sense. We are, for example, subjects of rights and laws and cultural expectations. So, even while there are autonomous choices, these choices are made and enacted dialectically, within a world of persons and commonsense situations that are present in both intelligent and obtuse ways, always asking something of us; and by this asking, they are already constitutive of the conditions of the choice. As a person, each of us is subject in the sense of existing-from a world of persons and nonpersons, deriving meaning or purpose from them. We say that we are shaped by our environment, or are subject to the authority of our parents, or live by obligations inherent in our own parenthood, in our friendships, in our workplaces, or are moved by the plight of the suffering, and so on. Yet in each case of what we are subjected to, each of us can choose or not choose to respond (and choose the manner in which we would) to that which we are subjected to in any moment. That is, the person alone chooses whether or how to respond to what the world, our own humanity, and that of others have subjected us to in their questions, demands, vulnerability, and so forth. Indeed, our wisdom, such as it might be, is in our picking up responsibility for how we respond to the cosmological conditions of lasting and passing that inhere in every subjection. We are subjects, but we are also selves. We choose our belonging. Personhood, we can say in a preliminary way, is a dynamic unity of subject-self. We can characterize personhood as a dialectical subject-self; we are subjects *in the cosmos*, but also a self-chosen mediator *of the cosmos*. In what follows, let us keep in mind the cosmological amplitude of meaning operative in the symbols "self" and "subject."

BELONGING AND CONSCIOUSNESS

I began this book by taking a phenomenological path—rather than an epistemological or metaphysical one—because belonging is, minimally, a perception of being-in-relation. Since phenomenology aims at a suspension or bracketing (*epoche*) of epistemological claims or metaphysical conditions for the purposes of elucidating the meaning of that relation from the first-person perspective, we can build upon the methods and insights from the field of phenomenology to think about the content of consciousness and the intentional acts of consciousness. Richard Kearney, in describing the beginnings of phenomenology in the work of Franz Brentano, writes that "phenomenology rests upon the radical conviction that meaning is neither in the mind alone, nor in the world alone, but in the intentional relationship between the two."[9] If Husserl more emphatically replaced the traditional metaphysical category of substance with relation, it was almost certainly inspired by Brentano's phenomenological method, which emphasizes relationality. Brentano emphasizes, for example, that sound presents itself in two ways—namely, as a physical phenomenon (a vibration) and as a mental phenomenon (such as a spoken symbol)—and in considering sound in these two ways, we have already grasped the meaningful signification of the relation between them. He explains,

> The presentation of the sound and the presentation of the presentation of the sound form one single mental phenomenon; it is only by considering it in its relation to two different objects, one of which is a physical phenomenon and the other a mental phenomenon, that we divide it conceptually into two presentations. In the same mental phenomenon in which the sound is present to our minds we simultaneously apprehend the mental phenomenon itself. What is more, we apprehend it in accordance with its dual nature insofar as it has the sound as content within it, and insofar as it has itself as content at the same time.[10]

Human consciousness is not a box containing perceptions within itself, but is already an act of reaching toward the reality of the world that it exists within and as part of. To be-in-relation, to reach toward that world, to meet or to encounter someone or something is already to find oneself in their presence in some meaningful way. Indeed, since presence is the precondition for relation and meaning and belonging, let us now clarify what is meant by presence by way of consciousness in the work of Bernard Lonergan.

Consciousness as Self-Presence

While we may be in the spatial-temporal proximity of another, we are not always conscious of that other. To be conscious of someone or something else means more than physical proximity and requires a

degree of intentional presence. Furthermore, in every act of consciousness, we are also present to ourselves. Therefore, if we recognize cosmological presence as a protean presence, then we can specify three
further meanings of presence. First, it can bear the rather ordinary
meaning of a juxtaposition or local proximity of one thing to another
in the sense that a stone rests beside a tree. Let me call this positional
presence. More pertinent for human beings are the further meanings
as dimensions of consciousness. So we can say that, second, presence
can mean intentionality in that we are conscious of something, someone, some event, or the like. Third, presence can mean self-presence
in a foundational sense.[11] Bernard Lonergan emphasizes this foundational character when he writes that "for anything to be present to me
I have to be present to myself at the same time. If I am not present to
myself, there is no one to whom the objects are present—we just have
the spectacle and not the spectator. The spectator is present to himself
not as a spectacle, but as a spectator."[12] There is some subtlety here.
Mark Morelli, working within the horizon that Lonergan has framed,
describes self-presence thus:

> Clearly, I must be present to myself if I'm to *come to know* any-
> thing at all, *pay attention* to anything at all, *understand* anything
> at all, or *mean* anything at all. If I'm paying attention or noticing
> anything, I'm present to myself. If I'm understanding, I'm pres-
> ent to myself. If I'm acquiring knowledge, I'm present to myself.
> If I am deliberating, I'm present to myself. If I'm intending any-
> thing at all I'm present to myself. Were it not for my presence to
> myself in these operations, the word "conscious" would not have
> been given so many different meanings. All of these operations,
> then, are *conscious* operations.[13]

Lonergan writes that "the presence of the object is quite different from the presence of the subject. The object is present as what is
gazed upon, attended to, intended. But the presence of the subject
resides in the gazing, the attending, the intending."[14] Consciousness
involves our self-presence in the performance of cognitive operations
such as noticing, wondering, questioning, conceptualizing, understanding, judging, deliberating, deciding, and so on. That is, in any act
of consciousness, I am present to myself, I am in relation to myself

while the object or person or event that I intend becomes present to me through that act of consciousness. Wilkins writes that "self-presence is not another kind of intentional presence, not the *intentio intenta*, but the *intentio intendens*, the presence of the subject to herself in and through the acts (operations and feelings) by which she intends the world."[15] To be conscious is always to be conscious of something, and in this conscious intending of something is both self-presence and intentional presence. One is always present to oneself in some intentional act of consciousness, in the process of cognitional operation.

Self-presence, we could say, is a quality of consciousness, and therefore a qualitative dimension of the cognitive operations of consciousness. Self-presence is intimately bound up with the operations of consciousness, driving, distracting, and otherwise affecting them as we intend our objects. Let us, then, consider these operations so that we may discern self-presence. Lonergan categorizes the various operations into four: experiencing, understanding, judging, and deciding.[16] For each of these, self-presence is a property of the operation. That is, if I enjoy a whiskey on a Friday evening after a hard week, I must be present to myself; I am the "enjoyment experiencer" in that moment. Or, I am present to myself as I try to figure out what to do about a flat tire on the highway; I am the "insight-seeker" in that moment. Or, I am present to myself as I try to ascertain if a particular word is the solution to 3-down in my crossword puzzle; I am the "judgment-making problem-solver" in that moment. Or, I am present to myself as I try to determine whether or not my nine-year-old daughter should eat all of her peas this dinnertime; I am the "paternal, daughter-loving, discoverer of the good" in that moment. In each case, I may be intending someone or something, but my presence in my own intending radiates a reflexive and multivalent quality to that intending.

As I experience the world, I may be tired, frustrated, jubilant, relaxed, anxious, and so forth—any of which feelings, affects, or moods influence what I perceive or notice or how I intend. I am an *experiencing self*. As I seek to understand the meaning of something, I am present to myself in yet another way: I am in search of an insight that would explain what I perceive, and my self-presence is a bearing of concern for intelligible meaning. I want to understand; I am present to myself and consequently to the object in the manner of curiosity; I need an idea that would explain what I perceive. This *understanding self* bears a quality of self-presence different from the quality of self-presence to the *experiencing self* or to the *judging self* (who is concerned to verify the truth of some idea) or to the *valuing self* (who is present in the manner of concern for choosing an appropriate course of action from a range of practical, possible courses of action). I am always present to myself, but in qualitatively different and varying ways, manifesting who I am both to myself and to the world, as I consciously engage and appropriate myself and the world. "My consciousness changes with changes *in* the operations I perform. My presence to myself seems to be *in* my operating, not something separate from my operations, and not something that my operations are in, as spectators and gladiators are in the Coliseum."[17] My presence to myself is always changing in the enactment of various cognitional operations of intentionality, but also in the functioning of these operations recurrently over time. The operations of intending consciousness—not necessarily the intended contents of the operations—recur over time; and it is in this recurrence of perceiving, understanding, reasoning, deliberating, deciding, and acting that I am a conscious person. As I become more experienced, I become more knowledgeable, more skilled, and (hopefully) more prudent, and this very development of my own personhood is always unfolding as self-presence. As I become more knowledgeable, I am present to myself as more knowledgeable; as I grow in virtue, I am present to myself as more virtuous.

In belonging, I must grasp who I am in my relations with others, with events, and even with aspects of who I am. In this, I must also attend to how, in relating to myself, I relate "from and toward" my own self. I am both intended and intending. If I am to belong here, to you, in these times, in this place, I must be able to relate to myself as one who would belong. Is there an aspect of my own subject-self, present in my intending, that must be reconciled first? Do I need to attend to my own conscious existence, with my own troubles, my own biases, my own blind spots, my own proclivities, all of which might militate against an existence-toward something or someone I would otherwise belong to? The self-relation means, so far, to be invariably present to myself in my varying modes or qualities of self-presence.

Nor are there several "I's" who become present in each of act of intentionality, as though there were no unity. Rather, I remain a personal unity even though I manifest myself in diverse ways. The person, as the invariable unity of subject-self, is also the dynamically variable and integrating complexity of a subject and a self in relation. Only an "invariable-I" can be present through the various and varying relations with the world: I am always present in a qualitatively reflexive relation to myself in all my relations to a varying concrete world that changes from moment to moment and from place to place. Consciousness as self-presence is foundational for belonging, as Augustine seems to demonstrate through his meditation on "memory": "That is called memory in things past which makes it possible to recall and remember them; so in a thing present, as the mind is to itself, that is not unreasonably to be called memory, which makes the mind at hand to itself, so that it can be understood by its own thought, and then both be joined together by love of itself."[18] For Augustine, memory is the principle by which each person is an integrated (yet always integrating, or disintegrating) conscious unity of subject-self. Yet memory and self-presence are not quite the same. While memory can be intended as an object of consciousness—delighted in, referred to, or even repressed as a source of shame—and while Augustine clearly means that such an object of consciousness is also constitutive of the intending self, nonetheless, even one without memory is always cognitively present in his or her cognitive operations, perhaps tragically in the mode of one who has lost their sense of identity and finds that they belong nowhere. The difference between memory and self-presence seems to be that the richly evocative set of image-laden meanings that relate the past to now can be lost, and what is left is a depleted reservoir, consciousness present to itself and its object without context or association. One intends one's world stripped of all belonging. One is present to oneself in one's cognitive operations as an exile, as an innocent, as an alien; and it is this quality of subjective homelessness that impacts intentionality. The loss of memory can amount to the loss of one's integration, to the diminishing of the unity of subject-self, which is also to lose one's hold on the bond and order by which the cosmos is present. Thus it is that we begin to grieve our loved ones as they suffer the disintegration of dementia. Without memory, they do not hold on to what they exist-from, and what they exist-toward in a succession of "nows" without context is by itself insufficient to be a belonging. In losing one's memory, one loses one's belonging. The home we cling to is functionally the microcosmos that shelters and renews us, but the fear of memory loss stokes the fear of losing our place in being and of becoming forever unmoored in a sea of chaos. There is, arguably, no greater loneliness than self-presence without memory.

Consciousness as Intentional Presence

One is present to oneself in the operations of consciousness, but we are also present to the world—and the world is present to us—in these operations.[19] Consciousness always intends some content. Lonergan refers to this content as "data," because it is the experienced material that we seek to understand and know. Data is what we are presented with; it is what we experience as subjects. Data is what we are subject to in experience, and as such, it is what we as meaning makers seek to render meaningful.

Let me introduce a distinction between two types of experienced data whose meaning we can make intentionally present. First, there is the data of sensation. We can be present to the reality (the materiality) of the world around us due to our senses. Like nonhuman animals with which we share sensation and corporeality, we are subject to the predicament of embodiment. Like animals, we can also act and react to a world of bodies "out there" (extroversion) that we find in our positional presence through sensation. What Lonergan calls experience involves more than sensation, as we'll see, but the point here is simply that our five senses present us with five streams of sensory data. Secondly, there is the data of consciousness. In every moment, in every situation and encounter, we experience the data already present in consciousness. Memory is data of consciousness, which is in part why we can say that we are "experienced," drawing as we do on recollections of previous experience and filling out the possibility of meaning in the present situation. Data of consciousness is the deep well of these memories, but also feelings, associations, biases, blind spots, and other affects, such as moods and predispositions. The data of sensation and the data of consciousness are the stuff that make us subjects. We are subjected to sensation and the content of our own consciousness.

Of course, we are also selves. Selfhood is the dynamic determination of who we are in relation to the world of things and to the mysterious origin of all things. That is, there is a relationship between what we are subjected to in experience and the "pure desire to know" what it is that we are subjected to. In striving to know the truth of things and in striving to enact the good of things, we are engaged in selfhood. Lonergan sets out his "Generalized Empirical Method" (G.E.M.), whose cognitive levels we have already met: experience, understanding, judgment, decision. The self-generating and self-correcting process of coming to judgments of fact and judgments of value, in which we affirm the truth and value of things respectively, is composed of these cognitive levels and the structured relations between them. If we would be authentic versions of ourselves—if we would belong to our world, our selves, and the cosmos that permeates everything—then we must concern ourselves with the structure and dynamism of consciousness. Because we are a self, what we *perceive from experienced data*, what we *understand in our percepts*, what we *judge to be real in our ideas* and in the light of previous judgments of truth and being, and what value we *decide is really worthy of enacting* are irreducibly one's authentic agency.[20]

G.E.M. is a phenomenology of inquiry, and it makes clear how belonging—that I both experience as a subject and must appropriate as my own self in openness to the real—is both a tension and an intentional process that is operative in each moment of waking consciousness. It is a tension because the experiences that we are subject to (that we exist-from) in the moment need to be understood, known, and appropriately valued. It is an intentional process because we seek to name patterns in the experiences that we have perceived, we seek to group and distinguish sets of insights that we have noticed; we strive to find correlations and causations among the data. Tad Dunne, in his account of this cognitional tension that drives the process of knowing and choosing and loving, writes, "An adult knows the subtle difference between resentment and jealousy, while a child knows only the elemental difference between feeling good and feeling bad."[21] That is, the unity of the "I"—or memory in Augustine's sense—is who becomes capable of differentiating the meaning of good and bad feelings through the repeated experiences of the similar data and the recurrence of cognitional acts. In understanding, we are inquiring. That is, we are interrogating the perception (experience) for an insight (understanding) into its meaning, and the meaning we seek to grasp depends upon whatever intelligibility is inherently available within the data we have perceived. Having achieved insight, having refined it into an articulate idea or concept, we now must make a judgment on the truth, the probability, or the falsity of the idea. We judge because we wish to affirm the real as truth and goodness. Human cognition does not stop at experience or understanding, because intelligibility and value are not "out there" in some extroverted sense. The dignity of every person is consonant with nothing less than an affirmation of the real (judgment). Human cognition involves judgment because we cannot belong to what is not real. We have to know so that we can love.

Let me provide a concrete example. The cacophony of noise I might suddenly hear from the kitchen bears within it the possibility of its being understood and known. *Experience.* (Who am I? Am I present to myself as someone who cares about noises emanating from the kitchen? If so, then I am authentic in paying attention to the noise I am subjected to.) In being attentive to the kinds of noises given in the data of sensation, I may discern patterns of shouting or crying or hissing or clanging, and so on. In being attentive to the data of my own consciousness, I am aware that I am also present to myself in a shocked, apprehensive manner.

Understanding. (Who am I? Am I present to myself as someone who cares to understand what the explanation of sudden kitchen outbreaks of noise is? If so, then I am authentic in seeking to interrogate the perception of noises and my own associated images of noisy kitchen goings-on for an insight into the intelligible meaning of the situation.) One insight that I may achieve is that the noise is a dropped pot—dropped, most likely, by my teenaged son, who, I previously affirmed, is in the kitchen; and this would bring with it possible implications, such as injury, damage, and, of course, a delayed dinner. A dropped pot would certainly explain the noise I just heard.

Judgment. But is my eminently plausible idea of the dropped pot correct? There is a relation inhering between experience and understanding, and there is a still further relation between judgment and what I have experienced and understood, since I really am driven to know the truth and grasp the reality of the situation. After understanding must come judgment as a determination of whether my idea is true or not since I find that I really am driven by a desire to know. My idea of a dropped pot certainly explains the noise from the kitchen, but so too would any number of other possibilities. A collapsed ceiling in the kitchen would explain the data of aural sensation that I just experienced, as might the discovery of a scorpion, a snake, or a large cockroach loose under the sink as a contributing factor to any sudden loss of control and crashing; but more likely again would be simple clumsiness, a trait that seems to run prolifically in my family. Achieving an insight and having grasped what is intelligible within the perceptual data, I am driven on by my pure desire to know toward a judgment of the veracity of my idea. In judgment, what I am seeking to grasp is the real. I want to know the truth. (Who am I? Am I present to myself in my eagerness to find the truth? Do I find that I am more worthy of truth than mere plausibility or clever ideas? Is not reality the home whose well-being is what I continually yearn for? If so, then I am authentic in seeking to establish the truth of what is going on in the kitchen.) I must seek sufficient evidence that my intelligible idea is correct if truth is my concern. Did a dropped pot cause the noise? If I go to the kitchen and look, I will gain sufficient evidence to determine whether or not the dropped pot is the true explanation of the experience of noise. I go and I find water and a pot on the floor, and a son with a sheepish look on his face who confirms my suspicion. If the idea (in understanding) fits the data (in experience) by way of validly fulfilling the conditions for establishing fact, then I have established the "virtually unconditioned." That is, I have grasped beyond reasonable doubt the truth (in judgment), and now I know what I did not know before. I have transcended my ignorance. I am neither simply a subject, nor simply a self, but a complex of both. I have achieved a contribution to knowledgeable selfhood through being attentive to the data of experience to which I was subject, through being intelligent in grasping what was inherently intelligible in the data through an act of understanding, and through being reasonable by judging my intelligible idea against the available data in order to affirm the real. As an authentic self, I was intentional. I aimed to affirm the truth of a real situation: Yes, my son dropped the pot.

Decision. What now? The knowledgeable self is thrown back into being-a-subject, but specifically now as a moral subject. I am subjected to a moral situation because the truth of the situation needs my decision and action; it awaits my moral self-determination. I feel the moral dimension of what I have established in fact. Now that I know that the floor is wet, that my well-meaning teenaged son is unhurt, and that the meal is gravely delayed, I feel the urgency of appropriate action. I must act. I must make some choices about the situation. Being subjected to a moral situation means that I must meet it as a moral self. (Who am I? Am I present to myself as someone who cares about his son, his wet floor, and our meal? Am I in search of the highest good available in this situation? If so, then I am authentic by making some responsible decisions.) I can mop the floor or give the mop to my son. (Choice.) I can reboil the water and cook something quickly or order something from a restaurant. (Choice.) In the end, my son mops the floor and I decide to order in some Lebanese food, and my family share a good meal and a good laugh at my maladroit son's expense. As a moral subject, I have achieved moral selfhood by being "response-able" (Levinas) for the situation. As one who responds to a moral need, who takes on the moral burden of the situation for the sake of the good, which is always calling to be brought into being, I was responsible. I was conscientious in my love of home. Being authentic here means that I was both present to myself and intentionally present to the concrete situation as attentive in experiencing, as intelligent in understanding, as reasonable in judging, and as responsible in deciding.

To be an authentic subject-self is to dispose oneself in maximal presence to the real. This is the work of philosophy. Beyond the naïve realism of presuming reality to be "out-there" and the idealism of eclipsing objectivity for subjective phenomena "in-here," Lonergan's method affirms the true and the good by the cognitional process of grasping objectivity according to the immanent norms of consciousness itself.[22] Lonergan's critical realism allows us to claim that consciousness is constituted by presence in two ways: (1) Dynamically, in that we make the world meaningfully present to us, and ourselves to the world, in affirming the truth of the real and the good of the real. Intentional presence is a relation to the world in which a self-determining agent seeks to know and to choose and act. (2) Reflexively, in that we are present to ourselves as worthy of truth and goodness, eager to appropriate the real. Self-presence is the invariant unity of the "I," but the "I" is present only through cognition of an object present.

Conscious presence—self-presence in intentional acts—is the pre-requisite to belonging. By conscious presence, we can, first, affirm or repudiate that we exist-from some aspect of the world—persons, places, things, times—to which we are subject and, second, affirm or repudiate that we exist-toward the real in authentic selfhood, realized in the intentional pursuit of the real.

Consciousness as Luminous Presence

The previous chapter discussed the differentiation of consciousness. One consequence of this differentiation was that the order of immanent, autonomous, existent things with their own natures or laws and their relations to other immanent, autonomous, existent things could become the main focus of a *theoria* that we would later refer to as philosophy and later again as the natural sciences. The achievement of the natural sciences in terms of our knowledge of the astrophysical universe is obvious, but it has not occurred without some damage to our belonging in a cosmos. Late medieval nominalism set the scene for thinking about nature as phenomena rather substance, and the subsequent modern-era advances of theoretical, scientific knowledge into these phenomena were so successful and were embraced with such enthusiasm that "Nature" could become an immanentized substitute for both the transcendent and immanent dimensions of the differentiated cosmos. The bond and order we call the cosmos were diminished in significance, its sacredness replaced by human mastery, and modernity became the era of great technological advances coupled with existential alienation or homelessness. It is easy in modernity for individuals to speak casually of reality as "out there" in the measurable and quantifiable world of Nature, while our consciousness is located "in here," somewhere behind the eyes. Under this model, reality is Nature, and Nature is what we can point to. The real loses its cosmological presence in between "God and world." In modernity, Being shifted into the mode of "a being" to be investigated. Its proper science, metaphysics, became frozen as a dogmatic set of self-referential propositions sundered from its animating experiences of cognitively dynamic participation where thought and being are luminously identical as the real. Under such a reification (being as "a being," albeit a very big being), reality has slipped into the mode of "thinghood." Again, as in the previous discussion of God, we find that there is a transcendental border problem. Yet reality is not another thing, even though things are certainly real.

Beyond the intentionality of the investigator and the scientist, consciousness has another structure by which the cosmos is present: luminosity. As discussed in the previous chapter, the differentiation of consciousness led to a refining of what it means to belong in the cosmos. Differentiation is not a dismantling of the cosmos but rather an opening to transcendent meaning and a clarifying of its immanence. Thus, the presence of the cosmos is a presence different in kind from the presence of things "in" the cosmos. There, I characterized cosmological presence as a luminosity. In this chapter, having shifted attention to consciousness, I must now treat the presence of the cosmos as luminously present in consciousness. With self-presence and intentional presence, I also name luminosity as the abiding presence of the cosmos in consciousness.

The luminosity of cosmological presence in consciousness is a subtle presence. It is easy to overlook since we are rarely disposed to the sort of contemplative thinking by which we might become aware of it. We think and communicate primarily in conceptual categories, language being supremely geared for the intentionality by which our lives are directed. Yet this intentionality communicated in language is notoriously problematic for those rare meditations on transcendent dimensions of reality because it tends to lead to semantic equivocations and paradoxes.[23] How do we communicate the nonthingness of reality as a Whole if not by language? The problems of language arise not from the structure of language itself, but more foundationally from the structure of consciousness.[24] Let us briefly consider consciousness as more than structurally intentional, as also luminous.

Eric Voegelin points out that in luminous presence of the cosmos, "reality moves from the position of an intended object to that of a subject, while the consciousness of the human subject intending objects moves to the position of a predicative event in the subject 'reality' as it becomes luminous for its truth. Consciousness, thus, has the structural aspect not only of intentionality, but also of luminosity."[25] For all its intentionality, consciousness is also an event "in between" the person and the cosmos. When the meaning of an event in the metaxy presses itself, consciousness acquires the character of luminous presence. "Luminosity" is Voegelin's term for awareness of the encompassing presence of the cosmos as a structure of consciousness. Moreover, it is not the passive presence of what merely surrounds us, a Whole in which we might participate, but is the active participation of the cosmos in us. Luminosity then is cosmological presence in consciousness. We catch a glimpse of ultimate meaning, of our place or role in the scope of all things and all time, in ways that can be unsettling, consoling, joyful, terrifying, as so forth, in each of those rare moments when luminosity surfaces into conscious awareness. Luminosity as presence is a recovering of the oneness of the cosmos with the subject-self where the subject-self has become the "predicative event" within the "flow" of the cosmos. Rather than the intentionality of participating in some event, luminosity is how we are participated in first. Luminosity is how the person becomes aware of herself as existing in between poles of immanence and transcendence, time and timelessness, ignorance and wisdom, and so on.

However, if it is a term that can symbolize the abyss of substance in the cosmos of which we are part, and the *Parousia* as the sacred flow of divine presence in the cosmos, then more precisely it names the depth and height of the cosmos both as aspects of consciousness itself. The amplitude of the cosmos in its transcendence and immanence, and in its sacredness and profanity, is present as a structure of consciousness. Each of us is *of* the cosmos in luminosity. It may be subtle, but it is by luminosity that the sacred divine ground manifests itself in mythic symbolization, erupts as *pneuma* in revelation, and gives rise to, and guides, the noetic questioning characteristic of philosophy, even as we age in our mortality and witness the perishing of all those who suffer the ravages of time.[26] Elusive and understated, the luminosity of consciousness operates like an undertow that enhances and heightens the role of self-presence and intentionality.

Voegelin writes, "The experience of divine reality . . . occurs in the psyche of a man who is solidly rooted by his body in the external world, but the psyche itself exists in the Metaxy, in the tension toward the divine ground of being. It is the sensorium for divine reality and the site of its luminous presence."[27] As site and sensorium, consciousness reveals itself as the in-between zone of the metaxy: on the one hand it is located as the consciousness of the concrete person in space and time, but on the other hand the encompassing and comprehending reality and mystery of the cosmos is always present in consciousness as a dimension of that concrete person. Luminosity is a structural constant of consciousness, even if we are normally unaware of it, because existence is never removed from the context of being-in-relation to itself, others, and its mysterious origin—that is, from the cosmos as that bond and order that hold us and draw us. As Voegelin puts it, consciousness "is the site in which the comprehensive reality becomes luminous to itself and engenders the language in which we speak of a reality that comprehends both an external world and the mystery of its Beginning and Beyond."[28]

Luminosity is why our wonderment arises. It is why we can outquestion all the available answers of proportionate being in pursuit of truth behind the veil of transcendent mystery; it is why we deeply revere the good of any person's inexhaustible worth; and it is why experiences of awe are possible in perceptions of the beauty that abides in existence. As a structure of consciousness, it functions as the ebbing and flowing tide of conscience that guards the cognitional drive toward the intentional truth and goodness of things from lapsing into the inauthentic traps of inattention, unintelligence, unreason, and irresponsibility. In short, the luminosity of consciousness is the possibility of love: love of the cosmos in communion with itself and through the existent beings who play their role in its drama. I will return to this in the next chapter.

We have considered three types of presence that constitute consciousness: self-presence, intentional presence, and luminous presence. We may say then that consciousness is that by which the individual person and the cosmological totality of being are simultaneously the same and different: respectively, luminosity signifies the identity, intentionality the nonidentity. Self-presence is the modulating self who can begin to understand his belonging in the metaxy of identity and nonidentity. Given the massiveness of intentionality, the abiding subtlety of luminosity, and the simultaneous operation of both in the self, consciousness can occasionally lose its hold on the real. Paradoxes inevitably arise, leaps of faith are required, and belonging can involve one in futile, if noble, efforts. Voegelin's recognition of the potential for imbalances and the need to navigate prudently in between the poles of existential tension has led him to write about the correlative need for "reflective distance." When a person grasps, explores, and knows himself as conscious both luminously and intentionally, then he has reflective distance. "Consciousness . . . is structured not only by the paradox of intentionality and luminosity, but also by an awareness of the paradox, by a dimension to be characterized as a reflectively distancing remembrance."[29] I have spoken of *anamnesis* above, and here we meet it again as reflective distance. Reflective distance is the anamnetic effort required of imagination to consider the significance of one's belonging as one participates in the reality of another person, or persons, or times, places, societies and histories, and always the cosmos, while allowing that one is also participated in concurrently by that reality. Voegelin points to the danger. Figuratively, unless a distance is maintained in reflection, a collapse of distance can occur. That is, the presence of the cosmos in consciousness as luminosity and the presence of the world in intentional consciousness constitute a precarious balance. Imbalanced reflection can lead to distortions and derailments where the tension in between luminosity and intentionality can be imaginatively obliterated. On the one hand, the world can be reimagined as a heavenly paradise on earth, awaiting militant action. On the other hand, transcendence can be sloughed off, leaving the world as an immanentized unit, subject to nothing more authoritative than the arbitrary or libidinous actions of anyone.

I may have characterized the person as potentially an "embassy" of the cosmos, but this does not render anyone an oracle. In belonging to the cosmos, one has not been commissioned to know the secrets of the cosmos, but to love its knowability and mystery even as its manifests itself through the persons and nonpersons of our lives. Reflective distance is important because awareness of luminosity is tenuous and fleeting, and the failure to recall in an anamnetic sense how we belong in between the cosmos and the world remains a perennial possibility. Such a failure amounts to an alienation of radical unbelonging, the imaginative oblivion by which we lose our grasp of the real, sometimes spurred on by others similarly alienated.[30]

Reflective distance involves the humility of remembering one's cosmological belonging that commissions the subject-self to think, speak, and act luminously and intentionally. By way of consciousness, we are always reflectively engaged in what has both luminously engaged us already as subjects, and what awaits our intentional engagement as selves.

BELONGING AND EMBODIMENT

We are conscious but we are also embodied, and it is appropriate to the dignity of every human being that we try to make sense of belonging in and through our bodies too. Let us now shift our attention to the complementary significance of bodiliness, the situation of being and belonging as an enfleshed subject-self. It is a shift not away from consciousness but toward the incarnation of consciousness. Maurice Merleau-Ponty's work on incarnate consciousness, by which we are in relation to our own selves and the world, has clear parallels with the work of Lonergan and Voegelin.[31] For Lonergan, cognition is operative upon both the data of consciousness and the data of sensation that we experience in each moment; for Merleau-Ponty, our "flesh" is the "sensible sentient" by which we perceive our own embodied presence even as we perceive the "flesh of the world."

> Whether we are considering my relations with the things or my relations with the other ... the question is whether in the last analysis our life takes place between an absolutely individual and absolutely universal nothingness behind us and an absolutely individual and absolutely universal being before us—in which case we have the incomprehensible and impossible task of restoring to Being, in the form of thoughts and actions, everything we have taken from it, that is, everything that we are—or whether every relation between me and Being, even vision, even speech, is not a carnal relation, with the flesh of the world.[32]

In Voegelin's theory, consciousness bears a luminosity that resonates well with themes of transcendence in Merleau-Ponty's work, where the "flesh of the world" is arguably totemic for cosmological presence. Moreover, embodied consciousness is precisely the "in-between," *l'entredeux*. Existence, for Merleau-Ponty, is always constituted by cosmological poles such as exteriority and interiority, the visible and the invisible, the material and the spiritual, and so on. In being consciously present to our selves and the world, within the cosmos that is paradoxically present in us, we have the conditions in place for belonging. Belonging emerges from the simultaneity of self-presence, intentional presence, and the luminosity of cosmological presence because we *exist-from* flesh (our own conscious embodiment, which is consonant with the corporeality of world) even as we *exist-toward* flesh (our perception of the world).

First-Order and Second-Order Expression

In *Phenomenology of Perception*, Merleau-Ponty contrasts intentional acts of reflection that result in scientific knowledge with prereflective perception. In Lonergan's language, the term "prereflective" describes conscious patterns of experience, percepts or images that have not yet been categorized or conceptualized by understanding nor verified and affirmed as fact by judgment. Merleau-Ponty stresses the importance of the prereflective as "first-order" expression. "Second-order" expression would be *theoria*, or differentiated scientific knowledge, because its work is the clarification and articulation of a prior living field of meaningful encounter that has already occurred in between the consubstantiality of flesh: mine and the world. He writes, "I cannot think of myself as a part of the world, like the simple object of biology, psychology, or sociology; I cannot enclose myself within the universe of science. Everything I know about the world, even through science, I know from a perspective that is my own or from an experience of the world without which scientific symbols would be meaningless."[33] Analysis (or *theoria:* scientific, philosophic, etc.) abstracts from first-order perception that is already a "living communication with the world that makes it present to us as the familiar place of our life."[34] Abstraction mitigates the spontaneity of "living communication with the world," but it adds intelligibility to our belonging in that world. Merleau-Ponty is strenuously emphasizing that existence and belonging are already perceptions whose first-order status tells us that they are concrete experiences that do not depend upon second-order theoretical development. Our embodiment is how we are always in prereflective encounter with the world and how we primordially participate in the drama of the cosmos. Indeed, for Merleau-Ponty, the term "world" reclaims a cosmological significance. The encounter with the world by way of conscious embodiment is *l'entredeux*: the endowing of, and being endowed by, the world with primordial meaning for one's incarnate existence as a subject-self. This prereflective, meaning-endowed vitality is what he refers to as the "phenomenal field" whose significance is easily and casually overlooked in the emphasis we place on the works of second-order expression. Perception for Merleau-Ponty has a subtlety to it that is suggestive of Voegelin's luminosity. It has a tendency to forget itself, which is why the phenomenal field of primordial, enfleshed meaning becomes eclipsed by the abstractions of analytic meaning. Since perception intends the perceived, it is the perceived that becomes the focus of attention. Perception offers its percepts to the cognitional process that culminates in the truth of the thing "in itself." The living communication in between the person as embodied consciousness and the world is submerged beneath the "in-itself." Merleau-Ponty points out that this perceptual projection of second-order truths can result in a forgetfulness of *l'entredeux*, the ever-present in-between character of existence that constitutes our primordial belonging in the world and belonging to one's own self, by way of flesh (which is nevertheless always conscious). The emphatic utility of "in-itself" truths can amount to a bias that the "objective world" (Lonergan's "already out there now real" of the naïve realists, empiricists, and, indirectly, of the idealists) is the home of truth and is therefore all that matters. Just as self-presence and luminosity are quite easy to overlook in the midst of the intentional operations of consciousness, but must be recovered for the sake of authentic self-appropriation and belonging, so in Merleau-Ponty's phenomenology is embodied subjectivity to be anamnetically recovered. Embodied subjectivity always stands in danger of being diminished or relegated to the realm of opinion, fiction, and essential untruths by the massiveness of intentional acts, or of being dissociated from the body in dualism, or indeed of being reduced to irrelevance through skepticism. The only way to overcome the alienation of subjectivity from its own embodiment, and thus from its place in between the flesh of the world, is to recover the richness of embodied meaning in and with the world through a phenomenology of embodiment, or, as the later Merleau-Ponty characterized it, an "ontology of the flesh."

Flesh as Living Communication

Merleau-Ponty's ubiquitous symbol for "intercorporeity," for belonging in between the flesh of the world, is the hand that can touch even while it experiences being touched. He asks rhetorically, "If my left hand can touch my right hand while it palpates the tangibles, can touch it touching, can turn its palpation back upon it, why, when touching the hand of another, would I not touch in it the same power to espouse the things that I have touched in my own?"[35] Our communication with the world is living communication. While it may be eclipsed by second-order expression, it is never obliterated. Embodiment is the *Gestalt* of living communication with the world through the senses. For Merleau-Ponty, recovering our prereflective "lived world" that is prior to scientific reflections is the "fundamental philosophical act."[36] Such an act is a recovery of the experiential meaning of embodiment by which we belong both reflexively to ourselves and to the cosmos. "The world is not what I *think* but what I *live through*. I am open to the world, I have no doubt that I am in communication with it, but I do not possess it; it is inexhaustible."[37] What Merleau-Ponty offers is an *anamnesis* or recovery of presence in the world and presence to oneself through an account of the body's "being-toward-the world."

In part 1 of *Phenomenology of Perception*, being-toward-the-world is demonstrated through how one experiences one's own body. The body, obviously spatial, is also temporal. Perception is openness to the living meaning that occurs "in between" the inexhaustible cosmos to which we are subjected and the self-determining "for-itself." My body, which is no mere spatiotemporal place, is an emplaced consciousness and as such is the zone of the metaxic in-between. I am present to myself and to the world as embodied. Merleau-Ponty's phenomenology recovers the significance of the body as "always present for me. . . . [It is] no longer an object of the world but rather . . . a means of communication with it." We can direct our bodies toward the world, but the world is no longer "the sum of determinate objects but rather . . . the latent horizon of our experience, itself ceaselessly present prior to all determining thought."[38] The body and the world have an elemental presence from which I exist and toward whose meaning I strain by my very existence.

While my body and the world are always what are present to me in any moment, there is a relation between them. Flesh has a "thickness" that is not monolithic, but layered; and the layers are related. The body-world relation is what can be cultivated or habituated over

time through the manner of repeated actions. Merleau-Ponty writes
that the "moticity" or moveability of the body is not a mere "servant
of consciousness," but that there is a sense in which one can claim
that "consciousness is being toward the thing through the intermediary of the body."[39] What he calls "original intentionality" is revealed
through how the body—its movements, its gestures, and so forth—
stylizes the relation with the world: "It shows that conversely those
actions in which I habitually engage incorporate their instruments
into themselves and make them play a part in the original structure
of my own body. As for the latter, it is my basic habit, the one which
conditions all the others and by means of which they are mutually
comprehensible. . . . In order that my window may impose upon me
a point of view of the church, it is necessary in the first place that
my body should impose upon me one of the world."[40] The window
unto the flesh of the world and the window unto the flesh of one's
body are joined in the conscious task of perception. "The flesh" is the
original unity of consciousness and the world.

Embodiment is the possibility of realizing both the meaning of
the world and the meaning of one's own selfhood in this place and
time. The body is permanently present, but not in the sense that it is
"*in* space, nor for that matter *in* time. It *inhabits* space and time. . . .
My body fits itself to them and embraces them. The scope of this
hold measures the scope of my existence; however, it can never in any
case be total."[41] The body is the primary expression of dramatic and
aesthetic experience. The body's gestures are all (personally, sexually)
stylized ways of carrying oneself when walking, talking, eating, and
so on. These gestures are all "signs" in space and time of what is not
limited (or "totalized") by space and time. My embodied presence is
not limited by time and space, but radiates through them, by means
of them. The inexhaustible open-endedness of the world (a term synonymous, I suggest, with "cosmos") is what is being mediated and
signified by the consciously incarnate person.

The living body is already a "mute language" that is always operative beneath spoken language and serves as the first-order foundation for the secondary expressions that the concepts and distinctions
of spoken language can communicate. In *Signs*, Merleau-Ponty underscores the importance of art as a language whose corporeality is
a primary expression, open to (but limited by) the conceptual clarity

of spoken language. Artistic expression—like the body itself, like all flesh—is a corporeal "stylizing" of perception. "As the artist makes his style radiate into the very fibers of the material he is working on, I move my body without even knowing which muscles and nerve paths should intervene, nor where I must look for the instruments of that action. . . . For me, everything happens in the human world of perception and gesture, but my 'geographical' or 'physical' body submits to the demands of this little drama which does not cease to arouse a thousand natural marvels in it."[42] Subject to natural processes and conditions whose meaning can be sought and clarified through science and analysis, I nonetheless *live* my embodiment prereflectively. The meaningfulness of my bodily existence is manifest through my flesh as it participates in between the flesh of the world. My embodied presence is a personal stylizing of elemental meaning, a primordiality that remains available in aesthetic experience. Lonergan wrote that "there is an artistic element in all consciousness, in all living."[43] Artistic experience for him is an aesthetic withdrawal from the world of practical living, a transforming of the practical, goal-oriented self into the purely experiencing, prereflective subject. Artistic experience involves a transformation in which "the subject in act is the object in act on the level of elemental meaning."[44] There is an elemental meaning, a primordiality, that opens *in* the artist and is the opening *of* the artist in this moment of primordial encounter. With Merleau-Ponty, elemental meaning is the "primordial expression" that bodily gestures and art signify. "Just as the thick and living presence of my body, in one fell swoop I take up my dwelling in space. And like the functioning of the body, that of word or paintings remains obscure to me. The words, lines, and colors which express me come out of me as gestures. They are torn from me by what I want to say as my gestures are by what I want to do."[45]

Flesh as Elemental

Although Merleau-Ponty never abandoned phenomenology, the thrust of his work brought him to suggest an ontology of the flesh within phenomenology. "Flesh," as we have seen, is the name he gives to what we exist within and of which we are a part. Not mere meat or physicality or matter, flesh is an incarnate prereflective encounter with the world that gives my elemental expressions or gestures their meaning and that ever arises from the continuity in between me and the world. By way of flesh is the world present and I am present in and to the world, as well as to myself: "The flesh is not matter, is not mind, is not substance. To designate it, we should need the old term 'element,' in the sense it was used to speak of water, air, earth, and fire, that is, in the sense of a general thing, midway between the spatio-temporal individual and the idea, a sort of incarnate principle that brings a style of being wherever there is a fragment of being."[46] Flesh has elemental meaning because, for Merleau-Ponty, it bears the quality of an element. Like the other elements, it is perceived as a principle of consubstantiality. Flesh is the common matrix in which all things are one and is always underlying the differentiations and distinctions among them. Flesh is how we are "of the world," subjected to its spatial conditions and temporalities, yet our embodied presence is never totalized by those conditions and temporalities. Flesh is perceived as bearing ontological significance; it is the manner of being and our only approach to the inexhaustible. Flesh—like our hands that can touch, and be touched while touching each other—is what is visible and tangible at the same time as being the intangible, invisible quality of the "vision" of touching. Flesh is elemental in that it can manifest itself both objectively and subjectively; it is the possibility of the distinction between mind and matter.[47]

Flesh, then, is Merleau-Ponty's symbol by which he elucidates the meaning of human embodiment in continuity with the embodiment of the bond and order synonymous with the cosmos. It is also a symbol that points, always phenomenologically, toward that primordial and elemental inexhaustibility beneath or beyond intentional perception, an inexhaustibility with which every human person, through their own conscious embodiment, is in continuity by participation. The unfinished nature of Merleau-Ponty's work leaves some interpretation open to his readers. Without its being written directly, there seems to be a numinous quality that radiates within his work, suggestive in ways of Voegelin's parallel symbol of luminosity as a structure of consciousness. Merleau-Ponty's philosophic engagement with embodiment directs attention to the modes of cosmological presence by way of elemental flesh. Furthermore, there is the suggestion that presence to one's own self and to the world—again, always by way of flesh—also invokes the paradoxical presence of what remains inexhaustible in the midst of what can be exhausted. Indeed, Merleau-Ponty's phenomenological work offers to us a recovery of the primordiality by which we are constituted, a glimpse of the cosmos from which we exist and which remains the ever-fertile basis of first-order, elemental expression beneath or within the operations of consciousness and spoken language. Every truth of a thing "in-itself," discovered by perception in its intentionality, in its "secondary expression," rests upon the elemental and inexhaustible—that is, the cosmological—for its very possibility.

HUMAN BEING IS irreducibly personal. By way of consciousness and the flesh, each person is present. The person is a unique and irreplaceable presentation of the cosmos in his or her very own incarnate and embodied presence. Nothing surpasses what the existence of the person presents because the body and soul bring forth in tandem the transcendence and immanence of all being. Nothing can surpass what has already surpassed all things, and it is this unsurpassability that personhood alone presents and channels into a world of things. I have discussed the person as a subject-self, an admittedly clunky term that aimed to demonstrate that the subject is precisely the one who is subjected to the sacred conditions of lasting and passing, to the flow of divine presence, and to the abyssal presence of all things within the cosmos, and that the self is the one who, in actualizing what is potential within him, strives to authenticate what is true, what is good, and what is beautiful. As a subject-self, we are in the presence of, and we present ourselves to, the reality of the cosmos. As a subject-self, we grasp what we exist-from and exist-toward, and in between these poles that constitute the conditions (and thus the tension) of our belonging, we are able to belong.

We exist and we belong by way of consciousness and the flesh. Lonergan and Voegelin offer us insights that tell us what consciousness presents: a self who is always already engaged with, and emergent within, his or her world; a world whose reality can be known and chosen; and the cosmos, whose absoluteness ungirds and illuminates the existence of the subject-self. These three kinds of conscious presence I separated out from one another for the purposes of discussion, but their integration is the conscious life of the person in whom the real is always operative and who must navigate her own path toward the real. Participation in the cosmos, and the participation of the cosmos, is personal existence. Without the reflectively distancing remembrance of personhood as the mediation of the cosmos, as the part in whom the whole is paradoxically made present, personal existence can lose its belonging and its direction. Humility and reverence maintain the reflective distance in which the person achieves the full status of their own dignity as a subject-self, who, in being able to grasp the real, is also able to fail to grasp the real. The humility and reverence of reflective distance also remind the person of the paradox that grasping the real is not the same as grasping all of the real, that our words, our actions, and our presence to one another are always pregnant with infinite possibility and endless meaning, that presence is an ongoing presenting that is never finally presented.

Merleau-Ponty's work on embodiment runs parallel to the ways that Lonergan and Voegelin's thought on consciousness runs. The body is emplaced by way of flesh and continuous with "the flesh of the world." We have seen how Merleau-Ponty's concern with primordial meaning—mediated as living communication in, through, and by the body—is a concern to rehabilitate our awareness of presence in and of the world that he names as "first-order expression." Flesh, then, is the elemental condition of belonging: we exist-from flesh even as we exist-toward flesh.

Presence is not yet belonging, but is the condition of belonging. It is the reason we belong or not belong. We can belong in the cosmos because of cosmological presence to us and in us as luminosity; and we can belong in and to the cosmos because we have presence by way of consciousness and the flesh. Furthermore, as embassies of the cosmos, we can belong with each other because we are present to one another. Let us now consider the meaning of presence in love.

CHAPTER FIVE

In Love

Love inheres in presence. We are not thinking of mere positional presence, but self-presence, intentional presence, and cosmological presence. Love inheres neither accidentally nor in the sense of a happy outcome. Rather, love drives presence. Like an engine, it provides the motive power to come into presence. Only by love can I be present. It is in love that I am humbly subject to you, a Thou (Martin Buber), and can be the self who acts for the sake of a Thou. If I am present to you, to the world, and to the cosmos, then I must be present to what is already ennobling and generative within me. Love is active: it works on me; it works from me. It is the force that, in generating presence, generates belonging. Thomas Aquinas famously wrote, "To love anything is nothing else than to will good to that thing."[1] Love is why I am disposed to will your good as my good, to take on your burden as my own, and to carry your cross with you. In this chapter, I consider love because, like the various types of presence I have already discussed—presence in and of the cosmos, by way of consciousness and the flesh—love too is primordial. In between you and me, we who are present to one another, there is no empty space. Love saturates proximity. In between the whole of the cosmos and its parts, love is their communion. Love welcomes. Or better, it opens the lover in the manner of greeting and receiving and giving. Love sees and embraces things as they are, in their own place. Love is why there is a cosmos rather than a chaos: in a cosmos, things not only exist but thrive in their proper place. One leaves the cosmos not by exiting, but by forgetting, but in love one never forgets. For the purposes of this study of belonging, one can say that one remembers one's home. To remember, in Plato's sense of *anamnesis*, is to recover oneself in the presence of the cosmos. Only in forgetfulness do we cease to be homeward bound.

Sometimes, we can forget. In pride, we can forget that our world is subject to the cosmological conditions of both lasting and passing. Like Ozymandias, we can will to forget that no project of ours lasts.[2] Yet in loving remembrance, we can recover the primal reasons for humility. The wisdom of love that moves in the lover reminds us that this too shall pass. Compassion for those who suffer, for the essential vulnerability of all who grow older and less able, and for those grieving what has passed is only possible in the one whose love is already attuned to the lasting and passing to which all are subject. Love itself becomes an embassy of the cosmos in that we can mourn what passes yet find sources of consolation in what lasts.[3] In the greeting and giving and receiving of love, we affirm the cosmos and cultivate our belonging together in what holds us all.

This chapter elucidates how love simultaneously involves the subject-self, the world of persons and nonpersons, and the sacredness of the cosmological ground, whether the lover is fully cognizant of this or not. I begin with Plato's mythical account of love in his *Symposium* and will concentrate on Socrates's speech in honor of *Eros*, which, in comparison to the speeches of the rest of the company, is more sober in its presentation of the provenance, nature, and goal of love. Not only is the beloved made present in love, but love reveals that it always moves in the presence of the divine Good too. I follow this with Aristotle's famous theory of friendship, emphasizing the importance he places on a proper self-love. A loving relation to one's own self opens the lover to the nobility of his own soul. This leads to virtue in relations not only with oneself but also with others who also properly love themselves. Furthermore, I consider this loving or erotic tension in relation to one's own soul as suggestive of the presence of the divine in the soul, or the soul in the divine. I will then return to phenomenology, or perhaps to what surpasses phenomenology, in the work of Emmanuel Levinas. His is the insistence that ethics is "first philosophy," rather than metaphysics, since it is the encounter with the Other that constitutes an encounter with transcendence. The "I" is ruptured by the radical alterity (otherness) of the Other, who cannot be assimilated or "totalized" as a mere being among beings, a thing to be known. The Other is utterly beyond any thinghood and transcends being itself. He is "otherwise than being." Love is desire of the desirable (Levinas's characterization of goodness). The face of the Other always manifests a primordial goodness, a trace of "holiness." I will finish with a meditation by David Walsh on how a metaphysics of love clarifies and amplifies the meaning of personal existence.

LOVE AND THE TENSION OF EXISTENCE

Socrates's Speech in Plato's *Symposium*

Socrates's speech is the sixth of seven speeches that Plato narrates in the *Symposium*. The first five are made in honor of the "great god, Eros," and they artfully recount the qualities of love that make a life of love highly desirable.[4] Socrates, arriving late, asks what the topic of discussion is, and when he is told, he rehearses a tale of love "I was given, once upon a time, by a Mantinean woman called Diotima—a woman who was deeply versed in this and many other fields of knowledge" (201d1–3). Diotima proved to Socrates that Eros cannot be a great god because, unlike a god, he is not only immortal, but mortal too. Eros is an in-between reality (*metaxy*) partaking of both eternity and time. Love is "a very powerful spirit, Socrates, and spirits, you know, are half-way between god and man. . . . Since they are between the two estates they weld both sides together and merge them in to one great whole" (202e4, 6–8). Love has a nature that is otherwise than divine and human. It is in-between them and can gather the two into a common horizon that holds them both. Through love, the god and the mortal regard each other from their proper place. The god, existing as the exemplar of the condition of lasting in the cosmos, responds to the mortal, who is subject to passing as the condition of their existence and who has poured out his heart in prayer and incantation to the god, who lasts. In love the proper place of god and mortal ceases to be mutually remote. It is not that love joins the contrary poles. Presence to the other becomes possible when love overflows the poles of divine and human, transforming remoteness into proximity and impossibility into possibility.

Socrates explains how Diotima proceeded to speak of the origin of love by recounting the mythic tale of how the parents of Eros came together. At the feast celebrating the birthday of Aphrodite, the goddess of beauty, the god Poros (Plenty or Resourcefulness) was present. Becoming intoxicated by taking too much nectar ("for this was before the days of wine"), Poros stepped out into the Garden of Zeus and fell asleep. Meanwhile Penia (Poverty), begging at doors, spied Poros resting and considered that she might raise her station in life by bearing a child by him, so she lay down at his side and conceived love (203b1–c1).

There are at least three aspects of love that are significant for us in the myth: Eros partakes not only of his parents' nature—plenty and poverty—but, because he emerged into existence on the birthday of Beauty, what he strains for is always the beautiful. So first, like his mother, Eros is rough and squalid. He has nothing; his heart is a hollow, molded in yearning for the beloved. Afterward, when the beloved leaves or dies, the lover is left empty, hurt, and lost. Considered under the aspect of his mother, love is vulnerability to pain and loss. Second, like his father, Eros is also "gallant, impetuous, and energetic, a mighty hunter, and a master of device and artifice" (203d4–5). Eros is what can also fill the heart of the lover, stirring his desire and imagination and spurring him to the most meaningful action. Love, in the nature of the father, is the unbounded joy of the presence of the beloved. Third, the beloved is always the beauty that the lover aims at, but Diotima advises the young Socrates not to confuse love with the beloved. Love and the beloved are not the same. Love gives the lover eyes to see the beauty of the beloved, and therefore "the beloved is in fact beautiful, perfect, delicate, and prosperous" (204c3–4). The beloved is always made beautiful in love. Yet whereas the beloved is fair and beautiful, love can sometimes be foul. It is the nature of Love to exist as a tension between otherwise remote or oppositional poles, bringing them into harmony in himself, and it is inevitable then that Eros "is neither mortal nor immortal, for in the space of a day he will be now, when all goes well with him, alive and blooming, and now dying, to be born again by virtue of his father's nature while what he gains will always ebb away as fast. So Love is never altogether in or out of need, and stands, moreover, midway between ignorance and wisdom" (203e1–204a1).

Plato tells us that love, the longing of love for the beauty of the beloved, constitutes "the one deathless and eternal element in our mortality" (206e8). It gives and receives from what is mortal and what is immortal. Love belongs strictly to neither, but participates in between both: it exists in time, forming the heart of the lover, but in the beloved, who is always present in love, the vision of the eternally beautiful is never lost. What love seeks is the beloved, who, as beautiful, is also the good and the source of happiness. "We may state categorically that men are lovers of the good? Yes, I said, we may" (206a4–5). Ultimately, "Love longs for the good to be his own forever" (206a11). Between lasting and passing, love equivocates. It is the memory of the timeless presence of the beloved in time, of a presence that sanctifies life itself and that radiates the sweetness of beauty beyond measure. Yet, while love grants a plenitude to the lover, whose heart is full, it can leave him broken, destitute, and poverty-stricken when the beloved has gone. Furthermore, relationships can die and belonging dissipate, not only because the beloved leaves but because the lover has too often fallen short of what love commands: giving and receiving, communion and generation. The lover—the subject-self who can choose not to be worthy of his love in thought, word, or deed—can fall away from what love requires, and when he does, he loses sight of the beauty of the beloved. But in love, in opening himself to love, the lover wants the beauty of the beloved to be his own forever and such beauty to last in spite of the devastation of the passing of time and in spite of the inexorableness of death.

Belonging, we can say, is grounded in a luminous beauty within the murkiness of the ordinary, simply because the beloved is a beloved and is present in our midst. From the beloved to whom we are now subject, we pick up the boundaries that demarcate the uniqueness of our selfhood. It is for the sake of the beloved that we choose to exercise our agency. We exist-from and exist-toward the beloved, whose presence invites us to be responsible and free, in that order. In the presence of the beloved, I am present to myself as *lover*, unfolding myself in ways that I might not have otherwise done. In such unfolding, I bring my own possibilities to light. What love opens to me is nothing short of the abiding cosmos as the horizon in which I find myself regarding the beloved. Indeed, the beauty of the beloved is consubstantial with the beauty of the cosmos. Hers is the beauty of the cosmos, a microcosmic bond and order, both lasting and passing at once. Love teaches the lover how to belong in the cosmos through beauty: "Whoever has been initiated so far in the mysteries of Love and has viewed all these aspects of the beautiful in due succession, is at last drawing near the final revelation. And now, Socrates, there bursts upon him that wondrous vision which is the very soul of the beauty he has toiled so long for. It is an everlasting loveliness which neither comes nor goes, which neither flowers nor fades, for such beauty is the same on every hand, the same then as now, here as there" (210e2–211a3). Diotima tells Socrates that our entrance into the life of love crosses first the threshold of the physical beauties of the world, and the beauties of the spirit second. But the embracing vision of divine beauty, the absolute, is the grand consummation of the life of love. Populated by the beauties of loved ones—beloved persons, places, and things—such a life is always played out against the vista of the absolute. Like climbing the rungs of a ladder, "the universal beauty dawns upon his inward sight, he is almost within reach of the final revelation" (211b6). Indeed, the in-between nature of love, in search of the beauty of the beloved, equips the consciousness and flesh of the lover to become "the friend of god, and if ever it is given to man to put on immortality, it shall be given to him" (212a5). Diotima asks rhetorically, "Would you call *his* . . . an unenviable life?" (211e4). In love of the beloved, we are mortals who put on immortality in contemplating the beauty that outlives death.

Aristotle: Love in Friendship and Truth

The Friendship of the Good Man
The question of immortality is an important theme for Aristotle too. This becomes clear in various places, including in his meditation on friendship. The eighth book of his *Nicomachean Ethics* is among the earliest and most sustained meditations on friendship. In his observational style, he records, describes, and classifies types of friendship. Some friendships are rich in belonging, and others less so. Yet Aristotle's consideration of types is demonstrative of more than a simple taxonomy of friendship. He demonstrates how genuine presence to

the friend involves an authentic friendship with one's own self as its very condition, and how such friendship is charged with divine presence. Thus, the highest type of friendship is a synecdoche of the cosmos itself. Or to put it another way, the highest type of friendship can last through and bear the vicissitudes of life because it is nothing less than a microcosmos of persons.

Aristotle famously describes three broad categories of friendship: pleasure, utility, and goodness (or virtue).[5] Friendship exists in each case for the sake of what it aims at. When pleasure or usefulness diminishes or is spent, friendships based solely on these must come to an end. The third type of friendship, unsurprisingly, endures and in fact deepens among friends. He writes, "Bad men will be friends for the sake of pleasure or of utility, being in this respect like each other, but good men will be friends for their own sake, i.e. in virtue of their goodness" (*Nicomachean Ethics* 1157b1–3). The most that bad men can achieve, to the extent that they are actually or intentionally bad, is pleasure or utility. Indeed, to the extent that these are the only goals that their friendships aim at and are all that bad men, qua bad, in fact strive for, only pleasure or usefulness is achievable. The friendships of bad men seem not to be friendships at all, and while they look to all intents and purposes like friendship, they assume only a superficial resemblance to the genuine friendship that is lived by good men for the sake of goodness. Good men have available to them the third type of friendship because it is already goodness that they aim for in life. Of good men who enter into friendship with one another, Aristotle writes, "These, then, are friends without qualification; the others are friends incidentally and through a resemblance to these" (1157b3–5).[6]

Aristotle is in search of the root of such friendships, and he conjectures that "friendly relations with one's neighbours, and the marks by which friendships are defined, *seem to have proceeded from a man's relations to himself*" (1166a1–2) (emphasis added). That is, the possibility of a meaningful friendship, a genuine belonging with a particular other, seems to emerge from an undergirding relation in which one is qualitatively present to one's own self in love or friendship. Thus, the implication in Aristotle's thought is that where one is lovingly present to one's own self, one not only relates well to oneself and desires what is worthy of love in oneself, but one can also recognize what is worthy of love in the other and relate well to that other. Correlatively, where one relates badly to oneself, not only has one missed what is genuinely noble in oneself and honors what is less than noble, but the possibility of relating well to others correspondingly degenerates or is perhaps extinguished. "Existence is good to the good man, and each man wishes himself what is good. . . . And such a man wishes to live with himself" (1166a19–20, 24).

Aristotle lists characteristics of genuine friendship that a good man also bears toward himself: he wants to be with himself, he enjoys his memories and weeps and rejoices with himself. "Therefore, since each of these characteristics belongs to the good man in relation to himself, and he is related to his friend as to himself (for his friend is another self), friendship too is thought to be one of these attributes, and those who have these attributes to be friends" (1166a30–34). On the other hand, "the bad man does not seem to be amicably disposed even to himself, because there is nothing in him to love" (1166b25). What is behind the pursuits of pleasure or convenience or profit or glory, and so on? The bad man seems to have hollowed himself out. He is to himself and others an empty shell, devoid of what is lovely. He does not pursue in friendship, or anywhere else, the good of existence that is worthy of the good man's love. In wickedness and deceit he may fool the world, but in the end he cannot fool himself. He may lie to himself, justifying each transgression with an appeal to pleasure or utility, but what he resists acknowledging is that with each transgression he becomes smaller in moral stature, weaker in conviction, a lesser version who he authentically could be.[7] The bad man may project strength and cunning to the world, but he is in flight from his own reality as a subject-self in and of the cosmos. In willfully forgetting what is desirable in himself, he is alienated from himself and, by extension, from the world and reality in which he is a participant. "So that if to be thus is the height of wretchedness, we should strain every nerve to avoid wickedness and should endeavor to be good; for so one may be both friendly to oneself and a friend to another" (1166b26–29). The good man, by contrast, intends the good that affirms the goodness of existence for its own sake, and thus is present to himself precisely qua friend of such a good; he holds a love of the good within himself, and it is this goodness that is the source out of which he can aim to enact goodness in the world. The term "conscience" was not available to Aristotle, but he is clearly motivated by the affective experience that such a term names. Goodness lives within the good man and invests him with its own authority, commissioning him to live and befriend for the sake of existence.

We don't need to divide humanity down the middle, demarcating the bad men from the good men, but instead we can recognize the quality of presence that characterizes our own personhood, which is always in relation. We can examine our own motives—the good we aim at—in our relations with others to whom we apply the title "friend." The "bad man" is as much a possibility of the emergent self as the "good man." Aristotle's account of the friendship in and of the good man is a splendidly attentive exploration of the presence that is required for belonging. If I am lovingly present to myself as I intend my own self, I can more likely recognize and affirm what in me is genuinely noble and desirable for its own sake. (With Lonergan, we can suggest the heuristically open normativities of attentiveness, of intelligence, of reasonableness, of responsibility, and indeed of love itself.) In this recognition of what is noble and desirable in my own personhood, I can recognize the same in the personhood of others. For Aristotle, virtue is the specifically human activity that leads to specifically human happiness, and the practice of virtue is the activity of the rational nature that leads to authentic friendship for human beings. The obvious potential for "wretchedness" would seem to follow from a failure of recognizing, knowing, choosing, and loving what is worthy of love in my own rational nature, in my own personhood. The good man is lovingly present to himself when he seeks to know the truth of himself and to enact the good within himself that he has discovered. He can relate well to himself because he loves what is lovely in himself, not what is base. It is not that there is nothing base in the good man, but he chooses to love what is not base and strives to live accordingly. The bad man, through lack of loving presence to himself, is inauthentic. He ignores the truth of his own rational nature, as fitted for happiness that is rational. So, he relates ill to himself, but he is still said to love himself, in the more narrow, self-centered sense of Augustine's *amor sui*.

In the case of *amor sui*, what does it mean to love oneself? Aristotle writes, "So those who are grasping with regard to these things [wealth, honors, bodily pleasures] gratify their appetites and in general their feelings and the irrational element of the soul" (1168b18). Since most people, according to Aristotle, are grasping for base things and seek self-gratification through the pleasure or utility of these, the term "self-love" has become associated with bad men and profane vulgarity. However, the self-love of a good man is categorically a different matter. It is ennobling, not vulgar and debasing.

> At all events [the good man] assigns to himself the things that are noblest and best, and gratifies the most authoritative element in himself and in all things obeys this. Besides, a man is said to have or not have self-control according as his intellect has or has not the control, on the assumption that this is the man himself; and the things men have done from reason are thought most properly their own acts and voluntary acts. That this is the man himself, then, or is so more than anything else, is plain, and also that the good man loves most that part of him. (1168b29–1169a3)

For Aristotle, one becomes a friend of one's own self to the extent that one is responsive to the highest part of the human soul—variously known as the rational, intellectual, or noetic part—which he also describes as ennobling and most authoritative. The intellect (*nous*) is what the good man becomes good by. By its authority, he is self-directed, seeking the happiness that corresponds with such a life. The life of the good man is the life of the intellect, which is nevertheless replete with the tension of existing in between what is noble and what is ignoble.

The love of a good man for himself is the choice to love what is noblest and best, and as such explains the perennial need for what we call a liberal education. Since the liberal arts aim at a cultivation or growth of the soul for the sake of the good life, they exemplify Aristotle's insistence that "excellence and the good man seem . . . to be the measure of every class of thing" (1166a11–12). The good man is already a friend of virtue: he can befriend excellence when he sees it because he knows and loves the measure of excellence already present and operative within him. He becomes excellent in loving excellence. He finds excellence, now constitutive within himself and others, to be worthy of his love; and he lives accordingly. Indeed, excellence is eminently lovable, and is the measure he directs himself toward, even as finds himself subject to it. Present to himself as a lover of what is highest and most authoritative, he befriends the world in an attitude of loving concern for existence itself. Indeed, excellence and the good of existence are rooted and unified in the man who relates well to himself. He is the good man who knows how to belong since he already belongs well to himself, affirming the good of existence and the good of virtue. Thus it is no surprise that friendships among good men partake of the lasting of the cosmos in their diachronic endurance, and eminently appeal to the nobility of the soul. Such friends, belonging together, find not only that each exists-from the nobility of what lasts, but that their friendship itself is saturated with a shared yearning for that nobility. In this way, friends ennoble each other. In belonging to what is most noble, they belong to one another. Their speech, their lives, their presence: in all things, the belonging of friends partakes of what is enduring and sacred.

The Intellect as the In-Between

But what is highest and most noble in the existence of the good man? As we know, Aristotle identifies the noblest and the best, the most authoritative element, as that which pertains to the intellect. I have discussed Lonergan's G.E.M., which tracks the dynamic norms of the cognitional process. Here, let us briefly consider Aristotle's thought on the intellect understood as a capacity of the soul in order to enter more deeply into the erotic (loving) tension in which the good man is thought to exist and belong.

In substantial agreement with Plato about the tripartite division of the soul—appetite, spiritedness, intellect—Aristotle undertakes an examination of the intellect (nous) as the highest part of the soul. In On the Soul, Aristotle differentiates between two types of intellect, or two categories of intellectual function: the "passive intellect" (nous pathetikos) and the "active intellect" (nous poetikos).[8] Aristotle considers the passive intellect to be passive because it is mixed and indelibly stamped with the incarnate experiences of mortal life. It is imprinted by these sensory experiences and becomes a repository of impressions—memories, behaviors, preferences, and so on. The active intellect, however, is that part of the intellect that works to render such experiences intelligible. As opposed to the passive intellect, the active intellect "is separable, impassible, unmixed, since it is in its essential nature activity (for always the active is superior to the passive factor, the originating force to the matter)" (On the Soul 430a17–19).

The account of the active intellect in *On the Soul* is often read in conjunction with the twelfth book of his *Metaphysics*, where Aristotle describes the active intellect as that part of the soul that "thinks of that which is most divine and precious and does not change" (1074b25–26). So, the active intellect not only works on grasping the intelligibility of experiences, but although located in the human person, it seems also to be more than human. For Aristotle, the active intellect is divine since it is a divine activity: it "thinks itself, if it is that which is best; and its thinking is a thinking of thinking" (1074b34). On the one hand, the active intellect is undoubtedly human since it is by the active intellect that we can come to know anything at all, yet on the other hand it seems to participate in divine nature too. The divine *nous* is, paradoxically, operative as a constituent part of human *nous*. The intellect seems to become the in-between zone of human-divine participation. So far from negating human nature, Aristotle's thought on intellect suggests that there is a metaxy called the intellect in which human and divine share. Like Voegelin's own later, differentiated account of the luminosity and intentionality of consciousness, Aristotle is comfortable with *nous* as an in-between reality. With the active intellect identified as "divine thinking," the human search for the truth of the real in thought seems to suggest the presence of divine reality, which is also in search of the real. But the real is what is highest and best, which is nothing other than the divine. The divine seems to be thinking itself, but present in the active intellect of each human thinker as he thinks. So it is that, while the active intellect is Aristotle's name for the highest capacity or function of the human soul, the most authoritative part, it can also be said to be the divine part of the soul. The active intellect is the dynamism of divine presence in the human soul, thinking divine thoughts. Thus the good man, who is friend of his own existence through love of what is highest and most authoritative in himself, finds the divine quality of his own intellect essentially desirable. In knowing, loving, and belonging to himself, he also belongs to the intimacy and activity of the divine. His choice to pursue goodness and the truth manifests the presence of divine sacredness operative within him.

Aristotle identifies the divine operation of the active intellect with the divine "first mover," which exists by necessity. The divine intellect, for Aristotle, is always active, contemplating its own necessary being. "The first mover, then, of necessity exists; and in so far as it is necessary, it is good, and in this sense a first principle" (*Metaphysics* 1072b11). The divine intellect contemplates itself, just as the human person can contemplate and love the divine as the highest. Necessary, divine being is the object of both the divine and human active intellect, always present as the first principle and constitutive element of human reason. "For the necessary has these senses—that which is necessary perforce because it is contrary to impulse, that without which the good is impossible, and that which cannot be otherwise but is *absolutely* necessary. . . . And thought [*nous*] in itself deals with that which is best in itself, and that which is thought in the fullest sense with that which is best in the fullest sense. And thought [*nous*] thinks itself because it shares in the nature of the object of thought" (1072b12, 17–20). The first mover is necessary being—it must exist since there are existing but contingent things that do not explain their own existence, and these must owe their existence to what necessarily exists. The first mover exists necessarily and is necessarily always present. This is another way to approach cosmological presence as the bond and order that generates, sustains, and governs all things. As divine *nous*, the first mover is present both as active intellect (*nous poetikos*) and as the highest object of *nous* (the good, the truth, and the beauty of the real, sought by the nobility of the good man's soul in pursuit of what is highest and most authoritative).

For Aristotle, the good man loves his own existence and the existence of his friends because they exist-from the *nous* that is operative within them; and in existing-toward the necessity, goodness, authority, and desirability of the divine *nous*, they have befriended divine sacredness, which binds and orders the cosmos and is necessarily and abidingly present within them, who are contingent beings. Voegelin comments that "Aristotle thus understands the tension of consciousness as a mutual participation (*metalepsis*) of the two *nous* entities in each other. On the part of the human *nous* the knowing questioning and the questioning knowledge, that is, the noetic act (*noesis*), is a knowing participation in the ground of being; the noetic participation, however, is possible by virtue of the preceding genetic participation of the divine in the human *nous*."⁹ *Nous*—ambiguously human, ambiguously divine—is an in-between reality of consciousness, strung out in a tension of eros between human and divine, time and eternity, immanence and transcendence. To contemplate humanly is to be drawn to participate—by way of consciousness and the flesh—in the ground of divine being, which is already present as desirable in that contemplation, as that contemplation. The identity of knower and known, we recall, is luminosity. Divine presence, for Aristotle, is manifest *in* human reason, not as a superaddition and not as mystical entity, but as luminously constitutive and substantial. It is what explains intentionality in its fullest sense: the unrestricted human desire to know (as Lonergan phrases it), since its objective is being itself.

As Socrates surmised, thinking is more than calculating or instrumental figuring out. It is to reach out in love for the real, by the real that is in act within us. Thinking is a "metaleptic" (or participatory) human-divine partnership. The essential human activity is itself an act that aims at belonging. Therefore, Aristotle advises us to attune ourselves to the divine thinking that is present and active within us. In continuation with Diotima's words to Socrates about becoming a friend of God, Aristotle himself instructs us not to listen "to those who tell us only to think of mortal things, but instead we ought to immortalize ourselves by thinking things divine" (*Nicomachean Ethics* 1177b31–35).

Present to himself as a friend of truth and goodness—in Plato, the lover of the beautiful—the "self-immortalizing" man is thereby a friend of divine being. The friendship or love of the good man is metaleptic and mutual. In self-presence, he finds himself subject to the erotic presence of the necessary, divine ground of the cosmos from which he exists. In intentional presence, he asserts his personal selfhood in the directedness of thinking toward the desirableness of truth and goodness that already forms the horizon of his thinking, the horizon of his specific humanity. In articulating the experience and understanding of the human-divine in-between nature of *nous*, and judging thought to be the area of unrestricted participation, Aristotle can be said to be articulating a noetic philosophy of cosmological belonging, a belonging that is enacted by the good man only because he loves or befriends what is authoritative and best. The good man is the measure of "every class of thing" because, in the midst of the passing of all that emerges in the astrophysical world, and as a committed player in the passionate social drama of meaning, he nonetheless lives in attunement to what does not pass.

The good man is ultimately a friend of the cosmos: in loving his friend, he seeks and affirms what lasts even as he uplifts and consoles the friends—and is consoled by the friend—in the midst of what passes. The belonging of good men in friendship radiates the meaning of both cosmological conditions. We can say that goodness is a divine measure that the good man—who is an authentic man, and who, in loving the real, is more properly characterized as a lover of divine goodness—mediates to himself and to the world by his love. He is not the ultimate source of goodness, but in discovering its necessary and authoritative presence in himself, his life is an originating value. Subsequently, the good man measures every class of thing with the necessary measure that he knows and welcomes as the measure of himself by way of love operative in the intellect. He is the presence of the measure because in love the measure belongs in him.

The love a good man has for his own existence (and that of his friend) is also a love of his share in being, or a love of his role in the drama of life in the cosmos. To love someone or something for their own sake is to love their existence, as the good man knows. It is to love their unique, irreplaceable share in the cosmos that holds them. Their life has intrinsic value because it is already a living out of the sacred bond and order that is present in all things and that finds its irrecusable channel in the being of the friend. The value of the friend's life is a value woven from the fabric of the cosmos, and to the friend we owe nothing less than the cosmos itself. In order to consider what it means to owe nothing less than the cosmos, or what the payment of such a debt would mean, let us now turn to the hermeneutics that Emmanuel Levinas's phenomenology offers us.

Emmanuel Levinas: Love and the Other

The Other as Transcendence

The "Other" is a ubiquitous term in twentieth-century continental philosophy.[10] Levinas does not thematize friendship as Aristotle does, but traces the pretheoretical and embodied movement of love in any encounter with the Other. The Other is the person who is in my proximity now. The Other is anyone who has what we called positional presence to me. Whereas "friend" refers to someone who has become dear to me, "Other" is a less exclusive term, attaching to him or her whom I happen to encounter face-to-face. What we owe to the Other in our proximity is nothing less than what we would owe to our friend.

One may be happily busy with one's well-made plans, but it is the Other who arrests the flow and the freedom of the self. The proximity of the Other, Levinas tells us, effects the "intersubjective curvature of space," a curvature that "inflects distance into elevation."[11] That is, the Other who comes before me is no mere object, like a stone thrown toward me. He is not grasped as something with a "'nucleus' to his objectivity." The Other looks upon me from what is more like height than distance. Objects may lie around me in space, but they lie outside intersubjective space. A nature, for Levinas, is what is given; it is comprehended and synthesized by me as knowledge. Levinas frequently refers to "being" as that which can be grasped and affirmed as knowledge, but the Other confounds my knowledge, because she comes to me from beyond being. Levinas's discussion of being has much in common with Lonergan. We have already met Lonergan's term "proportionate being." It is a useful term because, for Lonergan, "proportionate" not only refers to what can be known by human cognition, but is suggestive of reality that lies beyond being proportionate to our knowing, which is the meaning of transcendence. Levinas wants to demonstrate that the Other is always who is more than being, or indeed, "otherwise than being." Metaphysically, nature has being, or rather, it belongs to "being." The Other, for Levinas, does not belong to being; it is as though she comes into my presence from above, from "beyond being." Levinas makes the distinction between being and the Other primary.

"Being" signifies much of what has been discussed in terms of the primordiality of the cosmos: the ever-present threat of supervening chaos and the common matrix out of which all things come. For Levinas, being is the totality of all this. Being can be familiar, but also uncanny in ways that are reminiscent of Heidegger. "Being" refers to both the intelligible natures of things, encountered with their clear lineaments, and to the murky, nocturnal, incoherent rustling and rumbling of something oceanic or abyssal that fills the interstices between all things and their temporal moments; the terror of the insomniac,

the engulfing "*il y a.*" The Other, however, is of a different order entirely. She remains always and radically beyond my ability to assimilate in knowledge. She comes into my proximity, as it were, from an
elevation beyond being entirely. She is transcendence-in-immanence
because, in my proximity, she eludes my comprehension. The Other
is what Levinas calls "exteriority," and that which is utterly exterior
or transcendent is encountered as "infinity."[12] Phenomenologically,
there is ineffability in the encounter, a trace of holiness that is borne
in the face of the Other. In my encounter with her, the cosmological
condition of passing is suspended. It is as though time itself were suspended. She is "otherwise than being" and shockingly manifests the
absolute condition of sacred lasting that she brings "from above." In
a banal sense, as an other, she too must suffer and die like the rest of
us, but as the Other, she is the occasion of infinity, of transcendence
in my midst. "The Other is not the incarnation of God, but precisely
by his face, in which he is disincarnate, is the manifestation of the
height in which God is revealed."[13] Quite simply, I respond because
the Other presents herself as infinite value. Before her, I am no longer
free. I am response-able, I am response-ability.

If the Other is beyond being, then she is beyond metaphysics. It
is ethics, for Levinas, that necessarily precedes all else because ethics
is my inescapable responsibility for her who is otherwise than being. Before the building of all my projects, before politics, before
metaphysics, ethics is my priority. It is "first philosophy" because
intersubjective space—the place of encounter with the Other—is
where personhood begins. Philosophy, as a human pursuit, begins
in the reality of the person. The branches of philosophy proceed
from the person in whom wonderment occurs. In this vein, Levinas writes, "Morality [here, synonymous with ethics] is not a branch
of philosophy, but first philosophy."[14] The subject of philosophical
wonderment, the "I," is the subject approached by the Other, and
"I" am the one whose authentic selfhood emerges in response-ability.
Selfhood is thus always ethically in question. As the encounter that
welcomes the exteriority of the Other, ethics means nothing less than
who I must be when transcendent reality confronts me. The face of the
Other holds me. In the face-to-face encounter, I am floating. Without
my feet anchored upon my own ground, I am a hostage. I exist-from
the Other entirely, who has become the transcendent ground. The

face of the Other, Levinas writes, is "signification, and signification without context."[15] Context is what gives us characters with roles to play, but the Other cannot be a character, since she comes to us as a face without a context and without any known role. Whereas we can think of characters in relation to a profession, of what an address or biographical information would tell us about someone, and so on, the face is precisely what is not in relation to anything. It has no context because the alterity (otherness) of the Other is exteriority. "Here, to the contrary, the face is meaning all by itself. You are you."[16] Context is content, and content is what can be grasped and known. The face, however, is meaning that cannot be grasped. It eludes knowledge and being. It points beyond itself, making its "escape from being," or from what Levinas calls "totalization" as a synonym for knowledge. The Other evades synthesis or assimilation by me because she is always a surplus beyond my capacity to synthesize or assimilate in knowledge. Yet here I am in her proximity, she who is infinity because she gives the *ideatum* of infinity to me.

How do I respond to what is no longer an event in being? The impetus comes from her. The ethical priority holds me because the face of the Other has issued a very clear command: "Thou shalt not kill.... There is a commandment in the appearance of the face, as if a master spoke to me. However, at the same time, the face of the Other is destitute; it is the poor for whom I can do all and to whom I owe all."[17] At once powerful and frail, the face of the Other holds me and, in that holding, draws me into a response. I am rendered responseable. Responsibility before the Other and for the sake of the Other becomes my task, binding and ordering what I will find as my freedom. My freedom will have goalposts, will be directed and enriched by aiming at those goalposts. While the face commands, it is also what is exposed and defenseless, and such proneness seems to invite an act of predation or violence. The face of the Other pleads from her essential vulnerability, but again, the meaning carried by that same face is the prohibition of any act by me that would reduce her to another object in the world, totalized in being. Only because the face comes to me in penury and destitution can I be charged to respond to what is present in the face: transcendence, the trace of God. The face of the Other appears with overwhelming authority. It holds me, commissions me, and I find that I am able to respond. I find the resources.[18]

If I can exist-from the Other in the face-to-face encounter, I can exist-toward the Other too. Let us consider what loving and belonging to the Other means for Levinas.

Love, Desire, Goodness

Martin Buber writes, "Feelings one 'has'; love occurs. Feelings dwell in man, but man dwells in his love. . . . Love is a responsibility of an I for a You."[19] Is Levinas's Other synonymous with Buber's *Thou* (You)? Is love a responsibility I have for the Other? The answer to these questions is substantially yes, but there are subtleties in the answer that have great significance for the meaning of belonging.[20] Love, for Buber, lives between I and Thou, and in love, Thou is whom I exist-from and exist-toward. To Thou, I can belong because it is Thou who holds me in a tension of love and responsibility. In my belonging to Thou, the meaning of my life is renewed. Without Thou, I grieve. I am at sea. "This is no metaphor but actuality: love does not cling to an I, as if the [Thou] were merely 'content' or object; it is between I and [Thou]. Whoever does not know this, know this with his being, does not know love, even if he should ascribe to it the feelings that he lives, experiences, enjoys, and expresses. Love is a cosmic force."[21]

For Levinas, love is not obvious in the encounter with the Other. We have seen that he uses the harshest terms imaginable to describe the encounter: hostage, violence, rupture. The Other is always the Stranger whose alterity troubles me. Yet my response can only be an extravagant one. Love can be called goodness, and goodness is what the face commands.[22] It is a type of love that is not carried by a desire consonant with eros. I mean by "eros," in this instance with Levinas, desire that pursues the carnal beauty of the Beloved. For the sake of the goodness that is owed to the Other, who may not be the Beloved, who may not be Buber's Thou, let us make a distinction between love that is sexually erotic desire and nonsexual eros.

Love, Sex, and Holiness

"The epiphany of the Beloved is but one with her *regime* of tenderness. The *way* of the tender consists in an extreme fragility, a vulnerability" (Levinas's emphasis here and in the following quotations).[23] Erotic desire is a hunger that would impose itself upon the fragility of the Beloved, but if nested within love, erotic love allows itself to be nourished. The nourishment comes by a paradoxical route. Rather than sexual satisfaction in the proneness of the Beloved, erotic love feeds the desire of the lover by hunger itself.[24] It gorges itself on hunger. Sexually erotic desire strains toward what is not possible to grasp, but whose meaning radiates from the face of the Beloved. In such eros, "*The essentially hidden throws itself toward the light, without becoming signification.* Not nothingness—but what is not yet."[25] Desire reaches for the not-yet, the secret that appears without appearing, still clandestine but teetering behind the line of exposure.

This is an equivocation for Levinas that also amounts to profanation. The lover caresses the Beloved, "but the caress transcends the sensible. . . . The caress seizes upon nothing, in soliciting what ceaselessly escapes its form toward a future never future enough, in soliciting what slips away as though it *were not yet*. It *searches*, it forages."[26] In being both uncovered by erotic love and yet withholding the source of her evanescence, the Beloved is at risk of being profaned. The desire of the lover is to approach the limitlessly desirable, whose trace is caught in the face of the Beloved but always in the mode of withdrawing. Eros needs to be careful since it is given to a carelessness in which the lover grabs and clings to the Beloved as the limitlessly desirable, yet the source of limitlessness was never hers to give. The erotic equivocation between what is revealed and what remains concealed arises from the meaning of the caress. Caressing and being caressed is the way of tenderness, "the way of remaining in the *no man's land* between being and not-yet-being."[27] The erotic lover is forcing the secret, wants to consume what is holy, and bring what is veiled and precious in its concealment under the glare of the spotlight. Sexually charged eros wants to gaze upon ungazeable, to gulp from what the lover knows he should not. As the lover approaches the Beloved, there is a transgression at stake. The lover risks being swept away as he approaches holiness. "[The lover] dies with this death and suffers with this suffering. . . . Being moved is a pity that is complacent, a pleasure, a suffering transformed into happiness—voluptuosity. . . . Voluptuosity, as profanation, discovers the hidden as hidden."[28] In discovering the hidden, erotic desire brings the lover to an epiphany: he is standing on holy ground. Eros is sanctified in the epiphany. Erotic desire is the desire that seeks and approaches what is absolutely desirable, the very act of treading recklessly on holy ground.

Voluptuosity testifies to the proximity of holiness and to the possibility of profanation in the same moment. Holiness, present only as a trace, remains hidden and out of the reach of the lover, but erotic desire without love becomes lust, because it refuses holiness and hunger. It would proceed. It would profane absolutely what it has discovered if the hiddenness of the holy were not absolute. Lustful eros is the movement of profanation, but the face that expresses *Thou shalt not kill* expresses the command rather differently here in the context of erotic desire: *Thou shalt not pass.* There is a modesty that immodesty cannot reveal or render discoverable. The modesty of what remains hidden also remains insurmountable, but this is the proper geometry of love: to be angled toward the infinitely desirable that remains tantalizingly beyond what can be bisected. Absolutely remote, but not in the sense of vast distances across a horizontal plane, the face of the Beloved in the lover's emphatic proximity occasions the vertical tension of insatiability and hunger that love lives by. Keeping in mind Plato's originary notion of love as *metaxy*, as the in-between reality, love recasts its tension through Levinas's thought as that which is ever drawn from the possible to the impossible. Sexually erotic desire is the exuberance of coming into the presence of the absolutely desirable, of remote holiness and hiddenness, of the Good beyond being. Eros attempts the impossible, never daunted and always fed by the quixotic hunger that strains for a satisfaction that cannot ever be finally achieved.

The problem with sexually erotic desire is that it cannot wait as, in love, it must. Where love lives by the tension which nourishes and cultivates it, the urgency of eros risks its departure from such a love-nourished life. Erotic desire is centrifugal to the lows of love, dangerous if unguarded. Pornography as exhibitionist nudity serves as an inauthentic representation of what cannot ever be represented: the hidden in its ineffable, holy modesty. Indulgence in the pornographic gaze cannot satisfy the hunger for the not-yet. On the one hand, sexually charged eros can profane and destroy; but on the other, such eros is the very principle of fecundity. It partakes of the cosmos. It is the engine by which the lover enters "no man's land" and the occasion for beauty's great humbling of the lover in the encounter.[29] The lover must remain on guard: erotic desire is ignited by voluptuosity. The lover, suffused with sexual eros, would succumb immediately to the voluptuous seductions of pornographic dissimulation where "the face fades, and in its impersonal and inexpressive neutrality is prolonged, in ambiguity, into animality."[30] Erotic lust can bring the lover to an equivocation where profanation, in separating itself from love, leads away from goodness toward the totalizing of the Beloved as concept and being, and toward thematization in the nature of animality. But the erotic lover, qua lover, can harness eros for the sake of goodness too.

Love and Goodness

Goodness, according to Levinas, passes beyond being.[31] Goodness and the Other intervene in the flow of being, disturbing my plans and extending beyond my knowledge. Their intervention is enigmatic: it disturbs but does not remain. Indeed, the enigma of intervention is always already departing. "Desire, or the response to an Enigma or morality, is an intrigue," Levinas writes. "The I approaches the Infinite by going generously toward the You, who is still my contemporary, but, in the trace of Illeity [transcendent dignity], presents himself out of a depth of the past, faces, and approaches me."[32] This desire is self-forgetful, self-sacrificial love where I pass beyond the specter of my own death or mortal finality before the illeity of the Other. "Illeity" (from the French word for "he," the third person, the radically Other) is itself an enigmatic term that refers to the infinite dignity with which the Other approaches me. Dignity is the notion, operative in the contemporary world, that seems to function as an implicit affirmation of transcendent meaning and value, grounded in the consciousness and flesh of the Other. Illeity is the trace—the quality, the dimension—of transcendence that commands my reverence of, and respectful response to, the Other. As synonymous with dignity, illeity declares the transcendent dimension of meaning present in the face. As such, it is employed by Levinas as a symbol for how the "Infinite, or God," refers, "from the heart of its very desirability, to the nondesirable proximity of others."[33]

The infinite is a goodness that I find eminently desirable, but before I am caught by desire for it, I am arrested by the Other who enters my proximity. Such an entrance is a disturbance. The Other is a

Stranger whose entrance commands all of me. But I was busy. I had my own plans, and the proximity of the Other is not what I wanted. Yet I must look upon the face of the Other. That is, I must cease my projects when the Other walks into the room. It is always most inconvenient to have to pivot away from what I must do, in order to attend to the Other, whom I must now prioritize. The primordial command to respond is issued by the trace of illeity in the face of the Other. Illeity or the dignity of the Other always involves the proroguing of my desirable freedom for the sake of response-ability. Yet it is precisely by this illeity-mandated suspension, this pause, that I can recover the Good, the infinitely desirable. The proximity of others is less than desirable, and not because I am introvert, but because the good I had conceived had been directed toward my project but now must be set aside by a goodness that passes beyond projects and being. Even service of God must be interrupted by service of neighbor, which takes priority. "Through this reversal the Desirable escapes desire. The goodness of the Good—the Good which never sleeps or nods—inclines the movement it calls forth, to turn it from the Good and orient it toward the other (*autrui*), and only thus toward the Good. . . . [God's] absolute remoteness, his transcendence, turns into my responsibility—non-erotic par excellence—for the other (*autrui*)."[34]

The pivot from God to neighbor is a pivot from the God whose service I conceive and execute to the God who is otherwise than Other, "other with an alterity prior to the alterity of the other, . . . transcendent to the point of absence."[35] The presence of God amounts to the absence of God, an absence symbolized not as emptiness but as a trace. The trace of illeity in the face of the Other shatters my projects with the force that binds and orders the cosmos. Never convenient. I could choose to nullify goodness and reduce the Other to being and to history. I'd rather "forget what is better than being, that is, the Good."[36] Yet the Other is a reminder, a primordial recovery or *anamnesis*, that existence is called to belonging. Unless I set my jaw against belonging in order to foster alienation instead, I must respond to the eternal depth and the limitless value that the trace of illeity in the Other brings into my midst, and belong. To love the inconvenient Other is to respond to the illeity manifest in her face. It is to pick up the burden of the Other as one's own burden, and to love without obvious, affective desire. Affirming Aquinas's definition of love, this is to will the good of the Other. We did not desire it at first, but the Other implores us to draw from our resources all we can to recover the good. We did not intend it but, in the proximity of the Other, we are moving within the horizon that transcendent illeity in her face opens, "the glory of the Infinite."

DAVID WALSH: PERSONS IN THE BEYOND OF LOVE

Levinas's work is a phenomenology of hospitality.[37] Hospitality transcends being, welcoming persons who are never reducible to objects within being. We might say that hospitality, as personal encounter with the Other, is how we come to know love. It is not that we encounter and then love, but that love is already present in some sense, and this is why hospitable encounter can happen. Love has framed encounter before any encounter has taken place. That framing is hospitality. It is reminiscent of Buber's "cosmic force." Yet if encounters can be framed by hospitality, it is only because love is already a force present and operative in personhood. Love is already here, giving and receiving in the person who was always in relation.

Love is operative in between persons, but what the in-betweenness of persons could mean is what is in question in every encounter, permeated as it is by alterity. To love is to participate in the great fecundity that binds and orders interpersonal space. Such fecundity belongs not only to the in-betweenness of persons but also, as Levinas has glimpsed, to the in-betweenness that is the luminosity of cosmological presence. Recall that the in-betweenness of persons, according to Levinas, is an "interpersonal curvature of space." Why is interpersonal space curved? The answer surely lies in the ineffability of each person and of love. There is, first, the sacredness of the cosmos that flows in the uniqueness of each person. Second, love in between the "I" and the Other nullifies extension and distance for the sake of an unrestricted bond and order. The region in between persons is inflected into something like a "holy ground" on which encounter not only happens but envelops both in communion. I will discuss communion below, but for now, let us acknowledge that Levinas's "curvature" can be articulated as a paradoxical inversion whereby interpersonal space, proximity and hospitality, calls forth the cosmos in a movement of love that has already superseded the measurability of duration and distance. Love makes possible the apparently impossible. In love, the lasting and passing, time and eternity, suffering and flourishing of the Whole acquire a human face. Love is the indispensable mode of existing in the cosmos because it is in love that persons can exist-from and exist-toward one another both in time and out of time simultaneously. The interpersonal encounter is framed by hospitality, but hospitality is itself an enactment of the cosmos that love makes present.

In his *Politics of the Person*, David Walsh opens the fourth chapter with what seems like a lament. The quality of lament arises from a sense of homelessness or homesickness. "It is the elusiveness of the mystery by which we are held that renders the sense of being lost in the cosmos so unshakeable. We cannot quite drop the impression that what is most important has escaped us."[38] Finding ourselves unmoored and floating, alive but without meaning, is an uncomfortably uncanny feeling. Levinas's account of the *il y a*—the unnerving, saturating closeness of being, "the horrible eternity at the bottom of essence"—is a symbolic equivalent to uncanniness.[39] Walsh tells us something has been missed. We have overlooked mystery. Mystery is not meaningless. It is the name we give to what is present in the mode of absence, like the memory of a deceased parent or the megalithic monuments of a people long since gone from the earth; or as I mentioned above, like the trace of God. It is not so much that mystery troubles us, but that trouble arises when we choose to overlook the subtlety of presence-in-absence and to live in alienation from mystery. Acknowledgment of mystery would not only mitigate the uncanniness and console us, but possibly transform us. Walsh is engaged in an anamnetic recovery of the significance of the mystery that holds us, a recovery that could overcome alienation and bring about the prospect of a meaningful belonging. The impeccably modern and postmodern individual has overlooked the cosmos. In willed forgetfulness of the cosmos, we risk forgetfulness of love; but it is precisely in recovering love that we can recover the cosmos. Love, it appears, is the antidote to alienation.

Just as in the *Republic* where Plato prefaces the allegory of the cave with setting out the necessity of recognizing that thinking can only occur within truth—itself an echo of Parmenides—Walsh writes, "There is no way to understand thought but in relation to what makes it possible. Thinking cannot step outside of that by which thinking is. Truth is ... what surpasses thought because there is no thinking outside of it."[40] So too with love. In love, there is a cosmos that precedes the lovelessness of a universe of things. Indeed, the cosmos proceeds from love, from the infinite divine surplus of creative fecundity that not only frames but overflows the cosmos. All things are nested within that which is not itself a thing, but the transcendent-divine condition of thinghood. The cosmos is continually wrought in the flow of love from that cosmological partner who is more than a partner within the cosmos. Love flows because it is the condition of the existence of the cosmos.

We are brought to a grand metaphysics of love whose grandness risks becoming an impersonal, theoretical abstraction. Yet the reverberations of love are registered in the life of each of us. A metaphysics of love, recognized by Levinas as the meaning of ethics, is already grounded in persons who alone can give and receive love. In existing-from another person, place, or thing, persons live within the love that bonds us; in existing-toward that person, place, or thing, our longing orders us toward serving their good. We enter into a communion of belonging. Love is the stuff of belonging, because belonging is the name we give to how we live our love, and indeed are lived by that love. *Energeia* was Aristotle's term for the power of actualization by which something is brought from potentiality to a completion of itself.[41] Love is *energeia* because our belonging is achieved by the actualizing power of love. It is because we love that we belong, and nothing short of the possibilities of the cosmos becomes present in our belonging since love is the *energeia* of the cosmos itself. Walsh writes that "nothing originates with us, we merely constitute a moment of transparence within the whole."[42] Even the uncanniness of homelessness or alienation in the cosmos is just as transparent for the mystery we exist-from and exist-toward as our reposing in the arms of our beloved. By a conspicuous and troubling homesickness, we are being recalled to what we exist-from. Our belonging is in question, but the redirection onto the path homeward, should we pay heed to it, comes simply from a "turning around," one that Plato advises in the *Republic*.[43] Where do we begin to belong in the cosmos?

"Our point of access is the simultaneity of persons worthy of infinite love.... The question of whether the other is really deserving of such affection is moot since the question arises only because we have been seized by the imperative of love."[44] Persons are transparent for the love that the cosmos exists-from and -toward. All things must pass, yet love is. Love is what reaches from deep eternity and becomes incarnate as the love by which the person binds and orders what is given in space and time. "Love that outweighs all other reality impresses itself upon us so deeply that we see that we no longer live within space and time. Such are only the externals of an existence far more profoundly anchored in an eternal openness from which we cannot turn aside" (134).

While love—human, divine—binds and orders the cosmos, it is better said that the personal gift of self, given and received in love, is what vivifies and renews the cosmos. All of this is to begin to think of God as personal, as opposed to an impersonal force. If "first mover" was the symbol employed by Aristotle for the necessity that founds the conditions of existence and sets all things in motion, then love symbolizes the personalizing of that necessity, a necessity that makes all persons participants in the founding and movement of the cosmos. A first mover becomes a first lover. In the act of creation, God-as-first-mover brings all things to existence from nothingness, but in self-giving, God-as-love breathes each into life with his own *pneuma*. By that *pneuma*, love rejuvenates, restores, and redeems life. In creation, God makes present the massiveness of all things; in love, God is intimately present to all things. "Even before the encounter with God has occurred he is present as the silent partner *within* every meeting of persons" (135; emphasis mine). God is not a third party among those present to one another, but the indispensable foundation by which presence becomes possible. "Personal encounter cannot arise from what is merely impersonal" (136). Among persons, presence is a gift whose meaning is generated in love. Love, we remember, is the in-between reality that brings together the possible and the impossible, and presence is what makes possible the impossibility of self-giving. Love, presence, and belonging require the giving away of the self to the Other in order that one may receive the Other. Walsh wonders what it means to give away one's own self in love. After all, persons are not present to themselves or anyone else as well delineated commodities, as complete entities, as exhaustively proportionate beings, or as measurable by any instrument. Personal presence is metaphorically more like an unrestricted set of possibilities. Persons give face to mystery. In this sense, persons are paradoxically present to themselves and others in the mode of absence. That is, like a book, they occupy space and time, yet are never exhausted by space and time. If their presence in the cosmos is not reducible to spatiotemporal coordinates, it does not follow that their presence in the mode of absence amounts to some kind of half-heartedness. They exist in the cosmos with all of their heart since they must always suffer and rejoice with the cosmos, under the conditions of the cosmos.

"Without the need to share itself, divine being most of all shares itself out of love. . . . We can give what we do not possess, ourselves, because we have been given the gift of giving that is love itself" (137). If it is by their love that persons revitalize the existence of one another; it is by giving themselves away to one another in love that they affirm their transcendence as participation in the divine life that flows in the cosmos. Walsh writes that we are like God in our elemental, personal freedom. "No matter how limited the power of a person, even the smallest child or the dying patient, he or she can still give all that is needed. They can give themselves. Even God does not do any more for when one has given oneself one has given the whole world" (147). Our love is consubstantial with the *energeia* that binds and orders the cosmos. Our love is imperfect, not through a fault of love, but only because human existence lacks the perfection that only God must be. When we love, we love from more than we are able to love. "We could not love if love had not made it possible for us to love, for it is not we who love but love that loves within us" (138). Yet it is the choice to love—to give and to receive—that enables love to love within us. Present in the cosmos in the mode of absence, the life of the Trinity of divine persons is the life our love offers to the beloved. "Love is Trinitarian. This is an insight derived not from revelation but from the logic of love itself" (143). From Plato to Buber and Levinas, the insight that love is an in-between reality is an enduring one. Yet love is surely more fecund than its creative presence in the *metaxy* would suggest. Walsh notes that the Trinitarian life is symbolized by the Father who begets the Son, and nothing intervenes between Father and Son but love. In between the persons of Father and Son, who are present to one another in the mode of absence since they have already given themselves away to one another, their love is "so utterly personal that it must become a third person, the Spirit" (143). Our love generates belonging, but the love in which our love participates is what grounds our belonging in the divine life of love and cosmos. Home—our homes with one another in place and time—becomes a foreshadowing of the eschaton.

I HAVE TRIED TO BE EXPLICIT. Without love, there is no genuine belonging. Belonging is the in-between tension where existence-from and existence-toward are directional factors explicable by love alone. Only in love do we gain eyes to see the beauty of the beloved. Socrates's speech in the *Symposium* gives us the insight that love unlocks what is ordinary to reveal the beauty of what was always extraordinary. Love seeks the beautiful, driving the lover out in pursuit of the beloved whose beauty he alone can see. To love is to live within the horizon of beauty, and beautiful horizons call lovers to their mystery. For Plato, it is love that opens the lover to absolute, transcendent beauty through the participation of physical and spiritual beauties in that absolute. In this, we found our course. It is not that there is an immanent reality set against a transcendent reality, but that there is a dimension of transcendence in all that immanently exists. The revelation of transcendent beauty is the work of love.

With Aristotle, transcendent beauty becomes categorically divine. In the friendship of the good man with himself and other good men, and in the activity of the intellect, there is nobility, authority, goodness, and truth, all beautiful in that they are desirable, and desirable to every human being because they seem to reveal the joining of divine and human. The reach of human possibility is drawn in love beyond immanent meaning by the desirability of divine transcendence already operative within us.

I then made the jump from the ancients to representative thinkers in our own times because in their work we discern the same anamnetic remembrance of cosmological presence that was foundational to philosophy in its early centuries, as well as a differentiation of ancient insights in a manner that is fully cognizant of contemporary developments. Levinas, for example, picks up and extends the theme of beauty and desirability in the responsibility we bear toward the Other in our proximity. There is a condition of inexhaustibility that, in spite of ourselves and our busy distractedness, calls us to give all that can. The ethical obligation is prior to metaphysics, because before there is being there is alterity. We have seen that the radical otherness of the Other cannot be totalized. Indeed, the face of the Other reminds us that "deep is calling unto deep," and we find the resources to respond. Response is more willingly given when love is directed at the "voluptuous"; it is harder to give when it is not clear why love is required. Yet as the face of the Other regards me, the space between us allows its horizontal distances to open their fixed measurability to reveal the vertical height of transcendence that has always held us and now calls us forth.

Walsh probes this for the further insight that our love—like our truth-seeking knowledge and like the nobility of the good man's soul—is not merely our own. In love, the inwardness of persons resonates with the inwardness of persons. In love, there is a bridge between the inwardness of the Trinitarian divine persons and the human person. In love is God revealed because love is the communion of divine persons that constitutes the absolute. Human love participates in the absolute, revealing the limitlessness of the divine ground that gives rise to every possibility of the cosmos. We can love because, like God, we can give ourselves away and receive the Other. Like God, human personhood is inwardness. When Walsh writes that "personhood remains the unsurpassable mystery of our existence because all else is surpassed by it," we are reminded that only a person can love, and only persons can be the possibility of a cosmos for each other (155).

I HAVE CONSIDERED PRESENCE as the prerequisite of belonging, and found that presence is cosmological, is constitutive of consciousness and embodiment, and drives belonging by the *energeia* that is love. To extend this analysis of belonging, I must now move the focus of the study from the individual person to persons in society. To listen to Levinas one more time, we learn that "the concept of man has a single extension, and that is human fraternity."[45] Furthermore, "fraternity . . . does not arise out of any commitment, any principle, that is, any recallable present. The order that orders me to the Other does not show itself to me, save through the trace of its reclusion, as a face of a neighbor."[46] Fraternity is *philia*, a love among persons that binds them into a network of bonds of affection and orders them to one another. Let us now proceed to the second part of this exegesis of belonging: "Communion."

PART 2

Communion

CHAPTER SIX

Communitas

Each of us embraces and critiques community. It is a concern of ours. We are not indifferent to it. Even a lack of concern toward community does not remain unchallenged. Recall Levinas: we are always met with the face of the Other. The face undermines our apathy. The face is that to which we cannot remain unresponsive without mortgaging our very personhood. Moreover, behind the Other, there are always others (*le tiers*, the third party). "Men are absolutely different from each other; the concept of man is the only one that cannot be comprehended, since each man is absolutely different from the others. The concept of man has a single extension, and that is human fraternity."[1] This chapter will consider the inherent sociality of human existence, which Levinas calls fraternity and I will call *communitas*.

By "community" we mean our families, our friendships, our marriages, our neighborhoods, our cities and regions and nations, and more. "Community" has a specific meaning of belonging in common, but points unrestrictedly to the myriad of sets of relationships in our lives. Up until now, I have considered cosmological presence and personhood, but surely our communities also tell us something about the primordiality of existence and belonging. The cosmological conditions of lasting and passing bear on life in community as much as they do on individual persons. On the one hand, festivity, legend, and governance are replete with symbols that seek to embed the meaning of our communities in stability and lastingness in spite of the passing of times and event. On the other, there is the ephemerality of opinion, fashion, and sentiment, which can sometimes uproot and mesmerize because mere ephemerality is forgetfulness of the cosmos. Just as individual personhood is a field of tensions, so too is community. In the turbulence of community life, it can be hard to find one's feet and to live out one's convictions, to be simply an authentic person against the weight of groupthink, peer pressure, and collective modes of expression. Nonetheless, we also know that a community of persons is capable of love; and in love we belong. The question of belonging—the most human question—is also ultimately a question of the cosmos because the human desire to belong is the desire to find a sure resting place (*assiete ferme*) in the midst of cosmos.[2] This security and consolation is what belonging to a community offers; and this is what is jeopardized in the disintegration of belonging. There is a symbolic landscape that our inherent sociality is perennially in need of, turning our places and our times into a rich repository of shared, common meaning that binds us into a community and orders us toward serving the shared and common goods of existence.

I present a figure that hopefully illustrates the bond and order of community in general. C. S. Lewis wrote in 1943 that "it is when we are doing things together that friendship springs up—painting, sailing ships, praying, philosophizing, and fighting shoulder to shoulder. Friends look in the same direction."[3] Although we may initially encounter one another face-to-face, we place ourselves shoulder-to-shoulder. Lovers, family members, friends, neighbors, compatriots, fellow human beings: to be in communion is to face in the same direction together, confronting together what unites us. The next chapter, on political belonging, will explore what it is we face together and why a shoulder-to-shoulder position is the political position. In this chapter, however, I want to clarify the preliminary terms. In particular, I will need to explore the significance of "communion" for the constitution of "community."

The first task will be to set out what is meant by community. For this, I will employ the symbol *communitas*. *Communitas* has the specific meaning of the community that is sustained by its own communion. It is not merely an association. I will draw on the work of Michael Oakeshott as he differentiates between types of association. I will also follow Roberto Esposito's etymological analysis of the terms *communitas* and "communion" in order to gain a better appreciation of the relation between them. Belonging in any society, of course, is neither smooth nor straightforward, and the tensions by which the social communion exists must be considered. Lonergan's Generalized Empirical Method equips us well because, although we encountered it already in chapter 4 above in relation to consciousness, it shines light also on the dialectical tension that marks the restlessness of social existence. Then I will drill down more deeply into the meaning of communion itself. Martin Buber, Gabriel Marcel, and Jacques Maritain will be our guides here. The aim is to discuss communion as the good by which community exists and fellowship thrives. Building on the explorations of personal and cosmological presence in previous chapters, we must now think about the need to belong as the need that is met by community.

COMMUNITAS AND COMMUNION: PRELIMINARY DISCUSSION OF SYMBOLS

The Symbol *Communitas*

The historical development of the symbol *communitas* can tell us something about the deeper meaning of communion. The Latin term *communitas* was already in use in the Roman era and meant something qualitatively different from what was signified by the term *civitas*. *Communitas* generally meant community, but the meaning of the word referred specifically to that association formed in a preceding communion, fellowship, or like-mindedness. Whereas its counterpart, *civitas*, generally denoted a particular type of community—the *political* community—*communitas* connoted more the unifying condition by which the *civitas* could be a community. If *civitas* conveyed the empirical fact of a political unity, it was *communitas* that symbolized the formative and underlying unity that molded the plurality of political parts into a *civitas*. *Communitas* expressed that common condition of communion by which communities are formed. Two theological examples from the period illustrate the closeness of *communitas* and communion and the need of communion for community. In the fourth century, St. Ambrose of Milan wrote, "For if I shall believe that the Word is eternal, which I do believe, I cannot doubt about the eternity of the Father, whose Son is eternal. If [on the other hand] I think His generation to be temporal, He begins to have fellowship (*communitatem*) with us."[4] In other words, had Christ first begun to exist only in time through his birth, he would share only the mortality of the human condition. He would enjoy *communitas* with humanity, but not with divinity. In the early fifth century, St. Augustine discusses the *communitas* of the Trinity by way of communion. It is the Holy Spirit who is the essence or condition of communion of Father and Son.

> Therefore the Holy Spirit is a certain unutterable communion of the Father and the Son; and on that account, perhaps, He is so called, because the same name is suitable to both the Father and the Son. For He Himself is called specially that which they are called in common; because both the Father is a spirit and the Son a spirit, both the Father is holy and the Son holy. In order, therefore, that the communion of both may be signified from a name which is suitable to both, the Holy Spirit is called the gift of both.[5]

Later, *communitas* was a term used in the Rule of St. Benedict to refer to the monastic community whose community was formed in the observance of that Rule. The violation of the Rule could lead to excommunication, understood as a formal procedure against the antagonist that responds to the rupture of communion with the community.[6] That is, for Benedict, to be in community was still preeminently to be in communion with others, to be united-with others. To fall out of community—that is, no longer to participate in *communitas*, or to renounce one's belonging by not existing-toward that community—was to fall out of communion with other members as partners in that community. To be excommunicated is to be outside communion with the members of the community because one is no longer united with them.

Communitas did not remain the semantic privilege of the monastic life or of the *ecclesiam* in general; as medieval Christendom developed in the later twelfth and thirteenth centuries, it became significant for the kingdom (*regnum*) too. In the Magna Carta of 1215, for example, the English barons referred to themselves as speaking on behalf of the *communitas regni.* That is, the barons could claim for themselves a representative voice of the kingdom because the kingdom was itself a *communitas* formed and sustained already as a communion among many members. They, and not just the king, could speak for the kingdom. What the barons could take for granted in the Magna Carta was that England could be a kingdom only because it was already a nation, a *gens*, a plurality in unity. England was already a *communitas* achieved on a national level. Thus, *communitas regni* (the community of the kingdom) proved to be an evocative term in later popular revolts because even at the lowest social stratum of society, the peasants without property and without other realizable rights could still experience their existence as a participation or communion in the greater *communitas* of the English nation.[7]

Communitas and Enterprise

"Community" is obviously an old term, symbolizing forms of association among people for millennia. Forms of association can arise where particular locations and times become important to people. Forms of association are also recognized as being constituted by certain shared beliefs, a mythos of common memories, accomplishments, struggles and losses, and other experiences that also express fellowship among the members. Clearly, "community" is a term that has some flexibility but rests upon something valued in common. Furthermore, new associations form all the time and seek to articulate their presence for social, political, and historical action. New social groups, religious sects, political movements, and even supporters of sports teams, housing associations, consumers of particular commodities, and so on call themselves communities. How flexible is the term "community"? Does it extend to all forms of association?

It would seem that "community" is the term that confers a dignity that "association" does not. If this is true, why so? Perhaps the reason is that community is rooted in communion. The elucidation of what is meant by communion will follow, but for now, it is sufficient to point out that an experience of communion is an experience of something higher, more precious, more redolent of a sacred and enduring quality than an agreement or a joint purpose to achieve a practical outcome. In aiming to recover the deeper significance of community, one discerns a communion of belonging at its core, a heart of sacredness that invites recognition and reverence: families, local and regional cultures, national peoples, religious traditions. I will refer to the bond and order among persons who have achieved communion as *communitas*. *Communitas* signifies community that, in being bonded from, and ordered toward, communion (in Greek, *koinonia*), is always more than an association based on a common goal or interest. "Communion" means, quite literally, a union-with, and a *communitas* is therefore a community that forms as a consequence of a type of union of each member with every other member. Given the existence of different types of communion, it follows that there must be different types of *communitas*. It is the communion at the root of *communitas* that allows us to draw a hermeneutical line between "community" and other types of association. A *communitas* is already the community that manifests the prior and sustaining *communion* among members as its sociality.

There is, Gabriel Marcel writes, something like a "graduated scale" in the quality of human encounter, "with something like the mystical communion of souls in worship at the top end, and with something like an ad hoc association for some strictly practical and rigidly defined purpose at the bottom."[8] The graduation of this scale is one that measures the extent to which communion is the formative principle operative in the encounter. For Marcel, the corresponding good of the encounter, as we descend the scale he mentions, moves from intrinsic to extrinsic. Mystical communion is already the intrinsic good that constitutes the communion of worshipers, bringing them into *communitas*. It can be contrasted with the extrinsic good of a protest group that remains as the shared goal to be achieved by that group. Similarly, Michael Oakeshott distinguishes between "civil associations" and "enterprise associations."[9] Oakeshott notes that "civil association" refers to the spontaneous formation of bonds of fellowship among individual persons and groups in society. The civil association may be said to be a *communitas*, where each of its members is bound to every other member through the intrinsic good of the association. I will discuss the political dimensions of this in the next chapter, but fellowship among members of a civil association expresses belonging among those members who, shoulder-to-shoulder, are in communion with each other because they are already in communion with the good that is formative of that association. There are bonds of affection or sympathy or understanding between individual members because of the communion that already generates and sustains the society. The civil association is not a uniform collective because it remains cognizant of the plurality and uniqueness of individuals and of domestic, local, and other associations that participate in it. The unity of the civil association is a communion that precedes fellowship among the pluralities as the condition that accounts for the possibility of that fellowship. Because the civil association is already a communion, the pluralities find themselves bound to one another through belonging to the same *communitas* and guided by an order of responsible participation that does not depart from the obligations inherent in membership or citizenship. The enterprise association, on the other hand, also involves fellowship, but here fellowship is partnership in a well-delineated project, articulated to bring about a corporate aim. This aim extrinsically binds a plurality of participants into a unity of purpose and gives direction and value to their association. It is an association realized for the attainment of a particular goal or goals, an enterprise committed to the accomplishment of an identified end, and the association loses its *raison d'être* when the end is achieved or superseded.

Oakeshott's distinction points to associations that have communion as their intrinsic good and revitalizing source of life and to associations formed and organized in order to bring about a good that has not yet been achieved. The former association we may call a *communitas*, while the latter is an enterprise. Enterprises are perennially necessary to bring about adjustments and recalibrations of social relations due to emergent social forces, but these adjustments only make sense because there is already a *communitas* whose consequent social relations provide the context of those adjustments. A *communitas* and an enterprise are both associations, but the types of belonging that constitute each are not equally situated. The belonging that is a family, the belonging that is formed under the shared local conditions of particular places and times, the belonging of shared faith, the belonging of shared experiences, meanings, judgments, and commitments: these are all communities bound and ordered by communion. They are already a little world of order, what Voegelin calls a "cosmion."[10] The existence of the *communitas* is already its own good, and such a good clearly does not come from beyond the association but is already intrinsic to it. The good of the family, for example, is fundamentally the existence of the family, a domestic belonging, that underpins the goods of health, education, and other goods of well-being. The same can be said for the good of other types of *communitas*: the common good that provides for the flourishing of the city and the nation is fundamentally the intrinsic and sacred good of their existence, an existence forged and renewed in communion. By contrast, enterprise associations are formed not in communion but in the shared desire to articulate themselves as a social group in order to bring about a goal internal to the society. Their good is instrumental rather than intrinsic: they exist for the sake of concretizing a social, political, or economic interest.

"Community" is generally used as a term of convenience in referring to both types of association. Obviously, people associate and find commonality for many reasons, and they refer to the worthiness of their association as a community, but it is an open question whether or not there is communion at the heart of a particular association. The prevalence of the term "community" tends to obscure the distinction between *communitas* and enterprise. The dignity of any *communitas* is its communion, and the communion is already the justification of the *communitas*. The enterprise must make efforts to convince the wider society of the merits of its project, but the wider society does not seek a justification of its own good. It is already the *communitas* that exists-from and -toward its own communion, the good of its own existence. The goods that each type of association aims for are qualitatively different. On the basis of these goods, we can differentiate between types of association, as Aristotle did with his theory of friendship. Just as there are different forms of friendship at the interpersonal level of existence, so too there are different forms of association at the level of social existence. A *communitas* is the social, political, and historical analogue of the friendship cultivated and enjoyed by Aristotle's "good man" who already loves the good of his existence, whereas enterprises are the analogues of friendships rooted in pleasure or utility. Enterprises are important in their own right, crucially adding diversity, multifariousness, and dialectical responses to new discoveries; they challenge perceived injustices and shine light on blind spots; they aim to reconfigure formal arrangements and processes where necessary. However, enterprise associations do not substitute for the belonging of *communitas*, but only make sense because there is already a *communitas* that is worth their efforts.

Roberto Esposito: The Root of *Communitas* and Communion

Roberto Esposito, in researching the etymology of *communitas*, writes that there is an originary term from which "community" and "communion" (and other related words) ultimately derive: *munus*. *Munus* is a Latin root term that communicates a range of meaning: "service, duty; gift."[11] *Communitas* retains the semantic intricacy that was already present in *munus*.[12] Esposito proceeds to show this larger complexity among three terms that flow from *munus*. They are *onus*, *officium*, and *donum*. "For the first two the meaning of duty . . . is immediately clear: obligation, office, official, position and post. The third appears, however, to be more problematic. In what sense would a gift [*donum*] . . . be a duty?"[13] This cluster of meanings that are related to *munus* throws light on the also-related term *communitas*. Esposito tells us that

> it emerges that *communitas* is the totality of persons united not by a "property" but precisely by an obligation or a debt; not by an "addition" . . . but by a "subtraction." . . . As the complex though equally unambiguous etymology that we have till now undertaken demonstrates, the *munus* that the *communitas* shares isn't a property or a possession. . . . It isn't having, but on the contrary, is a debt, a pledge, a gift that is to be given, and that therefore will establish a lack. The subjects of community are united by an obligation, in the sense that we say "I owe *you* something," but not "you owe *me* something."[14]

For Esposito, etymology reveals the deeper semantic meaning of community as a *communitas* in which we find ourselves in communion when we acknowledge and act upon the moral debt that is owed to others by virtue of simply living and moving among them. It is the debt of responsibility that we have encountered with Levinas on an interpersonal level, but extended to "fraternity." It is a moral debt owed by way of one's freedom of action as a member of a community, as one whose membership of that community is already a dimension of one's own existence: I am a parent, and here is what I always owe to my children; I am your friend, and I choose to walk this extra mile with you; I am your compatriot, and here are the goods we cherish in common that have already bound us into a national *communitas*; you are an Other for whom I am an Other.

Esposito continues that our lives are gifts, rather than property in the Lockean sense that permeates modernity. If the ownership of property seems to be a poor model for thinking about the status of human life, the model of gift seems to move us closer to the cosmological dimension of meaning. We have received our lives as something like a gift, freely given, from both the encompassing mystery and the emergent astrophysical process of the cosmos. "It is only this first *munus* from on high that puts men in the position of having something in common with each other. And it is precisely this 'given'—what is given to us, we ourselves as 'given,' 'donated,' 'born from a gift'—that stands in the way of any hasty translation of *koinōnia* [communion] into a simple *philia*—'friendship,' 'fellowship,' . . . 'camaraderie,' or 'Freundschaft.'" The *Freundschaft* of the family, the sociopolitical community, the historical nation, all bear the trace of cosmological presence, but while fellowship and like-mindedness are certainly marks of association, in themselves they do not capture the element of gift, trust, or commissioning. Their *philia* is a hallmark of the shoulder-to-shoulder stance that characterizes *communitas*, but communion points to the bond and order that gives rise to *communitas*. Communion is what *communitas* and its *philia* continually spring from.

In the *Gorgias*, Plato writes, "The sages too say, Callicles, that the heavens and the earth, gods and men are bound together by communion, friendship, order, temperance, and justice, and for this reason, my friend, they call this universe order, and not disorder or intemperance."[15] Esposito frames his sense of what we are calling cosmological communion—bond and order, obligation and gift, gratitude and commissioning—with the richness of the Christian tradition: "Yes we are brothers, *koinonoi*, but brothers *in Christ*, in an otherness that withdraws us from our subjectivity, our own subjective property, so as to pin it, subjectivity, to a point that is 'void of subject' from which we come and toward which we are called, just as long as we remain 'grateful' so as to respond to that first *munus* with a corresponding gift."[16] Perhaps the purpose of *communitas* is the affirmation of the primordial gift of life and the obligation to cultivate the conditions in which of all those whose lives constitute *communitas* can flourish. There are, of course, always good pragmatic reasons to strive for the enrichment of the *communitas*—a stronger, more vibrant, successful, healthy community—but these are also more deeply the ways in which we attune ourselves to the cosmological process that gifted us life in the most primordial sense. To participate in the life of the *communitas* is to belong within its communion. By belonging in the *communitas*, we have gained not only membership that would authorize our speaking and acting in ways that keep that community accountable but an indispensable access to the cosmos in which the *communitas* is nested. Only by this access and participation do we find a universality in our belonging that prevents the particular community from closing in on itself and shutting out the wider world.

LONERGAN AND THE DIALECTIC OF *COMMUNITAS*

Communitas as the Achievement of Common Meaning

What Lonergan offers is a philosophical examination of the inner movements, developments, and derailments of the communion that constitutes any *communitas*. In chapter 4, I sketched his G.E.M. as the cognitional theory that takes account of the norms inherent in the various related and recurrent operations of consciousness. I wanted to demonstrate that authentic subjectivity is the process of following the pure desire to know and to love in our own cognitive operations, and by this authenticity, we achieve the genuine objectivity that is the affirmation of the truth and goodness of the real. Reality, then, is what we aim to grasp when we seek the truth or enact the good, but there can be multiple reasons why we would fall short. We routinely short-circuit our own pure desire to know and to love, because we experience many other desires, centrifugal in their effects on our knowing and loving; there may also be developmental stages or gaps in the growth of the person that preclude the attaining to higher viewpoints; there is ignorance of data or unavailability of data that would invite us to expand our field of meaning if it were available;

and so on. On the level of cognitive operations, there can be inatten-tiveness (in experience), or a lack of intelligence (in understanding), or an unreasonableness (in judgment), or an irresponsibility (in deci-sion). At any moment, we can stymie our own subjective process of coming to know and love.

With this in mind, Lonergan considers the social opening of the person to community from childhood to adulthood and nicely cate-gorizes the distinction between "the world," which is reality inde-pendent of my judgment, and "my world," in which I am living and developing and making sense of the real.[17] In the development of "my world," he discerns three levels. First, there is world of immediacy: "It is the world of the infant, the world of what is felt, touched, grasped, sucked, seen, heard—it is the world to which the adult returns when with an empty head he lies in the sun—it is the world of immediate experience . . . pleasure and pain, hunger and thirst, food and drink, surrender, sex and sleep."[18] Second, there is the discovery of a world mediated by meaning "that is known not just by experience but by the conjunction of experience, understanding and judgment [and commit-ment or value]."[19] By the operations of the intellect, we enter into a field of meanings where, third, we find that the world is not simply mediated by meaning but constituted by meanings already present and operative that encompass the full range of what human beings can experience of the real and have attempted to know and value about the real. The human world is already saturated with meaning. Language and action, constituted by meaning, occur in sociocultural context that itself is composed of meanings: "the family and mores, the state and religion, the economy and technology, the law and education." These are not reducible to the products of nature, because they are always determined from meaning. The world constituted by meaning is the product of self-constituting subjects; it is a world that emerges from the inward freedom of persons.[20]

Communitas then is no mere aggregate of individuals, nor can it be grasped by a sociological analysis of demographic trends alone. For Lonergan, community "is an achievement of common meaning, and there are kinds and degrees of achievement." Corresponding to experience, understanding, and judgment, he tells us that common meaning can be potential, formal, or actual. Potential common mean-ing can be achieved when "there is a common field of experience";

formal common meaning is the result of common understanding; and actual common meaning is the product of common judgments, "areas in which all affirm and deny in the same manner."[21] In each case, there are failures, derailments, oppositions, resistance. When we fall out of touch, we are not experiencing what is commonly experienced; when we misunderstand or do not have the means to comprehend properly, we cannot achieve the insight that leads to a common understanding; when we refuse to affirm or deny what others have affirmed or denied, we have departed from common judgment. To the extent that common meanings are achieved, the further decisions to love, to serve, to dedicate are decisions that, if made in common, realize the *communitas*. The *communitas* emerges—shoulder-to-shoulder, so to speak—from a common commitment to preserve a common set of meanings. "Community coheres or divides, begins or ends, just where the common field of experience, common understanding, common judgment, common commitments begin and end."[22]

Lonergan emphasizes *communitas* as a social emergence from the individual conscious and embodied lives of persons in communion, but he also emphasizes it in its historicity. However gradual and uncertain the achievement of common meaning may have been, its preservation and development are subject to the same slow and turbulent course. If *communitas* as common meaning is to endure through successive generations, inculturation and education are necessary. Effectively, in the course of time, each person in each new generation must experience, understand, judge, and commit to the manifold of meanings sustained by the *communitas* and expressive of the communion at its core. This exposes common social meaning to the further dialectical and historical processes of clarification or obfuscation, enrichment or disintegration, and transformation or encrustation. Each person enters into a world mediated and constituted by common meaning and finds that he and she already exist-from it. What they must discern is whether they wish to exist-toward it too. The belonging that *communitas* offers to individual members is a consensual matrix of meaning in which each member must deliberate whether such a matrix and its constituent parts are worthy of their commitment. Authentic deliberation necessitates that the member be attentive to common experiences, intelligent in inquiring into the meaning of those experiences that is already explained by common insights and ideas, and reasonable in verifying what common judgments have already affirmed about those common ideas. If the member can authentically do this, then he and she can authentically make a commitment to belong. It is this decision of subjectivity that objectively realizes their belonging because the decision is precisely the ground from which their contributions to the flourishing of the intrinsic common good of communion proceed.

The Dialectic of *Communitas*: Intelligence and Intersubjectivity

Lonergan's method rightly relates attentiveness, intelligence, reasonableness, and responsibility to the possibility of *communitas*, but the tension I alluded to in mentioning clarification or obfuscation, enrichment or disintegration, and transformation or encrustation is a key dimension of personal, social, and historical existence. Reminiscent of Madison's comment in *Federalist 51*, "If men were angels, no government would be necessary," Lonergan acknowledges that "man is not a pure intelligence," which necessitates accounting for factors other than intelligence at play in the *communitas*.[23] He writes that because human beings are "social animals," "the primordial basis of their community is not the discovery of an idea but a spontaneous intersubjectivity. . . . The bond of mother and child, man and wife, father and son, reaches into a past of ancestors to give meaning and cohesion to the clan or tribe or nation. A sense of belonging together provides the dynamic premise for common enterprise, for mutual aid and succor, for the sympathy that augments joys and divides sorrows."[24] Intersubjectivity is what is there before civilization, is sustained in families, friends, customs, language, humor, song, and so on, and therefore remains when civilization decays. There is, then, in *communitas* a communion that is constituted by both human intelligence and intersubjectivity—or, more precisely, a communion forged in the dynamic tension in between them that sometimes relaxes and sometimes heightens.

"Human society," Lonergan writes of nonprimitive communities, "has shifted away from its initial basis in intersubjectivity and has attempted a more grandiose undertaking," which has to include the operation of intelligence in achieving common meaning and the common good of practical discoveries in areas such as technology and

economics. Intersubjective groups are not only impacted by such discoveries, but their entire existence and set of common meanings are
confronted by the prospect of transformation. After all, practical intelligence at work in technology, capital formation, law, politics, and
so forth superimposes upon the intersubjective groups vast structures
of communication and interdependence. The particularity of intersubjectivity must find the means to develop and cope with the burgeoning
universality of intelligence. The transformation from particularity to
ever-wider universality continually confronts any *communitas* with a
notion of the good that "consists in an intelligible pattern of relationships" that reaches beyond the intersubjectivity of any group.[25] This
intelligible pattern of relationships is what Lonergan calls the good
of order, which is expressly not an order set apart from actions and
goals and particular objects of desire, nor is it placed above what is real
in the sense of an ideal point of light that would guide a community
toward a better future. Rather, order is what closes the circuit among
actual schemes of recurrence. That is, the good of order joins the various discoveries of practical intelligence together with a transformed
notion of dignified living.

If the human person is not a pure intelligence, nor is she purely
limited to spontaneous intersubjectivity. "For the bonds of intersubjectivity make the experience of each [member of a particular group]
resonate to the experience of others; and besides this elementary communion, there are operative in all a drive to understand and an insistence on behaving intelligently that generate and implement common
ways, common manners, common undertakings, common commitments."[26] Intelligence and intersubjectivity are dialectical, and it is
from this dialectic that the communion, as the basis of the *communitas*, can grow or diminish. Lonergan notes that "man is an artist. His
practicality is part of his dramatic pursuit of dignified living."[27] Even
if the good sought in the intersubjective group is particularistic—
making sense only within that sharply delineated community—it is
always attained by practical intelligence. Intelligence and intersubjectivity are bound to one another. They are elemental forces in the
communion that sustains the *communitas*, even if they strain in opposite directions: toward universality and particularity, respectively.
What this means is that every *communitas* is perennially pulled and
pushed between the universal and the particular according to the

unique elemental forces of its communion. In the history of societies, there are periods of peace and there are times of crisis, and Lonergan explains this through how well or ill the good of order accommodates the interests of intersubjective groups, and vice versa. "The alternations of social tranquility and social crisis mark successive stages in the adaptation of human spontaneity and sensibility to the demands of developing intelligence."[28] Where the goods of the group and the good of order more or less align, there results a social tranquility; but the intelligent discovery of new insights and the spontaneous adaptation of intersubjective attitudes inevitably disturb the precarious equilibrium. Thus, the life of *communitas* proceeds dialectically in the sense of both being subject to and responding to linked but opposed principles of change that bear upon the sustaining communion.

What the linked but opposed principles of intelligence and spontaneous intersubjective meaning set in constant motion is the elemental tension between universal and particular that expresses itself in the fellowship of persons in communion. Their *communitas* belongs to them, and they belong to it; and yet the communion that binds and orders its members drives them both inward and outward at the same time, across the threshold of their enclosures. The communion among persons is the commitment each has made to a shared, common meaning, even if this common meaning is subject to development or disintegration by the play of opposing principles. What belonging to any *communitas* invites us to is a higher viewpoint that is indifferent neither to intersubjective meanings that breathe life into particular groups nor the level at which their intelligence operates, but seeks to enter into the reality of communion itself. Like the notion of threshold in Levinas's work, belonging is a communion whose inherent liminality encompasses both the privacy of home and the hospitable embrace of the Other and others (*le tiers*). Communion is a "uniting-with" that ambiguously brings together inside and outside, the inhabitant and the stranger, and, in love, finds a way to accommodate intersubjectivity and intelligence in a higher viewpoint.

The "shoulder-to-shoulder" stance of persons and groups in *communitas* is not the quiescent obedience of members in a collectivity, but is more like a jostling. Life in society is fraught with difficulty, and this shouldering is caught well by the tension each must live between universal and particular. Whereas the effort required to work toward a higher viewpoint brings us to the notion of progress, the liminality of belonging means that progress unsurprisingly is found in dialectical tension with decline. Social tension is operative not merely on the horizontal plane between universality and particularity but also on the vertical plane of progress or decline, where higher and lower viewpoints are possible. Lonergan notes that "progress proceeds from originating value, from subjects being their true selves by observing the transcendental precepts, Be attentive, Be intelligent, Be reasonable, Be responsible."[29] In other words, the more that persons achieve authenticity in their self-transcending pursuit of relevant data, intelligibility, truth, and goodness, the more enabled will be their *communitas* to detect blind spots and to acknowledge their social failures; and thereby can they not only mend blind spots and failures cooperatively but improve upon what was already worthwhile. Progress, as a collaborative effort, is always a possibility.

However, since violations of the transcendental precepts are always possible too—personally and socially—the *communitas* also has to contend with the results of its own tendency for decline. Lonergan argues that biases are what interfere with insight and the subsequent achievement of fact and value by way of affirmative judgment and evaluation. "Evaluation may be biased by an egoistic disregard of others, by a loyalty to one's own group matched by hostility to other groups, by concentrating on short-term benefits and overlooking long-term costs. Moreover, such aberrations are easy to maintain and difficult to correct."[30] Aberrations, the derailment of the process of coming to know and to love, result from biases; and what is possible of personal cognition is possible in its social extension. The decline of the *communitas*, just as much as progress, is a result of the degree of authenticity or inauthenticity in persons, whose communion with one another is directly affected. When a *communitas* is in severe decline, some persons and intersubjective groups will have turned in a completely different direction away from a restoration of communion. Rather than making the normal social readjustments and corrections, *communitas* disintegrates into factional strife. Instead of the daily business of persons engaging in social bumping and butting, disputes and resolutions, there is the depersonalizing tendency to treat persons not as persons but as mere representatives of social groups. With depersonalization comes desocialization in the sense of losing the connection between social reality and persons. What follow are the myriad violations of personhood—silencing, vitriol, murder—and of the out-group. Where there was a communion of persons who achieved belonging and *communitas*, there is decline and alienation. As Lonergan puts it, "Inattention, obtuseness, unreasonableness, irresponsibility produce objectively absurd situations. . . . A civilization in decline digs its own grave with a relentless consistency."[31]

If there is a correlation between decline and alienation, so too is there a correlation between progress and belonging. "Self-sacrificing love will have a redemptive role in human society inasmuch as such love can undo the mischief of decline and restore the cumulative process of progress."[32] The only genuine remedy for a *communitas* in decline is love. To this we can add that if sufficient persons commit to self-sacrificing, self-transcending love, then they can find themselves in communion with one another. With communion comes *communitas*. With love, there is the substantive presence of each to the Other and others. There is hope for the redemption of *communitas*, which is always more than merely social. It is a home, a "cosmion" or microcosmos whose belonging anamnetically reminds each of us of the good of existence.

COMMUNION AS THE GOOD OF *COMMUNITAS*

Martin Buber's Basic Words: I-You and I-It

The thought of Martin Buber is suggestive of communion as the bond and order that can be both interpersonal and social. He primarily concentrates on the interpersonal relationship of I-Thou, but because he recovers what is basic or primordial in between I and Thou, he can extrapolate to broader relational contexts. His *I and Thou* begins with the following propositions:

The world is twofold for man in accordance with his twofold attitude.

The attitude of man is twofold in accordance with the two basic words he can speak.

The basic words are not single words but word pairs.

One basic word is the word pair I-You.

The other basic word is the word pair I-It. . . .

Thus the I of man is also twofold.

For the I of the basic word I-You is different from that in the basic word I-It.

Basic words are spoken with one's being.

When one says You, the I of the word pair I-You is said, too.

When one says It, the I of the word pair I-It is said, too.

The basic word I-You can only be spoken with one's whole being.

The basic word I-It can never be spoken with one's whole being.

There is no I as such but only the I of the basic word I-You and the I of the basic word I-It. [Emphasis added.][33]

Note that what Buber calls basic words are spoken, but only the basic word I-You is spoken with the whole of one's being. Note also that the I already belongs with You and It, whose realities are always constitutive of I. The two basic words or word pairs are spoken, but they are more than utterances. I can speak my existence-toward You because I already exist-from You. With You, what or who I am is I-You, which I speak with all of my being. I am present *to You and to myself* as I-You. This is who I am, and this is how I exist, since You are present to me in ways that are more significant than the positional presence of physical proximity. Even in your death, where I am, You are too, because "there is no I as such but only the I of the basic word I-You."

In belonging, there is for Levinas an ethics. For Buber, belonging is metaphysics: what You are, I am too. My being is essentially grasped in relation to You, and if your being speaks the basic word I-You in relation to me, belonging is the mode of our being. You are the Other with whom I belong, and I am the Other for You, because we exist-from and -toward each other in communion, and we grasp our being as belonging with each Other. Thus, "I" am never simply an individual in splendid isolation, but the entirety of my personhood strains for communion with "You," for whom I wait or seek, and whom I finally join. What You are, you are in relation to me and I am in relation to You. The words "I" and "You" are denatured and impoverished outside their prior, more fundamental relationality with one another. A communion then is no mystical entity, scaffold-ing, or a merely welcome guest or third party in our relationship. It is, existentially speaking, what we exist as. The freedom or responsi-bility that a practical situation asks of me or us finds its vital center of meaning in who we already exist as. I can be meaningfully free or responsible only because I am already in communion.

Nor does communion symbolize intimate relationships only. Indeed, Buber testifies to this in *Between Man and Man* where the topic of education is being discussed. The classroom is a formal set-ting—hardly a place of intimacy—yet is also the proper venue for a communion we call education. Buber remarks that the opposite of coercion or force is not freedom. It is communion. The student, pre-cisely qua student in participation with the educational effort of the teacher, is neither entirely passive, mindlessly receiving information and without regard to his or her own will, nor entirely active, self-determining, and creative. Since the student is partly both, education cannot be merely the pouring of data by the teacher into a receptacle, and neither can it involve a form of manumission of the student from obligation. Education instead must aim at a communion of student and teacher where the teacher's authority, ability, and knowledge are demonstrated in such a way that the potential of the student is real-ized by the student. Neither a threatening, tyrannical teacher nor an inert, distracted, resentful student is capable of educational commu-nion.[34] Education is operative in between the teacher and student, and both the dedicated teacher and the serious-minded student take care to cultivate a rich in-betweenness characterized by an edifying bond and order that is truly worthy of them both.

Note that Buber is clear that not every relation of the "I" is spoken with one's *whole being*. There is the basic word I-It too. "It" can most obviously refer to nonpersons, which, ontologically, lack personhood and therefore cannot be a You. The basic word I-It communicates relationality, and Buber uses it to refer to ways in which we fail, ethically and politically, to recognize or respond to the personhood of another You in some appropriate way. I can be in the proximity of another, yet not properly present by way of conscious-ness and the flesh, in love. Through some measure of unwillingness, the basic word I-You is not spoken, and something less than com-munion marks the relation between us. The failure occurs when I do not apperceive "You" or your personhood and instead reduce you to your role or consider you as no more than a replaceable, perhaps disposable, individual object unworthy of my concern. Yet the simple bifurcation of "I" into I-You and I-It covers over a complexity that is important for the tension of belonging. First, "It" can communicate more than the pejorative reduction of a You to an object and of I to inauthenticity and failure. The meaning of "It," I suggest, can be substantive for belonging too. For example, when we speak the basic word I-It, we may be relating to places and times, or taking delight in playing with toys or getting a rewarding job done, or indeed, enjoying the company of plants and animals, especially our pets. In each case, the basic word I-You cannot be spoken, though the value we invest in the "It" can sometimes lead us to repudiate this claim emotionally. Let us keep in mind that the "It" in the basic word I-It can mean much more than a reductive relation since nobody would choose to live without the natural world of rock and soil and flora and fauna, which renews their spirit, or without the equipment, furniture, and clothing that enchant, amuse, enable, and satisfy.[35]

Second, in addition to the deeply significant value of nonhumans as nonpersons, the complexity of belonging shows us that the basic word I-It can also refer to necessary interpersonal and social abbreviations or formalities that serve the good of order and mutual flourishing. The basic word I-It can be indicative of my relation to a function carried out by myself or somebody else, without reducing "You" to the "It" of the function or precluding the possibility of communion of some kind in between us. There are relations that are founded upon very definite limits, and these limits give rise to predictable ranges of action that provide for a well-functioning society. They constitute a major part of the common good of order. In a mundane sense, one's interaction with the cashier at the food store is ordinarily bounded within very set limits. Our encounter is set in advance by the utility of a transaction that we both require for our well-being. There are ways of transacting utility that are formative of social communion, and there are ways that militate against it. I do not need to be impolite or impatient with him, rude about his appearance, his accent, and so forth. Nor does he with regard to me. My clipped interaction with the cashier is limited by my role as customer and his as cashier. In this sense, we both speak the basic word I-It: he requires that I do no more than act as a customer, that I do not transgress that transactional boundary, while on my part, I require the same of him. Not every basic word I-It, spoken to another person, is a calamity. After all, behind the roles—the masks of the customer and the cashier—we are persons, and both a "You" for one another, but our interaction abbreviates the interpersonal communion of I-You into a socially sanctioned I-It where, as customer and cashier, we transact business from the position of mutual respect. We can be sincere when we thank each other.

This describes the shoulder-to-shoulder stance of social communion. It is less intimate than friendship or family relations, less spontaneous and more circumscribed, but it remains grounded in the interpersonal and no less important for the good of human flourishing. The basic word I-It can be spoken, then, as a social abbreviation of I-You that highlights the importance of particular transactions for social and mutual well-being and gathers both of us together, never collapsing our comfortable distance from each other. You and I speak the basic word I-It in relation to the importance of the social function we transact for each other, and it is this that allows you move at your distance from me while I move at my distance from you. Buber writes,

> The principle of human life is not simple but twofold, being built up in a twofold movement which is of such a kind that the one movement is the presupposition of the other. I propose to call the first movement "the primal setting at a distance" and the second "entering into relation." . . . Man, as man, sets man at a distance and makes him independent; he lets the life of men like himself go on round about him, and so he, and he alone, is able to enter into relation . . . with those like himself.[36]

The lack of intimacy in social relations is precisely what allows the common good of order to flow.

Adam Smith's famous distinction between self-interest and selfishness is itself a differentiation of social relations that constitute social communion: formal transactions assume the responsibility and liberty inherent in personhood, and they assume the mutuality of personhood that commands respect.[37] The self-interested customer and the self-interested cashier transact their roles for the sake of their personhood and their more intimate, domestic communion for which they are responsible, and in so doing, they participate in those goods that bind and order a wider social communion. What are these goods? They belong generally in the good of order and are individually the goods that serve the particular well-being of each person and association in the society. What is this particular well-being? The well-being of each person and association is a particular good best known by each of them alone. The social communion therefore requires a respectful distance, and the bond and order of the *communitas* is characterized by a vast interconnected web of respectfully distanced roles, all of which contrast with the intimacy appropriate to erotic, familial, or domestic forms of communion. There is no expected intimacy or coercive familiarity between me and the cashier in these few moments of our formal transaction, but the basic word I-You is not dispensed with. The basic word I-It is spoken with the breath of I-You. Indeed, what I owe the person whose function here is cashier is respectful distance. Distance, and not intimacy, opens a space in which we can belong to our *communitas* in our own way by leaving each other to participate, shoulder-to-shoulder in the communion for which we are both responsible.

Gabriel Marcel: The Primordial Need for Communion

Buber is not alone in prioritizing communion. Gabriel Marcel insists that "the fundamental datum of human existence is *man with man*," by which he means communion.[38] The openness of each in the encounter with another is a mutual availability (*disponibilité*) of each to the other.[39] The giving and receiving among persons is a participation in the mystery of the other, who, like oneself, exists by way of consciousness and the flesh and who is unlike oneself in his or her radical otherness. The communion is the horizon of encounter. Moreover, since communion is a presence of mutual participation rather than mere positional proximity, the "I" is freed from what would otherwise be a solitude of body among bodies. Instead of the contiguity of bodies, my freeing participation and communion—or my availability—not only opens me to others but also opens vistas of meaning within myself that solitude could never open. In communion, we are revitalized in being extended and deepened through participation in each other. In communion, I become more richly, more authentically, who I already am. Of course, *"it may be of my essence to be able not to be what I am*: in plain words, to be able to betray myself."[40] There is always also pride. Pride sees only independence and self-sufficiency.[41] It is an attitude that departs from the shoulder-to-shoulder position and looks in the opposite direction. Personal availability and dependency upon others have no place in pride. It is by pride that one puts oneself outside the belonging that is communion, and therefore beyond the *communitas*.

Marcel emphasizes the importance of bodily primordiality like Merleau-Ponty, finding in "incarnate being" something like a key to what is human about human reality. One's awareness begins in one's own here and now, which he tells us is a beginning in one's own body. One is present to oneself and to the world in incarnate being in a prereflective way that can move toward what he calls "primary reflection" upon the objects of the world and toward "secondary reflection" on participatory presence and availability rooted in the body as more than simply another object in the world. This prereflective consciousness, again similar to what Merleau-Ponty refers to as embodiment, is incarnate being in the world, an "Urgefühl or primordial feeling."[42] The modes of bodiliness—among which we can list vigor, fecundity, health, sickness, stages of development, pleasure, pain, vitality, and death—are the modes in which the primordiality of incarnate being is borne by every person in every moment. Marcel identifies the primordiality of the body as "the key datum, or rather a datum on which everything else hinges . . . my body in so far as it is *my* body."[43] With Levinas, he argues that *man with man* is a fundamental datum because it is an extension of primordiality into sociality, an extension that does not depart from incarnate being, but is a sharing of persons by way of the flesh and the consciousness that ensouls it.[44] It is a copresence where each becomes available to the reception of the other's incarnate being, a gift of another's existence under the conditions of the cosmos. In receiving one another, they receive the primordiality of the other, which is always an intrinsic susceptibility to the conditions of cosmos from which they are always emergent and toward which they proceed in aging, in wisdom, in death, and in hope. Marcel writes that, in asking the question "Who am I?" one issues an appeal before the very mystery of existence in the cosmos.

In this "*appeal qua appeal*, I am led to recognise that the appeal is possible only because deep down in me there is something other than me, something further within me than I am myself."[45]

Marcel's participatory philosophy, emergent from the primordiality of incarnate being, is an opening toward the cosmos that both holds us and moves within us. Communion with the other is more than a horizontal relation in between two or more. In embracing their incarnate being and primordiality in availability, communion is also a *disponibilité* to the cosmological conditions of existence in which incarnate being begins and ends. The cosmos is received and embraced in availability to the incarnate being of others. Furthermore, the embracing of cosmological conditions in communion—which is the apperception of the *conditio humana*—does not emerge as a by-product of embracing the bodiliness of the other first. It may be more accurate to say that we embrace the other in his or her bodiliness because of those cosmological conditions. That is, if the other were supremely powerful and never weak, if he were immortal, unbreakable, and invulnerable to suffering and loss, how could he be embraced? How can one receive an idol who cannot share in the simultaneous dignity and misery of incarnate being? Availability and communion means, at a minimum, to walk the road of both joy and anguish in the life we share.[46] To participate in life of each other, by way of consciousness and the flesh, is to participate in the cosmos in viscerally real and palpable ways. Our road is a road of mutual edification and truth telling, but it is also a road of violation, moral debt, insensitivity, and forgetfulness, all of which stand in constant need of anamnetic recovery, contrition, forgiveness, and redemption. In participatory presence with the other, one lives the bond and order of the cosmos—a primordial presence of each to the other—which is only heightened as our bodies grow older and weaker, but more venerable, under the conditions of the cosmos. Acceptance of aging opens the possibility of growing in wisdom and attunement to the cosmos whose conditions govern lasting and passing. The fragment of Anaximander's captures this well: "The source from which existing things derive their existence is also that to which they return at their destruction, according to necessity."[47] In communion, our belonging is a rendering unto each other of what is owed to our incarnate being—a bond and meaningful order—until we pass from each other into the great plenitude of substance in which we first originated. Such a rendering is impossible in solitude.

Jacques Maritain: The Common Good and Communion

Every *communitas* is already a communion. Communion does not mean the same as tranquility. I have referred to the jostling that is typical of *communitas*, and we recall that the very condition of jostling is the prior social communion of persons. To belong in *communitas* is to exist-from and exist-toward the intrinsic good of communion that holds all members, regardless of the saintliness or sinfulness of any of those members. Jacques Maritain writes that "the social unit is the person."[48] In contrast to the collective wholes that characterize hives or other animal colonies as well as the fantasies of ideological *Gestalten*, society is not composed of individuals but of persons. Maritain famously differentiates between the individual, who remains a unit within a whole, and the person, who is already a whole. "To say, then, that society is a whole composed of persons is to say that society is a whole composed of wholes."[49] The good of the *communitas* is neither the sum of individual goods nor some collective end. It must reside within the intrinsic good of the communion, which is realized only as a common good in the persons who are already the wholes who constitute its reality as a whole. The common good is the good common to both the social whole and the personal wholes. Indeed, it is the person who can be a whole within a whole only because the common good is what each person already carries within him or her. The common good is already present because there is already communion; "it is their communion in good living."[50] On the one hand, it is possible to list as included in the common good the collection of public commodities and services, the fiscal condition of the state and its military power, its laws and customs, symbols and treasures. On the other hand, Maritain also includes "the sum or sociological integration of all the civic conscience, political virtues and sense of right and liberty, of all activity, material prosperity and spiritual riches, of unconsciously operative hereditary wisdom, of moral rectitude, justice, friendship, happiness, virtue and heroism in the individual lives of its members."[51] It's not hard to see that the common good is suggestive of Lonergan's "good of order" since "it must flow back upon persons, and . . . it includes, as its principal value, the access of persons to their liberty of expansion."[52]

Still, no matter how neatly the common good can be described, there is an inescapable paradox in the communion that is the *communitas* that we have already caught in the dialectical tension between particular and universal, and progress and decline. The paradox is ultimately the relationship between the whole of the *communitas* and the whole that is the individual person. On the one hand, the common good is worth more than the good of each part; but on the other hand, since the common good is only realized in its "flow back upon persons," it is lost unless it resonates to the dignity of each. As David Walsh puts it, "No prescription of the common good, no matter how extensive the anticipated social rewards might be, can justify the abolition of the rights of a single individual along the way."[53] To belong in *communitas* is already an intrinsically meaningful mode of existence, because not only does our responsibility guide our freedom and render it meaningful, but a meaningful freedom happily bears the burden of responsibility that inheres in realizing one's belonging to a community. In the common good, there is a fortification of the meaning of "we." There are actions we happily commit and happily refrain from for the sake of the *communitas*, whose common good is the communion that is already a constitutive part of ourselves. We exist-from the community as members, and we exist-toward the realization of its common good as members who already carry, and are carried by, its communion within us. Therefore, we are neither egoists nor altruists; we simply belong. The common good "is both personalist and communal in such a way that these two terms call for and imply one another."[54] We belong because in the affirmation of our personal lives, which are also our lives in *communitas*, we affirm the good of those conditions of social life that allow both individual persons and their communities "relatively thorough and ready access to their own fulfillment."[55] Belonging means that the love I have for my own existence is intimately bound up with the existence of the *communitas* that holds me, and my actions are ordered toward enriching those conditions of the communion by which we, all of us in the *communitas*, flourish.

The common good, then, is neither an ideal nor an extrinsic good, but more properly the ontic good of our existence as persons who are inherently sociable. Nor is the common good an ideological enterprise since it does what no ideology can do: the common good expresses an affirmation of the fundamental good of existence. Maritain adds that "the common good of the city or of civilization—an essentially human common good in which the whole of man is engaged—does not preserve its true nature unless it respects that which surpasses it, unless it is subordinated, not as a pure means, but as an infravalent end, to the order of eternal goods and the supra-temporal values from which human life is suspended."[56] The common good is mentioned in social contexts, but the social context has already spilled over into what is more than social. *Communitas* mediates the sacredness of the cosmos in our midst because it is an affirmation of the good of life, and it holds open the horizon in which meaning, truth, and goodness become concrete. *Communitas* is the name for the cosmos we live in communion, because it is home, and the common good of the *communitas* was always the communion by which it exists. As a mirror of the cosmos, sacredness is a necessary dimension of the existence of any *communitas*. Communion, we may say, is the common good that bears dimensions of the sacred good of the cosmos by virtue of the existence of its constituting persons from age to age. Whatever serves the flourishing of its persons and associations and minimizes their unnecessary suffering is a good that reaches beyond the particularity of times and places and affirms the great good of existence and belonging. There is no greater nor more universal calling than service to the common good.

BOTH *COMMUNITAS* AND "COMMUNION" are words with a long history of development and use. Esposito offered us an insight based on the originary, root term *munus* (duty, office, gift). Its compactness houses possible meanings that have found expression in *communitas* and communion. To be in communion is to have a *communitas*, to hold a position of responsibility that amounts to the privilege of having a home to belong to. As with all privilege, we must make good on it. That is, our belonging is substantive and real to the extent that we commit to the common good of our community's bond and order. This etymological analysis framed the rest of the chapter.

The bond of common meaning is the achievement that Lonergan discussed by extrapolating personal authenticity to the *communitas*. Intentional consciousness is the capacity that consciously and unceasingly heads for and recognizes data, intelligibility, truth, reality, and value; and the determinations of these are reached through experience, understanding, judgment, and decision.[57] At the social level, questioning and answering result in the cultivation of common meaning, the dynamic basis of *communitas* and the locus of further developments or derailments. Lonergan employs the ubiquitous term "dialectic" to capture the tension that marks the vitality or turbulence of any *communitas*. I highlighted three related aspects of the dialectic: intelligence and spontaneous intersubjectivity; universality and particularity; progress and decline.

There arose the need to look more deeply at the meaning of communion, and this brought along three important contributors: Buber, Marcel, and Maritain. Buber's I-You and I-It provided the necessary distinction to think about social existence as both an extension and an abbreviation of the interpersonal communion. I emphasized the lack of intimacy in social communion as what provides for the respectful distance we maintain from one another, not as a rejection of others but as the space in which each is free to determine their own roles, including the possibility of choosing to enter from that distance into a more significant relation with particular others. The social communion then is marked by distance, but it is not a soulless vault reducible to solitude or individualistic selfishness. Buber shows us that it is a rich bed of meaning in which we can let the lives of others go on around us with a degree of confidence that our lives are ordered toward our mutual common good and bonded in a generally unspoken good will.

We listened to Marcel's reminder of primordiality. One of the claims of the chapter is that social existence is more than social, attesting to the metaxic reality of human existence in between all that lasts and all that passes. It is Marcel who explicitly grounds the primordiality of social existence in our embodied, conscious communion with one another. We exist in fundamental need of each other, because within each of us there is something that is more than us. Whatever this may be, Marcel refers to it as *Urgefühl*, and only in communion is the primordial depth reached that satisfies the need. While we have considered presence, Marcel's search for the primordial basis of communion emphasizes copresence. Only when we are shoulder-to-shoulder, mutually *disponible* for one another, can we find the resources to face the height and depth of the cosmos that holds us and lives in us.

Finally, Jacques Maritain ties the strands of the chapter together by laying out the most appropriate way to think about communion and its *communitas*. The person in community is a whole within a whole, and the inevitable difficulty of thinking about what a whole consisting of wholes is like leads him to rule out both individualism and collectivism. The common good is precisely the good of order that redistributes that good back to the individual persons in the community from whom it found its source. In the common good are the invitation to and the mechanisms for the attainment of the dignified living of all. Maritain's discussion is heuristic in the sense that he is acutely aware of the luminosity beyond merely sociological analyses and prescriptions. The common good of social existence open-endedly mediates transcendence because the persons in communion are already each the infinitely valuable good, each a unique embassy of the cosmos. For Maritain, the measurelessness of their dignity is that each has been made for God.[58] The end of the common good, then, is already the good of their existence in communion. Put another way, the end of the common good is the intrinsic good of the belonging we call *communitas*, which is both an analogue of and a participation in the mystery of divine communion that grounds the cosmos.

CHAPTER SEVEN

Political Goods, Political *Communitas*

To this point, we have considered the distinction between belonging in an association called *communitas* and belonging in an association that is not a *communitas*. I noted that this distinction is nicely caught by Michael Oakeshott, who differentiates between civil and enterprise associations. Whereas the *communitas* is sustained by the intrinsic good of its communion, the enterprise association is sustained by the extrinsic good of achieving some more or less specified end. This is not a trivial distinction. I also suggested the shoulder-to-shoulder stance as a helpful figure that characterizes social relations. Social life is proximity without intimacy and a proximity that gives rise to the sort of jostling or elbowing that makes it both restive and rewarding. In this chapter, I will reflect upon what it is that we face together in our shoulder-to-shoulder stance. That is, I want to think about what a specifically political communion means. Political belonging is why we stay in position and why we find it worthwhile to dialogue or wrestle with neighbors and compatriots.

The task of this chapter is to consider how even political belonging—for all of its fractures and divided loyalties—partakes of the bond and order of the cosmos. Therefore, this part of the study begins with extending the concern with primordiality, first discussed in chapter 3, to political reality. I will attempt to trace the abiding presence of the cosmos in political communion from cosmologically compact societies through to the *communitas* of today. Then what we can call "political goods" will be the focus of attention and, in particular, the foundational good of order. Political goods are Augustine's "objects" loved in common among the people. Love of political goods is the substance of the political communion by which our political *communitas* is formed, sustained, and renovated by every generation. As loved, these goods are worth our debating and struggling with one another. They are the concern of all. Since the political *communitas* is the bond that gathers the aggregate of persons into a people, we will need to consider political action as dynamically ordered toward service of those goods by which the communion of the people flourishes. I will argue that it is *by these political goods* that we have a *communitas* that is no less than a home where our belonging is both a beloved place in time and a shared yearning for the ground beyond all places and times.

POLITICAL PRIMORDIALITY

One of the major efforts of this study is to show that the primary experience and meaning of the cosmos does not vanish as human consciousness gradually differentiates transcendent and immanent dimensions of reality. In the process of differentiation, politics has crystallized as its own autonomous field of action. As such, politics is a clarification of a more compact bond and order, richly symbolized in myth in pretheoretical societies, but it is not a replacement of that bond and order. In cosmological compactness, divine or chthonic forces were symbolized as providing for us or depriving us; in the differentiation of the cosmos, politics is how we look after or deprive ourselves. Plato's myth of the rule of Cronos tells of an age when the god tended to our well-being and when human affairs were steered as though by a divine pilot. That age has now passed, and it falls to human beings to engage in a "mimesis of the God" by looking after themselves—that is, by becoming political.[1] Instead of an intracosmic drama saturated with gods, demons, and heroes, the differentiation of consciousness unfolds the possibilities of a differentiated political order: the autonomous political *communitas* that exists in relation to its own communion, that cultivates relations with other autonomous polities, and that derives dimensions of its meaning in relation with the sacred mystery of the cosmos in which it has its origin and role.

The overarching historical process in which politics emerges is the differentiation of consciousness, and properly political memory does not forget the images and evocations of the process, which continues in the communion of the people. Anamnesis is a recovery of the primordiality of existence, of the originary conditions of belonging in the cosmos. The function of political memory is derivative of this, re-presenting three abiding aspects of primordiality: it clarifies the meaning of the political *communitas* in the scope of the Whole, it circumscribes its authority, and it invests it with its proper competence. Let us very briefly consider the mythopoeic account of the meaning of kingship as political memory in the more compact environments of ancient Mesopotamia and Egypt.

Compact Kingship

Mesopotamia: Enuma Elish

The Enuma Elish is the creation myth of ancient Babylon. It tells of the paradigmatic beginning of all things and symbolizes the truth of the cosmos that ought never to be forgotten. Tiamat is the feminine *Ur*-divinity who is both the creative and mysterious source of all things on the one hand and, on the other, the destructive principle that consumes what it has brought forth.[2] As both creative and destructive, she seems to represent the mystery of both cosmos and chaos. She gives rise to both order and disorder. Tiamat is coupled with the masculine god Apsu, her consort in sexual union, and with him she brings forth a lineage of secondary gods. Apsu, the god of the known and the familiar, is the mythic symbol of culture, the god whose rules or structures or institutional patterns protect against all that is unknown and destructively chaotic. With Apsu, Tiamat's might is channeled into creation, life, and flourishing.

However, this neat arrangement merely sets the stage of a drama we know all too well. The lively and impatient younger gods tire of all that is familiar and steady. Apsu, knowing what is at stake, becomes increasingly harsh with them and tilts toward tyranny in his heavy-handedness. One of his descendants, Ea, slays him. Jordan Peterson writes, "This act of destruction, disguised as a blow for freedom, lets the terrible unknown flood back in. The Great Mother is a terrible force."[3] Tiamat's anger threatens to destroy the whole world.

She must be confronted and overcome, but there seems to be no match. One by one, all those who stand against her fall, until Marduk overcomes Tiamat.[4] Marduk is the young, heroic sun-god who voluntarily faces Tiamat and eventually overwhelms her. He is elevated forever to the position of king. His order is now the lasting, sacred order of the cosmos, in attunement to which life is restored. Marduk cuts Tiamat up into pieces, and from these pieces he constructs our known world. "Finally, he deigns to create man (out of Kingu, the greatest and most guilty of Tiamat's allies [a detail rich in implication]), so that 'upon him shall the services of the gods be imposed that they may be at rest.'"[5]

Mesopotamian kingship is an *anamnesis* of Marduk's sacred authority, and the royal role is enacted according to the order of Marduk, the order of the cosmos. Political authority is fused with spiritual authority because kingship is accountable to the cosmos— as abiding, if precarious, bond and order—on whose behalf it acts. Joseph Campbell notes that the destruction of Tiamat can also be regarded as something like the apotheosis of Tiamat by the kingly actions of Marduk.

> Tiamat, though slain and dismembered, was not thereby undone. Had the battle been viewed from another angle, the chaos-monster would have been seen to shatter of her own accord, and her fragments move to their respective stations. Marduk and his whole generation of divinities were but particles of her substance. From the standpoint of those created forms all seemed accomplished as by a mighty arm, amid danger and pain. But from the center of the emanating [cosmological] presence, the flesh was yielded willingly, and the hand that carved it was ultimately no more than an agent of the will of the victim herself.[6]

Tiamat is both creation and destruction, the unity of both lasting and passing. What the myth presents is cosmological justice. The distribution of Tiamat's body becomes a dissemination of a conditional fecundity: what is owed and enjoyed in life must be paid for by death. All are bound and ordered by such justice, the memory of which is embodied in the communion of the political *communitas*. Mircea Eliade elucidates the importance of reciting the Enuma Elish in the temple in Babylon on the fourth day of the New Year festival. The king's reenactment of Marduk's role was a crucial role that linked the gods in heaven with Babylon on earth. It recalled "the beginning" and the establishing of sacred authority. Kingship was thus a remembering of cosmological justice in the kingdom, and the kingdom was thereby renewed as an analogue of the cosmos. "Though the king recognized his earthly begetting, he was considered a 'son of god.' . . . This twofold descent made him supremely the intermediary between gods and men. The sovereign represented the people before the gods, and it was he who expiated the sins of his subjects."[7] Kingship was a sacred office, forged in the metaxy between gods and human beings to mediate the politico-spiritual meaning of right belonging in the cosmos.

Egypt: The Myth of Osiris

In Egypt, the myth of Osiris demonstrates structures of meaning similar to those found in the Babylonian. Osiris is the ancestral divine king over the four corners of Egypt, the earthly analogue of the cosmos. His *ma'at* is the force or energy that permeates and seals Egypt with order so that the kingdom is a consecrated microcosmos. He has a brother, Seth, whom he does not understand. Seth, devoid of *ma'at*, is a force of chaos, and he dupes the steady but somewhat naïve, somewhat lackadaisical Osiris, defeating him and taking control of the kingdom. In order to ensure that Osiris never returns, Seth dismembers his body. Much like Apsu in the Enuma Elish, Osiris represents a rulership, a code of values, or a constituting story that slides toward increasing irrelevance over time. Peterson notes that dangers accrue when we forget what evil and disorder are, and he notes how quickly chaos can ensue when we allow ourselves to become naïve. Isis, Osiris's mythic counterpart, representing creativity, enters the underworld and "gathers up Osiris's scattered pieces and makes herself pregnant with the use of his dismembered phallus. . . . Isis therefore gives birth to a son, Horus, who returns to his rightful kingdom to confront his evil uncle."[8] The battle between Horus and Seth results in the defeat of Seth, but Horus loses his eye. The way is open to Horus's ascension to the throne, but instead he descends to the darkness of the underworld with the eye that had been recovered. There he finds Osiris, "extant in a state of torpor. He offers his recovered eye to his father—so that Osiris can 'see,' once again. They return, united and victorious, and establish a revivified kingdom. The kingdom of the 'son and father' is an improvement over that of the father or the son alone, as it unites the hard-won wisdom of the past (that is, of the dead) with adaptive capacity of the present (that is, of the living)."[9] Osiris, like Tiamat, is not undone but reconfigured for a political order in which the bond of the cosmos is renewed in the work of kingship. Both Horus and Marduk are the heroes who symbolize the struggle to wrest order from a situation of chaotic breakdown and disorder, and their victory is a political one. However, the balance is always in danger, and the events of the beginning must be replayed through sacred ritual in the present so that the threat of disorder is not forgotten and so that order is secured for another year, another generation, another cycle. Such is the importance of political anamnesis. Whereas the myth dramatizes the abiding presence of both sacred divine order and the threat of chthonic disorder in all times as a truth of human existence, kingship is the great symbol of a hard-fought, precarious, but life-affirming equilibrium, an order of justice to which all are bound for the sake of life. Remembrance of the cosmos by which all things exist was the definitive political act. In the later differentiation of *theoria* from myth, the risk is always that we would forget the cosmos as that common matrix out of which a politics is delineated and to which it remains accountable.

Primordiality and the Differentiation of Order

Order as Foundational

In Christianity, political order undergoes an upheaval in meaning, a recalibration of how it relates to the Whole, where the Whole has been differentiated as a new and higher horizon of transcendence in tension with immanence. Politics must still contend with primordiality, which does not disappear, continuing to attend to the cosmological conditions of existence and to the balance between the common good of flourishing and the common evil of unnecessary suffering. Yet Christ admonished Christians to give to Caesar what is owed to Caesar and to God what is owed to God.[10] The Christian *communitas* comprehended a cosmos that now bore both of these immanent and transcendent dimensions of meaning. Thus, intracosmic kingship gave way to kingship differentiated by the meaning of existence in Christian civilization. What this means in the first instance is that the

political role was no longer burdened with sole responsibility for obligations owed to the gods for order, existence, and belonging in the
cosmos. In prescinding from such a burden, a separate sphere of appropriately political authority could emerge, its obligations directed
toward carrying out pragmatic and symbolic functions for the sake of
the community's well-being. To the communion of the *communitas*
in this place and this time were owed specifically political obligations,
and political authority was circumscribed by the meaning of that communion. Beyond the political, there remained also those obligations
owed to God. Differentiation in the Christian world thus led to the
development of a sphere of spiritual-religious authority with its own
set of obligations. Under such differentiated conditions, God was now
the transcendent ground of all things, and the divine-human relation
required the establishment of a church with its own authority.

Of course, making the neat civilizational distinction between different categories of authority—political and religious—did not mean
that there were no areas of dispute. Indeed, the frequent overreaches
of power, spurred by supererogatory claims from both princes, kings,
and emperors on the one hand and priests, bishops, and popes on the
other characterize much of medieval and Renaissance historiography.
However, what is missed in the pragmatic events of the noisy clashing
of church and empire is the quiet but sustained effort to set a standard by which every overreach and every abuse could be gauged and
resisted. This was the slow but sure recognition of personhood as a
third authority whose emergence as politically, legally, and religiously
significant could become the measure of church, empire, realm, and
state. The person emerged as an originating source of authority and
dignity, existing in the metaxy by way of consciousness and the flesh.
Institutional authorities in the Latin medieval and early modern West
gradually came to heighten their recognition of the person as the one
for whose life, well-being, and dignity their authority was exercised.[11]

Yet amid the civilizational clarification of political things from
ecclesial and religious things, and the historical emergence of personhood as authoritative amid a sea of other authorities, the cosmos persists. Transcendence and immanence, as dimensions of meaning in
human existence, bear also upon both politics and church. Therefore,
politics and church do not float without reference in a vacuum of
empty space, but are charged with providing a means of reconciling

human existence, in differentiated ways, to the cosmological conditions of lasting and passing to which all persons are subject and for which we are all responsible. Politics has a role. It functions as a practical recall of the cosmos in mediating those conditions that impact existence in the cosmos. Anamnesis is embedded in political life, and it is memory that commissions politics with authority to provide pragmatic and symbolic channels by which we respond as a *communitas* to the primordial predicament of mortality. The church too is a remembrance of the cosmos. Memory commissions the church to provide sacramental channels by which the *communitas* can receive and respond to God as the eternal mystery that illuminates, restores, and completes the communion of all things.

Politically anamnetic recovery of the cosmos is glimpsed in the following insight. Russell Kirk recounts a conversation with a Russian immigrant who had witnessed the Bolshevik Revolution. "At any moment, one's apartment might be invaded by a casual criminal or fanatic, murdering for the sake of a loaf of bread. In this anarchy, justice and freedom were only words: 'Then I learned that before we can know justice and freedom, we must have order,' my friend said. 'Much though I hated the Communists, I saw then that even the grim order of Communism is better than no order at all. Many might survive under Communism; no one could survive in general disorder.'"[12] The conversation reminds us that order is the foundational good, the primordial condition for politics. To stand shoulder-to-shoulder in *communitas* is to confront what unites each person in communion. The fundamental political good that bonds a *communitas* is order; disorder is an undoing of that bond. Order attends to the conditions of the existence of the *communitas* because order is formative of the bond that is communion. Order is the first and the foundational political good. This is surely communicated by the mythopoesis of the ancients, and it is here captured in Kirk's story. The insight of Kirk's interlocutor was that, before one might hope to cultivate further political goods such as liberty, justice, and equality, one must have order. Indeed, it is the primordial good inherent in the development of all the others, and without which these other goods disappear. Liberty, justice, equality, security, education, a territory, a common memory, and so on: each of these is more than an expression of an underlying order. They are differentiations of order, an unfolding of the possibilities of order under particular historical circumstances.

Order is the first and the foundational political good. It is the primordial good that secures the possibility of all other goods. It is primordial in three important senses: (1) genetically, (2) existentially, and (3) concretely.

First, political order is not primordial in the sense of being the first in a sequence. It can be understood in a genetic sense as the ground to which all things relate, and from which all things emerge. For example, liberty is a political good that is properly grasped as ordered liberty. Justice is another, but justice means a pervading order of justice where persons and groups have grounds for trusting the law, government, and administrative procedures. Again, security is always related to domestic and/or international order. One might continue, but the point is made: each political good is genetically related to order as its differentiation. Something primordial bears the quality of what persists from the beginning, a foundation without which the present cannot stand. This is one sense of primordiality that characterizes order.

Second, order becomes real because it is loved and sustained in the souls and lives of those who find themselves in political communion with one another in their common love of order. Such love of order gives rise to and justifies specifically political action. Political tasks may aim at the transaction of daily pragmatic business, in securing the recurrence of important social goods, and at the reconciliation of conflicting interests, but there is a higher viewpoint by which political order becomes luminous for a dimension of meaning that abides in what is otherwise the typical and ordinary. Political community exists in the fullness of the cosmos, and this horizon of meaning is not absent in the practice or science of politics. In attending to order, politics not only attends genetically to all of the subsequent political goods, but in an overlapping existential sense, it extends the meaning of the community to symbolic participation in the mystery of the encompassing cosmos. Order, as enduring as it may be through centuries of political development, can still be lost. The tension with chaos does not collapse. Existence in the fullness of the cosmos, because it is historical and not simply personal or political, remains precarious. Order is the precious good that is always at stake, its primordiality the very condition for political life and personal flourishing. Thus, order is what is emergent: never exhausted and never quite accomplished. It is the destination that, when political community arrives at it, points heuristically to what must still be uncovered. In its genetic differentiations, order is the work of justice that is never complete, of liberty that is never fully practiced, of security that is never absolutely accomplished, and so on. Yet, existentially, order is the object of our love in ways that matter personally, politically, and historically. It is the good whose praise redounds as an affirmation of being and belonging.

These are the genetic and existential characteristics of political order, but concretely, this genetic and existential character is also enfleshed. It is also the primordiality of embodied, creaturely existence. What politics seeks to attain it must attain within boundaries that are cognizant of the predicament of bodily need and limitation. What would crush the body in going beyond the limits of the body—violence, tyranny, caprice—is also what goes beyond the limits of politics. Politics keeps itself in order to the extent that it remains cognizant of the dignity of life as embodied. The disorder made explicit in, for example, directing the machinery of the state to jeopardize or to kill the bodies of unwanted persons testifies to what has been violated: the primordiality of order, which is always the order of existence in its embodiment.

Order is the primary task of politics because it is the primordial good. Politics serves and administers hard-won, precarious order and aims at securing the conditions adequate to life and to the full flowering of life. That is, politics retains an ancient but abiding cosmological role even under differentiated circumstances because the work of politics is the work of order—its renovation and renewal—and service of the good by which persons and communities flourish. In preserving the primordial good of order, politics is the work that provides for the *eu zen* (Greek: good life), in which further political goods can enrich the *communitas*. Aristotle gives the classical argument that only the *polis* is self-sufficient in the sense that only in political communion can our existential needs for order be securely met in abundant ways.

> Every state is a community of some kind, and every community
> is established with a view to some good; for everyone always
> acts in order to obtain that which they think good. But, if all

communities aim at some good, the state or political community, which is the highest of all, and which embraces all the rest,
aims at good in a greater degree than any other, and at the highest
good. . . . When several villages are united in a single complete
community, large enough to be nearly or quite self-sufficing, the
state comes into existence, originating in the bare needs of life,
and continuing in existence for the sake of a good life.[13]

Man, for Aristotle, is by nature a political animal who aims not at
mere survival but at a life of meaningful happiness.[14] Meaningful happiness is a flourishing that implicates the entire *communitas* of persons in communion, and necessarily involves the active embodiment
of order. For Aristotle, human beings exist-toward the good life "by
nature" and thus are necessarily political, since it is in the political
communitas that we direct ourselves toward securing the good of life
and what is good in life. However, we also exist-from a primordiality
that does not pass, but develops. Political belonging is how we coor-
dinate a life of developing order together.

Political Order and Need

Order is the foundational good that is formative of the bond of communion and that articulates the resulting *communitas* to refine itself
in myriad ways, and the development of political order does not lose
sight of threefold primordiality.

   Tilo Schabert holds that politics has to be a figurative "second
birth" that follows the first birth of the human person, bodily, into
the world. It is this bodiliness that requires a politics "by nature"
since the predicament of the body is characterized by natural need:
food, shelter, sociality, the knowledge, skills, prudence of others, and
so on. We need each other, so politics is figuratively a second birth
into the *communitas*. Politics, for Schabert, is how human beings care
for human beings. Just as the body is bounded—not so much by its
spatial extension but by its primordial predicament of need—so too
is politics bounded. What politics seeks to attain, it must attain within
boundaries that are cognizant of the predicament of bodily need and
limitation. The foundational political good of order extends to a regime of liberty and responsibility. These are all political goods that
are inseparable in attending to the dignity of bodiliness.

Schabert likens political reality to walking across a busy platform in a train station. On the platform are many persons, and in each of them there is intentionality and a sense of proximate chaos. Each aims for their next destination but has to negotiate their passage against the apparent disorder of many moving bodies that obstruct a straight path. Seen from a balcony, the chaotic platform begins to give way to an eloquent order opening in the space between bodies. Each passenger negotiates her and his way around others' bodies, still achieving their ends. They make their connections. Politics attends to that eloquence in which the needs pertaining to the predicament of embodiment among many persons are negotiated, and it does so through the good of order, an order that opens into the liberty of negotiating one's own way mindful of the proximity of others.[15]

In another place, Schabert writes that ordered liberty is the fundamental political good, because liberty is the political expression of the primordial order of embodiment: "Their bodies teach them that their bodies are a good that can exist only when free of restraints. This good—the intactness of the bodily existence—defines an absolute limit. The constitutional regime [a politics of ordered liberty] serves this limit. It is constructed with the limit in mind. The good in the center of the construction is liberty. Liberty is the political interpretation of the limit—the absolute limit grounded in our bodily existence—that unites all human beings in response to the teachings of their bodies."[16] Functionally, order is liberty, and liberty is order; and both are responsibility. By order and its genetic development as liberty, we respond to the bodily and existential needs of persons and communities for dignified living, for flourishing.

Emmanuel Levinas argues that politics is ordered toward the command issued in the face of the Other. The face is not limited to the incarnate singularity of the Other, but seems to be an aperture through which the universally human appears. He writes, "The third party [le tiers] looks at me in the face of the Other. . . . The epiphany of the face as face opens humanity."[17] Levinas's tone is grudging in his earlier work when he considers politics, recognizing that along with the fragility and essential vulnerability of others that politically mandate my response, violence and totalizing destruction are also characteristic of politics. However, we must resign ourselves to a politics because what I owe to the Other—and what I owe to le tiers—

is infinite; but I am not. So it is that a politics becomes inevitable, emerging, for Levinas, from the infinite ethical demand and mediating its infinity in ways that always call for justice. This call for justice is the priority of ethics over politics, the measure that ordains politics to its proper role.[18] Levinas writes, "It is extremely important to know if society in the current sense of the term [the political sense] is the result of a limitation of the principle that men are predators of one another or if to the contrary it results from the limitation of the principle that men are *for* one another. Does the social, with its institutions, universal forms and laws, result from limiting the consequences of the war between men, or from limiting the infinity which opens in the ethical relationship of man to man?"[19] For the later Levinas, there is no arbitrary freedom for political power. There is a limit, a boundary, a direction, consonant with the primordiality of the body and its needs. Human beings can suffer, and this suffering—though more than merely physical—is located in the body. Politics is not simply a matter of practical action. It is more fundamentally an order of justice that is owed to *le tiers*. If ethics is the response that the predicament of need cries out for in the face of the Other, then I require politics; humanity requires politics. Politics is the means by which we can respond to the primordiality of existence as a *communitas*.

Political Order and the Sacred

We have seen that in the cosmological myth of ancient societies, the political role of kingship was also a sacred role. The king represented the kingdom to the gods and the gods to the kingdom. Eric Voegelin writes of the Egyptian pharaoh that he was an *omphalos* or navel through which the divine substance of *ma'at* entered and sustained the kingdom as a microcosmic analogue.[20] The pharaoh performed a sacred role that made sense in ancient Egyptian society, as did the sacred rite of anointing kings among the medieval Germanic peoples. In compact, pretheoretical societies, governance was bound up with the exigencies of a kingdom existing in immediacy under the gods. With the removal of the divine from an order of intracosmic gods to a transcendent ground, political governance was no longer subject to the gods. Nonetheless, it remained accountable to something. The sacredness of the political role was not lost but differentiated. Governance of the political *communitas* no longer includes an intentionally redemptive role since that properly belongs to the spiritual authority of the church.[21] Rather than in the office of kingship, sacredness inheres in the communion of the *communitas*, a quality we intuitively discern when we hear about brutalities visited upon a people. The existence of the *communitas* is already the intrinsically valuable good, and as Maritain reminded us, the common good of any *communitas* has a meaning that extends from the pragmatic to the sacred.

Liberal thought, emphasizing the importance of consensus, has bequeathed to posterity the notion that a constituting social contract is what binds social existence into a political unit. The political bond then would seem to be derived from consensual social contract. If "social contract" can ever be a symbol adequately expressive of the life of the society, surely Edmund Burke is correct when he writes that it must be understood as a communion of generations present and absent. "As the ends of such a partnership cannot be obtained in many generations, it becomes a partnership not only between those who are living, but between those who are living, those who are dead, and those who are to be born."[22] The social contract is less a contract, signed at the end of a rational deliberation, and more a sacred covenant written in the lives of its members who belong together in communion. They remember their past with fondness and look to their future with hope. A social contract as sacred covenant binds not only many generations but also heaven and earth and all of nature. The bond that sustains the political *communitas* mirrors the bond of the cosmos, and therefore commands our reverence.

In light of this, Burke makes an important distinction and champions a spirit of "renovation" over a spirit of "innovation." A people renews or *renovates* itself for a new set of circumstances over and over again under dynamically changing circumstances, but always in the context of the underlying political bond and order that is loved in common among the dead, the living, and the unborn. In Burke's day, the Jacobin spirit in revolutionary France represented the contrary spirit of innovation. A people that *innovates* is a people that forgets its past, undoes its inheritance, and is heedless of its future. That is, innovation inevitably amounts to a dis-ordering of the *communitas* through a dissolution of its communion. Rather than a shoulder-to-shoulder stance where each is united in shared participation in a common political good, innovation replaces the uniting good with something else.

The spirit of innovation repudiates the sacredness of communion and dismantles the civil association. The association of innovation is an enterprise that aims at achieving an extrinsic set of goods. Mayhem and murder, rather than indifference, become characteristic of the loss of *communitas*. Innovating new political goods, on the other hand, is not unlike Marx's exhortation a century later that a class of people, in overthrowing its former masters, ought to rid "itself of all the muck of the ages."[23] Innovating new political goods rather than renovating order is how a people undoes itself in the enterprising hope of a new formation and how it enters "into the antagonist world of madness, discord, vice, confusion, and unavailing sorrow," where nothing is sacred because everything can be innovated.[24]

The themes of anamnetic remembrance and of imaginative oblivion stretch through Burke's reflections. For him, the adaptation of the nation's political goods according to the needs of each generation is a renovation characterized as a "world of reason, and order, and peace, and virtue, and fruitful penitence."[25] It is not difficult to discern that renovation is more properly the work of governance that seeks not to dispose of, but to adapt, the common meaning of order to new circumstances. That is always a sacred task, even if it is through the humdrum daily work of politics. It is not only how the political *communitas* makes itself a more adequate home for its people, and more hospitable to other peoples, but also how it dynamically renews itself as a microcosmos.

POLITICAL GOODS

The Communion of a People: Political Goods Loved in Common

Thomas Aquinas argued that "we must say that friendship among blood relations is based upon their connection by natural origin, the friendship of fellow-citizens on their civic fellowship, and the friendship of those who are fighting side by side on the comradeship of battle. Wherefore in matters pertaining to nature we should love our kindred most, in matters concerning relations between citizens, we should prefer our fellow-citizens, and on the battlefield our fellow-soldiers."[26] It seems not to be inordinate to enter into a communion of political friendship with fellow citizens, according to Aquinas. Nor does it seem to be inordinate to prefer those we happen to be more closely connected to. For Aquinas, the principle of charity has an order of preference appropriate to it. It does not exclude those with whom we are not like-minded or connected in some way, but the bond of communion naturally begins in closest connection and rightly proceeds from an intensity of charity "outward" in concentric circles, as it were, to embrace the universal. Without the intimacy of the closest connection, the universal exists nowhere. The universalizing tendency must first be rooted in what is rich and vital, which naturally is found in what is closest and most particular. That is, the bond of charity by which a particular *communitas* is constituted is ordered toward a universal sharing of its principle of charity, but the particularity of the *communitas* is where we first learn the value of belonging. Such is the reality of love. Let us then listen to Augustine discuss how the principle of charity is rooted in the intrinsic good of communion, which forms the political *communitas* as a political people.

In chapter 21 of *City of God*, Augustine first considers a definition of a people offered by Scipio, which Cicero finds compelling in his *On the Republic*. Scipio "defined a 'people' as a multitude 'united in association by a common sense of right and a community of interest.'" However, Augustine asserts that a "common sense of right" (*ius*) cannot be maintained without justice (*iustitia*). He finds that Scipio's definition inadequately symbolizes even the Roman commonwealth because the Romans do not adequately render what is owed in justice to God (as the transcendent-divine origin of the cosmos).[27] Yet Rome is certainly a people. Scipio's definition is not fit for purpose, and Augustine proceeds to offer his own definition. "A people is the association of a multitude of rational beings united by a common agreement of the objects of their love." He immediately follows this with this statement: "It follows that to observe the character of a particular people we must examine the objects of its love."[28] The objects of love of a particular people should be the focus of any attempt to understand the communion that forms and sustains a particular political *communitas*. The objects of love are the principles of unity among those who find themselves with others in their shared love. The objects of love are goods loved in common by rational persons who become a political people, bonded as such in their consensual love of these goods.[29] For Augustine, the objects bear both an affective and a rational quality of such a caliber that they are found worthy of the love of the multitude who consequently, in their love, become a people united by these objects. These objects can be considered political goods, because a shared love of them brings persons into a political communion. Love of these political goods forms the people, renews their communion, and potentially fits the *communitas* for dynamically changing times and circumstances.

On the one hand, political goods are goods particular to here, to us, to now. Our shared love of these goods is formative of the particular uniqueness of the political *communitas*. On the other hand, our political goods can comprise those goods that transcend our particularity, open a universal vista within our *communitas*, and direct our concern with what is loved in common by us to its relevance in a more expansive field of humanity beyond borders. I have already argued that order is the first political good because it rightly takes account of the predicament of existence in the cosmos. What are some other suitable candidates for "objects of love" or political goods that form a concrete people? Presumably, there are as many political goods as there are political societies. Historically, examples of these goods can include the Greek *aretai* (virtues or excellences) such as the "savage valor" of Sparta's warrior society and Athenian *sophia* (wisdom); there are the physical territories or homelands of particular nations or peoples, as well as the cultural expressions of memory of their common past, manifested in song, poetry, painting, statue, and other arts; there are civic recognitions and universal entitlements such as liberty and equality before the law; and so on. Political goods bind the multitude into a people or a political *communitas* who find themselves in communion with one another through a shared love for these goods.

Indeed, the multitude becomes a political *communitas* when their communion is formed not primarily by love of one another but by love of those political goods held in common. Indeed, theirs is not an intimate communion, but a political consensus on goods we share, goods that open political spaces between us. Schabert's "eloquence" between bodies is a political space that, as we saw with Martin Buber, keeps a respectful distance, but because it is distance, it is the condition of choice by which we can enter into relation with others. It is in the political spaces in between us—spaces for justice, spaces for liberty, for property ownership, for education, and so on—that political authority is wielded and that the stability or bond of the *communitas* is won or lost. John Courtney Murray calls the communion that establishes the political community a "constitutional consensus whereby the people acquires its identity as a people and the society is endowed with its vital form, its entelechy, its sense of purpose as a collectivity organized for action in history."[30] Furthermore, "this consensus is come to by the people; they become a people by coming to it." In love of those political goods, the political communion is formed and the *communitas* gives its members an earthly home in the cosmos, a way to live out and cherish their shared mortal existence against the immortal mystery of being itself.

Political goods are the basis of communion or constitutional consensus and are, therefore, the vitality of the political *communitas* and the means by which it realizes itself in the cosmos, belonging to itself, to humanity, and to God in history. Political communion on the basis of shared political goods is the vitality by which a multitude lives as a people, a principle whose vitality acts as the soul of a nation. Without political goods as objects loved in common, the people disintegrates into a multitude. Nations come apart when political goods are no longer loved in common. Let us consider two representative "objects of love" by which a political *communitas* lives: territory and liberty. Both territory and liberty are refinements of the primordial good of order.[31] By territory, the *communitas* can present itself to itself and to the world in its uniqueness and particularity. By liberty, the *communitas* knows itself to be universally accountable to the world within and without its borders. By goods such as these, the political *communitas* mediates the tension of belonging: what we exist-from and exist-toward is always affected by the interplay of particularity and universality.

Two Representative Political Goods

Territory

Territory is no mere spatial extension. It is a political good because the place of "home" is already imbued with sacredness. We must be careful. We remember the fascination of Heidegger with *Heimat*, which risked becoming an enclosure against the stranger. Sacredness restricted to the particular can foreclose openness to the universal and become petty and nasty. Nonetheless, home is a sacred place. The cosmological myth of pretheoretical societies often symbolized territory as a mirror of the bond and order of the cosmos. Territory, "our" territory, was a "cosmicized" place surrounded by an unknown and formless region akin to chaos.[32] "Cosmicized" is Mircea Eliade's term that indicates the requirement to consecrate, or make sacred, a place if it would be a home. The cosmicization of a home or homeland is an act that participates in and repeats the original divine cosmogony. Every homeland territory is "a work of the gods or is in communication with the world of the gods," and by the presence of the sacred is the territory "cosmicized":[33] "Whether it is a case of clearing uncultivated ground or of conquering and occupying a territory already inhabited by 'other' human beings, ritual taking possession must always repeat the cosmogony. For in the view of archaic societies everything that is not 'our world' is not yet a world. A territory can be made ours only by creating it anew, that is, by consecrating it. . . . To settle in a territory is, in the last analysis, equivalent to consecrating it. . . . Hence it shares in the sanctity of the gods' work."[34] The presence of the sacred interrupts the homogeneity of space and opens up the cosmos through establishing a territory where the "three cosmic zones" of underworld, earth, and heaven meet.[35] Thus, the sacred pillar or totem pole, the temple or the palace, or even the foundations of the house, are sunk into the earth that sits above the demonic realms of the underworld. The structure reaches toward the heaven that reaches down to it. Territory is founded as a participatory refounding of the cosmos in smaller scale. It is the *omphalos* or navel where the bond of the cosmos is located; it is also the point from which cosmic order radiates outward to the fringes of the territory along each of the four cardinal points or horizons. Territory is a mirror of the horizontality and verticality of the cosmos.[36]

Politically, the work of rulers is to govern the territory in ways that are appropriate to its cosmicization. That is, rulership is a mirroring or mimesis of the gods in their cosmogonic renewal of the world, which is constantly under threat of dissolution into formlessness by a lack of piety or apathy from within; rulership should prevent "an attack from without [which] threatens to turn [the territory] into chaos."[37] The ruler's victory is always a participation in the paradigmatic victory of the heavenly creator gods over the dragon of the underworld, who is just under the surface. Where the territory is well ruled, cosmic order on earth is maintained or strengthened; where the territory succumbs to chaos, it lapses into the ocean of disorder and disintegration.

According to Eliade, the primary experience of the cosmicized territory has not been lost in the process of differentiation, since "profane space" is still home to the nonhomogenous places that are consecrated by various personal experiences. (His examples include the childhood home and the scene of first love.) Similarly, the fear of reimmersion into a state of fluidity and formlessness, and of chaos in the abolition of order, are still caught in our clichés and choice of language when we speak about forces of chaos that threaten to overtake civilization or about darkness that overwhelms the world.[38] Territory is a political good because it meets the needs we have for our own place, an anchorage, in the cosmos. It is a political good because having a home to belong to is also a need of the political *communitas*; or at least, a shared yearning for a common homeland among displaced peoples demonstrates a political object of love that generates and sustains a *communitas*. Myth, legend, song: the territory is the locus of memory, the place that embeds the history of a people. The fields, the rivers, the mountains bear witness to a common past remembered through the generations. *Here* is where the nation emerges, now as in the past, the place itself—stable and continuous through time—being a partner in the nation's emergence. *Here* is the communion of the *communitas*, the locale in which the tribe, the *polis*, the nation, the state, the *ummah* is renewed. *Here* is home—a meaning of *communitas* harbored for the people who reach for it.

Alexis de Tocqueville acknowledges this when he writes that "there exists a love of country that has its source principally in the unthinking, disinterested, and indefinable sentiment that binds the heart of the man to the place where the man was born. This instinctive love is mingled with the taste for ancient customs, with respect for ancestors, and the memory of the past; those who experience it cherish their country as one loves the paternal home."[39] Territory can be a political good because it forms part of what Lonergan's intersubjective groups spontaneously identify with. It is, therefore, the home of a particular bond and a particular order. Territory can be a repository of other political goods too, goods that depend less on intersubjectivity and more on intelligence. For example, a system of justice requires a jurisdiction that can be mapped so that law can be applied. The borders of territories delineate the extension and limits of the territory, thereby demarcating the applicability of law. No borders, no law; no law, no legal expression of the communion that the political *communitas* lives by. For this reason, borders can be contentious, particularly in multinational states and regions that are home to many intersubjective groups whose intersubjectivity already extends beyond borders.[40]

Yet, more than a place of intersubjectivity, and more than a mere spatial extension of legality, territory is the earthly analogue of the cosmos. It is home whose loss we would grieve as a loss of the cosmos itself. This territory is the place we need as our point of luminous entry into the cosmos, where our *communitas* encounters the ultimate meaning of our shared belonging as a people. The territory, as mere place, is both mute and inanimate, but as home it sings aloud about the sacredness of our childhood, our heritage, our history, *les temps perdus* that bear witness to our lives together as intimately meaningful. A shared attachment to territory is how we recognize that our place is sanctified by the prayerful silence of the cloister, or how the unspeakable horror of what happened in a concentration camp still infests the place so many years later. The territory is haunted because we are already haunted by it. Territory is already the political good operative in our communion as a people. Shared love of territory is also how we can suffer from what Glenn Albrecht has called "solastalgia," profound anxiety in the despoliation or degradation of a place, which is always to lose something that we exist-from, and that we mourn because we still exist-toward it too.[41]

Still, we keep in mind de Tocqueville's admonition that because love of a territorial home is a romantic, intersubjective sentiment, it can come to resemble fanatic zeal: "It does not reason, it believes, it feels, it acts."[42] The potential for insularity and enclosure that would shut out the rest of humanity rests within a zealous love of territory. Yet the native land is a partner in the quest of the *communitas* for belonging. If it is the place that shelters the *communitas* from the world, then it is also the place whose threshold provides access to the world. Territory is a threshold that demarcates where "we" come from and therefore is historically invested with our own meaning and memory. It is from here that we go out to meet the world, and to greet the world when it comes to us. Territory becomes our particular home, suited to our unique existence as a *communitas*.

Liberty

Edmund Burke insists upon liberty as the most precious inheritance and responsibility of the English nation. The particularity of the English reaches out to the world by the political good of liberty. He writes that "from Magna Charta to the Declaration of Right, it has been the uniform policy of our constitution to claim and assert our liberties, as an *entailed inheritance* derived to us from our forefathers, and to be transmitted to our posterity."[43] Political liberty involves the privilege of self-government, and thus depends upon a government that knows its own proper limits. "By a constitutional policy, working after the pattern of nature, we receive, we hold, we transmit our government and our privileges, in the same manner in which we enjoy and transmit our property and our lives."[44] Liberty is a political good not simply because of its utility but because, for Burke, the English people have found—and continue to find—themselves as a nation through their shared love of liberty. Liberty is a "noble freedom" in which the past, the present, and the future are all parties to the communion that forms the political *communitas* that persists through the generations. That is, liberty is an object of love that has already formed, and continues to reform or renovate, a people. Liberty is not merely a useful accessory to a society, but is the vitality that the society already lives by.

Tocqueville remarks that "when one passes from a free country into another that is not, one is struck by a very extraordinary spectacle: there, everything is activity and movement; here, everything seems calm and immobile." "Scarcely have you descended on the soil of America when you find yourself in the midst of a sort of tumult. . . . Around you everything moves." "I am persuaded that if despotism ever comes to be established in America, it will find more difficulties in defeating the habits to which freedom has given birth than in surmounting the love of freedom."[45] In this remark, Tocqueville conveys the intrinsic quality of freedom as a dimension of America's cultivated political order, rather than an appendage with political utility. The American people cannot be understood without liberty. Even if the Americans come to pour scorn upon the idea of liberty, they will not overcome its practice and remain Americans. The price of narrowing liberty in America is the loss of American order itself. This is nothing less than dissolving the communion that sustains the American *communitas*. There is no American *communitas* in abstraction from liberty.

In the prerevolutionary struggle for independence from the crown, the American colonists were explicit that the good of independence was synonymous with the good of liberty. From the perspective of England, if it was difficult to accept independence from the crown, it was not difficult to understand the good of liberty. Burke's *Speech on Conciliation with America* sets forth the good of liberty as a continuity among the Americans of English order. For the English crown to resist the American colonists' desire for liberty was, in some sense, to denigrate the communion by which the English *communitas* exists. In putting down their revolution, England was inflicting harm on herself. Burke wonders what is to be gained in quelling the American uprising, except a loss of liberty in the meaning of English order. "To prove that the Americans ought not to be free, we are obliged to depreciate the value of freedom itself; and we never seem to gain a paltry advantage over them in debate, without attacking some of those principles, or deriding some of those feelings, for which our ancestors have shed their blood."[46] Political goods form, sustain, and renovate the political *communitas*, and liberty is one that renders the particular *communitas* perennially open to the universality of humanity, a tendency that Burke is giving voice to. By countering the spontaneity of intersubjective affection for England and its dominance, he is inviting his fellows to be intelligent and grasp the universal applicability of ordered liberty and to consider the self-damage in England's repudiating a political good constitutive of her own communion, the meaning of her political existence. In depriving others of liberty, the political *communitas* surely denigrates its own communion, stifles its own vitality, and contradicts the meaning of its own communion. The privilege of liberty is justified only in offering it to those who seek it.

However, just as the particularity of territory can be corrupted by group bias, so too can the universality of liberty.[47] We are always at liberty to deny liberty to others. It was Aristotle who was the first to sound the warning about the corruption of political goods. In setting forth the merits of democratic constitutions, he writes, "But there is a danger also in not letting [some share in governance], for a state in which many poor men are excluded from office will necessarily be full of enemies."[48] Similarly, Tocqueville warns the Americans of 1830 about the inevitable danger to the whole polity that the deliberate denial of liberty to some entails. "If liberty is ever lost in America, it will be necessary to lay the blame on the omnipotence of the majority that will have brought minorities to despair and will have forced them to appeal to physical force. Then you will see anarchy, but it will arrive as a consequence of despotism."[49]

POLITICAL COMMUNITAS

Hegel: The Bond and Order among Family, Civil Society, and the State

Political goods, as "objects of love," bind and order an aggregate into a *communitas*. This was famously Augustine's insight, but it was Hegel who offered us the further insight that I have been inching toward: belonging as an integrated synthesis of particular and universal patterns of membership. In his *Philosophy of Right*, Hegel places the political *communitas* of the state within the larger process he calls the ethical life (*Sittlichkeit*). It is only in the ethical life that existence and belonging can be maximally actualized because only here are particularity and universality (as subjectivity and objectivity) realized in the living good of freedom. That is, in freedom the particularity of individual "self-consciousness" is reconciled to the universality of an "ethical system." For Hegel, the state is the actualization of subjectivity in objectivity, and objectivity in subjectivity. "The ethical system is the idea of freedom. It is the living good, which has in self-consciousness its knowing and willing, and through the action of self-consciousness its actuality. Self-consciousness, on the other hand, finds in the ethical system its absolute basis and motive. The ethical system is thus the conception of freedom developed into a present world, and also into the nature of self-consciousness."[50] We cannot do more than point toward the major tripartite framework of belonging in which freedom drives actualization as *Sittlichkeit*: the family, civil society, and the state.

The family is the "direct or natural ethical spirit," whose first "phase" is marriage, where the family is actualized by a free decision of husband and wife. This leads to the "external reality" of property and goods, and ultimately to the education of children, who pass into civil society.[51] In the family, freedom or right accrues to the individual member by virtue of belonging in the family. Right does not appear as a right until the context has shifted from family to civil society or the state. Neither capital nor education is, in the first place, for the sake of establishing formal rights, but in a prereflective way, this is exactly how the family constitutes the beginning of what is realized fully in the state. The family is the first instance in which the particular persons find themselves existing-from a universality they exist-toward. The communion of the family *communitas* is an intense unity of persons. The family therefore is neither civil society nor the state since distance and formality do not characterize its communion; but nor is family other than the state since it endows its members with entitlements much like a state in miniature. Family is not quite the realm of the private since it is a communion that already holds family members as a unity that is always cognizant of their plurality; but nor is the family public either. The metaxy or in-betweenness of the family is due to its status as a living integration of particularity and universality, and without the family, civil society and the state would arise as merely abstract universals without the substance of belonging.

Hegel, in moving to the extension of the family into civil society, writes, "The concrete person, who as particular is an end to himself, is a totality of wants and a mixture of necessity and caprice. As such he is one of the principles of the civic community." The wants and needs of the particular person are necessarily connected to others since it is they who can provide for those wants and needs. The particular person "must call in the assistance of the form of universality," which is the civil society.[52] The relation between the individual and civil society is characterized by the provision of the individual's wants and needs, but never moves beyond that: "The interest of the individual as such would be the ultimate purpose of the social union."[53] However, Hegel is acutely aware of the human need to belong in communion.

If the state were no more than an exalted civil society, then it would be solely a voluntary membership. "But the state has a totally different relation to the individual. It is the objective spirit, and he has his truth, real existence, and ethical status only in being a member of it."[54] For Hegel, the state's rationality is the objective realization of what is most universal in the self-consciousness of its individual citizens. The relation between the particular person and the supreme universality of the state is categorically different from that between the individual and family or civil society. It is a real communion that dynamically synthesizes family and civil society by the mold of its universality. Political belonging, then, provides the "fit" in which individual persons, their families and civil society, their intersubjectivity and intelligence can find their own place and yet be shoulder-to-shoulder with others in their own place. "Union, as such, is itself the true content and end, since the individual is intended to pass a universal life."[55]

Hegel allows that the state is "not a work of art" and that this fully actualized state is rarely if ever the state that one encounters.[56] Political belonging is as messy and imperfect as any belonging, but as with Plato's ideal republic in the soul, and as with love itself, it is the spirit of the ideal that drives the will to belong through ever higher integrations toward perfect actualization. Although "yearning" is not a word that one would normally associate with Hegel, one might well be forgiven for thinking that his *Philosophy of Right* is aimed at exploring the extraordinary meaning of belonging that Spirit has opened up in the ordinariness of our various communities. There is desire and direction in Hegel's account of the in-between existence of human beings that recognizes the presence of the Absolute.

The Nation: Modernist and Perennialist Theories

For many recent theorists, it is not the state but the nation that holds the key to grasping the political communion. If we keep in mind that a political unit is a *communitas*, bound in political communion, then we need not overly concern ourselves here with problems like discerning which political constitution—monarchy, aristocracy, democracy—gives rise to the best political *communitas*. We recognize that, historically, political units have been *poleis*, *ethne*, geographic territories, linguistic groups, nation states, kingdoms, ecumenic empires, federations, groups of politico-religiously like-minded individuals and associations spread throughout the world, and so on, all of which can be called nations. John Stuart Mill gives the example of the un-conventionality of the Swiss nation as a political *communitas*. What bonds the Swiss in political communion is not easy to pinpoint. He writes, "Switzerland has a strong sentiment of nationality, though the cantons are of different races, different languages, and different reli-gions."[57] Political communion, we recognize, is not restricted to any particular constitution, and the political character of an unconven-tional, or to us unfamiliar, *communitas* is ignored at one's peril.[58] The particular constitution or communion of a political *communitas* will not be the concern here, but it is worth noting that in the absence of the bond of communion, there is no political *communitas* and thus no order that can be properly called political.[59]

In the West, the historical development of politics has been almost synonymous with the development of nations (and subsequently of states) from their origins in medieval kingdoms and empires and from the various ethnic peoples (*gentes*). I consider here the bond of politi-cal *communitas* in the West, which has been the nation predominantly. For most political theorists, the nation is the most well-known and concrete exemplar of political communion and *communitas*. Con-cerns in political theory with such topics as justice, legitimacy, and democracy raise profound questions about the nation as *communitas*. Among political theorists, questions about the nation compose a con-tested field that this study need not enter into, but a description of what contours demarcate the contest will help to clarify why a politi-cal unit is a bond and order of belonging, luminous with cosmological dimensions of meaning.

On the status of the nation, theorists tend to fall into one of two camps: "modernists" or "perennialists." Some can be classified as "modernist" because they hold that the nation—as the political unit—emerged in early modernity with the state.[60] The nation, by this thinking, is an offshoot of modernity along with the burgeoning success of other offshoots like the natural sciences and the growth of industrialization. For a modernist like Eric Gellner, "nation" is the name given to membership of a "high culture" that brings together the various strands of modernity. Regardless of a sense of nationality in the past, the nation is primarily an invention of modernity, and with it nationalism, the "principle that holds that the political and national unit should be congruent."[61]

Perennialists, on the other hand, insist upon the existence of the nation prior to modernity and statehood, insisting that the phenomenon of nationhood can only be understood if traced over *la longue durée*. The nation emphatically has historical existence since it has endured from a deep past and extends itself toward the future. Perennialism is theoretically close to a perspective known as "primordialism," but Daniele Conversi writes that they ought not to be "confounded." Perennialism and primordialism are opposed to modernism, and so, they are paired in their answering of a common question: When does the nation emerge? Primordialism, however, answers a further question in a way that perennialism does not: What is the nation? According to Conversi, primordialism refers to ethnic groups, "ethnie." Ethnie are the primordial political units that precede the development of modernity. Perennialists don't necessarily find organicistic or naturalistic threads of meaning, embodied by the various ethnie and their cultures, running from centuries past into the present, but whatever nations may be, they are much older than the state. Primordialists are "opposed to instrumentalism" or social constructionism.[62] Instrumentalists, on the other hand, tend to consider the nation as a fabrication of social engineers.[63] It is easier for modernists and more expedient for instrumentalists among them to think of nations in terms of modern statehood, while the perennialists and primordialists locate the political unit (the *communitas*) in the preexistent nation. For example, Johan Huizinga insists that "primitive instincts in human society" manifest themselves as patriotism and nationalism, and his work explores in the earliest political documents the phenomenon of yearning for a *patris* (Greek: fatherland, clan).[64] The tension between modernists and perennialists is important because questions of sovereignty, legitimacy, and democracy, among others, are all related to the particular order of the political *communitas*, and to the bond of communion that sustains it. What theorists know or assume about political communion becomes evident in their treatment of these other questions. Let us briefly survey some representative thinkers in both camps.

Hans Kohn is a good representative of modernism. While nationality may have existed prior to modernity, he argues that the nation becomes political only when the "idea of nationalism" becomes operative in modernity. He writes, "The continental Europe of the seventeenth century and of the first half of the eighteenth still lived in the prenationalistic age. But in the growth of centralized states in the secularization of political life, in the rise of individualism with its faith in liberty and its confidence in man's power, with the acceleration of economic life demanding the loosening of the static forms of traditional organization—the foundations were laid for the rise of nationalism."[65] Kohn recognizes that national consciousness—or "nationality"—existed in the "prenationalistic age," with the exemplars being Israel and Greece, but the nation that mobilizes itself for specifically political action supremely begins in modernity with the rise of the state. That is, nationalism transforms nationality by ideas of sovereignty, legitimacy, and democracy. Nationalism is bound up with statehood. Just as modernity is the era of political liberalism, so too is the nation compatible with a rational, civic, and liberal order. However, Kohn was also well aware of illiberal nationalism and its capacity for drawing upon the irrational biases and ethnocultural shortcomings of a people. The civic nationalism that Kohn identifies with the "West" is open to universal solidarity through human rights and international law, whereas the ethnic nationalism of the "East" is marked by a particularistic chauvinism. The Western state deserves the loyalty of its citizens because, by its civic and liberal nationalism, the nation transcends its ethnocultural particularity and begins to participate in cosmopolitanism. For a modernist like Kohn, the political *communitas* is the bearer of nationality because its members mobilize themselves through nationalism and the state, but he also keeps in view the larger—apparently more moral—field of universal humanity in which the nation moves.

While John Stuart Mill, in a perennialist vein, allowed that many nations preceded states, he acknowledged that governance often involved the governance of several nations within the borders of the state. For example, the "most united country in Europe, France, is far from being homogenous," composed as it is of "foreign nationalities at its remote extremities" and especially of its two dominant "portions, one occupied almost exclusively by a Gallo-Roman population, while in the other the Frankish, Burgundian, and other Teutonic races form a considerable ingredient."[66] Nations are composed in a variety of ways, sometimes mixed and blended with others, but for Mill, the sentiment of nationality by itself provides "a prima facie case for uniting all the members of the nationality under the same government, and a government to themselves apart."[67] The primary political *communitas* in the West is the nation, and, in principle, without the political communion—here, the sentiment of a common nationality—that forms the national *communitas*, "free institutions are next to impossible."

Mill recognizes that this principle is qualified by several considerations, among which are the close, local intermingling of nationalities on the one hand—for example, in the Balkans, where self-government seemed difficult at best; on the other hand, he recognizes that some members of the same nationality could be too distantly set apart from one another for a common governance to make sense. (He gives the example of Germans in East Prussia cut off from Germany by Poland.) For Mill, the political unit is, on principle, the nation, but the practical situation calls for prudence in government. Practically, the political unit, the *communitas*, may not be the nation, but something more pragmatic. Human universality and diversity beyond the particularity of the nation signifies the priority of prudence over principle in political governance. The political community is not a harmony, but a sometimes grudging, temporary alliance that, for now, places practical intelligence above a simmering set of hostilities among intersubjective groups. The resulting political *communitas* moves by institutions of governance that may be found by some to be disagreeable but that give voice to the people's better angels: their intelligent self-transcendence for the sake of the common good. Political friendship in a shoulder-to-shoulder stance does not call for a direct love of neighbor, as does Christian charity, but for mutual agreement on the available political goods we face together as objects loved in common.

The distinction between modernists and perennialists seems not so concrete for thinkers like Anthony D. Smith and Walker Connor. Connor writes that "the issue of when a nation came into being is not of key significance: while in factual/chronological history a nation may be of recent vintage, in the popular perception of its members, it is 'eternal,' 'beyond time,' 'timeless.' And it is not facts but perceptions of facts that shape attitudes and behavior."[68] For Connor, attitudes and behavior exemplify the spontaneous intersubjectivity of groups. His concern is with "ethnonationalism," a mass intersubjective sentiment. The ethnonationalist bond is experienced as belonging to a "fully extended family . . . not throughout time, but beyond time."[69] National belonging gives the people a sense of their place in the presence of the cosmos, and such a belonging is what ultimately legitimates the modern state. The modern state gives expression to the nation, but it is not identical to the nation. The nation is always a politicized ethnic group, and this is why the state is merely a construction, built out of a preexistent ethnic-national substance. The state seeks to address the practical problem of national self-determination. However, "national consciousness [may be] necessary [but it was] not a sufficient condition for the advent of national self-determination. Popular sovereignty — the notion that ultimate political authority rests with the people — was the other necessary part."[70] Consciousness of belonging to a nation, combined with an understanding that ultimate political authority is embedded in the nation, gives rise to national self-determination. The state is the mechanism by which the nation's self-determination is enacted. With Connor, the question of the nation brings us back again to the question of the communion of the *communitas.*

Anthony D. Smith, also occupying a middle position between perennialism and modernism, sees the modernist position as standing in need of correction, rather than replacement. He provides just such a "corrective and supplement" in his notion of ethnosymbolism. Whereas the modernists focus on the material and organizational factors conducive to the life of the nation, Smith insists that not only can culture not be overlooked, but a nation cannot be understood at all without its culture; and a culture is, elementally, a symbolic expression of an ethnie, or ethnic identity. For Smith, ethnies are "named human populations with shared ancestry myths, histories and cultures, having an association with a specific territory, and a sense of solidarity."[71] Smith's ethnosymbolism opens up the historical horizon of culture by shining the light of *theoria* on the ethnic roots of culture's national expressions as the communion of the *communitas,* geared for political action in time. Ethnosymbolism also offers something of a corrective to perennialism's tendency to treat nations as though their endurance through time amounts to some kind of permanence, as though nationhood is sewn into the political fabric of reality and in some ways exempt from the cosmological condition of passing. Smith suggests that the perennialist perspective is more accurate when it considers the symbolic continuity of a nation through time, rather than considering a nation as a fixed commodity. Every perennialist must acknowledge that particular nations come into and pass out of existence.

For the present purposes, Smith's ethnosymbolism provides a cosmological corrective to the lazy inclinations of perennialism while offering a remedy for the blind spots of modernism. An adequate understanding of a nation as a *political communitas* cannot exclude its symbolic vitality by focusing primarily on the mechanisms of state governance, and must include a consideration of its formative and sustaining communion. Smith defines the nation as "a named community possessing an historic territory, shared myths and memories, a common public culture and common laws and customs."[72] Some critics consider Smith's ethnosymbolism to fail in addressing the political, as opposed to the cultural, aspects of a nation. However, this consideration assumes a clear-cut distinction between culture and politics, perhaps assuming that politics is a modernist invention too.[73] What Smith's ethnosymbolism most clearly contributes to a grasp of national belonging is a thematic focus on a *communitas* whose communion is already cultural and political. More generally, what Smith helps to clarify is that a *communitas* is intrinsically political—regardless of the success or failure to achieve modern statehood—if we can admit that politics is a primordial ordering toward the flourishing existence of the bond of communion from which the *communitas* exists. Politics is anamnetic and primordial when it takes care to attend to those social conditions that impact the consciously embodied well-being of its individual and corporate members. Without political belonging, the *communitas* has neither bond nor order to sustain it.

Political *Communitas* as Mediator

Margaret Canovan writes that "questions of nationhood are not an optional extra for political theory, but should actually be at the heart of the discipline."[74] The illiberal chauvinism of much nationalism makes it an unattractive focus of study for many theorists. We are not naïve. We are painfully aware of the many brutalities against persons and communities that have been committed in the name of nationalism, and we know of the insidious methods of corrupting and manipulating the political goods operative in its communion. Still, as Canovan insists, illiberalism is not a necessary consequence of nationhood. While nationalism can be a murky topic, this does not absolve the theorist of responsibility to understand national belonging, and it does not grant them a license to dismiss it. Canovan suggests that, without understanding the bond of nationhood, we end up studying the branches without knowing the tree. Anyone interested in the study of democracy, social justice, and liberalism is already working with a (more or less acknowledged) set of assumptions about political power as a salient feature of the nation as the political unit. That is, suppositions about nations, nationhood, and nationalism all abound as untreated assumptions in otherwise well-crafted theories. For example, the problem that always arises in the study of democracy, social justice, and liberalism is the problem of power, and the theorist, in addressing power, must also address the political *communitas* in which power is stabilized. In spite of wielding great power, she writes, the modern state typically employs very little force due to the stability of the nation. The stable existence of the national *communitas* is a political belonging that allows for the study of its structures and content by academics, commentators, and practitioners. Democratic theory obviously relies upon the existence of a people as its most fundamental condition, and both social justice theorists and (classical) liberal thinkers require that political stability in which there can exist sufficient trust among citizens or between citizens and the mechanisms of the state (for the sake of just distribution or decision making respectively).[75]

Canovan pivots back and forth between the positions at stake in the modernist-perennialist divide and, in this, sets out reasons to think about the nation as an in-between reality. In spite of the contest between modernists and perennialists, Canovan, like Smith in his ethnosymbolist approach, wants to claim that the nation is cultural and political at once. While the nation is a *communitas* whose formative and sustaining communion may be rooted in some familial or local goods (ethnic, linguistic, mythic, geographic, etc.), as a state it measures itself by impartial and nonparticularistic rules. In this way, the nation-state mediates the cultural and the political, and by addressing the needs of both loyalty and legitimacy respectively, the nation-state is also mediating the tension between the particular and the universal. While it binds the aggregate of parts into a whole, it also, crucially, keeps the whole in a tension with its parts. Canovan employs Hannah Arendt's image of a shared table that presents what is universal or common to all while we take our own particular places around that very table.[76] Here is what is common; and our particular share depends upon what we do from where we are situated. The common table is an evocative metaphor for stability, power, and the political *communitas* itself as the beginning point for conversations about justice, rights, liberty, equality, and so on, germane to which is always our own particular situatedness at that table. Even though thinking about nationhood engages us in "a sticky cobweb of myths and mediations, guaranteed to repel the clearminded," the nation is also a hub of meaning that not only includes many experiences, stories, and phenomena but grounds and mediates them too.[77]

Canovan's notion of the nation as a mediator or hub of meaning aligns nicely with older lines of thought. Thinkers such as Kant, Johann Gottfried von Herder, Johann Gottlieb Fichte, and of course Hegel treat the nation similarly. Inherent within its political communion, the national *communitas* contains potentialities that, given expression, communicate something more than the local and particular: the possibility of its self-transcendence. I cannot survey this range of thought on the nation and its self-transcendence here, but it is worth highlighting Herder's notion of the nation as a medium in between humanity and the individual persons in political communion. The nation is worth studying not only because it reveals the intrinsic value of the nation's own uniqueness as a political belonging in the metaxy but also because, in doing so, we shine a light upon both the participating *communitas* and humanity as a whole. He writes that "in every one of their inventions, whether of peace or war, and even in all the faults and barbarities that nations have committed, we discern the grand law of nature: let man be man; let him mould his condition according as to himself shall seem best. For this nations took possession of their land, and established themselves in it as they could. . . . Thus we everywhere find man-kind possessing and exercising the right of forming themselves to a kind of humanity, as soon as they have discerned it."[78] The nation brings together what is particular and universal: it opens up the transcendent vista of a universal humanity from within its own particularity; and in the presence of *Humanität*, the *communitas* is able to take its place.[79] National belonging is a political tension that is maintained in a dynamic reciprocity of universal and particular.

Thus, for Herder, it is by nationalism that the universality of cosmopolitanism is realized, though not in an absolute and progressivist sense where nations are gradually superseded. *Humanität* seems to be Herder's term for the communion of a national *communitas*. It means humanity as both the abstract universal idea and the concretely realized *communitas* of persons in communion here and now. In living out its *Humanität*, a nation realizes and renovates its particularity through the generations. While *Humanität* transcends the limits of the nation, it does not surpass it because it is present as a dimension of meaning within the ordinary daily life of the nation.[80] The nation anchors *Humanität* in concrete living. It is in the nation that its people learn how to belong in between their own particularity as a *communitas* and the universality of shared humanity in the presence of the cosmos. In *Humanität*, Herder has found the abiding structure of meaning that gives the nation the resources to avoid stagnation and despotic prejudice by providing it with the means of substantive communication with other nations. For Herder, the communion of a national *communitas* is not racial (either in the sense of biological exclusivity nor of an ideologically closed circle), but primarily cultural or linguistic, and therefore never finished, but being well-grounded, is heuristically open to a field of communication and reciprocity with others. The inherent cosmopolitanism within nationalism drives and normalizes intercultural dialogue, refreshing and varying the nation itself. The inherent presence of *Humanität* to every nation renders every nation potentially an equal participant in a pluralist, nonhomogenous (and nonhomogenizing) cosmopolitanism. Since humanity is not set over and against the particular nation, the concern for universal humanity does not necessitate a progressivist, postnational order, nor does it result in a categorical set of uniform values applicable to every nation, regardless of traditions.

So it appears that we have here a convergence: what Canovan has diagnosed as mediation, and what Herder names as *Humanität*, are synonyms for cosmological presence. In the communion of the *communitas*, grounded in the consciousness and flesh of its individual persons who together face the objects of their political love, we disclose the metaxy as the conditions of our existence and belonging. We flourish and suffer, we live and we die, we measure our achievements to the degree that they raise what is subject to passing to the dignity of what is lasting. In the political belonging of the nation, there is present the Whole that binds and orders the universal and the particular to one another. That is, *in* the particular communion of the national *communitas*, there is a cosmos; but *in* the cosmos, the particular nation finds its response-ability to other nations and to the transcendent-divine origin. The fractious life of the nation is observable on the surface level of the day-to-day business of politics. Beneath the surface, however, is something more like the eloquence that Schabert described of navigating one's way across a crowded train station platform. The coordinated movements constitutive of the crowd are reducible to neither particular nor universal efforts alone, but involve a participation of each in a common predicament where the embodied conscious reality of humanity—in each person, each *communitas*, and universal humanity in all places and times—is present and operative. If the nation is the platform, then the order revealed as emergent from within the apparent chaos is a figure for the presence of the cosmos, or for Herder, of *Humanität*.

Undoing the Political *Communitas*

By belonging to the nation, persons simultaneously belong to what is more than the particularity of the nation, and they find themselves as participants in a universality that is mediated by the particularity of the nation. Universality and particularity are grasped only in tension with one another, mediating each other: the particularity of a national *communitas* filters out the generalities that would make talk of "universal humanity" irrelevant; the universality of humanity reminds the particular nation or its constituent social groups that the bigotry involved in denigrating others is also a self-denigration where keeping others out amounts to a commitment to keep ourselves small inside our enclosure, walled off from the ocean of humanity. Rather, it is in the nation as a metaxy of universal and particular that our political communion is affirmed and revitalized. Exodus is the great paradigm that dignifies national belonging. The going-out, the crossing of one's threshold, the embrace of *Humanität* is not a political self-evacuation but a forging of stronger national belonging in service to a universal humanity that awaits us. On the one hand, there is the crossing of one's own threshold. The exodus of Israel from Egypt is the story of a particular nation, but as the paradigmatic story of political belonging, it is the exodus of a nation, a gift of itself, from itself to the world. Only a firmly rooted nation can give itself as a gift. On the other hand, the world crosses one's threshold, comes in. There is the way of reciprocity: invitation and reply. There is also the way of violence: we were not ready for ravenous wolves, but they came in anyway. They desecrate our holy ground, the goods that bind and order us into a people. In their wanton savagery is our homeland destroyed, but ironically our national belonging is strengthened as our *communitas* is attacked. Invasion, oppression, and defilement are murderous in principle and in act, but also generate endurance. Political communion is already the good of the existence and belonging of the *communitas*, and the blows of the hostile stranger against the *communitas* serve only to intensify the communion, even through centuries of repressive treatment. Exodus and invasion both testify to the strength of political communion.

However, not every *communitas* can withstand national disintegration of its communion. The coming undone of the communion that sustains a people in unity is what we must consider finally, even if only to underscore the sacredness of political belonging in the presence of the cosmos. We have seen that the national *communitas* mediates between the particular and the universal—however these are conceived—but is always vulnerable to ideological militants who would destroy the nation from within or without. Implicit in the well-loved political goods that bring an aggregate into communion as a *communitas* is the tension between the universal and the particular. The disintegration of any political unity culminates in a collapse of the tension in between particularity and universality that forms the communion of the *communitas*. In the destruction or subversion of political goods loved in common, the tension between universal and particular is loosened and communion disintegrates. In the presence of the cosmos, not only is this the loss of a *communitas*, but in losing the belonging-in-tension expressive of the national communion, we lose the key to loving what is worthy of love in all nations. The cosmos becomes opaque.

This is framed acutely in the twentieth-century experience of loss through the violence of militant ideologues. In working to break belonging by collapsing the tension between the particular and universal that we exist-from and -toward, ideology eschews the mediating character of the national *communitas*. Whereas national belonging is a communion enriched by the tension, the work of ideology is, functionally, the loosening and collapse of the tension. From one side, National Socialists in Germany hypostatized and exalted a particular set of ethnic traits (biophysical, linguistic, cultural, geographic), subordinating those who did not share the traits; and from another side, Soviet Socialists in Russian and Eastern Europe excoriated and diluted the uniqueness of any particular nation in striving to attain a uniform international order. As in the poetry of Anna Akhmatova and the searing truth-telling of Aleksandr Solzhenitsyn, one weeps for one's nation and suffers its sufferings, because one is already in communion with all in the *communitas* who writhe in agony together as the nation is picked apart.[81] Experiencing national disintegration amounts to revulsion at the coerced loss of home and at the prospect of homelessness and exile at the hands of activists, rapacious and reckless with power. By what authority is the sacredness of national belonging undone? According to Hannah Arendt, appeal to the laws of Nature (National Socialism) and of History (Communist Socialism) is what is thought to justify every ideological act, including the suffering inflicted on the nation. On this, Solzhenitsyn comments that "the imagination and the spiritual strength of Shakespeare's evildoers stopped short at a dozen corpses. Because they had no ideology. Ideology—that is what gives evildoing its long-sought justification."[82]

In corrupting political goods, one corrupts the political communion, destroying the tension by which the national *communitas* exists. In destroying the mediating function of the nation, ideology destroys the microcosmos of home, leaving the people existentially adrift in the cosmos. One can deny cosmological presence, eclipse the in-between constitution of one's own personhood and the *communitas* of persons in communion, and accede to the ideological subduction of humanity into an abyss of violence and forgetfulness; or one can resist the lie by anamnetically recovering one's existence in the cosmos.[83] Anna Akhmatova, already famous for her love poetry in prerevolutionary Russia, became known for her solidarity with and love for her nation after the Bolshevik Revolution. "She loathed the new regime for its atheism and what she saw as its disdain for culture, but decided nevertheless to stay in Russia, to do what she could to defend and maintain its culture."[84] In 1922, Lenin offered intellectuals and dissenting voices an opportunity to flee that, not unlike Socrates in response to Crito, Akhmatova refused.

> Not where the sky's dome enclosed a foreign space,
> Nor where foreign wings sheltered and reassured,
> But among my people I took up my place,
> There, where by an ill fate, my own people were. . . .
> Not for myself alone, for all I pray,
> All those who stood beside without fail,
> Alike in bitter cold and sweltering haze,
> Beneath the brick-red blind walls of the jail.[85]

Brendan Purcell notes that Akhmatova "remarked to Isaiah Berlin . . . that she felt 'it was important to die *with* one's country. Compared to this dying *for* one's country was easy.'"[86]

The phrase "to die with one's country" raises four points of interest relevant to political belonging in the presence of the cosmos: (1) Akhmatova expresses the visceral pain of experiencing the sociopolitical chaos under which one's own national *communitas* is disintegrating. (2) Her spirit of existential resistance to the great lie at the heart of the chaotic undoing of communion arises from the depths of her own soul. (3) Her sense of belonging to a people or nation is expressed not only in solidarity with her contemporary neighbors but in finding her own fate as intimately bound up with the fate of the pangenerational nation in Burke's sense. (In the intensity of this communion, she experiences escape and exile as inauthentic, absurd, and unworthy of who she knows herself to be.) (4) Hers is a stark sense that the nation—even in its demise—participates in a reality higher, or is more luminous with meaning, than the experienced distortion or foreshortening of reality that the Bolsheviks, in their zealous recklessness, were inflicting on Russia. There is a sad, but revelatory, irony in Akhmatova's willingness "to die with one's country": to choose to share in the death of the nation is also her way of choosing to affirm the cosmological bond and order of existence, the primordial good of the life of the nation. For Akhmatova personally, by being prepared to die with her country, she is able to bear witness to the deepest meaning of the Russian nation. Her sentiments suggest that the nation's meaning, its role, its obligation is to be a political *communitas* that mirrors the cosmos in its own intrinsically valuable and uniquely Russian way (and emphatically not as a temporary arrangement, a state destined to wither away after the revolution when the terrestrial paradise is scheduled to emerge). That is, Akhmatova's horizon of meaning grasps the nation as having its proper place and its proper role and its proper time as a mediator of the cosmos, which itself does not pass.

Nor is Akhmatova's situation and response an idiosyncratic spectacle. In the *Crito*, Socrates educes the spirit of the laws of Athens, a spirit of justice that renders Athens accountable to the gods beyond Athens. The laws speak to Socrates, to whom Crito has offered a clandestine escape from imminent execution, and they exhort him to remember that the political *communitas* of Athens finds its justification only as a mirror of the cosmological bond and order that links the world and God.

> Be advised by us your guardians, and do not think more of your children or of your life or of anything else than you think of what is right, so that when you enter the next world you may have all this to plead in your defense before the authorities there. It seems clear that if you do this thing [escape from the sentence], neither you nor any of your friends will be the better for it or be more upright or have a cleaner conscience here in this world, nor will it be better for you when you reach the next. As it is, you will leave this place, when you do, as the victim of a wrong done not by us, the laws, but by your fellow men.[87]

Like Socrates in responding to Crito as he considers who he is in relation to the cosmos through his relation to the political communion of Athens, Akhmatova found the meaning of her existence in a personal vocation to stay and suffer, bearing witness to the good of existence and belonging. The meaning of her existence was found to culminate in her dying-with, a nobility of purpose that did not countenance a flight into exile.[88] Her poetry is a *cri de coeur*, expressing her belonging to the disintegrating Russian nation as conspicuous for her belonging in the cosmos that endures. The common good of communion may deteriorate and die, but the cosmos in whose presence it has existed does not. Akhmatova and Socrates find the resources within them to face death for the sake of their political *communitas*; their deaths are an act of remembrance and resistance because they die as embassies of the cosmological bond and order that cannot die.

If we listen to Solon, there is an unseen measure—glimpsed in the soul—by which a politics succeeds or fails in being, genuinely, a politics.[89] I will conclude by returning to Plato's myth of the rule of Cronos, where I began this chapter. The myth begins with a description of the age of Cronos. It was he who presided over human beings and provided for their every need. This was truly a prepolitical age, since Cronos's care for humanity meant that there was no need for politics. However, his divine care reached its due limit, the age came to a close, and he, the pilot, let go of the handle. In the withdrawal of Cronos, human forces were released and power was utilized, but utilized in confusion and chaos. Plato tells us that Cronos, as the god of care, had to intervene—though his time was over—in order to obviate the destructive course human beings had stupidly given to themselves. There was, however, to be no more divine intervention. The gods indeed have withdrawn for good. Human beings have no choice but to look after themselves. Tilo Schabert, in his commentary on the myth, writes, "There is one word for the care of human beings for themselves: politics. . . . Or, to put it differently, there are two ways of naming the care of human beings for themselves. One is 'politics.' The other is 'mimesis of God.'"[90] By way of consciousness and the flesh, we belong to one another, we are in need of each other, and we are of service to each other. Politics can mirror the bond and order of the cosmos in mimesis of Cronos, the paradigmatic god of care. "Human dignity is closely connected with the dignity possessed by politics in human life," writes Schabert. "When politics is despised or abused, human beings despise or abuse themselves. But if they understand politics as their most important activity, and if they act accordingly, human beings make themselves in fact worthy of themselves."[91]

HAVING CLAIMED, in the previous chapter, that *communitas* is constituted by communion, the task here was to think about what it is that brings a multitude of persons into communion. Why, after all, would anyone want to stand shoulder-to-shoulder with anyone else? Yet, here we are, in our communities. This necessity of figuring out that by which communion and its *communitas* exist was precisely a political one, and it was Augustine who directed attention to the shared love of political goods that brings an aggregate into a people. Without a common love, there is no obvious reason for a common stance. Whereas Christian love is centered on love of neighbor as *imago Dei*, even when the neighbor is an enemy, political love is directed at common political goods, the very condition of neighborliness. The neighbor is the one who most clearly evinces the shoulder-to-shoulder stance, which is not without its troubles but has a solidarity that becomes possible when we are both confronted by common goods. Our jostling with each other over the precise meaning of those goods is the normal business of politics, transacted on the basis of a shared love of common political goods.

These common goods, I argued, are not limited to utilities and commodities, but include existence, meaning, mystery, mortality, and the human predicament in the cosmos generally, which is why recognition of the primordial function of politics is necessary. Through considering the mythic status of cosmological kingship, we could discern that politics is not simply any form of governance, but is the name we give to the maintenance of bond and order in our midst, a microcosmos in which all may flourish against the threat of disorder, fragmentation, destruction, and chaos that is never finally dissipated. Political anamnesis is surely a commitment to remember that what was hard-won can be easily undone. Order (*kosmos*) is the fundamental political good because this is the good that gives rise to and sustains the bond called communion. Order is the good that attends to the primordiality of existence, which does not disappear but abides through all times and places. From the genetic unfolding of the good of order, according to the particular situation of the *communitas*, do the further political goods emerge by which a common dignity can be achieved.

I wanted then to demonstrate how political goods, in being loved in common and bonding persons into a people, bear an in-between status. Political goods bear on the well-being of individual persons and on the society at large; they bear on the particular *communitas*

and on the universality of humanity; and they bear on the immanent givenness of times and places as well as on the transcendent
dimensions of meaning implicit in them. I attempted to show this
in-between tension in representative examples of political goods, territory and liberty, and to consider how any political good can be sub-
verted by the corrupting of its meaning, with the consequent negative
impact on political communion.

I then needed to turn to consider the political *communitas* in
light of the tension between particular and universal in each of its
sustaining political goods. Since the focus of this study is on belonging, it was possible to avoid some of the more contentious debates
and instead draw valuable insights from various, disparate thinkers
who were each concerned with what the tensions implicit in political
goods mean for belonging to a nation. Inversely, the sentiments and
actions of partisans and ideological militants threw into relief the sacred value of political belonging as that which is being destroyed.
Anna Akhmatova, we saw, was a representative figure whose lamen-
tations for a people subject to a machinery of violence rose aloft in
poetry. Sacredness lies beyond the reach of murderous jackals, but
not beyond the reach of political *communitas*. Indeed, we find it in
the communion of our political belonging.

CHAPTER EIGHT

Sacramentality

There remains one more aspect of communion to consider: its consummation. While this has been implicit throughout, it is appropriate now to ask what it means to consummate a communion since every *communitas*—lovers, families, and friends; civic, religious, and political communities; and humanity itself—seeks its own flourishing. This chapter concentrates on the meaning of consummation as a realization—a perfection, or a completion—of communion. When we belong to a *communitas*, we become both participants in and agents of its consummation. That is, we become responsible for the good that is communion. *Communitas* is perfected to the extent that each person exists-from its communion in bonds of love and chooses to exist-toward the good of order that sustains them in communion. This is our belonging. It is precious to us. Belonging is the indispensable experience that functions as our point of access to the sacred. We find that sacredness, as absolute value, abides in our communion. It is probably more difficult to argue that sacredness does not subsist in communion than that it does, because in communion, those who belong to us are worth living for, and if put to the test, we find that they are worth dying for too. One need not have traditionally religious convictions to have experienced the sacred. One need only love. In this chapter, I will consider this sacredness and the presence of its inexhaustible quality within every *communitas*. Put another way, if every *communitas*—for all its occasions and extensions through place and time—is already structured by a dimension of sacredness in its communion, then this study remains incomplete unless we consider the *communitas* as straining toward the realization of what remains absolute within it. We are therefore still grappling with the in-between, with existence and belonging as metaxy.

Eric Voegelin points out, "At the border of transcendence the language of philosophical anthropology must become the language of religious symbolization."[1] We have already seen that the symbolization of compact, intracosmic religious experience offers us resources to discuss belonging in the cosmos, as do the noetic philosophical tradition and the revelatory religious traditions. The key symbol in this chapter will be "sacramentality." By sacramentality, I intend the metaxy, but am deliberately transposing the Greek noetic insight of the in-between of time and the timeless to the Christian environment in which both faith and reason interpenetrate one another as the life of each person. One does not lose the metaxy in the shift, but gains this further dimension of meaning: persons and *communitas*. By sacramentality, I am therefore referring to the quality of sacredness that permeates communion among persons and every *communitas*, and whose presence in all belonging invokes the struggle for completion or perfection.[2] "Sacramentality" is a term that combines the Latin term *sacer* (holy, sacred) and the Greek term *mysterion* (mystery) to underscore that the cosmos is a mysterious reality manifesting absolute value and that existence-as-belonging intrinsically partakes of that absolute value of the cosmos. The discussion below will aim to probe the philosophical significance of sacramentality that radiates through the heart of communion. "Probe" is the correct word in this context because, with sacramentality, one is essentially confronting a dimension of meaning whose very transcendence eludes our ability to capture that meaning. Again, one is probing a transcendent border problem because the communion of belonging meets our existential needs, is worthy of our deepest aspirations, and renews itself by glimpsing the sacred that already lives within it; but the intentionality of putting words to this complex of luminous experience is fraught with difficulty.

The discussion begins with a consideration of the meaning of a general sacramentality by setting out the philosophical significance of a specific sacrament, the Eucharist. I argue that this significance lies in its framing of all sacramentality. I will add to this a metaphysical account of consummation as telos. By then, we should have sufficient clarity to consider the sacramentality of belonging. We will need a concrete example, and for this I have chosen matrimony. We will consider matrimony because of its apparent ordinariness and obvious sacramentality, but also because it exemplifies an intensity of communion between two spouses who, in the intimate consummation of their self-sacrificial unity and fecundity, mediate the cosmos to one another and to the world. Matrimonial communion provides an exemplar of belonging that lives and is renewed by its consummation. Every communion, lived by every *communitas*, has its own proper consummation, but to grasp the meaning of matrimonial belonging is to grasp very clearly the importance of consummation more generally for the life and renewal of any *communitas*. This will set up the final discussion on the sacramentality of politics and history. What I want to add to the discussion in the previous chapter is a consideration of sacramentality in politics, which necessarily brings us to history. History, I will claim, is the story of the general sacramentality of human existence.

Sacramentality: Communion and Its Consummation

Communion as Sacramental

According to Thomas Aquinas, "every sign of a sacred thing is a sacrament."[3] Something may be called a sacrament "either from having a certain hidden sanctity . . . or from having some relationship to this sanctity."[4] The seven sacraments of the Eastern and Western Christian *ecclesia* are a heightening of what I am here recognizing and naming as the general sacramentality of belonging. It is worth considering the sacrament of the Eucharist for what it can tell us about sacramentality in general. Regarded as the "source and summit" of faith, the Eucharist is the sacramental presence of Jesus the Christ, who himself was the sacred human-divine person, the Way, the truth, and the life in between heaven and earth.[5] The Eucharist is the preeminent sacrament of the metaxy. Not only does it render Christ's invisible presence visibly present in the "species" of bread and wine, but human participation in the Eucharist efficaciously presents to the participant his or her own in-between existence too. Consumed and consuming, our participation in the Eucharist is existential nourishment because, in the sacramental act, we ourselves *are participated in* by the body, blood, soul, divinity, and metaxy of the Christ who is consumed. Thus, the Eucharist is food sacramentally disposed to human embodiment and to the luminosity of human consciousness. As the Pasch, the Eucharist re-presents the sacrificial lamb of the Passover whose completion is announced in the death of the Christ: "Consummatum est" ("It is finished"; John 19:30). In consuming the Paschal sacrifice, we sacramentally participate in Christ's passion and death.

It is rightly called communion, because in being sacramentally nourished by the same food, we come into communion with one other across places and through times because, more foundationally, we are in communion with the Trinitarian-divine *communitas* that grounds the existence of all things. Of sacramental presence, Thomas writes that the Eucharist extends from the past and into the present and future. With regard to the past, it

> is commemorative of our Lord's Passion, which was a true sacrifice, . . . and in this respect it is called a Sacrifice. With regard to the present it has another meaning, namely, that of Ecclesiastical unity, in which men are aggregated through this Sacrament; and in this respect it is called "Communion." . . . With regard to the future it has a third meaning, inasmuch as this sacrament foreshadows the Divine fruition, which shall come to pass in heaven. And according to this it is called "Viaticum," because it supplies the way of winning thither. And in this respect it is also called the "Eucharist," that is, "good grace."[6]

The flow of divine presence in the Eucharistic sacrament is a "threefold significance" of temporal efficacy: it is self-sacrificial love, the death of Christ that consummates the life of Jesus and the meaning of baptismal consecration from which we exist in each moment; it is the achievement of spiritual communion with one another that perfectly realizes a *communitas* of persons in between time and eternity; and it anticipates the final consummation of the cosmos itself, toward which we exist in each moment. It comprehends and meets the deepest human yearning, articulated by Augustine as final tranquility: addressing God, he writes that "our heart is restless until it rests in you."[7] Gathering reality together in the totality of its immanence and transcendence, the Eucharist is the great icon of the general sacramentality of existence-as-belonging, and it is the presence of sacred divine mystery in and of the cosmos that ennobles existence. The Eucharistic presence of Christ heightens the general sacramentality of personhood and belonging, but personhood and belonging are essentially eucharistic (lower case) in their sacramentality, because *communitas* is itself a reality of our lives that can direct us toward the threefold significance of sacredness in time: in love, we exist-toward the persons and places of home self-sacrificially; we know ourselves as existing-from all that constitutes home for us in bonds of communion; and we are fortified for existence in the metaxy, ennobled in purpose and direction. The Eucharist brings forth nothing less than a joining of "Christ's true body, and Christ's mystical body."[8] It teaches that the general sacramentality of belonging with one another in *communitas* is already a disclosing or foreshadowing of our stake in that final consummation together.

Belonging in communion is a mode of existence that is "us" and more than "us" simultaneously, because in communion we become more who we already are: persons who live out the bond and order that sustains all things. We are, and are more than, persons standing shoulder-to-shoulder. With Maritain, we can say that we are brought into communion by a common good that extends to the transcendent-divine good, which thereby becomes our mode of participation in eternity in every present moment. Communion in *communitas* reveals itself as sacramental when the inwardness of communion—for example, the exclusivity of lovers or the particularity of a political people—opens onto a vista of universality and transcendence for which we become responsible. By the inwardness of communion is the bond and order of the cosmos unveiled in the midst of the world. It was love that did this, that softened the heart. Love did the impossible: by the turning of lovers, friends, and compatriots toward the unitive and fecund common good of all, love elucidates communion as the reality by which the world flourishes.

Consummation as the Perfection of Communion

Consummation as the Tension between What Is and What Will Be
"Consummation" is a symbol that bears a meaning equivalent to the Greek symbol *telos*. *Telos* translates typically as "end," but it is an end that means more than a simple terminus or closure. It means, in addition to a terminus, an end in the sense of what Aristotle calls a final cause. With regard to an intentional act, a final cause would be the purpose of the act. So, for example, if we are concerned about our health, and we choose to incorporate more walking into our daily lives, then we can say that health is the final cause of walking. We do more walking for the sake of health, which means that health would be the desired end that walking aims at.[9] Health is the end, fulfillment, or consummation of walking, and prior to the incorporation of walking into our daily lives, health was the perfection that was desired. It motivated our plan to walk more. Generally speaking, a consummation as telos was the reason we engaged in some action in the first place, the end for which sake the action aimed. A consummation in this teleological sense explains the purpose and remit of the action. It also demonstrates that the desirability of a particular consummation—such as health—precedes the intentional action. As desire, it is the pivot from knowing to choosing; as value, it is the motivation for choosing a course of action. Consummation in this sense means an antecedent telos.

Yet *telos* can mean more than a final cause as the antecedent purpose for some action. *Telos* also has the meaning of the completion of that action, the actual satisfaction or realization that the action has now accomplished. This is a shift of meaning of consummation from the *conceptually prior* end to be aimed at in action to the realized, *posterior actualization* of the end. Such a shift is paradigmatically, though not exclusively, characteristic of the operation of final causes in the nonintentional realm of nature, according to Aristotle. For example, when he writes that "it takes a human being to generate a human being," he is indicating that the form, essence, or nature we call "human being" or humanity is the final cause of the natural reproduction of human beings.[10] By the movement, action, or change inherent within some natural thing (a hylomorphic unity of matter and form), some new thing of the same nature has been generated. The new, natural thing is the consummation or telos. In this posterior sense of *telos*, a new generation is the actualization that has consummated what was latent in the natural movement, action, or change of the older generation. "For the generation," Aristotle writes, "is for the sake of the substance and not this for the sake of generation."[11] The consummation of the change we call human generation or reproduction is the substance of a naturally generated human being. This is consummation in the sense of a subsequent perfection. The natural offspring is the consummation of the reproductive movement, action, and change in its parents. The natural world contains within it the processes or means to its own consummation or telos, not as purpose in the intentional sense, but as the actualization of form. Thus, Aristotle can conclude that, although final, formal, material, and efficient causes are different types of cause, nonetheless the same being can, by nature, act as different causes simultaneously.[12]

So far, I note that a consummation is a telos that bears at least these three shades of meaning: (1) an end in the sense of a terminus to movement or change; (2) an antecedent purpose; and (3) a subsequent perfection.[13] Yet there is a further shade of meaning in consummation that *telos* brings out. "Consummation" connotes a dynamic *tension* in between what has been realized and what is still to be realized. The antecedent realization, such as a desired purpose, contains within itself a potentiality that strains for its subsequent perfection as actualization. A consummation is certainly already a telos in the former sense, yet it also generates a tension by which a telos in the latter sense would be actualized. To the tension operative in consummation from antecedent to subsequent, Aristotle gives the name *entelecheia*. It is a term that etymologically contains *telos* within itself. It is the power in a being to self-actualize what was always potentially in it. The related term, *energeia*, used above in the discussion of love, is crucial here. Although there is a distinction between the meanings of *energeia* and *entelecheia*, Aristotle uses them quite interchangeably because *energeia* is the activity or motion that makes a thing what it is; "entelechy" is the consummation that has been realized by *energeia*. An entelechy is a consummation completed in *energeia*, the bringing-to-actuality.[14] I will continue to use *energeia* because I want to focus on the tension of "bring-ing" (as gerund, being in motion) a communion from its antecedent to its subsequent consummation, and this is better symbolized by *energeia*. With any *communitas*, the *energeia* of consummation is the inner straining from its beginning in communion toward its end as the perfection of that communion. *Communitas* begins in a communion consummated in the antecedent sense: these are our commonly desired political goods, and in loving them we become a people. *Communitas* is bonded in the consummation or realization of its communion by this shared love of political "objects." Yet every belonging can grow or wither. Every *communitas* flourishes, develops, and renovates itself to the extent that it continues to consummate its telos. Every *communitas* is in motion, reaching toward the end it was originally consummated by. It exists-from and -toward its consummation. It is in tension, and lives by the tension that makes it restless, self-critical, and acutely aware of the political goods to which it, as *communitas*, approximates itself, but which are never finally achieved. A *communitas* more likely exhausts itself before it exhausts its political goods.

Consummation, we could say, is the perfection of a fit where persons, families, institutions, and communities of all sorts have already been fitted from the start to come to their proper place. That is, the life of belonging in communion is the *energeia* of its consummation. Every communion has already had, and yet reaches out for, its consummation. The life and belonging in communion is what has begun in consummation; and thereby imprinted, formed, and commissioned, that same communion strives for its ultimate consummation. Thus, the sacramentality of communion and the *energeia* that generates and sustains it: a life of belonging that exists-from the consummation by which it is realized, and yet exists-toward the consummation that finally perfects it. The *communitas* is already a share in that perfection, formed as it was for the sake of perfection.

Here again, the Eucharist presents itself as icon and reality of a heightened sacramentality of belonging. The Eucharist clarifies that the love that first found perfection in the human incarnation of the Christ, and that subsequently drove the passion and redemptive death as its completion, is the *energeia* that was always striving toward consummation. Participation in that consummation is the remembrance that not only brings us into communion but is what feeds our communion: the nourishment it offers is less a satisfaction and more a hunger for the great belonging that is the personal culmination of our life, framed by the mortal boundary of death on the one hand and, on the other, the eschatological completion of the cosmos when time and timelessness are consummated in God. It is not difficult to find shades of Aristotle's metaphysical meaning of *telos* and *energeia* resonating in meditations on the Eucharistic. Thus, there are two metaphysical claims to make about belonging by reference to the Eucharist as the iconic framing and paradigmatic *typos* of the general sacramentality of belonging. The first is that belonging in *communitas* is born of a communion already consummated in some way. The good we love in common has already placed us shoulder-to-shoulder, and the resulting *communitas* is the sign of a communion already realized. The second is that every *communitas* has a quality of sacredness because its communion is generally sacramental. What could this mean? In between the visible and invisible presence of perfection, the *communitas* is the sign of communion; and we experience our belonging as what is most sacred to us. Our belonging together as a *communitas* is how we come to experience and understand our lives *sub specie aeternitatis*. Since *communitas* has already been consummated in the former, antecedent sense among these persons, in these times and places, communion is not simply what we exist-from in *communitas*, but must also entail a meaning not yet perfectly realized. Communion is sustained by its own *energeia* toward a final consummation, already inherent and operative within itself. The communion of *communitas* anticipates, in its very living, a communion of belonging unrestricted by time and place as what it is already existing-toward. Our belonging, prosaic and ordinary, nonetheless is the sacredness in our midst that we often take for granted; but by this sacredness is disclosed finality in the direction of the unrestricted or eschatological.

Wisdom and Death

It was in this vein that Aristotle wrote of wisdom in his *Nicomachean Ethics* as the consummation of knowledge: "Therefore wisdom must plainly be the most finished [the consummation] of the forms of knowledge. It follows that the wise man must not only know what follows from the first principles, but must also possess truth about the first principles. Therefore wisdom must be comprehension combined with knowledge—knowledge of the highest objects which has received as it were its proper completion."[15] Wisdom is a perfection. It is already complete, and it draws the soul by the *energeia* of love: by its perfection, wisdom affords knowledge and knowers their purpose and their rest. If wisdom is the consummation of knowledge in the sense of completion, then it was also already the perfection that initiated the striving for knowledge, gave that striving its particular form and purpose, and made the knower, desirous of knowledge, worthy to enter under its roof. Because wisdom was prior to the particular search for knowledge, and because it was wisdom that first stirred, ignited, or participated in the soul or consciousness of the particular person, there arose the *energeia* of existential tension I call the love of wisdom, the pure desire to know, that gathered and guided the one who began to strive for knowledge.

The love of wisdom that calls the philosopher, qua philosopher, into existence in the first place and sustains her in the philosophical life is also formative of the communion we call philosophical friendship. The love of wisdom is the communion of the soul or souls with wisdom. Philosophy—in its deepest sense of a life sprung from and commissioned by a love of wisdom—begins in a communion of the soul and wisdom, the conspicuous moment when wonderment is experienced, according to Socrates and Aristotle; yet the soul continues to reach out for that very wisdom in erotic tension.[16] By the philosophical life are knowledge and the knower consummated in wisdom. The philosophical life is an *energeia* because the communion of the soul and wisdom is also *that by which* knowledge and the knower are consummated in wisdom. If their communion was formed in an antecedent consummation, it is by the life of communion that their consummation is renovated and renewed in desire. The philosopher exists-from that wisdom, yet exists-toward it in love. Her life, conducted as a love of wisdom, is a communion consummated and consummating by the *energeia* of philosophy. The philosophic life bears sacramental witness in its striving toward the perfection that is more than either ignorance or opinion. It strains for the perfection that is wisdom, that not only calls it now, but that sanctified and commissioned it from the beginning. It was for the sake of wisdom that knowledge was sought. Indeed, it was wisdom that awaited the homecoming of the philosopher who would be the knower. Knowledge and knower have found their proper place in wisdom, which is their perfection.

In writing about the philosophical life in the *Phaedo*, Plato too writes about consummation. As he awaits the arrival of the executioner, Socrates has the courage to meet death because the separation of the soul from the body in death is an event that he understands precisely as a homecoming. Pregnant with hope, he understands death to be nothing less than the consummation of life, and the death of the lover of wisdom to be the homecoming of the philosopher to divine wisdom: "The true philosophers, Simmias, are always occupied in the practice of dying, wherefore to them least of all men is death terrible. . . . How inconsistent would they be if they trembled and repined, instead of rejoicing, at their departure to that place where, when they arrive, they hope to gain that which in life they desired—and this was wisdom."[17] The philosopher is the lover of wisdom: from the start it was wisdom that structured and drove the life of the philosopher; and it was always for the sake of wisdom that one lived as a philosopher. It was wisdom that Socrates existed-from and existed-toward. He lived in intimate communion with wisdom— what could be more intimate than urgings of wisdom in the soul?— obediently listening for the wisdom of the *daimon* within him. It was to wisdom, indeed, that Socrates belonged in love.

So, wisdom and death acquire a sacramentality in the *Phaedo*. Because wisdom straddles the divide that is mortal life and death, wisdom in communion with the soul in life does not fall out of communion with the soul in bodily death. Death is more likely the occasion for the fullest embrace: the perfection of the soul. That is, death as consummation of life reveals an extraordinariness that was always available in ordinary life. It is philosophy, as the Socratic "art of dying," that was the ongoing lived testimony of extraordinariness that precedes, sustains, and perfects the ordinary. At the end of the *Phaedo*, the sacramentality of death requires a ritual dressing of the body and an almsgiving that we see Socrates enacting because, in gratitude that outweighs sorrow, Socrates anticipates the consummation of his life lived in sacred communion with wisdom. He dies in the hope that in death he will now meet the god who is wisdom and be perfected. Sacramentality radiates through the philosophical life in love with wisdom just as it illuminates the death of the philosopher. Death is a consummation because, in the *Phaedo*, it is literally the final homecoming of the lover of wisdom into the divine home of wisdom. Socrates had cultivated this belonging all his life long.

In communion, perfection is present, but subject to the imperfections of original, defective human wills. We cannot all be Socrates, but for the purposes of this study, it suffices to point out that every belonging in communion is already a participation in its own subsequent perfection because that perfection has already participated in each human life, generating that life and belonging. We are touching the sacred that has already touched us; we are touching the sacred *because* it touched us first. Belonging in communion is where the differences between perfection and imperfection are both manifest and managed. Yet communion is also an *energeia* where perfection is the extraordinariness that drives the ordinary stuff of life even if by way of the imperfections inherent within the individual person and the individual *communitas*.

MATRIMONIAL BELONGING

Let us turn now to matrimonial communion since a consideration of matrimony will serve as a familiar and concrete instance of the rather abstract foregoing discussion about belonging in communion and its consummation. In general, let us keep in mind that the life of any communion is as unique as the individual circumstances of those particular persons in communion. Let us also keep in mind that, while there are many types of *communitas*, each existing in its own communion, there are many types of consummation appropriate to those many types of communion. In discussing matrimony, I do not make any claims vis-à-vis other articulations of marriage, such as gay marriage (involving the legal negation of the significance of biological sex) or polyamorous marriages (involving the legal negation of restriction to two spouses). The effort here is solely concentrated upon a reconsideration of *matrimonial* marriage, where both biological sex and a restriction to two spouses do matter. The discussion aims to chart the contours of matrimonial communion as a special form of belonging between one man and one woman. The consummation of this particular kind of communion—primordial in its fecundity by way of consciousness and the flesh, and driven by the *energeia* of love—bonds the spouses in intense intimacy and intrinsically orders their communion toward the generation of life. As a *sui generis* form of belonging, matrimony stands as a figure of the cosmos and, like the Eucharist, clarifies the sacramental meaning of belonging in general. It is also worth saying that the symbol "matrimony," rather than "marriage," is the more appropriate symbol because it keeps within its orbit of meaning this inherent fecundity that pertains naturally to the communion of a man and a woman.[18] By matrimony-as-communion, I intend a sacramental dimension of meaning that marriage-as-civil-contract overlooks.

Every communion, of course, is intrinsically unitive and generative in its own way, but here, the meaning of sexual love merits special attention. By sexual congress do spouses consummate their matrimonial communion. This is the act by which the *communitas* of spouses becomes more than an interrelation between those spouses, an act of belonging in between the spouses and the cosmos. Matrimony is rooted in the communion of husband and wife, but the consummation of their communion is how they elevate their *communitas* to what is more than either of them. Husband and wife become one flesh—paradoxically overcoming their sexual differences by way of their sexual differences—and merge into a higher, unitive whole. It is a whole that mirrors the Whole, mediating the cosmos in such a way that matrimony becomes a cosmogony, their conjugal bond intrinsically ordered toward the generation of new life, their bond the embrace that extends beyond them. Indeed, the matrimonial embrace of spouses is a gathering of the fertile possibilities of the cosmos itself into their mutual love. Their act of sexual love consummated and consecrated their unity in the beginning, but is the means by which they continue to consecrate one another in communion. Their intimate communion is how they set out upon the great cosmological communion of all things, as though an ocean, their conjugal unity a seine that trawls the abyss of transcendent mystery that brings all things forth. Here we must consider both of these uniquely unitive and generative aspects of matrimony by referring to what Kierkegaard has written on marriage in his *Either/Or*, which endures as one of the most extended philosophical exegeses of this unique type of communion.

Matrimonial Consummation as Unitive

In responding to A (the writer of the first part of Kierkegaard's *Either/Or*) Judge William, or B, writes a defense of marriage—what I am here calling matrimony—as a correction of the severe shortcomings articulated by A.[19] A's realm is the realm of the aesthete and dreamer, forever fleeing boredom. Love, for A, is about the thrill of seduction, and he will not yet recognize that, instead, love is more properly a movement (or *energeia*) that tends toward communion. B accuses him of becoming intoxicated by the aesthetic-intellectual mode of existence that is attuned to the pride and hubris of one who will not give or receive what is required in order to love the other and, for the purposes of this discussion, who repudiates belonging (391). The refusal to love anything but the grand project of his own life amounts to the refusal to enter into any type of communion. As B reminds A, "Bear in mind your life is passing; there will come a time even for you when it draws to its close, when you are offered no further ways out in life, when recollection is all that is left. Yes, recollection, but not in the way you so much love it, this mixture of poesy and truth, but the serious and faithful recollection of conscience. Take care that it does not unroll a personal record, not indeed of genuine crimes, but of wasted possibilities, phantom-images which it will be impossible for you to chase away" (390). B diagnoses the malady of a self-imposed limitation in A's heart whose inescapable consequences are regrets. "What you are drawn to is the first rapture of love.... As for marriage, you have always remained simply an observer" (384–85). What A has missed in his rapture, his dedication to pleasure, is that matrimony is not something separate from the excitement of "first love." Rather, matrimony is lived in continuity with first love, or better, with the abiding meaning of falling in love. Matrimony is "a matter of continual rejuvenation of [that] first love" (387). Indeed, in stories about romantic love, "the lovers finally fall into each other's arms, the curtain falls, the book ends, ... the reader is none the wiser" (392). For Judge William, this may be where the audience leaves the story, but not the lovers. For them, this is not where the story ends, but is the beginning point from which a life of love is unfurled. The curtain falls where love's sensuality becomes ecstatic and radiates its meaning outward from a moment of love to a life of love.

A life of love makes sense only because of what is latent in the sensuality of first love. Sensuality is consummation in the antecedent sense because it already expresses the telos that calls the communion of matrimony into existence. Sensuality is a whole-person language in which intimacy is communicated by touch or by a look or by words. It is a language spoken not merely for sake of delighting in the beauty of the body of the beloved but also for the sake of the mutual giving and receiving of the entire personhood, the enfleshed consciousness, the very life of the lovers.[20] The giving, the receiving, the forging into communion: this is the consummation of sensuality, the meaning articulated by the grammar of intimacy that was already the reason for its expression. The sensuality of first love speaks an intimate yearning that wants nothing less than to possess the beauty of the beloved forever. The fecund moment that speaks its yearning for intimacy by way of consciousness and the flesh to the entirety of the beloved's life is a sensuality that is fed by its hunger rather than its satisfaction, and thus it will seek to realize its consummation again and again and, in so seeking, will bind the lovers in the most fitting, most self-sacrificing communion.

Matrimony is the name of this communion. Only in the belonging of matrimony is the meaning of sensuality consummated in its full amplitude across a lifetime. Thus, it is not matrimony that justifies sensuality, but sensuality that commissions and renews matrimony. From the erotic sensuality of first love does matrimony proceed as the dynamic tension by which the perfections of sexual congress that express themselves in intimacy find their realization on the scale of life itself. As Levinas told us, it was *eros* that brought the lover onto holy ground. Eros has already swooped for what is desirable beyond measure: beauty whose sacred presence-as-hiddenness can become profaned, unless voluptuosity is elevated into the higher orbit of encounter with alterity. It is the sensuality of *eros* that discovers sacredness, and it is sacredness that calls for matrimony. Sensuality needs matrimony because *eros* by itself would have the lover tread recklessly on holy ground, but the communion of matrimony lifts *eros* to its sacramental height. Kierkegaard writes of first love that, "though based essentially on the sensual, this love still has a nobility by virtue of the consciousness of the eternal it takes up in itself. For what distinguishes love from lust is its having the stamp of the eternal" (393).

Sensuality is the *energeia* that not only consummates first love in the sanctity of matrimonial communion, but in the continual renewal of the meaning of first love—and the continual erotic rediscovery of the beauty of the beloved—drives that communion as a visible pattern of sacramentality in the midst of the world. The sensual intimacy of spouses is hidden from view, but by virtue of this hiddenness does matrimony become a visible sign of the sacredness that binds and orders all belonging.

The communion that holds the spouses was always more than a consensual interrelationality. Their matrimonial "I do" was spoken with the authority of what is eternal in and of the cosmos, but spoken to what must remain bound by temporality: the mortality of each spouse. Spouses must die, and their matrimony must expire with them. But for now, their communion with one another is effectively their intermediation of cosmological lasting and passing to one another. As every human person is an embassy of the cosmos, so too is the heightened communion of spouses a matrimonial embassy that mirrors the cosmos in a heightened way. The sensuality that finds its renewal and sanctification in the consummation of matrimony is thereby heightened and becomes luminous for its sacredness. "In marriage the spiritual is higher than in first love, and the higher the heaven over the marriage bed the better, the more beautiful, the more aesthetical it is, and the heaven that overarches the marriage is not this earthly one but the heaven of the spirit" (414). Sacramental love that gathers the sensuality of first love into a "higher concentricity" is both the participation of the lovers in the sacred bond and order of the cosmos and, crucially, also the flow of cosmological presence as the very love of the lovers. The breakdown of matrimonial relationships, it appears, is not a failure inherent within love but a failure of one or both of the spouses to belong in communion.

Belonging involves anamnetic remembrance of cosmological presence with its conditions of lasting and passing. Lasting is present in matrimony as the heaven that sacramentally overarches the marriage bed—the efficacy of conjugal consummation which always united and renewed them—but in the living of life, lovers can be swamped with the concerns, passions, and affairs of the passing world. Matrimony is a high calling, in part because it is difficult one. A life of communion is a life of self-sacrificial love. For those called to it, matrimony is the point of entry into the metaxy of existence, a calling of each spouse toward the perfection of the communion that both is theirs and was always more than theirs. They are accountable to themselves, to each other, and to their matrimonial communion in which the cosmos is sacramentally present through them. "As with everything eternal, it has in itself the twofold character of presupposing itself back into all eternity and forward into all eternity. [First love] is the unity of freedom and necessity. The individual feels drawn to the other with an irresistible power but precisely in this feels his freedom. It is a unity of the universal and the singular, it has the universal *as* the singular, even to the verge of the contingent" (404–5). Matrimonial communion unites the duality and alterity of male and female because its sacramentality is an efficacy that flows from the metaxy that already unites eternity and time, freedom and necessity, particularity and universality, perfection and imperfection. To live such a calling requires everything that can be given and received through the lives of the spouses. They become, in effect, channels of the flow of divine presence for each other.

Matrimony is "sensual but spiritual at the same time, free and also necessary, absolute in itself and also, within itself, pointing beyond itself" (414–15). Kierkegaard does not use the word "sacramentality," but he does emphasize that matrimony carries its telos within itself. It is because of this that there is no point in asking what the point of matrimony is. Belonging in matrimonial communion is neither a question to be answered nor an answer to anyone's question. To insist upon asking "Why matrimony?" is to reduce matrimony with its character of the eternal to "rational calculation," which is always and irredeemably temporal (397). To ask "why" of matrimonial communion is to instrumentalize, to engage in finiteness, to weigh up the pros and the cons, to miss radically the sacramental bond and order of the cosmos that is already present in the inner life of matrimony. "For marriage there is only marriage's own 'why,' but that is infinite. . . . [If] someone could unite all finite 'whys' at the beginning of his marriage, he would be the basest of husbands just for that reason" (415). The "why" of matrimony is the "why" of the cosmos. The decision to marry is a free choice, but one that discovers its meaning in that which is more primordial than the autonomy of choice. The decision to stitch one's life to another is also to consent to live in a state of heightened belonging where the most intimate movement of the cosmos—which has already moved the lovers from love's first stirrings to its consummation in matrimonial communion—moves their matrimony in the direction of the consummation of the cosmos itself. The choice to marry is genuinely an autonomous free choice, but in the choice, the spouses live in the tension toward the eschaton that draws them matrimonially into the finality of the cosmos itself. The hidden life of matrimony is an intimacy that flows with a cosmological exigency.

The matrimonial communion lives by the uniqueness of its consummation: it is already the consummation of the communion of spouses that is renewed and affirmed over the course of a lifetime; but the communion, participating in the cosmos, also joins the cosmos in straining toward the perfection and culmination of all things in the transcendent-divine ground. The affirmation of matrimonial love in the choice to marry is the affirmation of a sacramental life, but also of the sacramentality of existence in general. The richness of matrimony is its sanctification of life and death under the conditions of the cosmos, and that sanctity is luminous with cosmological presence that moves with finality within it. The cosmological horizon that joins the perishing to the everlasting is the tension of the metaxy. Matrimony lives this unitive embrace and manifests itself as the image of sacramental belonging or the sign of contradiction to a world that has largely accommodated itself to a *saeculum* of loneliness and alienation.

Matrimonial Consummation as Generative

Take away love, Kierkegaard writes, "and a shared life is either just a satisfaction of sensual desire or an association, a partnership in the interests of some goal" (399). We marry because we already love, but it is possible to discern in advance some probable and desirable outcomes of matrimony, none of which by themselves or together—in separation from love—could convert an enterprise association into a communion. Such outcomes are not reasons for matrimony; they are not a telos in an antecedent sense that drives matrimony toward its subsequent perfection. Kierkegaard's B proceeds to list three commonly supposed reasons "why" someone might marry. The first reason is that "marriage is a school for character; one marries in order to elevate and improve one's character" (399). The second is that one marries "to have children, to make one's humble contribution to the propagation of the human race upon earth" (417). Third, "one marries to acquire a home" (423). Each of these three reasons is a consequentialist approach to matrimony, but the problem is that matrimony cannot ever be approached, simply because, as a communion of love, matrimony has already arrived in the authenticity of first love in the lovers, sensually unfolding with an intensity from an embryonic state in the direction of perfection. Love alone is the infinite "why" of communion. We love, and by the consummation of love, we have entered communion with our spouse and with the cosmos for the sake of love's finality.

Kierkegaard's B is right to consider each discrete "reason to marry" as insufficient because to marry for the purposes of achieving a better character, children, or a home *apart from love* is to consider character, children, and home wrongly. Each of these is more properly a manifestation of the consummation of the matrimonial communion in its sensual and spiritual fecundity, which is always a fecundity of love grounded in the metaxy that joins two persons. To think of character, children, a home, or anything else as a reason for matrimony is to separate them from what anchors, sustains, and gives meaning to them. It is a bland point, but not everyone who marries will gain a better character; conceive, bear, and raise children; or establish a home. (Nor, for that matter, is matrimony necessary for the mere generation of any of them.) That is, character, children, and home are not ends that retroactively justify their means. The "why" of matrimonial communion is not one that emerges post hoc from a subsequently more virtuous character, is not drawn from the existence of the children who eventually came along, is not granted by the stateliness, tranquility, or otherwise of the home acquired. Still, if these nonetheless remain as possible outcomes of the fecundity of matrimony, it is only because of the prior matrimonial communion of which they are not simply effects in some causal sense, but are witnesses. What they are—character, children, home—they are in continuity with the communion in which their existence is rooted. They testify, by their existence, to the communion that was always more than the spouses themselves. The love by which the communion is consummated is the love that continues to move the communion into a myriad of sacramental expressions, among which we may indeed find character, children, and the home.

To claim that children are consequences, by-products, or effects is to fall short of properly recognizing their generation, existence, and emergence within the matrimonial communion, which is a sacramental microcosmos. If the mistake of scientism is to think that the natural sciences can account for all that the human person is, so too is the mistake that presumes that the meaning of procreation within the matrimonial communion has no more than a merely physical, chemical, or biological basis, a meaning separated from the sacramentality of the communion. By way of consciousness and the flesh, the meaning of procreation must certainly include generation among the physical, chemical, and biological manifolds of reality, but extends to the intellectual and spiritual height of the human-divine encounter in the cosmos.

Even procreation per se cannot be discussed properly on its own terms, because the terms of procreation are more properly the terms of the sacramental consummation by which matrimonial communion is renewed. Procreation can only be weighed in the context of love's tension by which the spouses already belong to one another and by which they belong in communion to a cosmological richness that unites them by erupting within them as love, the consummating *energeia*, but that remains forever more than each of them. Procreation signifies the silence of the deepest givenness and mysterious reception in the open heart of matrimonial existence. What is given and received on the one hand is each spouse to the other, the mutual promise of each spouse's consciousness and flesh to the other, today and for a lifetime. On other hand, what is given and received is also the infinite fertility and abyss of mystery in and of the cosmos. Through the sensuality and sacramentality of matrimonial consummation, the matrimonial communion mediates cosmological infinity to the world. To a "modernist" world that knows only the mechanics of scientific and technological progress, matrimony acts as a reminder of what has been filtered out by attesting to the primordial mystery of new life and the renewal of life; to a "postmodernist" world that seems to focus on power dynamics and social construction, matrimony radiates the sacramentality of self-sacrificial love that may have been forgotten. While "procreation" is the name for the begetting of the child, the child is begotten in the communion whose consummation was never merely a moment in time, never merely a biological act, but was the moment that—as Kierkegaard might say—impossibly captured eternity. The matrimonial consummation is what immerses the communion in the eternal and now procreates, of the eternal, the new life of the child.

If the meaning of procreation is to be found within the meaning of matrimony, then it is significant to note Kierkegaard's claim that "the proper light" in which to view marriage is Christianity (398). For Kierkegaard, the meaning of matrimony is embedded within the larger scope of the meaning of communion in Christianity. What Kierkegaard discerned as the "character of the eternal" in marriage was the eternal as grasped in Christian experience and symbolization. The eternal then is characterized as the Trinitarian communion, and the Trinitarian communion is the divine ground of the cosmos. It is most deeply symbolized as a *communitas* whose love is consummated in absolute perfection and absolute completion among three divine persons.[21] Love and communion in Christianity unavoidably pivot back and forth between persons human and persons divine. Matrimonial communion, with the uniqueness of its consummation, is a participation in the pivoting simply because communion is already a life of sacramental attunement to the interpersonal and cosmological bond and order of love. The cosmos exists-from the fecundity of divine persons in communion, yet exists-toward an eschatological order of perfection in that Trinitarian ground. In Christianity, matrimonial communion is a mirror of the divine communion because, consummated in a moment of love for the sake of a life of love, the giving and receiving of spouses reach out for nothing less than the sacredness of the perfection and completion of the other, whether they acknowledge this or not. Like God, the spouses have already given themselves away in love.

Matrimony is worth discussing because, as a familiar form of belonging, it serves to exemplify why belonging in communion is sacramental. The two spouses grow together in time. In time, they grow older and frailer. Their communion was always more than an interrelationality because they confronted the good of existence together, and through their sheer ordinariness from day to day and year to year, they have tackled the vicissitudes of living the lasting and passing of the cosmos. They delight and they grieve with each other, and they bear the weight of the years with one another. Their communion deepened its structures into the structure of the cosmos by way of a consummation at once primordial in its sensuality and sacramentality. What else but matrimony is worthy of the spouses? What else, but the cosmos itself? Indeed, matrimony recovers the meaning of time by consecrating the time of the spouses to the eternity that has erupted in between them. Of the spouse, Kierkegaard writes that "eternity is something that he has had in time, preserved in time. Only he, therefore, has triumphed over time. . . . As a true victor, the husband has not killed time but saved and preserved it in eternity" (463). As a mirror of the cosmos, matrimony recovers an eternal bond and an order of lasting in the midst of the passing world that, in the end, must perish too with the spouses. Matrimony presents itself as a visible sign of the Solonic "unseen measure."[22] This is why matrimony is both a consolation to a perishing world and a visible sign of the cosmos whose transcendent-divine ground of Trinitarian communion does not perish. Antoine de St. Exupéry writes that "experience shows us that to love is not simply to look at one another, but to look together in the same direction."[23] Those in communion—spouses, friends, communities—are looking together in the same direction, but what matrimony teaches us is that what they look at was, in some deeper sense, always looking upon them. This is the matrimonial sacramentality and heightening of communion.

SACRAMENTALITY IN POLITICS AND HISTORY

It is obvious that the consummation of matrimonial communion is an intimate act, but not every communion is consummated in intimacy. The sacramentality of existence permeates all belonging. Playing with metaphors derived from vertical and horizontal planes, we can say that if matrimony is a sacramental heightening of an intimate communion between two spouses, then the widest conceivable communion involves us in considering the structure of sacramentality in the belonging proper to politics and history. Politics and history are not obviously sacramental in the way that matrimony is, but since they are constituted by *communitas*, there is communion; and every communion strains toward its consummation. This study has considered presence and *communitas* in the context of ordinary living and belonging, which nonetheless participates in the finality of the cosmos. What then do politics and history have to do with sacramentality? A better question might be, From what viewpoint do we recognize politics and history as sacramental? Politics and history evince that more universal viewpoint, and it is this that enables the widening of our belonging to include what we can call universal humanity. It is in universal humanity that we seek the sacramental.

Politics as Sacramentality

On the pragmatic level of action, politics can refer to the coordination and machinery of governance in service of the goods by which the *communitas* flourishes; on the symbolic level, politics is an attunement—to a greater or lesser degree of transparency—to the cosmos as a dimension of the meaning of the *communitas*. "Every society," Voegelin writes, "has to cope with the problems of its pragmatic existence and, at the same time, it is concerned with the truth of its order."[24] Recounting the pragmatic action of any society in the historiographic record calls forth the meaning of its history. The history of any particular *communitas* is concerned with the meaning of its constituting communion.

Voegelin discusses the continuity of political representation of cosmological or transcendent order from the earliest historiographic record to the present. From the evidence of the earliest documentation, he writes that "all the early empires, Near Eastern as well as Far Eastern, understood themselves as representatives of a transcendent order, of the order of the cosmos; and some of them even understood this order as a 'truth.'"[25] Voegelin quotes the Behistun Inscription, which records the feats of Darius I, whose victories are representatively the victories of the god Ahuramazda. He also quotes a letter from Kuyuk Khan to Pope Innocent IV in response to an earlier letter from the pope.

By the virtue of God,
From the rising of the sun to its setting,
All realms have been granted to us.
Without the Order of God
How could anyone do anything? . . .
And if you do not observe the Order of God,
And disobey our orders,
We shall know you to be our enemies.[26]

The problem with political representation of transcendent reality, according to David Walsh, is that "by naming the transcendent, human language and especially public language already renders it as something immanent." He adds that "the failure of all political theologies is that they inevitably render the divine as a figure within the partisan conflicts of the day. God is hardly God when he becomes the deity of a particular people or party."[27] For this reason, we acknowledge that, in the environment differentiated by Christianity, where things owed to Caesar are administered separately from the things owed to God, political projects that aim at representing transcendent reality are necessarily a failure, just as religious projects that aim at representing a mundane political order fail too.

However, this does not imply the conclusion that the realm of the political is devoid of transcendent meaning. While the epochal differentiation of political from religious results in the circumscription of political authority to its own proper remit and the religious to its own, the differentiation is more deeply centered upon, and takes account of, the human person who exists in between things political and things religious. To the extent that politics attends to the predicament of suffering and flourishing of the persons and communities over whom it has proper authority, it is concerned with what transcends it, because persons and communities are themselves more than merely political. (Similarly, to the extent that religion attends to the same predicament, it has to be concerned with pragmatic socio-political conditions that fall outside its zone of authority.) For example, a political emphasis upon the inexhaustible worth of each person is an opening of politics to a dignity that extends further than the judgment of the politician.[28] Walsh notes that "no higher aspiration prevails in the contemporary world than to create a political order that is derived from and ordered towards the preservation of individual dignity and respect."[29]

The apparent weakness of the *liberal* political order, Walsh argues, derives not simply from its divestment of any orthodox religious or ideological purpose but also from its fragmentary character as a collection of embedded abbreviations of a deeper knowledge about human reality in the cosmos that it cannot find the language to articulate coherently. Liberal political order appears as incoherence, turbulence, and philosophic feebleness, unable to explain itself; but these are the surface-level phenomena that conceal the ocean current of meaning from which they arise. The practice of liberal politics, rather than the theory of liberal politics, marks the sacramental nature of a genuine politics. Only on the surface of liberal order is the spectacle of debate, partisan division, and squabbling. In the depth, however, is found the swell of concern for the person and *communitas* of persons that reveals the meaning of liberal politics. Liberalism's very shortcomings act as an invitation to persons and communities to enter the political depth for the more-than-political meaning that sustains the practice of liberalism. The liberal invocation of rights, for example, abbreviates the need for human autonomy and freedom in practice, and therefore, rights resonate with the deepest reverence for the transcendent dignity of the person and *communitas* of persons in communion. Other abbreviations include the "rule of law" or "democracy," both of which act as compressions of the full life of responsibility and autonomy, consonant with a philosophical anthropology of human dignity that has been developed over millennia. Liberalism is politics that moves by the abbreviation of this range of meaning that radiates from an anthropology of human dignity, folded down into categories that authorize political action in the present. "Liberal principles emerge . . . as the residue of resonances that remain of the Christian evocation of the transcendent finality of the person" (34).

Walsh continues, "The rightness of a moral and political language in which the inexhaustible worth of the person is placed at the center still lives from a sense of the movement of participation in the life of God" (34). In making persons the central focus of its concern, liberal political order ministers to what is sacred. Walsh rhetorically asks, What, after all, is more valuable than a human being? We call movements that aim at establishing a final order of truth by way of intimidation, violence, and piles of corpses failures because we are already convinced that we move within the larger insight that there is nothing more valuable than a human being. Dehumanizing human beings in the name of religion, progress, or some other deity is utterly unjustifiable when our fundamental political orientation emerges from and is directed toward the flourishing of the person. Indeed, any political order becomes sacramental in its explicit service of the person and *communitas*. Walsh writes, "Without the Christian illumination of the transcendent worth of each human being, it would be impossible to conceive the inexhaustible dignity of each individual" (37). Liberalism does not become Christianity by another name, but only makes sense if the transcendent value of the person illuminated by Christian experience constitutes the depth in which it moves. The problem, the source of the suspicion of liberal vacuousness and weakness, is that a public language of abbreviations does not, of itself, have the capacity to make the link between its practice and its underlying sacramentality, centered in the measureless dignity of the person. The liberal political order is plagued by its own theoretical ambivalence. It is a politics, not a philosophy and certainly not a religion; but it is also a wisdom tradition in its own right. The liberal is the one who has received the invitation to authenticate the deeper intuitions of transcendent value embedded in the compressed language of liberalism, but embodied in persons and fully decompressed in the concrete belonging of *communitas*. The liberal is the one who can practice service of the common good, who has grasped that all deserve to flourish by virtue of their very humanity, and who has glimpsed the value of that humanity in each person without exception.

A sacramental dimension of political order is precisely what cannot be articulated politically, and this incapacity renders political sacramentality vulnerable. Not everyone is prepared to look into the depth out of which sacramentality comes. Walsh points out that "liberal ideology" is what is always on hand to threaten liberalism's sacramental order of persons. Liberal ideology effectively abstracts an order of liberty from an order of sacredness grounded in persons. In the case of Abraham Lincoln and the abolition of slavery, the rights of property owners and the self-determination of states were liberty claims conspicuously framed in liberal language. Ideology bowdlerizes liberal language by deliberately narrowing its horizon of meaning from an autonomy nested in cosmological presence to an autonomy bounded only perhaps by a measure of consent among peers. Slaveholders who argued on liberal terms for the legal nonrecognition of personhood of some humans seemed to demonstrate the inconsistency, emptiness, and ease of manipulation of the liberal order. However, "whatever rags of justification might be invoked under property and choice, the liberty claim of slaveowners could not withstand the implication that they undermined the whole possibility of an order of rights. Preservation even of the right of popular liberty cannot be sustained when the choice extends to the derogation of the right to liberty" (44–45). Walsh writes that Lincoln did not take recourse to the Bible or natural law in his public statements, but re-presented the liberal foundations of the American republic in a more evocative, more authentic way. "Even when the abuse of human beings is relatively confined, the damage caused is universal since the abrogation of humanity in one instance eliminates the basis for opposing its extension to all others" (45). If the sacramentality of liberal political order is luminously centered in its treatment of the human person as qualitatively beyond the metrics of cost-benefit calculations, then its ideological corruption is surely arbitrariness about who is entitled to the full protection of the law from such calculations.

If ideology could create a useful category of nonperson human that legally underpinned the particular practice of slavery, then it would remain a corruption generally available at all times within the arc of liberal meaning. The unborn and the trafficked; the elderly, infirm, and severely disabled; the racial, ethnic, sexual, or religious Other are often subject, in the name of liberalism, to treatment that begins with the illiberal assumption of their nonpersonhood. The greatest test of a properly political sacramentality in liberalism surely requires confronting and reversing the assumption of nonpersonhood among any human group, securing their existence and responding to all that the vulnerability of their personhood asks of us. The sacramentality of existence and belonging is at stake in every instance. Commitment to serve the goods of personhood is how a liberal communion is consummated again and again.

Walsh points out that the liberal invocation of rights results in a "growth of the soul." The pragmatism of politics may see to the fixing of potholes in the roads and to the building of bridges and tunnels, or to the reconciliation of conflicting interests, but by far the greatest outcome of a liberal order is its provision for the inner enlargement of the person, which cannot remain merely a private affair since the growth of the soul manifests itself throughout a lifetime of choices. "It puts the individual participant in touch with the most real dimension of reality, providing an indubitable sense of contact with what is most enduring" (46). It is not hard to see that politics does not have to become a theology nor proceed by religious precepts in order to serve the sacred when what is sacred is the life and belonging of persons and their *communitas*. As Walsh writes, "The best that can be done from a political perspective is to point silently toward that about which our mundane discourse can say nothing. In this way the liberal reverence for the inviolable dignity of the person preserves intact and conveys more powerfully the sense of awe before the mystery by which we are held" (50).

History and Universal Humanity

Every politics is historical. History, like personhood and *communitas*, is a structure of human existence and belonging. As I shift my final focus to historicity, I must ask how history has a role to play in sacramentality. Still following Walsh, history is present in every human person and *communitas* in every moment. "History itself hangs in the balance of every human action. There is no need to wait for an apocalypse at the end of time for time has reached its culmination in every human action. The revelation of what *is* is being proclaimed in every instant."[30] The eschatological consummation of the cosmos is already what is present in some prefigured sense in the lives of persons and communities. Thinkers such as the medieval Joachim of Fiore and Karl Marx have sought the meaning of history *in* history. By a critical analysis of historical material, they went in search of the inner meaning of history. Such searches are doomed to success. As Joachim could decode the Old and New Testaments for the secret knowledge that would reveal him as the prophet of the third and final age, so too could Marx announce communism as the solution to the riddle of history.[31] However, the apocalypse of history or of the cosmos is what cannot happen in time since it is an apocalypse of time. The final consummation of all things, if it is thought to have a location, can only happen in God. History does not reveal a secret redemptive code within its structures, but rather strains for what surpasses it.

So what then is history? Negatively, history is not historiography. Whereas historiography is the record of memory, history is the very possibility of memory itself. As Walsh puts it, "Motives, incentives, interests may be the stuff of history, the warp and woof of its fabric, but they are not the cloth itself. That is visible only from outside of it."[32] Positively, "History is the history of what in every instant exceeds history."[33] Since human existence is participation in and belonging to the limitlessness of the cosmos, history is the story of immanent human action set against the intersecting, heuristic dimension of transcendent meaning. History comprehends the finite in its setting against the backdrop of the infinite. The struggles of a marriage, the quarrels among friends and families, the inflamed group passions in politics and sects, the international conflagrations of violence: these are the transactions of history in which the common bond of humanity among persons and communities is loosened or tightened. Working through the scale from fractious to harmonious, history is the story of humanity's presence to itself in the cosmos as persons and communities, oscillating between the particular and the universal, between beholding and turning away from that which beholds all. The hard-bitten cynicism of the academic historian is not enough to deprive historiographic details of the memory, the anamnetic retrieval, of cosmological presence that makes the details of historiography possible. History is the very possibility of *anamnesis* because "history is the possibility of persons. In their existence they already live beyond themselves; they are never simply present in what they say or do."[34] Persons are present to each other, but never fully present since the deepest intimations of their souls and the truth of their existence and belonging remain hidden and largely undocumentable; yet the traces of these intimations and this truth can be glimpsed within the (very much present) words and actions chosen and documentable in the historiographic record. Historical existence involves the recovery or loss of what sustains us in our belonging together in the cosmos of lasting and passing, the truth that was present from the beginning but must be continually realized.

Prior to the epochal differentiation of consciousness, discussed in chapter 3, mythic and pretheoretical thinkers expressed personhood, humanity, nature, and divinity—the cosmological communion of primordial partners—in symbols well suited to intracosmic existence and belonging.[35] However, the opening of the cosmos to its own transcendence and immanence through the differentiation of consciousness yields three principle categories that we, with Eric Voegelin, can name as universal humanity, universal world, and universal divinity. These correlate with differentiated consciousness, immanence, and transcendence respectively. First, universal humanity is the discovery that eventually results from elevating consciousness or the soul to attention and theoretical comprehension. The differentiation of consciousness is the central event that marks the epiphany of specifically human being from the underlying common matrix of the cosmos. The differentiation of the cosmos clarifies the consubstantiality of all things, revealing the existence of the human being in its bond and order: autonomous existence, relationality to other persons and nonpersons, and immediacy under the transcendent-divine mystery we call God. According to Voegelin, "Humanity means man in a mode of understanding himself in his relation to God, world and society, and these modes change. And history would be the drama (if a meaning in it can be discovered) of humanity, of the self-understanding of man."[36] History emerges from the differentiation of consciousness as the ongoing drama of humanity enacting the possibilities of its own belonging in the context of the cosmos. History and myth play equivalent roles as memory that recalls the ultimate conditions of existence, but history diverges from myth in its breakthrough from a particular cosmological society to a universal humanity.

Second, if the differentiation of consciousness led to the discovery of itself as soul or consciousness, then it was a discovery that emerged parallel with the discovery of universal divinity. Voegelin writes of differentiation that it was a process that concentrated the intracosmic divinities into a world-transcendent divinity. As a result, "there is only one divinity, the one world-transcendent divinity, to be found nowhere within the world. Thus, you have an idea of universal divinity corresponding to the universality of man."[37]

Third, along with universal humanity and universal divinity, there arises a universal world, a common world structured by a universality of intelligibility. "You get the three as a unit or you get nothing at all. If you surrender one or the other, that whole system, or this whole apparatus of ideas which is inherent in the exegesis of such an experience, will collapse."[38] Together, this threefold, differentiated emergence is the discovery of history as a structure of human existence. This emergence in experience, developed as a mutuality of universal categories, is played out as the stuff of history. Necessarily implicit within any notion of universal humanity at play in history are universal divinity and universal world.

As Herder argued, every political society is a particular representative of this wider, universal humanity within which it has its place and time. The struggle to secure the political goods that sustain the communion of the particular *communitas* is the work of political order, which, as we have seen, bears within itself tendencies toward serving its own particularity as a unique political *communitas* and the *Humanität* that is universal and present within it. The drama between the particular and the universal, according to Voegelin, "is the very substance of history; and in so far as advances toward the truth are achieved by the societies indeed as they succeed one another in time, the single society transcends itself and becomes a partner in the common endeavor of mankind."[39] A humanity of persons and communities is also a universal humanity whose history can only be told in the context of the whole of the cosmos, since a universal humanity only arises in tandem with a universal world and a universal divine ground. I suggest that universal humanity is genuinely a communion, but it is a communion consummated only in history.

That is, universal humanity is brought into communion not as a worldwide political *communitas* but as a dimension of universality implicit in the political existence of every *communitas* in time. *Communitas* is a communion consummated in facing together, in a shoulder-to-shoulder stance, the universal divinity of God, who faces us. The consummating historical realization is that a universal divinity faces every person in every *communitas*. The universal divine ground is the protean and foundational good of being that first brought each *communitas* into existence as a communion and draws them toward an ever-fuller realization of themselves as both a particular and a universal people. We learn to belong in the particular by putting down our roots, affirmatively existing-from and -toward what is given to us and achieved by us, and it is *through* the affirmation of the particular that we reach toward the universal in each of its three extensions. It is the universality of humanity, divinity, and world that is affirmed in the affirmation of belonging in the particular, because universality is a dimension of meaning, equivalent to cosmological presence, that abides in the particular political goods that bring us into communion. This, I suggested, was Herder's insight, symbolized as *Humanität*. Belonging in the particular is how we exist historically, because historical existence is the concretizing of the universal through the particularity of persons in *communitas*. A universal humanity of particular persons and communities exists in the metaxy as a tension in between what is finite and perishing on the one hand and what is infinite and enduring on the other, and history is surely the drama of belonging in this essentially human-divine intersection.

In belonging, not only is the truth of historical existence achieved, but in belonging is the historical existence of truth lived. Voegelin catches this nicely when he writes, "Hence, the play of order is always enacted, not before the future but before God; the order of human existence is in the present under God even at the times when the consciousness of that present has not yet disengaged itself from the compactness of the myth. . . . The millenniums in which the mystery of history has reached the level of consciousness have not diminished the distance from its eternity."[40] History, I conclude, is a story of the sacramental belonging of one humanity in between one world and one God. It is the story that supersedes the myth, but like the myth, it is a remembering of the dynamic, permeating, and sacramental presence that gathers us all into the communion of a common *Humanität*.

THE TASK IN THIS CHAPTER was to think about sacramentality. I needed to conclude the book with this because the persons and communities whom we belong to and those who belong to us originate a value that we experience as nothing less than sacred. A communion among persons lies at the heart of every *communitas*: family, civil society and the city, the people, universal humanity. That very communion is already a sacred bond and order for those in communion, but what every communion reaches out for is its own consummation or completion. I attempted to show this by considering the sacrament of the Eucharist as an exemplar of a sacred communion and its necessary consummation. Grasping the meaning of consummating a communion, it turned out, was no simple affair. On the one hand, a communion exists by its having already been consummated. On the other hand, every communion is sustained by its straining toward its own consummation. In this case, there is a perfection that has not yet been finally attained, even if it has been imperfectly prefigured. The difficulty is that "consummation" is a multivalent term that captures the somewhat paradoxical tensions that are the life of communion. Furthermore, a consummation is what Aristotle understood by variously employing *telos*, *entelecheia*, and *energeia*. However, to this I added the recognition that the end for which the communion exists is also a quality of perfection, a value beyond measure synonymous with sacredness. The ambiguity to contend with is that a consummation is both present and not yet present in the communion of every *communitas*. Each *communitas* holds its own perfection within itself, a sacredness by which it anticipates its own perfection.

Clearly, the line of thought was entering a thicket of meanings through which there was no clear path. Fortunately, matrimony provided an example of a familiar communion in our midst whose intimate consummation is hidden from view but whose *communitas* is a public witness to sacramental belonging. Kierkegaard's account was the perfect complement, treating as it does the unity and fecundity of matrimonial communion and uncovering it as occupying an in-betweenness of time and eternity.

Politics, history, and universal humanity were the themes toward the end because matrimonial belonging manifests a sacramentality that is conferred by spouses in the seclusion of their conjugal union. The task was to show that sacramentality is also present even in the least intimate and most broad of communions and bears upon the belonging of all human beings at all times. The general sacramentality of belonging can be experienced in any communion. Politics and history, for all their troubles, are more substantively the achievements of belonging among persons in *communitas* whose consummation is the realization of the presence of, and the participation in, universal humanity.

Epilogue

Unbelonging: The Refusal of Presence and Communion

The study is at an end. The topic of belonging, however, remains, and inexhaustibly so.

An epilogue functions as an addendum, most often a conclusion. I ask the reader to consider this epilogue as a supplement, and not as a denouement. All along, I have characterized this study as a moving viewpoint. I found that I had to spiral back over previously discussed topics in order to bring out what was not ready to be exposed in the earlier discussion. My concern throughout has been the presence and communion involved in belonging, and only indirectly have I addressed the negation or refusal of these. Here, I briefly consider the meaning of alienation from the viewpoint of chapter 8. In chapter 2, I had referred to alienation as homelessness. I briefly return to it to calibrate those earlier comments to the later horizon of meaning. I will set out in summary form how the term "alienation" was originally used, before proceeding to make the distinction that I think is necessary: there is alienation as *not-belonging*, discussed in chapter 2, and there is alienation as *unbelonging*. This is no trivial distinction. While I regard the former as an occasional outcome of the tension of belonging itself, the latter I hold to be a nihilistic repudiation of belonging *tout court*.

The Differentiation of Alienation and the Case of Marx

Existence-from and existence-toward are the useful phenomenological structures for providing a simple hermeneutic of belonging, a

265

hermeneutic that now clarifies the distinction between the alienation of not-belonging and the alienation of unbelonging. Belonging is the in-between tension of finding oneself both, on the one hand, *existing-from* a person, a *communitas*, a place, a time, and crucially, the cosmos itself, and on the other, also *existing-toward* these in bonds of affection. If we would belong, we must become cognizant of how persons and nonpersons affectively, intelligibly, and spiritually live within us, holding us, not letting us go, and constituting who we are; but we must also care, and in doing so, choose to cultivate the vitality of our relations. When we live in the tension between whom or what we exist-from and whom or what we exist-toward, we belong. However, as discussed in chapter 2, belonging is also dynamic. Neither of these two structures of belonging is frozen; they are both always in play. Persons can fall in and out of love, gain and lose friends, move houses, work in different cities, states, continents, and so on. In the course of our lives, very little stays the same. There are times when we know we belong, and there are times when we are acutely aware that we don't. When we don't belong, we are—in some figurative sense—homeless. We find ourselves alienated.

Unlike belonging, "alienation" has been a well-considered and explicit theme in philosophy and across the humanities, arts, and social sciences because exclusion and exile are problems; conspicuous, painful, and sometimes endemic problems. Richard Schacht's study on alienation locates Hegel's *Phenomenology of Spirit* as its point of entry into philosophical discourse. Schacht writes, "An examination of the uses of 'alienation' and *Entfremdung* in philosophy and theology prior to Hegel's use of the latter in his *Phenomenology of Spirit* will show that he was the first to use the term systematically in anything like the special ways in which it is used today."[1] In introducing alienation as a philosophical problem, Hegel has bequeathed to posterity a twofold meaning. "At times [Hegel] uses it to refer to a separation or discordant relation, such as might obtain between the individual and the social substance, or (as 'self-alienation') between one's actual condition and the essential nature. . . . He also uses it to refer to a surrender or sacrifice of particularity and willfulness in connection with the overcoming of alienation and the reattainment of unity."[2] Karl Marx gave the term a wider, more practical currency. In his *Economic and Philosophic Manuscripts of 1844*, in the course of discussing estranged labor in the working conditions of the time, Marx speaks of alienation as an all-encompassing estrangement: self-estrangement, estrangement from the fruit of one's labors, estrangement from others, and estrangement from nature.[3] Alienation is clearly one of the most dehumanizing experiences. It is a problem that cries out for a remedy. I add nothing here to the corpus of extant works on the theme except to ask why it is that alienation is dehumanizing. I suggested in chapter 2 that the experience of alienation can only assert itself qua problem if there is originally a will to belong. In this sense, alienation points up belonging as an absence, analogous to Augustine's example of blindness as a privation, the evil that functions as an indicator of sight as the original good that is missing. Alienation here is the discovery or acknowledgment that we don't belong. Belonging is the good that we are prevented from having. We find that our state of alienation is not unlike a state of limbo, as discussed in chapter 2. Marx's prolific writings remain a rich source for understanding the possibilities inherent in a state of alienation. On the basis of this study, one finds that he has used the term in two contrasting ways. The most common characteristic of alienation is a sense of disturbance and of being haunted by the lack of what is proper or by the absence of a fit. This is not-belonging. Not-belonging is a state of being at odds with oneself and the world. To be alienated involves experiencing and knowing what one is alienated from and, to some degree, caring that one is alienated. Alienation as not-belonging is haunted by the fit that it isn't. One finds oneself as a misfit, lacking one or both of the structures of belonging. As Linn Miller put it, one finds oneself in a troubling "misrelation." In not-belonging, one is ultimately out of kilter with the cosmos and its primordial communion of partners, an anxiety that reaches into the soul. The communion of cosmological partners, we recall, involves the person in relations with oneself, with others, with the natural world, and with the transcendent-divine mystery. In not-belonging, the communion yearned for remains unconsummated, and those relations, which are constitutive of personhood, are unsettled, in motion, or in confusion. In excommunication, one remains outside the *communitas*. Marx's diagnosis of alienation as not-belonging remains a key insight. Alienation is a homelessness defined entirely by the home from which we are sundered or separated but for which we long. It is a homelessness that can arise only in tension with the original home.

However, there is another meaning of alienation at work in Marx's writings. Where not-belonging is the problem to be remedied by belonging, where limbo and excommunication can be overcome by being guided homeward, Marx eschews such "homely" remedies as contributing to the problem. His remedy suggests a new category: unbelonging. Unbelonging does not solve the problem of not-belonging by reconciliation and by beginning to belong but departs entirely from the tension of belonging. While Marx advocates for a situation—inevitably postrevolution—in which all the alienating and dehumanizing conditions of the workplace have been flattened, the way toward this situation involves not a reform or "renovation" (Burke) of those conditions but an "innovation." Home in the broadest sense of *communitas* is to be innovated in the revolution.

Marx presents an interesting case. On the one hand, his comments on alienation as not-belonging are evocative and move within the sacramentality of a universal humanity. (Who, after all, is not moved by the sufferings of the oppressed in our world? For the sake of a genuinely better, more equitable world, do we not wish to reconcile workers and the oppressed to themselves, to others, and to nature?) On the other hand, Marx's writings express an urgent and even apocalyptic spirit furiously at work to overturn the historical *communitas* that has resulted in bourgeois capitalism and politics. Burke recognized that innovation goes far beyond the adjustments and dialogues of reform. For Marx, only revolutionary consciousness can truly bring forth a final overcoming of alienation, and the work of the revolution will be successful only if it ushers in a postalienated realm of peace and freedom. This realm of freedom is the image of a consciousness transformed whose innovated "home" is the telos that gives direction to the revolution in the present and gives to the revolution itself the unconsummating *energeia*. The riddle of history with its complicated dialectic of ongoing oppression has been solved in principle. The communist solution will attend to both the realm of necessity (bodily needs) and the realm of freedom, and the terrestrial paradise will unfold where the state withers away. The communist will thus no longer live in history, but beyond history.

Clearly, there is more to alienation in Marx's thought than overcoming the estrangement of not-belonging. Nothing short of a transformation of human consciousness is necessary. Once human consciousness has been transformed, Marx expects that alienation will be overcome. "Both for the production on a mass scale of this communist consciousness, and for the success of the cause itself, the alteration of men on a mass scale is necessary, an alteration which can only take place in a practical movement, a *revolution*; this *revolution* is necessary, therefore . . . because the class overthrowing the [ruling] class can only in a revolution succeed in ridding itself of all the muck of ages and become fitted to found society anew."[4] Marx's writings, then, move precipitously at the edge of not-belonging's estrangement and unbelonging's innovative annihilation. For the sake of innovation and the realm of freedom, the revolution will need to be directed by a vanguard enterprise association to pull apart the civil association of the existing historical *communitas*. From our present perspective, we know that vanguard dictatorships of the proletariat do not easily relinquish the powers of the state. We also know that any program whose revolutionary violence aims to tear down all the old filth of history does not so much solve history's problems as destroy the lives of those persons and communities whose existence constitutes history. In the bloodlust of revolutionary consciousness, Marx's diagnosis of not-belonging does not result in belonging, but in vast unbelonging, where every *communitas* it touches has disintegrated or has been destroyed.

Marx is merely a single example. From Lenin and Stalin, through Mao, Pol Pot, the Kim dynasty, Fidel Castro, and others to Hitler, Mussolini, Franco, Pinochet, and so forth, the violence and murder of unbelonging is a desecration of the sacred. The sacramentality of belonging, I have concluded, is the consummation of a communion of persons. If social remedies for social problems do not penetrate to the level of persons, then the exercise of power can amount to the refusal of presence and the repudiation of communion. A sense of the sacred is an affirmation of belonging. It is the luminosity that calls for justice and ongoing renovation in order to resolve problems of alienated estrangement as not-belonging. There is no necessary connection between not-belonging and the unbelonging of revolutionary consciousness that knows only the manipulation of reality on a social level, hypostatized from persons. The required transfigurative violence of the revolution proceeds toward its goal not by reform or argument but by trampling on holy ground in the mass murder of persons. In *anamnesis*, we recall that only in persons is there a cosmos, a history, humanity; and only among persons can there be belonging and sacramentality. The method of ideological violence results in more than a "decosmicization" of belonging; it leads to the nihilism of unbelonging, which is measured in corpses and where persons and the *communitas* are uprooted, ungrounded, shorn of an encompassing cosmos, rendered malleable for ideological ends, and disposed of as so much waste. When we have lost a sense of the sacred, we have lost our concern for belonging.

Unbelonging and Loss of the Sacred

In chapter 7, I emphasized that order is the first and fundamental political good, from which all other political goods stream. Order generates and sustains a bond, and a bond generates and sustains order; disorder not only reverses order but undoes or prevents the bond of communion. Eric Voegelin tells us that if we would understand disorder in our day, we must consider it a work of undoing. That is, we must look at the civilizational substance that is being undone. Western civilizational order was differentiated by many developments, but most substantially by the sacramentality of Christian *communitas*, and so it is that within the arc of Christian meaning that formed a medieval Christendom and informed the cultures of the West we can gain insight into the meaning of order as it has unfolded historically. Inversely, it is within the same arc of meaning that we will gain insight into the meaning of disorder and unbelonging.

In the most general terms, Voegelin writes that what Christianity contributes to a civilizational bond and order is both (a) a notion of consummation as a final state of transcendent perfection and (b) a sacramental value that gives purpose to human life in this world as a movement toward that perfection. In other words, a telos and a "pilgrim progress."[5] However, Voegelin also reminds us, "the bond [of Christian faith] is tenuous, indeed, and it may snap easily. The life of the soul in openness toward God, the waiting, the periods of aridity and dullness, guilt and despondency, contrition and repentance, forsakenness and hope against hope, the silent stirrings of love and grace, trembling on the verge of a certainty which if gained is loss—the very lightness of this fabric may prove too heavy a burden for men who lust for massively possessive experience."[6] The divine presence of the cosmos, the luminosity of consciousness, the subtlety of the embracing and embraced "flesh of the world," the bond of communion that underpins the jostling of sociality, the primordiality of order, the mystery of humanity in history: all of these are a "lightness of fabric," a hiddenness of the sacred that remains abidingly present in our midst. They characterize the sacramental horizon that our belonging opens to us. The corruption or degeneration of Christian civilization in the wake of "massively possessive experience" results from a disintegration of differentiated consciousness. Inevitably it leads to an isomorphic disintegration of the insights and achievements of differentiated consciousness and, in its extreme, to an evacuation of any quality of sacredness and a resultant a vacuum of order into which rush several "solutions." Nietzsche's symbol, the "death of God," does not necessarily mean the death of religiousness, but the generation of a *substitute religion* to fill the vacuum. Into the mold of two millennia of Christianity, the substitute religions enter.

Substitutes for Christian perfection and progress are generated in the imaginations of the unbelonging. Rather than cosmological presence and the communion of *communitas*, substitute religions are ideological enterprise associations. They are formed to provide a common goal of building substitutes for the sacredness of cosmological presence by generating equivalent symbols (Orwellian Newspeak language, liturgies, rites, etc.) that evoke (a) substitute perfections and (b) substitute means to progress toward such perfections. Where cosmological presence is eclipsed, persons are reduced to individual members of the corporate enterprise, and the sacred bond and order that is consummated in every communion is forgotten. Instead, the promise is a final state of unbelonging, where a *communitas* of belonging in the metaxy is overshadowed by the glory of the ideological movement, and the tension or "lightness of fabric" of existence in between time and timelessness is collapsed for membership in the vanguard. The ideological telos evokes a decosmicized Arcadia, a paradise without presence or communion, cast in the imaginative oblivion of the substitute religionists.

The unbelonging of Marx provides a clear example. Voegelin writes,

> The revolution in "history" is made to substitute for the theophanic event in reality. The turbulence of the encounter between God and man is transformed into the violence of an encounter between man and man. In the imaginary reality of the ideologists, this killing of men in revolutionary action is supposed to produce the much desired transfigurative, or metastatic, change in the nature of man as an event in "history." Marx has been quite explicit on this point: Revolutionary killing will induce a *Blutrausch*, a "blood-intoxication"; and from this *Blutrausch* "man" will emerge as "superman" into the "realm of freedom."[7]

Unbelonging in the West has a typical form and content because it adapts itself to the mold set by millennia of Christian civilization. First, Voegelin explains that there are three ideal forms of ideological unbelonging. There is the enchantment of utopianism, where the *final perfection* of a heaven-on-earth is clearly seen, but the means of arriving there is not so clear. There is the urgency of progressivism, where the emphasis lies on *progress* from a benighted past toward an enlightened future state, but what that perfected state will be need not be well defined because we have the direction, the means, and the confidence to get there. Then there is the intoxication of social revolutionism, in which *both the final perfection and the means of getting there* are clear.[8]

Second, there is the corresponding content of ideological unbelonging. Divested of sacramentality and historicity, substitute religions aim themselves at the substitute gods that seem to correlate with time or place. The Aryan fantasy of the National Socialists imagines a racially pure human stock that arose in the past from the Germanic soil, to be renewed by a racially purified *Reich* that knows itself in service of the *law of Nature* that commands that only the strongest have earned their survival. Then there is the Communist revolution and the Marxist realm of freedom that awaits us. Communism is activated in service of the *law of History* as its "scientific" solution. The *law of Progress* rules the present as a process of revolutionary social progress. Its theorists critically slough off sources of regressivism wherever they are found. Hannah Arendt picks up on the apocalyptic content of totalitarian substitute religions. "Totalitarian lawfulness, defying legality and pretending to establish the direct reign of justice on earth, executes the law of History or of Nature without translating it into standards of right and wrong for individual behaviour."[9] Arendt points out that presence and communion are abolished by the defacing of persons and the manipulation of *communitas* into groups or collectives. This is the method and the sign of unbelonging because the collective is that which has no face and remains distended in time without the possibility of historicity or consummation. The substitute religion "applies the law directly to mankind without bothering with the behaviour of men. The law of Nature or the law of History [and presumably, the law of Progress], if properly executed, is expected to produce mankind as its end product."[10] Contriving a mankind as the ideological product throws the spotlight on the contrasting, unengineered "imperfection" of persons and the grubby sacredness of ordinary life in *communitas*. The person and the *communitas* of persons are the adversary of ideological glory since their ordinariness is the sign of contradiction: their belonging partakes of the cosmos, the presence that remains infinitely beyond the reach of manipulation and domination.

NIHILISM AND THE ABSURD

Whereas *anamnesis* recovers cosmological presence, imaginative oblivion results in cosmological absence. It is the experience of absurd existence in a void, without a ground, without any point of orientation. It is what makes relativism possible. Unbelonging becomes a movement of absurdity, but it is important to point out that it does not have to become nihilistic. Albert Camus, we might say, is something of a liminal thinker whose writings exemplify both the absurdity of unbelonging and cosmological absence on the one hand and the strongly antinihilistic desire to counter the inevitable despair that emerges from absurd existence on the other. We want to exist in a cosmos that knows us, holds us, and consoles us, but in fact we are alone in an empty universe without meaning and direction. Camus sees that the resulting futility of our lives can only be overcome by the solidarity of a universal humanity that shares the same predicament. Happiness begins not in illusion or baseless fantasy, but only when we accept that there is no cosmos and no God.

Camus imagines that we are each like Sisyphus in his underworld punishment as he returns from the mountain heights to retrieve the rock that he has been condemned to roll forever. The rolling of the rock is a meaningless, futile task, destined always to fail, and it is during the descent to retrieve the rock that Sisyphus has moments of lucidity. He can fully contemplate his fate, and inevitably despair sets in. In the early moments of his punishment, Sisyphus might have clung to the false hope that his suffering could end some day, or he might have continued to wallow in the sweet memories of his life on the surface of the earth. In either case, there could only have been further soul-crushing desolation since his fate can never change, and he knows this. Both hope and memory fail because they do not console. According to Camus, the only path that avoids despair comes from the abandonment of hope and memory and from acceptance of the ultimate tragedy that is one's life. Camus urges us always to have compassion, because we are all rolling our own rock in some way, just like Sisyphus. Death is the despicable destiny of each of us, but aside from that one fate, we are the masters of our days only if we absurdly embrace the tragedy of our existence. The cosmos we would belong to, or the God who would bring us to everlasting life, does not exist, and our happiness—perhaps our happiness in belonging with one another in the days before our doom—begins in accepting the reality of an ultimate unbelonging that is existence without ground and purpose.

Again, Camus is a liminal figure because, in spite of this unbelonging related to God and cosmos, there is a way in which we can share our absurdity with one another. If we must imagine that Sisyphus, who scorns the gods and his fate, is happy, all the more so should we support one another in our absurd joys, sufferings, and scorn.[11] Camus may repudiate cosmological presence and communion, but the predicament of absurdity compels him to presence and communion with other human beings; and each human person, let us remember, is one *in whom* the cosmos abides even if the cosmos *in which* we exist is not recognized or acknowledged. In spite of his efforts and his embrace of the absurd, the human solidarity that Camus champions belies his absurdity.

Sisyphus is the absurd hero who can find happiness in the embrace of tragedy. Yet there are other moods of the absurd that don't result in happiness and solidarity, but can become mendacious. Disenchantment, *ressentiment*, arrogance, and the will to dominate are expressions of unbelonging that can deteriorate into nihilism.[12] Whereas not-belonging can adopt a stance toward particular and well-defined sociopolitical injustices and drive reform for the sake of reconciliation, unbelonging can lead to revolution rather than reform, as Marx demonstrated. Indignation and envy at the particular set of injustices can metastasize into a willed rejection of the possibility of a cosmos, sacramentality, and any bond and order among persons and communities. This is nihilism, as the grandest expression of imaginative oblivion. Nihilism is not itself therefore simply value-neutral in the sense of holding that nothing matters. In its maximum, nihilism can manifest itself in the will to reduce everything to nothing, a rage to destroy as the deepest revolt against the cosmos, which will not conform to the distorted libidinous image of the unbelonging individual or group. As Nietzsche wrote, "Nihilism is . . . not only the belief that everything deserves to perish; but one actually puts one's shoulder to the plough; *one destroys.*"[13] Nihilism is the attitude of disgust. The violence visited upon children in their schools, upon innocents and the vulnerable; upon institutional arrangements generated by a *communitas*, traditions, customs, and lore; and upon natural environments: this is the logical outcome of nihilistic unbelonging. In the alienated attitude of cosmological absence, it is belonging that becomes absurd, but it is disgust that drives nihilism to reject not simply belonging but existence itself. The rejection of the good of existence is implied in the rejection of belonging. Again, Nietzsche, as the preeminent prophet of nihilism, traced the direction of disgust into civilizational catastrophe. The death of God means the evacuation of all that is sacred by the mediocrity of nineteenth-century European herd-mentality, and the shell of Christian culture without substance leaves a vacuum. "What I relate is the history of the next two centuries. I describe what is coming, what can no longer come differently: *the advent of nihilism.* . . . For some time now our whole European culture has been moving as toward a catastrophe, with a tortured tension that is growing from decade to decade: restlessly, violently, headlong, like a river that wants to reach the end."[14]

The claim I made at the beginning of the book was that belonging is the human mode of existence. Alienation can be dehumanizing, as Marx rightly diagnosed. Not-belonging dehumanizes because it prevents our entering into the communion of *communitas* we yearn for. However, the remedy named unbelonging dehumanizes too because it kills persons and *communitas* to the tune of millions. Without the sacramentality of belonging and existence, with the loss of a sense of the sacred in our midst, we lose the cosmos. If the person is an embassy of the cosmos, then its absence amounts to the loss of responsibility for personhood. Outrage and cold calculation both mask the despair of unbelonging: like barren rock hurtling ever further into the cold recesses of space, nihilist disgust at existence and belonging marks the hellish loneliness in the heart where there might have been communion, wrought in the embrace of the sacredness that has embraced us first.

NOTES

Introduction

1. *The Barnhart Dictionary of Etymology*, ed. Robert K. Barnhart (New York: H.W. Wilson, 1988), 88.

2. Ibid., 839.

3. See my chapter "Existential Authority, Belonging, and the Commissioning That Is Subjectivity: A Medieval Philosophical Anthropology," in *Subjectivity: Ancient and Modern*, ed. R. J. Snell and Steven F. McGuire (Lanham, MD: Lexington Books, 2016), 205–26.

4. Aristotle, *Nicomachean Ethics* 1.1.

5. Augustine, *Concerning the City of God against the Pagans* 19.12, trans. Henry Bettenson (London: Penguin Books, 1984), 866.

6. Ibid., 869.

7. Ibid., 870.

8. In "Peace and Proximity," Levinas writes, "Philosophy here is a *measure* brought to the infinity of the being-for-the-other of peace and proximity, and it is like the wisdom of love." In *Basic Philosophical Writings*, ed. Adriaan T. Peperzak, Simon Critchley, and Robert Bernasconi (Bloomington: Indiana University Press, 1996), 169. Also, he writes that "philosophy is the wisdom of love at the service of love." *Otherwise than Being, or Beyond Essence*, trans. Alphonso Lingis (Pittsburgh: Duquesne University Press, 2011), 162.

Chapter 1

1. Karen F. Osterman, "Belonging," in *Encyclopedia of Educational Leadership and Administration*, ed. Fenwick W. English (Thousand Oaks, CA: SAGE Reference, 2006), 1:74–75. See also the "belongingness theory" in evolutionary psychology in, e.g., Roy Baumeister and Mark Leary, "The Need to Belong: Desire for Interpersonal Attachments as a Fundamental Human Motivation," *Psychological Bulletin* 117, no. 3 (1995): 497–529, https://doi.org/10.1037/0033-2909.117.3.497.

2. Gabriele Pollini, "Social Belonging," in *Encyclopedia of Sociology*, 2nd ed. (New York: Macmillan Reference USA, 2001), 4:2630–37.

3. Nadia Lovell, "Belonging in Need of Emplacement," in *Locality and Belonging* (London: Routledge, 1998), 1.

4. Belonging is treated as a psychological motivation across many fields in developmental psychology. Abraham Maslow's hierarchy of needs, Erik Erikson's psychosocial theory, and Urie Bronfenbrenner's ecological systems theory are three dominant sources. A philosophy of belonging takes the social and scientific insights seriously, and from here attempts to clarify the meaning of belonging.

5. A starter bibliographic list might include Vicki Bell, ed., *Performativity and Belonging* (London: Sage Publications, 1999); Roger Bromley, *Narratives for a New Belonging: Diasporic Cultural Fictions* (Edinburgh: Edinburgh University Press, 2000); Sheila L. Croucher, *Belonging: The Politics of Identity in a Changing World* (Lanham, MD: Rowman and Littlefield, 2004); Joel S. Migdal, *Boundaries and Belonging: States and Societies in the Struggle to Shape Identities and Local Practices* (Cambridge: Cambridge University Press, 2004); Nina Yuval-Davis, *The Politics of Belonging: Intersectional Contestations* (London: Sage Publications, 2011).

6. Georg Wilhelm Friedrich Hegel, *The Philosophy of History*, trans. J. Sibree (New York: Dover, 1956), 353.

7. Ibid., 354.

8. For an excellent account of the theme of homelessness in Heidegger and Levinas, whose main line of analysis I am following here, see C. L. Eubanks and D. J. Gauthier, "The Politics of the Homeless Spirit: Heidegger and Levinas on Dwelling and Hospitality," *History of Political Thought* 32, no. 1 (Spring 2011): 125–46.

9. See the discussion in division 2 of Martin Heidegger, *Being and Time*, entitled "Dasein's Possibility of Being-a-Whole, and Being-Towards-Death," in *Being and Time*, trans. John Macquarrie and Edward Robinson (Oxford: Blackwell, 2001), 279–311. See especially section 49, "How the Existential Analysis of Death Is Distinguished from Other Possible Interpretations of This Phenomenon," 290.

10. Heidegger, *Being and Time*, 436.

11. Martin Heidegger, *Introduction to Metaphysics*, trans. Gregory Fried and Richard Polt (New Haven: Yale University Press, 2000), 162–63.

12. Cosmopolitan universalism is a common theme in Kant's writings. In particular, see Immanuel Kant, "Idea for a Universal History from a Cosmopolitan Point of View," trans. Lewis White Beck, in *On History*, ed. Lewis White Beck (Indianapolis: Bobbs-Merrill, 1963; first published 1784).

13. Martin Heidegger, "Letter on Humanism," trans. Frank A. Capuzzi, in *Pathmarks*, ed. William McNeill (Cambridge: Cambridge University Press, 1998), 260, quoted in Eubanks and Gauthier, "Politics of the Homeless Spirit," 128. See also Nicolai Krejberg Knudsen, "Depopulation: On the Logic of Heidegger's *Volk*," *Research in Phenomenology* 47 (2017): 297–330.

14. See Heidegger's remarks in his preface in William J. Richardson, *Through Phenomenology to Thought* (New York: Fordham University Press, 1993), viii–xxiv.

15. Martin Heidegger, *Building Dwelling Thinking*, in *Poetry, Language, Thought*, trans. Albert Hofstadter (New York: Harper Colophon Books, 1971), 147. For an extended consideration of the fourfold and an impressive discussion of the major themes of the later Heidegger, see Andrew J. Mitchell, *The Fourfold: Reading the Later Heidegger* (Evanston, IL: Northwestern University Press, 2015).

16. Martin Heidegger, *Contributions to Philosophy (Of the Event)*, trans. Richard Rojcewicz and Daniela Vallega-Neu (Bloomington: Indiana University Press, 2012), 200.

17. John D. Caputo, *Demythologizing Heidegger* (Bloomington: Indiana University Press, 1993); Theodore Kisiel, *The Genesis of Heidegger's "Being and Time"* (Berkeley: University of California Press, 1993). For a summary account of this tension, see Paul Harrison, "The Space between Us: Opening Remarks on the Concept of Dwelling," in *Environment and Planning D: Society and Space* 25 (2007): 625–47.

18. Heidegger, *Being and Time*, 99.

19. Ibid., 105.

20. Martin Heidegger, "What Calls for Thinking?," in *Basic Writings*, ed. David Farrell Krell, 2nd ed. (London: Routledge, 1993).

21. Ibid., 379.

22. Ibid., "Building Dwelling Thinking," 157–58.

23. Martin Heidegger, "The Question concerning Technology," in *Basic Writings*, 330.

24. Martin Heidegger, *Hölderlin's Hymn "The Ister,"* trans. William McNeill and Julia Davis (Bloomington: Indiana University Press, 1996), 49.

25. Emmanuel Levinas, *Totality and Infinity*, trans. Alphonso Lingis (Pittsburgh: Duquesne University Press, 1969), 152.

26. Ibid. 153.

27. Ibid. 156.

28. Ibid. 156, 157. Significantly, Jacques Derrida refers to Levinas's philosophy as a "treatise of hospitality." See Derrida, *Adieu to Emmanuel Levinas* (Stanford, CA: Stanford University Press, 1999), 21.

29. Levinas, *Totality and Infinity*, 172.

30. Emmanuel Levinas, "The Trace of the Other," trans. Alphonso Lingis, in *Desconstruction in Context*, ed. Mark Taylor (Chicago: University of Chicago Press, 1986), 348, quoted in Eubanks and Gauthier, "Politics of Homelessness," 143.

31. I will discuss history as a structure of existence and belonging in chapter 8.

32. Patrick Deneen uses the *Odyssey* as a symbol for the assumptions and tensions that plague Western politics. Learning to navigate between the particularity of loving one's home and the universality of cosmopolitanism, for example, is one of the characteristic features that a political education and life must grapple with. Patrick Deneen, *The Odyssey of Political Theory: The Politics of Departure and Return* (Lanham, MD: Rowman and Littlefield, 2000).

33. René Girard, "Belonging," *Contagion: Journal of Violence, Mimesis, and Culture* 23 (2016): 2.

34. Ibid., 4.

35. Ibid., 8.

36. Ibid., 10.

37. Ibid., 12.

38. Ibid., 9.

39. I mentioned cosmopolitanism in reference to Immanuel Kant in n. 11. Cosmopolitanism has been an attractive and recurrent theme in philosophy since at least the Stoics. This suggests a dimension of belonging that is truly universal in its bearing. For Girard, universality is the overcoming of belonging. I will argue against this by discussing universality as an intrinsic dimension of belonging. See chapters 6 and 7.

40. Concerning the natural condition of mankind Thomas Hobbes writes that, while nature has made human beings equal in the faculties of body and mind, such equality naturally leads to a condition of war and the life of man being "solitary, poor, nasty, brutish, and short." The Leviathan power of government exists to short-circuit the inevitable violent outcome and to impose an order restricting an absolute right of nature for the sake of life and "commodious living." *Leviathan* (Indianapolis: Bobbs-Merrill, 1958; first published 1651), 104–5 (pt. 1, ch. 13).

41. Girard, "Belonging," 5.

42. Ibid., 7–8.

43. Ibid. 12.

44. Ibid. 3.

45. Linn Miller, "Belonging to Country—a Philosophical Anthropology," *Journal of Australian Studies* 27, no. 76 (2003): 215.

46. Ibid., 217.

47. Ibid.

48. Ibid.

49. Ibid., 218.

50. Kierkegaard contrasts objective and subjective approaches to life. Where objectivity seeks certainty, it loses passion; whereas subjectivity lives by uncertainty and passion. "Christianity is spirit, spirit is inwardness, inwardness is subjectivity, subjectivity is essential passion, and in its maximum an infinite, personal, passional interest in one's eternal happiness." *Concluding Unscientific Postscript*, trans. D. F. Swenson (Princeton: Princeton University Press, 1941), 33.

51. The fragment of Parmenides (B3) records the insight that "it is the same to think and to be." He warns against separating thinking and being since then thinking would be concerned with not-being. There are many interpretations of Parmenides's poem. For example, see Martin Heidegger, *The Beginning of Western Philosophy: Interpretation of Anaximander and Parmenides* (Bloomington: Indiana University Press, 2012); Eric Voegelin, *The World of the Polis*, vol. 2 of *Order and History*; vol. 15 of *The Collected Works of Eric Voegelin*, ed. Athanasios Moulakis (Columbia: University of Missouri Press, 2000), 274–91; and more recently, Nestor-Luis Cordero, *By Being, It Is: The Thesis of Parmenides* (Las Vegas: Parmenides Publishing, 2004).

52. I will return to Kierkegaard and the eternal in chapter 8.

53. Miller, "Belonging to Country," 220.

54. Indeed, as we shall see, the question of self is a question that opens into the question of the cosmos, and ultimately into the question of God.

55. "Liberality consists in the use which is made of property." Aristotle, *Politics* 1263b12, in *The Complete Works of Aristotle*, ed. Jonathan Barnes (Princeton: Princeton University Press, 1995), 2:2005.

Chapter 2

1. Ludwig Wittgenstein, *Tractatus Logico-Philosophicus* (London: Routledge & Kegan Paul, 1963), 149e; Wittgenstein, *Culture and Value*, ed. G. H. von Wright (Chicago: University of Chicago Press, 1984), 62e.

2. Heidegger, *Being and Time*, section 16, "How the Worldly Character of the Environment Announces Itself in Entities Within-the-World," p. 105.

3. In *Being and Nothingness*, Jean-Paul Sartre writes that the "essence of the relations between consciousnesses is not the *Mitsein*; it is conflict." *Being and Nothingness* (London: Routledge, 2003), 451. The "look" of the other, upon whom I would make my claim to belong, is a derisory and unwelcoming one, and beneath that look, my desire becomes the occasion of shame. For a discussion of shame and belonging, see Luna Dolezal, "Shame, Vulnerability, and Belonging: Reconsidering Sartre's Account of Shame," *Human Studies* 40 (2017): 421–38.

4. See the epilogue, where I contrast "not-belonging" with "unbelonging."

5. Augustine discusses the cardinal virtues of prudence, justice, fortitude, and temperance as "great goods" because they alone, of all the created order, are incorruptible. All other goods are either intermediate (such as free will and reason) or low goods (such as material things). Genuinely good, these are nonetheless susceptible to corruption because they can be employed by a deficient will in the pursuit of evil. See Augustine, *On Free Choice of the Will* 2.19, trans. Thomas Williams (Indianapolis: Hackett, 1993), 67.

6. The growth of the soul is an interesting concept that Kurt Vonnegut describes in a 2013 letter to students at Xavier High School in Chicago. In the letter, he urges them to use poetry to push out their personal boundaries and challenge themselves, in the course of which they will find that they have made their souls grow, already itself a reward for the effort. "Make Your Soul Grow," posted by Shaun Usher, Letters of Note, November 5, 2021, https:// lettersofnote.com/2013/10/28/make-your-soul-grow/.

7. Bernice Johnson Reagon, "Coalitional Politics: Turning the Century," in *Home Girls: A Black Feminist Anthology*, ed. Barbara Smith (New York: Kitchen Table/Women of Color Press, 1983), 358–69.

8. See Chandra Talpade Mohanty's commentary on Reagon's "barred room," and contrast with Robin Morgan's notion of a barred room, in *Feminism without Borders: Decolonizing Theory, Practicing Solidarity* (Durham, NC: Duke University Press, 2003), 117.

9. Mariana Ortega, *In-Between: Latina Feminist Phenomenology, Multiplicity, and the Self* (Albany: State University of New York Press, 2016), 200.

10. Ibid., 201. Ortega goes on to advocate "hometactics" as a way to make what is not home more homely. The quality of homeliness is surely what is generated by the transcendent reality of belonging, which involves what is, and what is more than, one's membership of social groups.

11. See my discussion of Margaret Canovan's thought in chapter 7. She argues that without first understanding nationhood (or national belonging), we cannot grasp what stabilizes and directs the exercise of power in a society.

12. "The existential experience is that there is an element of human searching (the *zetesis*, in the classical sense) and an element of being drawn by God (the *helkein*). These are the two experiences you have. There's a dynamics in your existence. The tension is that of being drawn not only by a force of which you have never heard anything but by a force which you are seeking." Eric Voegelin, "Conversations with Voegelin at the Thomas More Institute for Adult Education in Montreal," in *The Drama of Humanity and Other Miscellaneous Papers, 1939–1985*, ed. William Petropulos and Gilbert Weiss, vol. 33 of *Collected Works of Eric Voegelin* (Columbia: University of Missouri Press, 2004), 294.

13. Eric Voegelin, "Eternal Being in Time," in *Anamnesis: On the Theory of History and Politics*, ed. David Walsh, vol. 6 of *Collected Works of Eric Voegelin* (Columbia: University of Missouri Press, 2002), 324, 329.

14. For example, see the discussion of the nature of love in Plato, *Symposium* 201d–204c.

15. Eric Voegelin, "Reason: The Classic Experience," in *Published Essays, 1966–1985*, ed. Ellis Sandoz; vol. 12 of *Collected Works of Eric Voegelin* (Columbia: University of Missouri Press, 1990), 279.

16. Nicholas of Cusa, *De coniecturis*, quoted in Pauline Moffit Watts, *Nicolaus Cusanus: A Fifteenth Century Vision of Man* (Leiden: Brill, 1982), 109.

17. Glenn Hughes, *Transcendence and History: The Search for Ultimacy from Ancient Societies to Postmodernity* (Columbia: University of Missouri Press, 2003), 70.

Chapter 3

1. *Anamnesis* is most famously discussed in Plato's *Meno*. Here, Socrates responds to the question about how he can seek something he does not know. His answer proceeds from observing the apparently ignorant slave boy who works through a problem of geometry. Under the questioning of Socrates, the boy moves from total ignorance and the absence of curiosity, to a middle ground of frustration and perplexity, to the eventual, correct solution. Socrates tells Meno, "And if the truth about reality is always in our soul, the soul must be immortal, and one must take courage and try to discover—that is, to recollect—what one doesn't happen to know, or more correctly, remember, at the moment." *Meno* 86a–b, in *The Collected Dialogues of Plato, Including the*

Letters, ed. Edith Hamilton and Huntington Cairns (Princeton: Princeton University Press, 1999), 371.

2. "Cosmos" is the more appropriate term for my purposes, and preferred to its close synonym, "being." I will discuss this below. For now, "being" is more suited to the differentiation of transcendence and immanence, which is a more fitting symbol for the later philosophical and revelatory theory. See Gregor Sebba, "Prelude and Variations of the Theme of Eric Voegelin," in *Eric Voegelin's Thought: A Critical Appraisal,* ed. Ellis Sandoz (Durham, NC: Duke University Press, 1982), 56–57.

3. Dupré continues, "The modern translation of *kosmos* as 'physical nature' is quite misleading since originally *kosmos* included theological and anthropic and well as physical meanings. The loss of the former two reflects the disintegration of the ancient ontotheological synthesis." Louis Dupré, *Passage to Modernity: An Essay in the Hermeneutics of Nature and Culture* (New Haven: Yale University Press, 1993), 17, 18.

4. Glenn Hughes, *Mystery and Myth in the Philosophy of Eric Voegelin* (Columbia: University of Missouri Press, 1993), 47.

5. Ibid.

6. "There is the experience of separate existence in the stream of being, and the various existences are distinguished by their degrees of durability.... Under this aspect, being exhibits the lineaments of a hierarchy of existence, from the ephemeral lowliness of man to the everlastingness of the gods." Eric Voegelin, *Israel and Revelation,* ed. Maurice P. Hogan, vol. 1 of *Order and History*; vol. 14 of *The Collected Works of Eric Voegelin* (Columbia: University of Missouri Press, 2001), 41, 42. (Hereafter, *Israel and Revelation*).

7. Pseudo-Dionysius, *The Mystical Theology,* ch. 3, Sophia Project, Philosophy Archives, 2001, http://www.sophia-project.org/uploads/1/3/9/5/13955288/dionysius_mysticaltheology.pdf. Accessed March 2021.

8. Louis Dupré gives a convincing account of the Greek derivation of form from *kosmos,* intrinsic to which is the notion of "limit." He writes, "In early Greek thought the idea of form had always implied definiteness, that is, limitation. The unlimited was considered a negative category." *Passage to Modernity,* 21.

9. Voegelin, *Israel and Revelation,* 41–42.

10. See Homer, *Iliad* 2.167–82, 3.371–82, respectively.

11. Voegelin, *Israel and Revelation,* 39.

12. Ibid., 41.

13. Mircea Eliade, *The Sacred and the Profane* (New York: Harcourt, Brace & World, 1959), 30.

14. Ibid.

15. Ibid., 31.

16. See Eliade's discussion in "Sacred Time and Myths," in *Sacred and the Profane,* 68–113. See also Voegelin's discussion of *omphalos* in the context of Sumerian civilization in *Israel and Revelation,* 67–69, and the treatment of political symbolism in chapter 7 below.

17. Eliade, *Sacred and the Profane,* 69.

18. Hughes, *Mystery and Myth*, 44.

19. See Brendan Purcell, "In the Beginning . . . ," ch. 2 in *From Big Bang to Big Mystery: Human Origins in the Light of Creation and Evolution* (Dublin: Veritas, 2011).

20. Karl Jaspers, *The Origin and Goal of History*, trans. Michael Bullock (New Haven: Yale University Press, 1953). The relative contemporaneity of "spiritual outbursts" in China, India, Persia, Israel, and Greece is the pattern that the term "axis-time" refers to. There have been attempts to explain it by cultural diffusion, so that a causal connection of sorts between the likes of Heraclitus and Lao-Tzu, for example, would explain the apparent plurality of the irruptions. See Voegelin's words of caution in using such categorical devices "to reduce a diversified field of spiritual centers to the oneness of an event in history. . . . A *horror*, not *vacui* but *pleni*, seems at work, a shudder at the richness of the spirit as it reveals itself all over the earth in a multitude of hierophanies." *The Ecumenic Age*, ed. Michael Franz, vol. 4 of *Order and History*; vol. 17 of *The Collected Works of Eric Voegelin* (Columbia: University of Missouri Press, 2000), 47–48. See also Bruno Snell, *The Discovery of the Mind* (New York: Harper, 1960); S. N. Eisenstadt, ed., *The Origins and Diversity of Axial Age Civilizations* (Albany: State University of New York Press, 1983).

21. Voegelin, *Ecumenic Age*, 381–82. Karl Jaspers holds that the window of axis-time extended only from 800 BCE to 200 BCE. Voegelin writes that "Jaspers distinguishes between the reality of the existential tension in Jesus toward God and the theological construction of the reality, after the death of Jesus, by the early Christians" (383). However, Jaspers excludes Christianity from the axis-time because "the Christian 'view of universal history can be valid only for believing Christians" (381). Voegelin notes that Jaspers "forms an oddly doctrinal conception of 'Christian faith' that will permit him to remove Christ from his epochal status together with a 'religion' in which the majority of mankind does not believe anyway" (382). Voegelin allows that the spiritual outbursts of the time were certainly epochal, but the restriction of the Axial Age to those outbursts obscures the further differentiations that occurred outside Jaspers's axis window that were just as epochal. "If spiritual outbursts were to be recognized as the constituents of meaning in history, the epiphanies of Moses and Christ, or of Mani and Mohammad, could hardly be excluded from the list" (49).

22. See Voegelin's analysis of "non-existence" as a compact symbol for what would later be differentiated as transcendence, in "Immortality: Experience and Symbol," in *Published Essays, 1966–1985*, 52–93.

23. Voegelin, *Ecumenic Age*, 127.

24. Ibid., 77.

25. Xenophanes, fragments 14, 15, 11, respectively, in *Ancilla to the Pre-Socratic Philosophers: A Complete Translation of the Fragments in Diels, "Fragmente der Vorsokratiker,"* ed. and trans. Kathleen Freeman (Cambridge, MA: Harvard University Press, 1996), 22.

26. Xenophanes, fragments 23–26, in ibid., 23.

27. Voegelin, *Anamnesis*, 165.

28. See Dupré, "From Cosmos to Nature," in *Passage to Modernity*, 15–90.

29. Glenn Hughes, "Nature, Human Nature, and Human Dignity," in *Concepts of Nature: Ancient and Modern*, ed. R. J. Snell and Steven F. McGuire (Lanham, MD: Lexington Books, 2016), 45.

30. Eric Voegelin, "What Is Political Reality?," in *Anamnesis*, 357, quoted in Hughes, "Nature, Human Nature," 45.

31. Matthew 22:21; Mark 12:17; Luke 20:25. This claim of separation does not preclude the ultimate provenance of authority in the world-transcendent God, but functions as a further subsidiary (but crucial) differentiation of transcendent from immanent meaning, and of both transcendence and immanence from cosmological compactness. I will discuss this in chapter 7.

32. Voegelin, "What Is Political Reality," 357. "Being" is the preferred term because "being" has the two dimensions of transcendence and immanence, which "cosmos" does not.

33. See Voegelin's discussion in *Anamnesis*, 149.

34. John J. Ranieri, "Grounding Public Discourse: Eric Voegelin's Contribution," in *The Politics of the Soul*, ed. Glenn Hughes (Lanham, MD: Rowman and Littlefield, 1999), 36.

35. Glenn Hughes, *Mystery and Myth*, 25.

36. Ibid.

37. Voegelin, *Anamnesis*, 165.

38. Eric Voegelin, "What Is Nature?," in *Anamnesis*, 163.

39. Ibid.

40. Ibid., 164.

41. Hughes, "Nature, Human Nature," 45. He continues, "The terms are 'exegetic, not descriptive' in their function and so must 'never be used in isolation' from each other" (46). See also Eric Voegelin, "The Beginning and the Beyond: A Meditation on Truth," in *What Is History? And Other Late Unpublished Writings*, vol. 28 of *The Collected Works of Eric Voegelin*, ed. Thomas A. Hollweck and Paul Caringella (Baton Rouge: Louisiana State University Press, 1990), 185.

42. The depth and height of the cosmos are indices. On the abyssal depth, Anaximander used the term *apeiron*. Voegelin comments, "Reality was experienced by Anaximander (fl. 560 B.C.) as a cosmic process in which things emerge from, and disappear into, the non-existence of the Apeiron. Things do not exist out of themselves, all at once and forever; they exist out of the ground to which they return. Hence, to exist means to participate in two modes of reality: (1) In the Apeiron as the timeless arche of things and (2) in the ordered succession of things as the manifestation of the Apeiron in time." *Ecumenic Age*, 174.

43. Thomas begins his *Summa Theologica* with the frank admission that natural reason has limits in probing the mystery of existence, which is always a divine mystery. For this, the "sacred teaching" of revelation is a necessary complement to philosophy, as grace is to nature. We probe the mystery of existence because our pure desire to know is the relentless pursuit of happiness, the end of which Aquinas identifies as salvation and the beatific vision. "But the end must first be known by men who are to direct their thoughts and actions to the end. Hence it was necessary for the salvation of man that certain truths which

exceed human reason should be made known to him by divine revelation. . . . It was therefore necessary that besides philosophical science built up by reason, there should be a sacred science learned through revelation." *Summa Theologica* I.1.1, trans. Fathers of the English Dominican Province, 3 vols. (New York: Benziger Brothers, 1947), 1:1. All quotations of *Summa Theologica* will be from this edition.

44. Exodus 3:13–15 (New American Bible, revised edition).

45. Parmenides, fragments 2, 3, 7, in Freeman, *Ancilla to the Pre-Socratic Philosophers*, 42, 43.

46. Augustine, *On Free Choice of the Will* 2.6–15 (Williams, 40–58).

47. Augustine, *City of God* 12.2 (Bettenson, 473).

48. Anselm, *Proslogion with the Replies of Gaunilo and Anselm*, trans. Thomas Williams (Indianapolis: Hackett, 2001). See chs. 2 and 3. See particularly Anselm's reply to Gaunilo's objections with his emphasis on God as perfect, necessary being. For all of its logical coherence, arguably Anselm's argument continues to resonate because the heuristic of God-as-being, which is operative in the *Proslogion*, is a heuristic of the transcendent ground of all being, and therefore perfect and necessary.

49. The fuller quotation reads, "It remains that there can be only one such thing that is its own existence. Apart from this exception, then, in the case of anything else whatsoever, it is necessary that its existence is one thing and its quiddity or nature or form another. . . . It cannot be the case that the existence itself is caused by the very form or quiddity of the thing—I mean 'caused' as by an efficient cause—since then some thing would be the cause of itself and make itself exist, which is impossible. Therefore, every such thing whose existence differs from its nature must have existence from another. And since whatever is through another is reduced to that which is through itself (per se), as to a first cause, there must be some thing that is the cause of being (causa essendi) for all things, in that it is existence only. Otherwise one would proceed to infinity in causes, since every thing that is not existence only has a cause of its existence, as just stated. Therefore, it is clear that an Intelligence is form and existence, and that it has existence from the first being that is existence only—and this is the First Cause, which is God." Thomas Aquinas, *On Being and Essence*, ch. 4, in *Aquinas: Basic Works*, ed. Jeffrey Hause and Robert Pasnau (Indianapolis: Hackett, 2014), 26–27.

50. Etienne Gilson writes, "God exists in virtue of Himself (*per se*) in an absolute sense. . . . Just as His existence is not derived from any other than Himself, so neither does He depend on any kind of internal essence, which would have in itself the power to bring itself to existence." *The Spirit of Medieval Philosophy* (Notre Dame, IN: University of Notre Dame Press, 1936), 54.

51. Thomas Aquinas, *Summa Theologica* I.13.11 (Benziger, 1:70). Aquinas quotes Damascene's *De fide orthodoxa* 1.

52. Aquinas, *Summa Theologica* I.13.2–11 (Benziger, 1:60–71). Rather than having aseity, all contingent existence receives its being *ab alio* (not from itself, but from elsewhere), and ultimately from He Who Is. The existence of all creation bears—in the particularity of its existence and in essence—some degree

of "likeness" to God, who is the fullness of being through Whom they exist, so that when Aquinas writes, "Hence any creature represents Him [God], and is like Him so far as it possesses some perfection," he is primarily clarifying that "Now since our intellect knows God from creatures, it knows Him as far as creatures represent Him. … Damascene says that these names signify the divine substance, and are predicated substantially of God, although they fall short of a full representation." *Summa Theologica* I.13.2. (Benziger, 1:61).

53. Pseudo-Dionysius, *Dionysius the Areopagite: "On the Divine Names" and the "Mystical Theology,"* ed. Clarence Edwin Rolt (Grand Rapids, MI: Christian Classics Ethereal Library, 2000; first published 1920 by SPCK [London]), Documenta Catholica Omnia, https://www.documentacatholicaomnia .eu/03d/0450-0525,_Dionysius_Areopagita,_On_The_Divine_Names_And _The_Mystical_Theology,_EN.pdf. See also John Scotus Eriugena, who writes that God is beyond all names. "He is called God, but He is not strictly speaking God; … He is hypertheos, that is, more-than-God." *Periphyseon* 1.459D, trans. I. P. Sheldon-Williams (Montréal: Éditions Bellarmin, 1987), 47. According to Aquinas, *Summa Theologica* I.13.3, when we predicate names of God, we do so metaphorically. (Benziger, 1:62). See also Aquinas's discussion in *Summa Theologica* 1.13.5.

54. Gilson, *Spirit of Medieval Philosophy*, 53. Here he quotes Bonaventure: "Ipsa caligo summa est mentis illuminatio."

55. David Bentley Hart writes, "God so understood is not something posed over against the universe, in addition to it, nor is he the universe itself. He is not a "being," at least not in the way that a tree, a shoemaker, or a god is a being; he is not one more object in the inventory of things that are, or any sort of discrete object at all. Rather, all things that exist receive their being continuously from him, who is the infinite wellspring of all that is." *The Experience of God* (New Haven: Yale University Press, 2013), 30.

56. George Eliot captures the rare conspicuousness of what I mean by cosmos: "Here was a man who now for the first time found himself looking into the eyes of death—who was passing through one of those rare moments of experience when we feel the truth of a commonplace, which is as different from what we call knowing it, as the vision of waters upon the earth is different from the delirious vision of the water which cannot be had to cool the burning tongue. When the commonplace 'We must all die' transforms itself suddenly into the acute consciousness 'I must die—and soon,' then death grapples us, and his fingers are cruel; afterwards, he may come to fold us in his arms as our mother did, and our last moment of dim earthly discerning may be like the first." George Eliot, *Middlemarch*, ed. Bert G. Hornback (New York: W.W. Norton & Company, 1977), 293.

57. Eric Voegelin, *In Search of Order*, ed. Ellis Sandoz, vol. 5 of *Order and History*; vol. 18 of *Collected Works* (Columbia: University of Missouri Press, 2000), 120.

58. Glenn Hughes, *Transcendence and History* (Columbia: University of Missouri Press, 2003), 153.

59. Ibid., 131.

60. I will discuss luminosity as the presence of the cosmos in consciousness in the following chapter.

61. Voegelin, *Ecumenic Age*, 17.

62. Ibid., 17–18.

63. Voegelin, *In Search of Order*, 45 (emphasis added).

64. Voegelin, *Ecumenic Age*, 16–17. On "immortalizing," see my comments on Aristotle in chapter 5.

65. See Joseph Campbell, *The Hero with a Thousand Faces* (New York: Pantheon Books, 1949); Mircea Eliade, *Myth and Reality* (New York: Harper and Row, 1963); Jordan Peterson, *Maps of Meaning: The Architecture of Belief* (New York: Routledge, 1999).

66. Aquinas, *Summa Theologica* I.2.3 (Benziger, 1:13–14).

67. This argument was first formulated by Aristotle in *Metaphysics* 12.6–10.

68. See chapter 7 for a discussion of creation myths and their political importance.

69. See Purcell, *From Big Bang to Big Mystery*, 90.

70. Bernard Lonergan, *Insight: A Study of Human Understanding*, ed. Frederick Crowe, S.J., and Robert Doran, S.J., vol. 3 of *The Collected Works of Bernard Lonergan* (Toronto: University of Toronto Press: 1992), 144–51.

71. Ibid., 281.

72. Purcell, *From Big Bang to Big Mystery*, 90; Barrow and Tipler, *The Anthropic Cosmological Principle* (Oxford: Oxford University Press, 1986), 252–53.

73. Purcell, *From Big Bang to Big Mystery*, 96.

Chapter 4

1. The term "flesh" is employed by Merleau-Ponty in his later works, in particular *The Visible and the Invisible*, ed. Claude Lefort, trans. Alphonso Lingis (Evanston, IL: Northwestern University Press, 1968), although the implications of its meaning are present in various forms throughout his career. See below for a discussion of the meaning of the phrase "flesh of the world."

2. Bernard Lonergan, *Method in Theology*, vol. 14 of *Collected Works of Bernard Lonergan*, ed. Robert M. Doran and John D. Dadosky (Toronto: University of Toronto Press, 2017), 273.

3. Jeremy D. Wilkins writes, "For the phenomenologies of perception and of language, being is identified as 'what appears,' and insofar as it cannot handle the problem of judgment, 'phenomenology is an inadequate method.' But Lonergan's intentionality analysis does not bog down in the precritical morass; it brings to light that being is what is attained through correct judgment; it is able to connect the remote issue of being in the truth, the truth of existence, with the proximate issue of true judgment, predicative truth." *Before Truth: Lonergan, Aquinas, and the Problem of Wisdom* (Washington, DC: Catholic University of America Press, 2018), 142. See also Fred Lawrence, "The Fragility of Consciousness: Lonergan and the Postmodern Concern for the Other," in *The Fragility of Consciousness: Faith, Reason, and the Human Good,*

ed. Randall S. Rosenberg and Kevin M. Vander Shel (Toronto: University of Toronto Press, 2017); Bernard Lonergan, *Phenomenology and Logic: The Boston College Lectures on Mathematical Logic*, ed. Philip J. McShane, vol. 18 of *The Collected Works of Bernard Lonergan* (Toronto: University of Toronto Press, 2001), 277–78.

4. Immanuel Kant, "Autonomy of the Will as the Supreme Principle of Morality," in *The Moral Law*, ed. H. J. Paton (London: Unwin Hyman, 1989), 101–2; John Stuart Mill, "Of Individuality, as One of the Elements of Well-Being," chapter 3 in *On Liberty*, ed. Currin V. Shields (Indianapolis: Bobbs-Merrill, 1956), 67–90. Autonomy is a central concern for much contemporary social thought, especially within feminist and cultural theories. For example, see John Christman and Joel Anderson, eds., *Autonomy and the Challenges to Liberalism* (Cambridge: Cambridge University Press, 2005); Gerald Dworkin, *The Theory and Practice of Autonomy* (Cambridge: Cambridge University Press, 1988); Marilyn Friedman, *Autonomy, Gender, Politics* (Oxford: Oxford University Press, 2003); Catriona Mackenzie and Natalie Stoljar, eds., *Relational Autonomy* (New York: Oxford University Press, 2000); Alfred R. Mele, *Autonomous Agents: From Self-Control to Autonomy* (New York: Oxford University Press, 2001).

5. See Tilo Schabert, *The Figure of Modernity: On the Irregularity of an Epoch* (Berlin: de Gruyter, 2020). In this volume, Schabert discusses modernity as the epoch that eclipsed existence in the cosmos through mastery over Nature.

6. Levinas, *Otherwise than Being, or Beyond Essence*, 127.

7. Emmanuel Levinas, *Existence and Existents*, trans. Alphonso Lingis (Pittsburgh: Duquesne University Press, 2001), 78–79.

8. I will discuss Levinas under the rubric of love in the next chapter.

9. Richard Kearney, *Modern Movements in European Philosophy* (Manchester, UK: Manchester University Press, 1994), 15. See also Edmund Husserl, *Ideas Pertaining to a Pure Phenomenology and to a Phenomenological Philosophy: First Book; General Introduction to a Pure Phenomenology*, §135, "Object and Consciousness: The Transition to the Phenomenology of Reason," ed. F. Kersten (The Hague: Martinus Nijhoff, 1983), 322–25.

10. Franz Brentano, *Psychology from an Empirical Standpoint*, ed. Tim Crane and Jonathan Wolff (London: Routledge, 1995), 98.

11. I am indebted to Jeremy D. Wilkins, who emphasized these three meanings of presence during the course of his masterful response to a chapter I wrote about subjectivity. See Wilkins, "Response to James Greenaway," in *Subjectivity: Ancient and Modern*, ed. R. J. Snell and Steven F. McGuire (Lanham, MD: Lexington Books, 2016), 231–32.

12. Bernard Lonergan, "The Human Good, Meaning, and Differentiations of Consciousness," in *Early Works on Theological Method 1*, ed. Robert M. Doran and Robert C. Croken, vol. 22 of *Collected Works of Bernard Lonergan* (Toronto: University of Toronto Press, 2010), 47.

13. Mark D. Morelli, *Self-Possession: Being at Home in Conscious Performance* (Chestnut Hill, MA: Lonergan Research Institute of Boston College, 2015), 80.

14. Lonergan, *Method in Theology*, 8.

15. Wilkins, "Response to James Greenaway," 231.

16. Lonergan adapts Thomas Aquinas's insights into human cognition to the contemporary situation, which has benefited from developments since Thomas's day in the fields of the natural and social sciences, as well as in philosophy, theology, and the humanities. Lonergan's adaptation of Thomas's cognitional theory intentionally shares Thomas's original concern to affirm both the reality of the world and the reality of the individual cognizing person. In particular, see questions 75 to 86 in the first book of *Summa Theologica*.

17. Morelli, *Self-Possession*, 86.

18. Augustine, *On the Trinity* 14.11.14, New Advent, http://www .newadvent.org/fathers/130114.htm. I will discuss the importance of memory below, and it will carry with it the self-presence that is my focus here.

19. For Lonergan, this is the key to overcoming (1) naïve realism that posits an "already out there" version of truth, whereby only the mathematically measurable and the empirically tangible can be real, and (2) idealism, which tends to lock up the real in an "already in here" solitude. See Bernard Lonergan, "Cognitional Structure," in *Collection*, ed. Frederick E. Crowe and Robert M. Doran, vol. 4 of *Collected Works of Bernard Lonergan* (Toronto: University of Toronto Press, 1988), 205–21. Instead, Lonergan lays out a "critical realism" that affirms the reality of the world in intellection and judgment and affirms the reality of the embodied conscious person who arrives at judgments of facts and values.

20. Although Lonergan sets out the Generalized Empirical Method in detail in *Insight*, he provides a neatly accessible summary in *Method in Theology*, 17–22; see also Lonergan, "Cognitional Structure," 205–11.

21. Tad Dunne, *Lonergan and Spirituality* (Chicago: Loyola Press, 1985), 14.

22. "Men in their living can be organized more on the level of experience, or more on the level of intelligence, or more on the level of rational reflection; and so there arise three basic classes of philosophy. The tendency to organize on the experiential level is manifest in the materialist, the empiricist, the sensist, the positivist, the pragmatist, the modernist. [Naïve realism.] . . . On the second level, there are the philosophies of the Platonist, idealist, relativist, essentialist varieties. [Idealism.] On the third level, there are the realists, where what is meant by the real is what is known when one truly affirms, 'It is.' [Critical Realism]." Bernard Lonergan, "The Theory of Philosophic Differences," in *Topics in Education*, vol. 10 of *Collected Works of Bernard Lonergan*, ed. Robert M. Doran and Frederick E. Crowe (Toronto: University of Toronto Press, 1993), 178–79; Lonergan, "Cognitional Structure," 231–36.

23. The literature on apophatic thought is rich with paradox, straining as it does beyond logic in the attempt to unsay what can be said. Apophatic thought has a long history from ancient to postmodern times in many fields of expression. In particular, William Franke has pulled together a first-rate compendium of apophatic writings with essays: *On What Cannot Be Said: Apophatic Discourses in Philosophy, Religion, Literature, and the Arts*, vols. 1 and 2 (Notre Dame, IN: University of Notre Dame Press, 2007). See also Catherine Keller and Chris Boesel, *Apophatic Bodies: Negative Theology, Incarnation, and*

Relationality (New York: Fordham University Press, 2010); Denys Turner, *The Darkness of God: Negativity in Christian Mysticism* (Cambridge: Cambridge University Press, 1999).

24. Glenn Hughes comments that there are other types of language than conceptual analysis. These listen "to what reality has to say and [let] its 'story' be told. 'Mythic and revelatory symbols' fall into this category, as do . . . the many voices of art." *Mystery and Myth in the Philosophy of Eric Voegelin* (Columbia: University of Missouri Press, 1993), 35.

25. Voegelin, *In Search of Order*, 29–30.

26. "Noetic experience, interpreting itself, illuminates the logos of participation [in reality]." Voegelin, *Anamnesis*, 352.

27. Eric Voegelin, "The Beginning and the Beyond: A Meditation on Truth," in *What Is History?*, 184.

28. Ibid.

29. Voegelin, *In Search of Order*, 55. See also ibid., 116–17; Voegelin, "Wisdom and the Magic of the Extreme," in *Published Essays, 1966–1985*, 345; Hughes, *Mystery and Myth*, 36–37. Very succinctly, Hughes writes that "'reflective distance' [is the structure that] enables consciousness to grasp and articulate its own nature" (111).

30. See epilogue.

31. Other embodiment thinkers notably include Simone de Beauvoir and Karol Wojtyła. See de Beauvoir, *The Second Sex*, trans. Constance Borde and Sheila Malovany-Chevallier (New York: Vintage Books, 2011); Wojtyła, *The Acting Person*, trans. Andrzej Potocki (Dordrecht, Holland: Reidel, 1979). On the significance of embodiment in the thought of Wojtyła and Merleau-Ponty, see Nigel K. Zimmerman, "Karol Wojtyla and Emmanuel Levinas on the Embodied Self: The Forming of the Other as Moral Self-Disclosure," *Heythrop Journal* 50, no. 6 (2009): 982–95. Also John McNerney, *John Paul II: Poet and Philosopher* (London: Burns and Oates, 2004); John Paul II, *Man and Woman He Created Them: A Theology of the Body*, trans. Michael Waldstein (Boston: Pauline Books & Media, 2006).

32. Merleau-Ponty, *Visible and the Invisible*, 83–84.

33. Maurice Merleau-Ponty, preface to *Phenomenology of Perception*, trans. Donald A. Landes (New York: Routledge, 2012), lxxi–lxxii. Richard Kearney writes of Merleau-Ponty, "By thus reversing the tendency of both traditional metaphysics and modern science to subordinate the 'aesthetic' (our prereflective carnal experience) to the 'analytic' (our reflective conceptual judgement), Merleau-Ponty denies that objective ideas are born *ex nihilo*. He rules out the possibility of cognitive autonomy. Ideas are neither otherworldly (Platonism), innate (Cartesianism), *a priori* (Kantianism), nor indeed mechanical combinations of impressions made upon some *tabula rasa* of the mind (Empiricism)." *Modern Movements*, 77.

34. Ibid., 53

35. Merleau-Ponty, *Visible and the Invisible*, 141.

36. Ibid., 57. This is anamnesis that is, arguably, more primordial than the ancient understanding of *anamnesis*. For example, in Plato's *Meno*, Socrates

talks to Meno about a remembrance that can be conceptualized. "And if the truth about reality is always in our soul, our soul must be immortal, and one must take courage and try to discover—that is, to recollect—what one doesn't happen to know, or more correctly, remember, at the moment." *Meno* 86b, in *Collected Dialogues of Plato*, 371. See also Mircea Eliade on Hindu and Greek *anamnesis* in *Myth and Reality*, 114–32. Merleau-Ponty is pointing to a communication that is always operative but in a preconceptual manner.

37. Maurice Merleau-Ponty, *Phenomenology of Perception*, trans. Colin Smith (New York: Routledge, 1962), xvi–xvii.

38. Ibid., 92.

39. Ibid., 139–40.

40. Ibid., 91.

41. Ibid., 139–40.

42. Maurice Merleau-Ponty, *Signs* (Evanston, IL: Northwestern University Press, 1964), 66.

43. Lonergan, "Art," in *Topics in Education*, 217.

44. Ibid.

45. Merleau-Ponty, *Signs*, 66.

46. Merleau-Ponty, *Visible and the Invisible*, 139.

47. "We must not think the flesh starting from substances, from body and spirit—for then it would be the union of contradictories—but we must think it . . . as an element, as the concrete emblem of a general manner of being." Merleau-Ponty, *Visible and the Invisible*, 147.

Chapter 5

1. Thomas Aquinas, *Summa Theologica* I.20.2 (Benziger, 1:115).

2. Percy Bysshe Shelley, "Ozymandias." In particular, "And on the pedestal, these words appear: / My name is Ozymandias, King of Kings; / Look on my Works, ye Mighty, and despair! / Nothing beside remains. Round the decay / Of that colossal Wreck, boundless and bare / The lone and level sands stretch far away." Poetry Foundation, https://www.poetryfoundation.org/poems/46565 /ozymandias.

3. The Stoic *memento mori* remembers the condition of passing that attends to presence in the cosmos, a presence casually forgotten in the hubris of our projects. Seneca wrote, "Therefore, let us so order our minds as if we had come to the very end. Let us postpone nothing. Let us balance life's account every day. . . . One who daily puts the finishing touches to his life is never in want of time." "On the Futility of Planning Ahead," letter 101 in *Moral Letters to Lucilius/Letters from a Stoic*, trans. Richard Mott Gummere (Loeb Classical Library edition, 1915), https://onemorelibrary.com/index.php/en/?option=com _djclassifieds&format=raw&view=download&task=download&fid=16913. Epictetus similarly wrote, "Let death and exile, and all other things which appear terrible be daily before your eyes, but chiefly death, and you will never entertain any abject thought, nor too eagerly covet anything." *Enchiridion*,

section 21, http://www.perseus.tufts.edu/hopper/text?doc=Perseus%3Atext
%3A1999.01.0237%3Atext%3Denc%3Achapter%3D21. Marcus Aurelius:
"Since you may depart from life this very moment, regulate every act and
thought accordingly." *Meditations* 2.8, ed. Richard Miller, https://archive.org
/details/meditations-marcus-aurelius-2020-edit-pdf/mode/2up?q=%22leave
+life%22. For an excellent commentary on the Stoics, see Brad Inwood, ed.,
The Cambridge Companion to the Stoics (Cambridge: Cambridge University
Press, 2003).

   4. Plato, *Symposium*, in *Collected Dialogues of Plato*, 526–74. In order of
presentation, the first five speeches describe love as fortifying; as enduring and
heavenly; as healing; as yearning; and as fertile. Socrates's speech is the sixth.
The seventh speech is made in honor of Socrates as the embodiment of love
and the lover of the loveliest reality of all, wisdom. Subsequent citations of the
Symposium are in the text.

   5. Aristotle, *Nicomachean Ethics*, books 8 and 9, in *Complete Works*,
2:1825–52. Subsequent citations of *Nicomachean Ethics* are in the text.

   6. John von Heyking discusses the crucial political importance of Aristotle's friendship of *synaisthesis*, a friendship that lives by a conjoint love of,
and active search for, the good. See Heyking, *The Form of Politics: Aristotle and
Plato on Friendship* (Montreal: McGill-Queens University Press, 2016).

   7. In Boethius's *The Consolation of Philosophy*, Lady Philosophy explains
why the bad man is to be pitied for his unhappiness. "Hating evil men would
make no sense. Viciousness is a kind of disease of the soul, like illness in the
body. And if sickness of the body is not something we hate, but rather regard
with sympathy, we have much more reason to pity those whose minds are af-
flicted with wickedness, a thing worse than any sickness." *The Consolation of
Philosophy* 4.4, trans. Richard Green (Indianapolis: Bobbs-Merrill Educational
Publishing, 1978), 88.

   8. Aristotle, *On the Soul* 430a17–19, in *Complete Works*, 1:684. One cannot overestimate the importance of the Aristotelian differentiation. It is the
source of a tradition that took on a life of its own, especially in the Islamic
intellectual world of the *falasifa* (most famously in Averroës) and in those in-
fluenced by them in Latin Christendom such as Siger de Brabant, while the
Scholasticism from Albert the Great and Thomas Aquinas onward appropri-
ated the differentiation for Christian anthropology and theology. Furthermore,
we recall Lonergan's cognitional method, which, although appropriating and
adapting Thomas Aquinas's theory of the intellect, can legitimately be considered a further differentiation of the Aristotelian passive and active intellects.

   9. Voegelin, "What Is Political Reality?," 348.

   10. The "Other"—capitalized—is the conventional English translation of
each of Levinas's four French terms: *l'autre, l'Autre, l'autrui* and *l'Autrui*. The
"Other" will be used throughout the book to refer to the person in one's proximity. It should be noted that there is (a) a difficulty in capturing in English the
differing nuances of each of the French terms, which do not easily translate,
and (b) a difficulty in rendering Levinas's intention in his choice of term. Dino
Galetti explores these difficulties and their consequences in interpretation of

Levinas in "The Grammar of Levinas' other, Other, autrui, Autrui: Addressing Translation Conventions and Interpretation in English-Language Levinas Studies," *South African Journal of Philosophy* 34, no. 2 (2015): 199–213.

11. Levinas, *Totality and Infinity*, 291.

12. "The idea of infinity is the mode of being, the *infinition*, of infinity. Infinity does not first exist, *then* reveal itself. Its infinition is produced as revelation, as a positing of its idea in *me*. . . . Subjectivity realizes these impossible exigencies—the astonishing feat of containing more than it is possible to contain." Ibid., 27.

13. Ibid., 79.

14. Ibid. 304.

15. Emmanuel Levinas, *Ethics and Infinity: Conversations with Philippe Nemo* (Pittsburgh: Duquesne University Press, 1985), 86.

16. Ibid. In a similar vein, Martin Buber writes, "The relation to the You is unmediated. Nothing conceptual intervenes between I and You, no prior knowledge and no imagination; and memory itself is changed as it plunges from particularity into wholeness. No purpose intervenes between I and You, no greed and no anticipation. . . . Only where all means have disintegrated encounters occur." *I and Thou*, trans. Walter Kaufmann (New York: Touchstone, 1996), 62–63.

17. Levinas, *Ethics and Infinity*, 89.

18. "Whence came this shock when I passed, indifferent . . . under the Other's (*Autrui*) gaze? The relationship with the Other (*Autrui*) puts me into question, empties me of myself and empties me without end, showing me ever new resources. I did not know I was so rich, but I no longer have the right to keep anything for myself." Emmanuel Levinas, "Meaning and Sense," in *Basic Philosophical Writings*, 52.

19. Buber, *I and Thou*, 66.

20. For an extended consideration of both convergence and divergence between the two thinkers, see especially Peter Atterton, Matthew Calarco, and Maurice Friedman, eds., *Levinas and Buber: Dialogue and Difference* (Pittsburg: Duquesne University Press, 2004).

21. Buber, *I and Thou*, 66.

22. Emmanuel Levinas, "God and Philosophy," in *Basic Philosophical Writings*, 140.

23. Levinas, *Totality and Infinity*, 256.

24. "The Desirable does not gratify my Desire but hollows it out, and somehow nourishes me with new hungers." Levinas, "Meaning and Sense," 52.

25. Levinas, *Totality and Infinity*, 256.

26. Ibid., 257–58.

27. Ibid., 259.

28. Ibid., 260.

29. See my discussion of matrimony in chapter 8.

30. Levinas, *Totality and Infinity*, 263.

31. Emmanuel Levinas, "Enigma and Phenomenon," in *Basic Philosophical Writings*, 74.

32. Ibid., 76.

33. Levinas, "God and Philosophy," 140–41.

34. Ibid., 141. In his *Otherwise than Being, or Beyond Essence* (190), Levinas writes of God, "But the name outside of essence of beyond essence, the individual prior to individuality, is named God. It precedes all divinity, that is, the divine essence which the false gods, individuals sheltered in their concept, lay claim to."

35. Levinas, "God and Philosophy," 141.

36. Emmanuel Levinas, "Essence and Disinterestedness," in *Basic Philosophical Writings*, 125.

37. In *Adieu to Emmanuel Levinas*, Jacques Derrida writes, "Although the word is neither frequently used nor emphasized within it, *Totality and Infinity* bequeaths to us an immense treatise on *hospitality.*" *Adieu to Emmanuel Levinas* (Stanford, CA: Stanford University Press, 1999), 21.

38. David Walsh, *The Politics of the Person as the Politics of Being* (Notre Dame, IN: University of Notre Dame Press, 2016), 123.

39. Levinas, *Otherwise than Being, or Beyond Essence*, 176. Levinas uses the term *il y a*, a derivation of Heidegger's *Es gibt*, but these contemporary symbols of uncanniness are preceded by Pascal's exploration. "The eternal silence of these infinite spaces frightens me" (206). Pascal is confused, because the modern human being has fallen from his proper place in the cosmos and cannot find it again. "True nature being lost, everything becomes its own nature" (426); "[Man] has plainly gone astray and fallen from his true place without being able to find it again. He seeks it anxiously and unsuccessfully everywhere in impenetrable darkness" (427). Pascal, *Pensées*, intro. T. S. Eliot (New York: E. P. Dutton and Co., Inc., 1958).

40. Walsh, *Politics of the Person*, 124. We can grasp the finite as finite only because we have already surpassed the finite. "Thinking takes its stand within the absolute whose reach is infinite. This does not mean that we are able to think the absolute, since we are not absolute, merely that our thinking occurs within the absolute" (128). See Plato, *Republic* 509b6, in *Collected Dialogues of Plato*, 744: "In like manner, then, you are to say that the objects of knowledge not only receive from the presence of the good their being known, but their very existence and essence is derived to them from it, though the good itself is not essence but still transcends essence in dignity and surpassing power."

41. In *Metaphysics* 1048a25, Aristotle makes the distinction between two kinds of power: *kinesis* and *energeia*. Whereas *kinesis* is the exercise of a power that brings about a change, *energeia* is the power to bring a thing from potentiality to actuality. By *energeia* is a thing brought to its proper end. In *Metaphysics* 1050a21–23, Aristotle writes, "For the action is the end, and the actuality [*energeia*] is the action. Therefore, even the *word* 'actuality' [*energeia*] is derived from 'action' [*ergon*], and points to the fulfillment." In *Complete Works of Aristotle*, 2:1658.

42. Walsh, *Politics of the Person*, 133.

43. *Periagoge* is Plato's term for a turning around of the soul, or an openness, to the light that beckons it toward a higher caliber of truth and being. Plato, *Republic* 518d.

44. Walsh, *Politics of the Person*, 133. Subsequent citations are in the text.

45. Emmanuel Levinas, "Transcendence and Height," in *Basic Philosophical Writings*, 27.

46. Levinas, *Otherwise than Being, or Beyond Essence*, 140. Levinas clarifies the meaning of "the other" with a lower-case "o": "The other is from the first the brother to all the other men" (158).

Chapter 6

1. Levinas, "Transcendence and Height," in *Basic Philosophical Writings*, 27.

2. "Nous brûlons du désir de trouver une assiette ferme." Fragment 43 in *Pascal's Pensées*, trans. H. F. Stewart (New York: Pantheon Books, 1950), 24.

3. C. S. Lewis, "Equality," in *Present Concerns*, ed. Walter Cooper (New York: HarperOne, 2017), 11.

4. Ambrose, *De incarnationis Dominicae sacramento* 3.18. For the translation of Ambrose, see *The Sacrament of the Incarnation of Our Lord*, in *Saint Ambrose: Theological and Dogmatic Works*, trans. Roy J. Deferrari, The Fathers of the Church: A New Translation 44 (Washington, DC: Catholic University of America Press, 1963), 219–62, http://www.strobertbellarmine.net/books/CUAPS--044.pdf.

5. Augustine, *On the Trinity* 5.11, trans. Arthur West Haddan, in *The Nicene and Post-Nicene Fathers*, Series 1, ed. Philip Schaff (Buffalo, NY: Christian Literature Publishing, 1887), rev. and ed. Kevin Knight, New Advent, http://www.newadvent.org/fathers/130105.htm. Adam Kotsko explores the theme of the Holy Spirit as *communio* and therefore as a gift mutually given and received and considers the implications of this both for the church as a community and for the notion of proprietorship in the political community more generally. See Adam Kotsko, "Gift and Communion: The Holy Spirit in Augustine's *De Trinitate*," in *Scottish Journal of Theology* 62 (2010): 1–12.

6. See Rule of St. Benedict, chs. 23 and 24, "On Excommunication for Faults" and "What the Measure of Excommunication Should Be," respectively, Online Guide to Saint Benedict, http://www.e-benedictine.com/rule/#ch23.

7. See Linda Clarke and Christine Carpenter, *Political Culture in Late Medieval Britain* (Woodbridge, UK: Boydell Press, 2004), 160. For further commentary on the historical development of "community" see Warren C. Brown, "Community," in *Encyclopedia of Political Theory*, ed. Mark Bevir (Thousand Oaks, CA: SAGE Reference, 2010), 1:256–60.

8. Gabriel Marcel, *The Mystery of Being*, vol. 1, *Reflection and Mystery*, trans. G. S. Fraser (Chicago: Henry Regnery, 1950), 178–79.

9. Michael Oakeshott, "Character of a Modern European State," in *On Human Conduct* (Oxford: Clarendon, 1975), 197–203, 314–15.

10. Society is a "cosmion of meaning, illuminated from within by its own self-interpretation." Eric Voegelin, *The New Science of Politics*, in *Modernity without Restraint*, vol. 5 of *The Collected Works of Eric Voegelin* (Columbia: University of Missouri Press, 2000), 129.

11. *Collins Latin Dictionary* (Glasgow: HarperCollins, 2004), s.v. "munus."

12. Roberto Esposito, *Communitas: The Origin and Destiny of Community Cultural Memory in the Present* (Stanford, CA: Stanford University Press, 2010), 3–4.

13. Ibid.

14. Ibid., 6. This is reminiscent of the nineteenth-century thinker Giuseppe Mazzini, who exhorts his compatriots, "Workingmen, brothers—understand me well. When I say that the consciousness of your rights will never suffice to produce an important and lasting progress, I do not ask you to renounce those rights. I merely say that such rights can only exist as a consequence of duties fulfilled, and that we must begin with the latter in order to achieve the former.... Hence, when you hear those who preach the necessity of a social transformation declare that they can accomplish it by invoking only your rights, be grateful to them for their good intentions, but distrustful of the outcome." "The Duties of Man," in *Joseph Mazzini: A Memoir*, ed. Emilie Ashurst Venturi (London: Alexander and Shepheard, 1885), 46.

15. Plato, *Gorgias* 508a (Bekker, 136), in *The Works of Plato*, trans. Henry Cary (London: Henry G. Bohn, 1848), 211. The word "communion" is curiously absent in later translations.

16. Esposito, *Communitas*, 10.

17. Bernard Lonergan, "Existenz and Aggiornamento," in *Collection*, 243.

18. Ibid.

19. Ibid., 224–27. Lonergan notes that the three classic styles of philosophy are framed by how each approaches the world mediated by meaning: for the naïve realist, such a world is merely an abstraction; for the idealist, such a world "is the only world we know intelligently and rationally, and it is not real but ideal; and for the critical realist it is the world we know intelligently and rationally, and it is not ideal but real" (225).

20. Ibid., 244.

21. Ibid., 245. At the time of writing "Existenz and Aggiornamento," Lonergan had not fully developed decision as the fourth level of cognition. Presumably, common value would correspond to this fourth level, which Lonergan is here implying by "common commitments."

22. Ibid.

23. Bernard Lonergan, *Insight: A Study of Human Understanding*, ed. Frederick Crowe, S.J., and Robert Doran, S.J., vol. 3 of *The Collected Works of Bernard Lonergan* (Toronto: University of Toronto Press: 1992), 237.

24. Ibid.

25. Ibid.

26. Ibid., 240.

27. Ibid., 237. Lonergan tells us that "a dialectic is a concrete unfolding of linked but opposed principles of change" (242).

28. Ibid., 243.

29. Lonergan, *Method in Theology*, 52.

30. Ibid.

31. Ibid., 55.

32. Ibid.

33. Buber, *I and Thou*, 53–54.

34. Martin Buber, "The Education of Character," in *Between Man and Man* (New York: Routledge, 2002), 123–39.

35. Aldo Leopold refers to the natural world as a "biotic community" of which we are citizens along with everything else. His "land ethic" urges a moral perspective of community that would include the natural world and supersede the utilitarian calculus of land as commodity. *A Sand County Almanac: And Sketches Here and There* (Oxford: Oxford University Press, 1977), 201–26.

36. Martin Buber, *The Knowledge of Man*, trans. M. S. Friedman (New York: Harper & Row, 1965), 60, 67.

37. Surely this was what Adam Smith had in mind when he wrote, "It is not from the benevolence of the butcher, the brewer, or the baker, that we have our dinner, but from their regard for their own interest." "Of the Principle Which Gives Occasion to the Division of Labour," in *An Inquiry into the Nature and Causes of the Wealth of Nations* (1776), available from the Online Library of Liberty, https://oll.libertyfund.org/title/smith-an-inquiry-into-the-nature-and-causes-of-the-wealth-of-nations-cannan-ed-vol-1#preview.

38. Gabriel Marcel, "I and Thou," in *The Philosophy of Martin Buber*, ed. Paul Arthur Schilpp (Cambridge: Cambridge University Press, 1967), 43.

39. "Let us say that the *ego* . . . is ruled by a sort of vague fascination, which is localised, almost by chance, in objects arousing sometimes desires, sometimes terror. It is, however, precisely against such a condition that what I consider the essential characteristic of the person is opposed, the characteristic, that is to say, of availability (*disponibilité*)." Gabriel Marcel, *Homo Viator*, trans. Emma Craufurd (Chicago: Henry Regnery, 1951), 23.

40. Gabriel Marcel, *Being and Having: An Existentialist Diary*, trans. Katharine Farrer (New York: Harper and Row, 1965), 106.

41. In fact, Marcel criticizes Spinoza's definition of *superbia* in the *Ethics*: "'Pride in an exaggeratedly good opinion of oneself which arises from self-love.' In reality this is a definition of vanity. As for pride, it consists in drawing one's strength solely from oneself. The proud man is cut off from a certain form of communion with his fellow men, which pride, acting as a principle of destruction, tends to break down." See Gabriel Marcel, *The Philosophy of Existentialism* (New York: Kensington Publishing, 1984), 32.

42. Gabriel Marcel, *Metaphysical Journal*, trans. Bernard Wall (Chicago: Henry Regnery, 1952), 247.

43. Marcel, *Mystery of Being*, 1:91–92 (emphasis original).

44. Margaret M. Mullan, quoting Marcel, writes that "communion of presence forms ground for community. Every experience of being *with* an other person is a meeting and 'within the meeting there is created a certain community.'" She continues by invoking belonging directly: "One who recognizes presence of others, communicates to the others, 'you belong' and 'you belong *with* me.' When we mutually acknowledge the presence of others, that they belong, our beings are refreshed." *Seeking Communion as Healing Dialogue: Gabriel Marcel's Philosophy for Today* (Lanham, MD: Lexington Books, 2021), 112.

45. Marcel, *Being and Having*, 125.

46. Emmanuel Levinas wryly notes that "the incarnation of human subjectivity guarantees its spirituality (I do not see what angels could give one another or how they help one another)." *Ethics and Infinity*, 97.

47. Anaximander, fragment 1, in Freeman, *Ancilla to the Pre-Socratic Philosophers*, 19.

48. Jacques Maritain, *The Person and the Common Good*, trans. John J. Fitzgerald (New York: Charles Scribner's Sons, 1947), 436.

49. Ibid., 444.

50. Ibid., 437.

51. Ibid., 438.

52. Ibid., 439.

53. David Walsh, *The Priority of the Person* (Notre Dame, IN: University of Notre Dame Press, 2020), 80.

54. Maritain, *Person and the Common Good*, 444.

55. Paul VI, *Gaudium et spes*, ch. 2, section 26, available at the Vatican website, https://www.vatican.va/archive/hist_councils/ii_vatican_council/docu ments/vat-ii_const_19651207_gaudium-et-spes_en.html.

56. Maritain, *Person and the Common Good*, 442.

57. Sources of meaning are divided into transcendental and categorial: "The transcendental notions ground questioning. Answers develop categorial determinations." Lonergan, *Method in Theology*, 71.

58. Maritain writes, "Man is constituted a person, made for God and life eternal, before he is constituted a part of the city; and he is constituted a part of the family society before he is constituted part of the political society." *Person and the Common Good*, 448.

Chapter 7

1. See Tilo Schabert's discussion in *The Second Birth*, trans. Javier Ibanez-Noe (Chicago: University of Chicago Press, 2015), 57–58.

2. While the Enuma Elish probably dates to some time in the second millennium BCE, scholarly research has opened the veil on older symbolisms dating from well before the end of the Paleolithic period (approx. 11,000–12,000 years before present). Marie König, Alexander Marshack, Jean Clottes, Henri Breuil, and André Leroi-Gourhan, for example, examined and interpreted the meanings of many artefacts, discovering in bones and petroglyphs a potentially vast field of meaning. Human beings may always have been toolmakers, but as Marshack once said, we are primarily "symbol-makers." For a comprehensive account of the earliest attempts to symbolize an order of meaning, see Barry Cooper, *Paleolithic Politics: The Human Community in Early Art* (Notre Dame, IN: University of Notre Dame Press, 2020). Furthermore, see Tilo Schabert's work on enduring cosmological symbolism from the architecture of early cities onward: "The Cosmology of the Architecture of Cities," *Diogenes* 39, no. 156 (December 1991): 1–31.

3. Jordan Peterson, *Maps of Meaning: The Architecture of Belief* (New York: Routledge, 1999), 116.

4. Enuma Elish, quoted in Peterson, *Maps of Meaning*, 117. See Voegelin's commentary in *Israel and Revelation*, 78–84. On Tablet 2 of the Enuma Elish, lines 127 and 128, the god Anshar addresses Marduk on behalf of all gods, importuning him to save the entire order of the cosmos, generated from Tiamat, that she would now destroy. Anshar says, "Oh my [son], who knoweth all wisdom; Pacify [Tiama]t with thy pure incantation." From *The Seven Tablets of Creation*, transliterated by Leonard William King, 1902, https://www.sacred -texts.com/ane/stc/stc05.htm.

5. Peterson, *Maps of Meaning*, 123. King's translation is slightly different: "that the services of the gods may be established and that [their] shrines [may be built]." *Seven Tablets of Creation*, tablet 6, line 8, https://www.sacred-texts .com/ane/stc/stc09.htm.

6. Campbell, *Hero with a Thousand Faces*, 287–88.

7. Eliade, *A History of Religious Ideas*, vol. 1, *From the Stone Age to the Eleusinian Mysteries*, trans. W. R. Trask (Chicago: Chicago University Press, 1978), 75, quoted in Peterson, *Maps of Meaning*, 126. Compactness is an apt metaphor for the consubstantiality of cosmological consciousness in which we can see that the sacred and the political roles were operative, one within the other. The differentiation of things of Caesar from things of God had not yet occurred. See below.

8. Peterson, *Maps of Meaning*, 130.

9. Ibid., 131.

10. Matthew 22:21; Mark 12:17; Luke 20:25.

11. See my study on the development of order and civilizational consensus in medieval Latin Christendom in James Greenaway, *The Differentiation of Authority: The Medieval Turn toward Existence* (Washington DC: Catholic University of American Press, 2012).

12. Russell Kirk, *The Roots of American Order* (Washington, DC: Regnery Gateway, 1991), 6–7.

13. Aristotle, *Politics* 1252a1–6, 1252b28–30, in *Complete Works*, 2:1986–87.

14. In his *Nicomachean Ethics* 1094a24, Aristotle considers *eudaimonia* or happiness as the target at which all people, like archers, aim. *Complete Works*, 2:1729.

15. Tilo Schabert, *The Second Birth: On the Political Beginnings of Human Existence*, trans. Javier Ibañez-Noé (Chicago: University of Chicago Press, 2015), 17.

16. Tilo Schabert, *The Figure of Modernity* (Berlin: de Gruyter, 2020), 166.

17. Levinas, *Totality and Infinity*, 213.

18. See Levinas's closing remarks in "Peace and Proximity," 168–69.

19. Levinas, *Ethics and Infinity*, 80. Not all commentators on Levinas agree with him that politics is derived from ethics. Simon Critchley argues that politics is not founded on the ethical, or at least politics cannot be deduced from the ethical obligation. He proposes, with Jacques Derrida, that there is a gap, a "lacuna," a "hiatus" between ethics and politics, rather than a passage between

them. See Simon Critchley, "Five Problems in Levinas's View of Politics and the Sketch of a Solution to Them," *Political Theory* 32, no. 2 (2004): 172–85. Other commentators, such as Annabel Herzog, emphasize that there is passage from ethics to politics. Herzog names this passage "misery." See Annabel Herzog, "Is Liberalism 'All We Need'? Lévinas's Politics of Surplus," *Political Theory* 30, no. 2 (2002): 211–12.

20. See Voegelin's discussion of the adaptability of the symbol *omphalos* as a portal through which the stream of divine being flows into the world, including its political order. Voegelin, *Israel and Revelation*, 67–69.

21. Thomas Aquinas argues that governance indirectly retains its role in redemption. This is realized most clearly through law. In his *Summa Theologica*, his treatise on law appears in the sweep of his larger discussion of human actions, differentiated by internal and external principles. All human actions aim at some end, the highest of which is the good of salvation, the happiness of the beatific vision. All human actions participate to some degree in this. Law is an external principle of action, and in the course of his treatment, Aquinas writes, "But since some are found to be depraved, and prone to vice, and not easily amenable to words, it was necessary for such to be restrained from evil by force and fear, in order that, at least, they might desist from evil-doing, and leave others in peace, and that they themselves, by being habituated in this way, might be brought to do willingly what hitherto they did from fear, and thus become virtuous." I-II.95.1 (Benziger, 1:1013–14.)

22. Edmund Burke, *Reflections of the Revolution in France* (London: J. M. Dent and Sons, 1910), 93. By the time Burke was thinking about the meaning of *communitas*, the category of "social contract" was well set. From intuitions of social compacts and consensus in Thomas Hobbes's *Leviathan* and John Locke's *Second Treatise in Government* respectively to the extended meditation of Jean-Jacques Rousseau in *On the Social Contract*, Burke was merely utilizing an adaptable symbol for the unity of the political *communitas*. The health of social contract theory continues to this day. As well as famous contemporary accounts by John Rawls in *A Theory of Justice* (Cambridge, MA: Belknap Press, 1999) and David Gauthier in *Morals by Agreement* (Oxford: Clarendon, 1986), the social contract has been put to use in recent feminist and race theory. For example, see Carol Pateman, *The Sexual Contract* (Cambridge: Blackwell, 1997); Charles Mills, *The Racial Contract* (Ithaca, NY: Cornell University Press, 2022).

23. Karl Marx, *The German Ideology*, in *The Marx-Engels Reader*, ed. Robert C. Tucker (New York: Norton & Co., 1978), 193.

24. Burke, *Reflections*, 94.

25. Ibid., 94.

26. Thomas Aquinas, *Summa Theologica* II-II.26.8 ("Whether We Ought to Love More Those Who Are Connected with Us by Ties of Blood?" [Benziger, 2:1300–1301]).

27. Augustine, *City of God* 19.21 (Bettenson, 881). The Latin original is available at the Latin Library, https://www.thelatinlibrary.com/augustine/civ19 .shtml: "Ubi ergo iustitia uera non est, nec ius potest esse." Bettenson translates

this as "Where there is no true justice, there can be no right" (881–82). Further-more, for Augustine, the term "God" is largely convertible with "being," as I discussed above. The justice at stake can be understood as Rome's inadequate attunement to the divine order of being, which Augustine himself, as a Christian, experienced as eminently worthy of our love and life.

28. Ibid., 19.24 (Bettenson, 890).

29. "Political communion" is my term for what sustains the political community. Aristotle referred to like-mindedness. Frederick D. Wilhelmsen and Willmoore Kendall use "political orthodoxy" to signify the "tacit agreement on the meaning of the good life, and, therefore, on the meaning of man within the total economy of existence" within the political *communitas*. See Wilhelmsen and Kendall, "Cicero and the Politics of the Public Orthodoxy," in *Christianity and Political Philosophy*, ed. Frederick D. Wilhelmsen (Athens: University of Georgia Press, 1977), 35. Bruce Douglass renders like-mindedness as "civil theology" and maintains that it is the entirety of beliefs "through which the members of a political society relate their political experience to the ultimate conditions of human existence." See Bruce Douglass, "Civil Religion and Western Christianity," *Thought* 55 (June 1980): 169.

30. John Courtney Murray, *We Hold These Truths: Catholic Reflections of the American Proposition* (New York: Sheed & Ward, 1960), 9.

31. Johan Huizinga writes, "Freedom as a purely political principle seemed not only to combine easily with that of nationality, but to demand recognition of nationality as an indispensable basis, for freedom needed a subject." "Patriotism and Nationalism in European History," in *Men and Ideas: History, the Middle Ages, the Renaissance* (Princeton: Princeton University Press, 1959), 147. Huizinga characterizes the political landscape of the later eighteenth century in the West as a struggle to achieve an equilibrium among three political goods: freedom, nationality, and the administrative institutions of state.

32. See Eliade's discussion of chaos and cosmos in *The Sacred and the Profane* (New York: Harper & Row, 1959), 29–32.

33. Ibid., 30.

34. Ibid., 31–32, 34.

35. Ibid., 42.

36. From this experienced sacred center, Eliade elucidates a sequence of cosmological images that form a "system of the world": (a) sacredness forms a break in the homogeneity of space; (b) the break is also an opening from heaven to earth, from earth to the underworld, and vice versa; (c) communication with these other planes becomes possible; and (d) around this axis lies the territory as "our world," which is always the center of the cosmos. Ibid., 37.

37. Ibid., 47.

38. This is reminiscent of Stanley Rosen's thought on the importance of ordinary speech for communicating, in inchoate and never quite graspable ways, the *logoi* of human existence. See in particular Rosen, *Metaphysics in Ordinary Language* (New Haven: Yale University Press, 1999); Rosen, *The Elusiveness of the Ordinary: Studies in the Possibility of Philosophy* (New Haven: Yale University Press, 2002).

39. Alexis de Tocqueville, "On Public Spirit in the United States," in *Democracy in America*, ed. Eduardo Nolla James, trans. T. Schleifer (Indianapolis: Liberty Fund, 2014), 384–85 (vol. 1, pt. 2, ch. 6).

40. See Walker Connor's analysis of the twofold difficulty faced by multinational states: national self-determination and assimilation of various ethnic groups (ethnie). "Self-Determination: The New Phase," *World Politics* 20, no. 1 (1967): 30–53.

41. Glenn Albrecht, "Solastalgia: A New Concept in Human Health and Identity," *Philosophy Activism Nature* 3 (2005): 41–55.

42. Tocqueville, *Democracy in America*, 385.

43. Burke, *Reflections*, 31.

44. Ibid.

45. Tocqueville, "Activity Reigning in All Parts of the Body Politic of the United States: Influence That It Exerts on Society," in *Democracy in America*, 395, 396, 398 (vol. 1, pt. 2, ch. 6).

46. Edmund Burke, "Speech on the Conciliation with America (1775)," in *The Philosophy of Edmund Burke*, ed. Louis I. Bredvold and Ralph G. Ross (Ann Arbor, MI: Ann Arbor Paperbacks, 1970), 81.

47. See my remarks in the epilogue.

48. Aristotle, *Politics* 1282b27–30, in *Complete Works*, 2:2034.

49. Tocqueville, "That the Greatest Danger to the American Republics Comes from the Omnipotence of the Majority," in *Democracy in America*, 425 (vol. 1, pt. 2, ch. 7).

50. G. W. F. Hegel, *Philosophy of Right*, §142, trans. S. W. Dyde (Kitchener, ON: Batoche Books, 2001), 132.

51. Ibid., §160 (Dyde, 139).

52. Ibid., §182 (Dyde, 154).

53. Ibid., §258 (Dyde, 195).

54. Ibid.

55. Ibid.

56. Ibid., §258 (Dyde, 198). Hegel writes, "The state is not a work of art. It is in the world, in the sphere of caprice, accident, and error. Evil behaviour can doubtless disfigure it in many ways, but the ugliest man, the criminal, the invalid, the cripple, are living men. The positive thing, the life, is present in spite of defects, and it is with this affirmative that we have here to deal."

57. See John Stuart Mill, "On Nationality, as Connected with Representative Government," in *On Considerations on Representative Government*, ch. 16 (London: Electric Book Company, 2000) 284.

58. Aleksandr Solzhenitsyn told a commencement audience at Harvard University in 1978, "Every ancient and deeply rooted self-contained culture, especially if it is spread over a wide part of the earth's surface, constitutes a self-contained world, full of riddles and surprises to Western thinking." "Harvard Address," in *The Solzhenitsyn Reader: New and Essential Writings, 1947–2005*, ed. Edward E. Ericson Jr. and Daniel J. Mahoney (Wilmington, DE: ISI Books, 2006), 563.

59. Pierre Manent's concern with "depoliticization" becomes relevant with regard to governance. The smoothness of the bureaucratic and/or technocratic

governance in the European Union depends upon a politically disengaged population. See "Current Problems of European Democracy," *Modern Age* 45, no. 1 (Winter 2003): 7–16.

60. See Hans Kohn, *Nationalism: Its Meaning and History* (Malabar, FL: Krieger, 1982); Ernest Gellner, *Nations and Nationalism: New Perspectives on the Past* (Ithaca, NY: Cornell University Press, 2006); Benedict Anderson, *Imagined Communities: Reflections on the Origin and Spread of Nationalism* (New York: Veros Books, 2016).

61. Gellner, *Nations and Nationalism*, 1.

62. Daniele Conversi, "Mapping the Field: Theories of Nationalism and the Ethnosymbolic Approach," in *Nationalism and Ethnosymbolism: History, Culture and Ethnicity in the Formation of Nations*, ed. Athena S. Leoussi and Steven Grosby (Edinburgh: Edinburgh University Press, 2007), 27n4.

63. See Eric Hobsbawm, *The Age of Extremes* (London: Abacus, 1995).

64. Johan Huizinga, "Patriotism and Nationalism in European History," in *Men and Ideas: History, the Middle Ages, the Renaissance* (Princeton: Princeton University Press, 1959), 97–156.

65. Hans Kohn, *The Idea of Nationalism: A Study in Its Origins and Background* (London: Routledge, 2005), 204.

66. Mill, *On Considerations on Representative Government*, ch. 16.

67. Ibid.

68. Walker Connor, "The Timelessness of Nations," *Nations and Nationalism* 10, no. 1–2 (2004): 35.

69. Walker Connor, *Ethnonationalism: The Quest for Understanding* (Princeton: Princeton University Press, 1994), 202. Friedrich Meinicke provides a naturalistic notion of the state as "a natural core based on blood relationships." *Cosmopolitanism and the National State*, ed. Felix Gilbert, trans. R. B. Kimer (Princeton: Princeton University Press, 1970), 9.

70. Walker Connor, "Nationalism and Political Illegitimacy," in *Ethnonationalism in the Contemporary World: Walker Connor and the Study of Nationalism*, ed. Daniele Conversi (New York: Routledge, 2002), 29.

71. Anthony D. Smith, *The Ethnic Origins of Nations* (Oxford: Blackwell, 1986), 32.

72. Anthony D. Smith, "When Is a Nation?," *Geopolitics* 7, no. 2 (2002): 15.

73. See Montserrat Guiberneau, "Nations and National Identity," *Nations and Nationalism* 10, no. 1–2 (2004): 125–41.

74. Margaret Canovan, *Nationhood and Political Theory* (Cheltenham, UK: Edward Elgar, 1996), 1.

75. Margaret Canovan, "Sleeping Dogs, Prowling Cats and Soaring Doves: Three Paradoxes in the Political Theory of Nationhood," *Political Studies* 49 (2001): 203–15.

76. Canovan, *Nationhood and Political Theory*, 71.

77. Ibid., 139.

78. Johann Gottfried von Herder, *Reflections on the Philosophy of the History of Mankind*, abridged with an introduction by Frank E. Manuel (Chicago: University of Chicago Press, 1968), 84.

79. In discussing the tension between particularism and universalism, I have purposely avoided entering into the ongoing debate among communitarians and liberals. I am not aiming to set out a position, but to recover belonging as the human mode of existence in the cosmos. Both communitarian and liberal insights seem to be valid to the extent that they recognize that sociopolitical-historical belonging is born of the in-between tension of particularity-universality. It's worth noting, at least in passing, that liberals of a neo-Kantian persuasion, such as John Rawls in his *A Theory of Justice* and Francis Fukuyama in *The End of History and the Last Man* (New York: Free Press, 2006), emphasize a universal liberal egalitarianism, constitutive of universal progress, but seem to prescind from cultural and historical concreteness. Among communitarians, Alasdair McIntyre emphasizes a notion of *communitas* that binds and orders its people in ways reminiscent of Aristotle's discussion of the *polis*, while Michael Walzer in *Spheres of Justice* (New York: Basic Books, 1983), aware of the Western focus of most political theory, attempts to highlight the cultural concreteness of non-Western polities. See Alasdair McIntyre, *After Virtue: A Study in Moral Theory*, 3rd ed. (Notre Dame, IN: University of Notre Dame Press, 2007).

80. Frederick Barnard comments that Herder stressed the connectedness of nation and *Humanität* "as a performative principle, which enters into and enriches human aspirations within their particular milieu and sphere of endeavour." *Herder on Nationality, Humanity, and History* (Montreal: McGill-Queens University Press, 2003), 77. See also Hans Kohn's commentary in *The Idea of Nationalism: A Study in Its Origins and Background*, with an introduction by Craig Calhoun (New Brunswick, NJ: Transaction, 2008), 427–51.

81. It may, however, be a sorrow hard to evoke in observers who are secure on their perches above their own political arrangements. Margaret Canovan characterizes political theorists' attitudes toward nations and nationhood as letting sleeping dogs lie. Typically, theorists take "for granted the presence of nations at the same time as ignoring or disparaging them." But the option of letting sleeping dogs lie "is no longer available: for the past decade the dogs have been awake and barking, roused by events outside the control of academics." Canovan, "Sleeping Dogs, Prowling Cats and Soaring Doves," 206.

82. Hannah Arendt, *The Origins of Totalitarianism* (New York: Meridian Books, 1962), 462; Aleksandr Solzenitsyn, *The Gulag Archipelago: An Experiment in Literary Investigation*, abridged by Edward E. Ericson Jr., with a foreword by Anne Applebaum (New York: Harper Perennial Modern Classics, 2007), 77.

83. The latter characterizes the work of Charter 77 in late twentieth-century Czechoslovakia. See Jan Patočka, "Two Charta 77 Texts," in *Jan Patočka: Philosophy and Selected Writings*, ed. Erazim Kohák (Chicago: University of Chicago Press, 1989); Michael Zantovsky, *Havel: A Life* (New York: Grove Press, 2014).

84. Geoffrey A. Hosking, *Rulers and Victims: The Russians in the Soviet Union* (Cambridge, MA: Belknap Press, 2006), 186.

85. Anna Akhmatova, "Requiem," in *The Word That Causes Death's Defeat: Poems of Memory*, trans. Nancy K. Anderson (New Haven: Yale University Press, 2004), 135, 144.

86. Brendan Purcell, *From Big Bang to Big Mystery*, 282–83.

87. Plato, *Crito* 54b2–c, in *Collected Dialogues of Plato*, 39.

88. The story of Blessed Franz Jägerstätter is an equivalent evocation of the meaning of a life and death in the presence of the cosmos. Like Akhmatova, Jägerstätter bore authentic witness to the good of personal and political existence and belonging under the conditions of Nazi disintegration. See Gordon Zahn, *In Solitary Witness: The Life and Death of Franz Jägerstätter* (Springfield, IL: Templegate, 1986); Franz Jägerstätter, *Letters and Writings from Prison*, ed. Erna Putz (Maryknoll, NY: Orbis Books, 2009).

89. Attributed to Solon is the fragment, "'Tis very hard to tell the unseen measure of sound judgment, which yet alone hath the ends of all things." In *Elegy and Iambus: With the Anacreontea*, part 1, "Elegiac Poets from Callinus to Critias," ed. and trans. J. M. Edmonds (London: William Heinemann, 1931), 133.

90. Schabert, *Second Birth*, 57–58. See Plato, *Laws* 713b1–714a8, in *Collected Dialogues of Plato*, 1304–5.

91. Schabert, *Second Birth*, xvi.

Chapter 8

1. Eric Voegelin, *Plato and Aristotle*, vol. 3 of *Order and History*; vol. 16 of *The Collected Works of Eric Voegelin* (Columbia: University of Missouri Press, 2000), 419.

2. There is a wealth of literature on the topic of sacramentality by theologians. Among the works most notable for their extension beyond Christian doctrine are Alexander Schmemann, *Church, World, Mission: Reflections on Orthodoxy and the West* (New York: St. Vladimir's Seminary Press, 1979); Graham Hughes, *Reformed Sacramentality* (Collegeville, MN: Liturgical Press, 2017); Bernard Cooke, *Sacraments and Sacramentality*, 2nd ed. (New London, CT: Twenty Third Publications, 1994); Lizette Larson-Miller, *Sacramentality Renewed: Contemporary Conversations in Sacramental Theology* (Collegeville, MN: Liturgical Press, 2016).

3. Thomas Aquinas, *Summa Theologica* III.60.2 (Benziger, 2:2346).

4. Aquinas, *Summa Theologica* III.60.1 (Benziger, 2:2345).

5. Catechism of the Catholic Church, 1327. "In brief, the Eucharist is the sum and summary of our faith: 'Our way of thinking is attuned to the Eucharist, and the Eucharist in turn confirms our way of thinking.'" In the Catechism of St. Philaret, 317, the Eastern church says: "What is to be noticed of the Sacrament of the Communion in regard to divine service in the Church? This: that it forms the chief and most essential part of divine service."

6. Aquinas, *Summa Theologica* III.73.4 (Benziger, 2:2436–37). Thomas then adds, "In Greek, moreover, it is called Metalepsis, i.e. 'Assumption,'

because, as Damascene says (*De Fide Orth.* iv), 'we thereby assume the Godhead of the Son.'"

7. Augustine, *Confessions* 1.1, trans. Henry Chadwick (Oxford: Oxford University Press, 1992), 3.

8. Aquinas, *Summa Theologica* III.60.3 (Benziger, 2:2346).

9. A final cause is the fourth of Aristotle's four causes (material, formal, efficient, and final), which he defines as "the end [*telos*], that for which a thing is done" (*Physics* 194b33ff., in *Complete Works*, 1:332; *Metaphysics* 1013a33ff., in *Complete Works*, 2:1600).

10. Aristotle uses this example in various places: *Physics* 194b13; *Metaphysics* 1032a25, 1033b32, 1049b25, 1070a8, 1092a16.

11. Aristotle, *Parts of Animals* 640a.18–19, in *Complete Works*, 1:996.

12. For example, in *On the Soul*, Aristotle characterizes the soul as the principle of life, the nature or substantial form of the body, and purposiveness (or that for which the body is shaped). Thus, the soul is simultaneously the efficient, formal, and final cause of the human being. "The terms cause and source have many senses. But the soul is the cause of its body alike in all three senses which we explicitly recognize. It is the source of movement, it is the end, it is the essence of the whole living body." *On the Soul* 415b9–12, in *Complete Works*, 1:661.

13. James Allen writes about the meaning of consummation in each of these senses in ancient Greek thought generally: "For in paradigm cases of action it will be the fulfillment or consummation of the action that both brings it to a close and was the reason or that for whose sake the agent undertook it in the first place." "Why Are There Ends of Both Goods and Evils in Ancient Ethical Theory," in *Strategies of Argument: Essays in Ancient Ethics, Epistemology, and Logic*, ed. Mi-Kyoung Lee (New York: Oxford University Press, 2014), 240.

14. As I noted in chapter 5, Aristotle writes, "For the action is the end, and the actuality [*energeia*] is the action. Therefore, even the *word* 'actuality' [*energeia*] is derived from 'action' [*ergon*], and points to the fulfillment [*entelecheia*] [being-at-an-end]." *Metaphysics* 1050a21–23, in *Complete Works*, 2:1658.

15. Aristotle, *Nicomachean Ethics* 1141a16–19, in *Complete Works*, 2:1801.

16. Wonderment as the beginning of philosophy appears in Plato's *Theaetetus* 155d2 and Aristotle's *Metaphysics* 982b12.

17. Plato, *Phaedo* 67e, in *The Dialogues of Plato*, trans. B. Jowett (Oxford: Clarendon, 1892), 207.

18. There are two etymological elements in the word "matrimony" that are suggestive for its meaning. The first part derives from the Latin word *matrem*, meaning motherhood. The second part is *-monium*, a suffix meaning "a condition of" or "a function of" or "an action of." Thus, "matrimony" is a well-suited symbol by which we can only intend one-man, one-woman marriages of which motherhood or parenthood is an inherent possibility.

19. Why B should engage in a defense of marriage is explained in his statement, "It is indeed my vocation as a husband to fight for marriage—*pro aris et focis*." Søren Kierkegaard, *Either/Or: A Fragment of Life*, trans. Alastair

Hannay (New York: Penguin Books, 2004), 386. Subsequent citations of this work are in the text.

20. All that A allows himself to enjoy is the libidinous abstraction of consciousness from flesh. Sensuality for him means the isolated but thrilling moment of seduction, the enjoyment of the flesh of the woman. It does not extend beyond that moment to the consummated and consummating communion of conscious incarnate life in between the spouses and the cosmos.

21. David Walsh writes, "If there is love between the two then it must become so real that it too is other. Only as an other person is the love between them so real that they set themselves aside for its sake. . . . Love itself must be a third person as the only surety that love belongs neither to lover nor beloved." *Politics of the Person*, 144–45.

22. Solon, in *Elegy and Iambus*, 133.

23. "L'expérience nous montre qu'aimer ce n'est point nous regarder l'un l'autre mais regarder ensemble dans la même direction." Antoine de St. Exupéry, *Terre des Hommes*, 146, BiblioVox, https://www.bibliovox.com/reader/docid/45000818/page/146.

24. Voegelin, *World of the Polis*, 68.

25. Voegelin, *New Science of Politics*, 130–31.

26. Kuyuk Khan to Pope Innocent IV, ca. AD 1246 , quoted in Voegelin, *New Science of Politics*, 133. Voegelin notes that the pattern of claiming to represent the truth—the truth of the cosmos, the truth of nature, the truth of progress, the truth of history—is a principle that drives contemporary ideological movements too. "In Marxian dialectics, for instance, the truth of cosmic order is replaced by the truth of a historically immanent order" (*New Science of Politics*, 134).

27. David Walsh, "Are Freedom and Dignity Enough? A Reflection on Liberal Abbreviations," in *Priority of the Person*, 49–50.

28. Levinas evocatively reminds us that there are "the tears that a civil servant cannot see." *Otherwise than Being, or Beyond Essence*, 213.

29. Walsh, *Priority of the Person*, 31. Subsequent citations to this work are in the text.

30. Walsh, *Politics of the Person*, 194.

31. Marx announces in the *Economic and Philosophic Manuscripts of 1844* that "Communism is the riddle of history solved, and it knows itself to be this solution." *The Marx-Engels Reader*, ed. Robert C. Tucker, 2nd ed. (New York: Norton, 1978), 84. On Joachim of Fiore, see especially chapters 9–12 in his *Book of Concordance*, in *Apocalyptic Spirituality: Treatises and Letters of Lactantius, Adso of Montier-en-Der, Joachim of Fiore, the Franciscan Spirituals, Savonarola*, trans. Bernard McGinn (New York: Paulist Press, 1979), 129–34.

32. Walsh, *Politics of the Person*, 194. Walsh reiterates the point that neither persons nor history is simply present, simply there to be read. For example, he writes that "history comes into view from the perspective of a viewpoint outside of it, but endures under the shadow of its own supersession" (210).

33. Ibid., 194.

34. Ibid., 197.

35. See Voegelin's discussion of an Egyptian case of a man in despair struggling to articulate his experience in available symbols in "Dispute of a Man, Who Contemplates Suicide, with His Soul," in *Published Essays, 1966–1985*, 58–68.

36. Voegelin, *Drama of Humanity*, 186.

37. Ibid., 204.

38. Ibid., 206.

39. Voegelin, *Plato and Aristotle*, 68.

40. Ibid., 71–72.

Epilogue

1. Richard Schacht, *Alienation* (New York: Anchor Books, 1971), 15; see also 43.

2. Ibid., 43.

3. See Marx's discussion of the various dimensions of alienation or estrangement in "Estranged Labour," in *Economic and Philosophic Manuscripts of 1844*, 70–81. Walter Kaufmann notes, "While Marx uses 'alienation' in several different senses, the phenomenon that concerns him most is the dehumanization of man. Man's loss of independence, his impoverishment, his estrangement from his fellow men, and his involvement in labor that is devoid of any originality, spontaneity, or creativity are so many aspects of man's estrangement from his true nature." "The Inevitability of Alienation," in Schacht, *Alienation*, xxiv–xxv.

4. Marx, *German Ideology*, 193.

5. Voegelin, *New Science of Politics*, 186.

6. Ibid., 122.

7. Voegelin, *Ecumenic Age*, 253–54.

8. Voegelin, *New Science of Politics*, 186.

9. Arendt, *Origins of Totalitarianism*, 462.

10. Ibid.

11. See Camus, *The Myth of Sisyphus* (London: Penguin Books, 1975), 107–11.

12. *Ressentiment* is Max Scheler's term for resentment and envy that degenerate explosively into malice fueled by a sense of one's present impotence. Max Scheler, *Ressentiment* (Milwaukee: Marquette University Press, 2007).

13. Friedrich Nietzsche, *Will to Power* (New York: Vintage Books, 1968), 18.

14. Nietzsche, preface to *Will to Power*, 3.

INDEX

Abraham, 30–31, 48. *See also* Levinas,
  Emmanuel
absurdity, 273–75
  and Lonergan, 176
  See also alienation; unbelonging
Akhmatova, Anna, 226–29, 231
Albrecht, Glenn, 209
alienation
  from cosmos, 112, 116, 150, 151
  and decline, 176
  Entfremdung, 266
  need to differentiate, 265
  as not-belonging, 17, 20, 51, 249,
    265–67
  opposite of philosophy, 3–5,
    148
  of self, 80, 119, 266
  as unbelonging, 17, 116, 268–76
  See also Girard, René; Marx, Karl;
    Schacht, Richard
alterity, 28–30, 128, 143, 144, 148,
  149, 155, 246
Ambrose, St., 161
anamnesis, 62, 64, 69, 95, 127, 148,
  191, 226, 247, 270, 273, 282n.1,
  291n.36
  and history, 260
  political, 192, 194, 196, 220, 230
  and reflective distance, 116, 203
  See also Merleau-Ponty, Maurice;
    Walsh, David
Anaximander, 280n.51, 285n.42

Anaximenes, 78
Anselm, 83, 286n.48
Aquinas, St. Thomas
  cosmological proofs, 86
  definition of love, 126
  on Eucharist, 16, 234–36,
    306n.6
  on laws, 301n.21
  names of God, 83, 286n.49,
    286n.52, 287n.53
  on principle of charity, 203–4
  on sacred scripture, 285n.43
  See also Lonergan, Bernard
Arendt, Hannah, 222
  totalitarianism, 226, 273
  See also Canovan, Margaret
Aristotle
  on *eudaimonia*, 7, 300n.14
  on friendship, 132–36, 154, 166
  on intellect, 136–39, 293n.8
  on liberality, 39
  polis, 198–99, 212, 302n.29
  on soul, 307n.12
  and *telos*, 237–38, 264
  on wisdom, 240–41
  See also association; *energeia*;
    wisdom
association, 160, 161, 163, 168, 18,
  203, 219, 249
  and political community, 204
  types of, 163–66, 189, 269
  See also Oakeshott, Michael

311

JAMES GREENAWAY is the San José-Lonergan Chair
in Catholic Philosophy at St. Mary's University.
He is the author of *The Differentiation of Authority:
The Medieval Turn Toward Existence*.